JAPAN'S INVISIBLE RACE

THE CENTER FOR JAPANESE AND KOREAN STUDIES of the University of California is a unit of the Institute of International Studies. It is the unifying organization for faculty members and students interested in Japan and Korea, bringing together scholars from many disciplines. The Center's major aims are the development and support of research and language study. As part of this program the Center sponsors a publication series of books concerned with Japan and Korea. Manuscripts are considered from all campuses of the University of California as well as from any other individuals and institutions doing research in these areas.

PUBLICATIONS OF THE CENTER FOR JAPANESE AND KOREAN STUDIES

Chong-Sik Lee
The Politics of Korean Nationalism. 1963.

Sadako N. Ogata
Defiance in Manchuria: The Making of Japanese Foreign Policy, 1931-1932. 1964.

R. P. Dore
Education in Tokugawa Japan. 1964.

James T. Araki
The Ballad-Drama of Medieval Japan. 1964.

Masakazu Iwata
Okubo Toshimichi: The Bismarck of Japan. 1964.

Frank O. Miller
Minobe Tatsukichi: Interpreter of Constitutionalism in Japan. 1965

Michael Cooper, S.J.
They Came to Japan: An Anthology of European Reports on Japan, 1543-1640. 1965.

Postwar Economic Growth in Japan. 1966.
Edited by Ryutaro Komiya
Translated from the Japanese by Robert S. Ozaki

Robert A. Scalapino
The Japanese Communist Movement, 1920-1966. 1967.

Soon Sung Cho
*Korea in World Politics, 1940-1950:
An Evaluation of American Responsibility*

JAPAN'S INVISIBLE RACE

Caste in Culture and Personality

GEORGE DE VOS
AND HIROSHI WAGATSUMA

Revised Edition

UNIVERSITY OF CALIFORNIA PRESS
Berkeley, Los Angeles, London

University of California Press
Berkeley and Los Angeles, California

University of California Press, Ltd.
London, England

© 1966, 1972 by The Regents of the University of California
ISBN: 0-520-00306-3

Library of Congress Catalog Card Number 66-16422

Revised Edition, 1972

Printed in the United States of America

CONTRIBUTORS

Gerald Berreman
Professor of Anthropology
University of California
Berkeley, California

John B. Cornell
Professor of Anthropology
University of Texas
Austin, Texas

George De Vos
Professor of Anthropology
University of California
Berkeley, California

John Donoghue
Associate Professor of Anthropology
Michigan State University
East Lansing, Michigan

Kazufumi Fukumoto
Staff Photographer
Kobe Shinbun
Kobe, Japan

Hiroshi Ito
Member of the Technical Staff
The Aerospace Corporation
El Segundo, California

Edward Norbeck
Professor of Anthropology
Rice University
Houston, Texas

John Price
Assistant Professor of Anthropology
University of California
Los Angeles, California

Yuzuru Sasaki
Probation Officer
Osaka Family Court
Osaka, Japan

George O. Totten
Associate Professor of Political
  Science
University of Southern California
Los Angeles, California

Hiroshi Wagatsuma
Associate Professor of Sociology
  and of Anthropology
University of Pittsburgh
Pittsburgh, Pennsylvania

Preface

This volume is an interdisciplinary application of various social science methods and perspectives, first to a general examination of the nature of caste segregation and racist ideology, and second to the little known but significant incidence of such phenomena in Japanese culture.

Adequate discussion of caste segregation and demonstration of how it manifests itself in Japan require competent application of methods from more than one discipline. Advice and collaborative assistance were obtained from several colleagues, scholars specializing in Japanese or Indian culture who have made relevant studies of one or another phase of outcaste phenomena.

Our interest in the Japanese outcaste as an "invisible race" grew out of our ongoing comparative research on delinquency and social deviancy in Japan and the United States. We needed to gain some cross-cultural understanding of the effects of minority status on psychological adjustment and social adaptation, and we wondered whether the obvious correlations of minority status and deviant behavior apparent in the United States were also apparent in Japan.

Negro Americans have not been thoroughly accepted since slavery was legally abolished as a result of the American Civil War. Instead, by the close of the nineteenth century the efforts to relegate Negroes to a position of a special caste within the American social structure had taken on the rigidities not only of established custom but also of legal sanctions. Segregated by caste barriers, prevented from easy assimilation into the modern industrial, socially mobile American society, the Negro American has been prone to manifest various forms of socially deviant behavior. Negro youth has manifested a very high rate of delinquency. Was there an analogous relationship between minority status and delinquency to be found in Japan?

As a source of comparative evidence, we considered studying either

vii

the Koreans, or the former untouchables, still treated as outcastes who were rumored to comprise from one to three percent of the present population in Japan. Fortunately, circumstances permitted us to initiate studies of outcaste subjects in urban ghettos in the Kansai area (which contains the principal Japanese cities of Osaka, Kobe, Kyoto, and Nara) where there is the highest concentration of outcaste settlements. Our own empirical work consisted of first, a survey of arrests and arraignments of delinquents within one urban area; second, a study of social stratification in the outcaste communities of another; and third, interviews with various informants in three cities to ascertain the effects of outcaste status or background on social self-identity. These interviews were conducted both with individuals who are seeking to pass into the majority culture and with those who are openly maintaining their outcaste identity.

The more we learned about the present conditions of the Japanese outcaste, the more we perceived that the problems encountered were indeed parallel to social problems found in India and the United States. So much interest was shown in our particular studies that we decided to prepare a more general report covering the subject from as many aspects as possible. At first we thought we might simply add to our own materials a number of already published reports on the history and ethnography of the outcaste. Our first attempt at editing such a compilation was unsatisfactory. The result was much too disjointed and could please only a specialist on the subject of Japanese culture who would be given the convenience of finding in one place various completed researches on the outcaste not otherwise readily available. Since we considered the subject matter to be of sufficient general interest, we decided to completely rework and reorganize these previously published specialized materials within a new overall perspective.

We were fortunate enough to obtain further assistance from a number of our colleagues who altered their previous reports or prepared new material. For some chapters we prepared complementary or supplementary material germane to a particular subject. We did not alter the intent or viewpoint of our collaborators in any way, although several individual viewpoints are not as likely to produce a work as smoothly integrated as one produced by the effort of a single mind. To relate the various sections of the book better to one another, De Vos did a final editing to reduce repetitions and wrote brief introductory remarks to each section (excepting Section V) to help the reader relate the material to the framework held in the minds of the authors.

To Hiroshi Wagatsuma fell the burden of going through what has been published in Japanese on both the past and recent history of the outcastes, regardless of the approach or discipline involved, so as to integrate these materials with those published in English. To this end he was responsible for the organization of Sections I and II.

In Section I, John Price, a history-oriented anthropologist, has written for us a general cultural history of the Japanese pariah up to the time of official emancipation in 1871. His presentation draws heavily on a number of sources. Acknowledgments must be made to the published material provided by Shigeaki Ninomiya and Herbert Passin, whose reports supplied particularly helpful summaries of available historical documentation on the subject up to the time of their writing.

Section II is concerned with the more recent, post-emancipation, social history. It brings together various materials on political movements and attempts at social improvement from the time of the official emancipation. George Totten, a political scientist, provided guidance for us and also provided some of his own original material from his continuing research in Japanese politics.

The ethnographic section, Section III, assembled by George De Vos, brings together the results of several anthropologists who did field work in outcaste communities. The opening chapter of this section assembles general materials on the human ecology of such communities, and is a joint effort by Wagatsuma and De Vos. We would like to express our thanks especially to Robert B. Hall, a geographer, who made available to us detailed charts and other material from his own research on Buraku ecology. Yuzuru Sasaki, a probation officer of the Kobe Family Court, did the field observations that made the following chapter on the urban Buraku of Kyoto possible. John Donoghue, an anthropologist, permitted us to republish the results of his previous work, which appeared in the *American Anthropologist*. John Cornell, an anthropologist, added new materials to those he has already published in several papers on the rural community that he has been studying over a period of years. The anthropologist Edward Norbeck prepared a chapter on non-Eta-Hinin outcastes stemming from both his own field materials and secondary sources.

Hiroshi Ito's paper, which ends section three, was included in the first printing of this book without Mr. Ito's knowledge. Further, his name was mistakenly labelled a pseudonym and permission to publish was erroneously attributed to Professor Leonard Broom. Mr. Ito's study was not intended for publication in the form in which it appeared. In this printing a few editorial changes have been made within the constraints of printing economy, changes largely concerned with informant privacy, the violation of which was unknown to Mr. Ito and Professor Broom.

The editors deeply regret their serious errors in this matter and apologize to Mr. Ito, to Professor Broom under whose supervision the study was conducted, and to any informants who may believe themselves or their communities identified.

The social psychological material in Section IV has been the joint work of Wagatsuma and De Vos with the able assistance of Mr. Sasaki. Interviews were conducted directly with various members of the outcaste community, both those who had learned to disguise their identities and so pass as ordinary Japanese and those who maintained open contact with their community. Without Mr. Sasaki's continual direct involvement and facilitation, the gathering of social-psychological materials from informants would have been impossible. Through him we were able to gain the confidence, acceptance, and participation of other members of those communities contacted. We are greatly indebted to the trust that many of these individuals placed in us, and hope that nothing in this volume will be felt as a betrayal of that trust. We have in all instances sufficiently disguised the material obtained in direct interview to guard the privacy of our informants.

The difficulties of obtaining materials of a psychological or developmental nature from the outcaste community are considerable. We did not succeed in many instances in gathering the types of material that would satisfy scientific criteria. Nevertheless, the cogency and pertinence of the material we did obtain, fragmentary though it might be, made its inclusion seem warranted.

We did not feel that our task ended with the presentation of the material obtained from Japan, but rather decided to place the discussion of caste within a comparative perspective. To this end we included as Part Two of this volume a theoretical discussion of caste in culture and personality. The final two sections attempt to define in general terms the social, organizational, and motivational components of caste wherever it occurs. Section V, including its introduction, was written especially for this volume by Gerald Berreman, an anthropologist with considerable experience in India. His exposition affords a thorough comparative perspective on the structure of caste-segregated behavior, whether in India, the United States, Japan, or elsewhere. Finally, in Section VI, De Vos has attempted to examine caste from within a theoretical framework concerned with psychological motivation as well as social structure.

We are indebted to the following people who rendered their able and kind assistance at various stages of our data collection: the Reverend Francis A. Diffley, Catholic priest at Hope House in Kyoto; Mr. Lawrence H. Thompson, former Director of the Hiroshima Christian Social Center; Mr. Toyo Ichikawa, our Research Assistant; Mr. Seiichi Muratsu, Mr. Haruo Nagashima, and Mr. Yōtarō Takeda, editorial writers of *Kobe Shinbun;* Mrs. Motoko Sasaki, Probation Officer at Kobe Family Court; Mrs. Yōko Hotta, Kasei Gakuin College in Tokyo; Mr. Kyoshi Nishimura, Nishi Honganji Temple, and Mr.

Kun-ichi Minobe, Higashi Honganji; and Mr. Hidehiko Yaoi, Mr. Kenji Nakamura, and Mr. Haruo Oshitani, Kansai Headquarters of Sōka Gakkai.

Finally, we would like to profess our gratitude to the numerous individuals, both in the United States and in Japan, who have helped to improve this book by their suggestions and criticisms. We wish to thank our typists, Miss Jill White, Mrs. Carolyn Kohler, Miss Suzanne Allen, Mrs. Kathleen Wilson, Miss Frances Hammond, and Miss Felicia Hance who have had patience with us through the various drafts of the manuscript. We are also extremely grateful for the editorial assistance given by Mrs. Winnifred De Vos.

This investigation was supported by Public Health Service Grant MH-04087, from the National Institute of Mental Health, and carried out at the Institute of Human Development of the University of California at Berkeley.

Berkeley, California
February, 1966

G. D. V. and H. W.

Contents

xiii

Introduction

The Problem: Caste and Race, A Syncretic View

In comparing systems of social segregation in various of the world's cultures, those based on alleged caste impurity and those based on alleged racial inferiority are found to be the most fixed and immutable. One can too quickly conclude that these two concepts have very different bases for the classification and separation of two or more segments of a particular society. Instead of stressing the obvious surface differences, one might do well to consider whether there is a curious similarity between these concepts, whether they are not, indeed, two dissimilar faces of identical inner psychological processes that seek external expression.

The concept "race" as used in modern physical anthropology has come to be very different from the common usage of the term. Until recently it had been concluded in Western societies that human character and temperament, intellectual and moral qualities, were produced by genetic transmission. Individuals with desired characteristics were said to have "good breeding." With increased knowledge about the role played by human learning and the socializing processes that occur within the primary family, physical anthropology—the discipline that concerns itself with the biological nature of man—no longer seriously holds that moral or social traits have a genetic origin. Anthropological explanations of social behavior are now based almost solely on concepts of cultural transmission. Anthropologists have become almost universally convinced that *Homo sapiens*, be they of Mongoloid, Caucasoid, or Negroid stock, can be socialized to become functional members within any human society. Race as a concept, though still useful in designating particular physical features of skin or hair color, face or body proportions, has lost its scientific value as a differentiator of mental or moral patterns.

xix

At first glance, racism may seem to bear no direct resemblance to the social segregation found in a caste system. But it is a major proposition of this volume that the contrary is true, that from the viewpoint of comparative sociology or social anthropology, and from the viewpoint of human social psychology, racism and caste attitudes are one and the same phenomenon. To make clear the basis of this judgment, we discuss our definition of caste and the essential elements of caste segregation in the chapters comprising the theoretical section of this volume.

Our syncretic approach to caste and racism is based on two further propositions. First, racist as well as caste attitudes and resultant social practices of discrimination are not necessarily related to actual physical differences among definable groups. Second, there are no essential psychological differences between the rationalizations for social discrimination based on race and those based on caste distinctions. Racism is usually based on a secularized pseudo-scientific biological mythology, whereas caste, as we shall shortly demonstrate by the instance of Japan or India, is often based on a pseudo-historical religious mythology. But from a psychological point of view race and caste attitudes are one, and their effects on a pariah caste are the same, given sufficient time for these effects to become culturally self-perpetuating.

The essence of a socially prevalent emotional concern over racial differences is a deep-seated, psychologically primitive, vaguely conceptualized fear of contamination and loss of purity as a result of possible interbreeding. This fear is evidenced by a secondary rejection of some unacceptable physical difference, such as skin color. The observable physical differences in themselves are not the prime source of rejection.

This volume concerns the extreme case that tests these propositions —Japan's "invisible race." It is not widely known that Japan has discriminated in the past and continues to discriminate against a pariah caste that is completely indistinguishable in any physical sense from the population as a whole, whose segregation nevertheless has long been justified in racial terms. There is a commonly shared social myth that the *Eta*, as they were termed, are descendants of a less human "race" than the stock that fathered the Japanese nation as a whole. Up to the time of their official emancipation, they were visibly distinguished by the special garb they were forced to wear and by other social attributes that prevented them from becoming invisible. Today, free of visible clues to their identity, they nevertheless remain a distinguishable segment of the Japanese population and bear the same social stigma as that borne by the American Negro. Both are internally if not externally branded with the same marks of oppression. There are various social practices which still serve to keep outcastes sexually and socially apart from the Japanese society generally.

For the ordinary modern Japanese, the existence of this caste within their society is a source of embarrassment—a source of discomfort, of visceral reactions—and is never mentioned in polite company. No scientific fact substantiates the myth that there are hereditary biological factors that separate ordinary Japanese from the former pariahs. Attempts to find anthropomorphic differences have all failed, yet no social mechanism exists within Japanese culture today by which the members of the pariah caste can obtain open social equality without resorting to some form of social disguise.

While many educated Japanese readily add their voices to the chorus of world disapproval of racist attitudes and practices toward American Negroes, they still continue to feel a deep abhorrence at the thought of intimacy with a Japanese pariah. Incidentally, in today's India, where caste remains a much more central problem, many well-educated, intellectually sophisticated Brahmans also decry racism in the United States and at the same time cannot relate freely to an Indian untouchable without physical discomfort. This uneasiness occurs even though there is no difference in physical appearance or intellectual quality between the Brahman and the pariah.

After we have thoroughly explored the political, social, economic, and psychological conditions of the Japanese outcaste, we will return to this underlying issue. It is our final proposition that theoretical understanding of caste phenomena cannot be fully obtained without comprehension of its psychological matrix within the individual.

From what social scientists call the "functionalist" standpoint, the attitudes toward caste in Japan have outlived any possible usefulness for Japanese society. They persist without legal sanctions in spite of the fact that they no longer make economic or social sense. In premodern times quasi-religious attitudes could justify the maintenance of some separate occupational groups, each of which carried out ritually impure activities; no such occupational differentiation makes sense in a secularized, industrial society. In the past, economic and social circumstances could reinforce such occupational differentiation; in the present there is no such justification. Nor is there any serious support in religious proscriptions for the feeling that the pariahs are somehow ritually impure. The concept of caste remains a social force because it exists in the emotional structure of individual Japanese.

We have here, therefore, an example of what we term "psychological lag" in social attitudes. Caste feelings remain affectively strong, although they have ceased to make sense even to the individuals who are subject to such feelings. In Japan, outcastes evoke gut reactions;

in the United States, reactions to Negroes rest upon an identical primitive emotional base. The persistence of such emotions in a society cannot be explained by a simplistic Marxian interpretation of caste as a form of economic or social exploitation. This interpretation fails to note the essential difference between caste and class: that caste is not simply an *instrumental* exploitation of particular segments of the population, but rather that it is an enforced differentiation based on deeply felt, emotionally *expressive* aspects of individual psychology.

Lastly, one needs to consider from both a social and a psychological viewpoint the cultural history of an exploiting group. Events that challenge the integrity of a group may cause it to make a scapegoat of a submerged segment of its population as a form of expressive exploitation, in addition to its economic and political instrumental exploitation of the subjugated group. In our final chapter we will discuss both the social and psychological functions of what we term "status anxiety."

In the United States the plight of the American Negro persists. Despite ameliorative changes that are taking place, the segregating barrier of caste status has not been completely lowered. The social and psychological stigmas of a hundred years of oppression after slavery are still visible and will remain so for some time to come. The persistent effects of caste, social and economic exploitation, and the continuing prejudice in American society are reflected in the statistics of illiteracy, unemployability, family dislocation, illegitimacy, disease, drug addiction, mental illness, as well as delinquency and crime. Such statistics not only reflect present social conditions but are also the inheritance of the past crime of enslavement. The *karma* of this crime is transmitted from one generation to the next. On the descendants of the oppressors it bestows a brutalizing burden of unfaced guilt yet to be expiated. But the true horror is more keenly felt by the descendants of the victims; in many cases a debilitation of the human spirit is passed on from mother to child. It will take the concerted effort of the total American society to break this chain of causation.

If we generalize from American studies on the subject, we find that the psychological and social destiny of a member of a disparaged caste unfolds early. Increasing self-knowledge in the context of social pathology wounds and debilitates, stunts and perverts. However, this volume is not about the American Negro, but about his counterpart in Japan, a group of over two million real or fancied descendants of an untouchable pariah caste. These Japanese were supposedly liberated from their special status to become "new citizens" in 1871, less than ten years after the American Civil War was fought to settle the issue of slavery in the United States. How have they fared? We will tell their story and draw some generalizations and conclusions which may promote better understanding of the universality of the effects of a social exploitation that is based on the false premise of the moral inequality of man.

Part One:

Caste in Japan:
A Descriptive Cultural
Analysis

SECTION I

Historical Perspective

INTRODUCTION

The first chapter of this volume summarizes available knowledge concerning origins and history of outcaste status in Japan. The cultural diffusion by Buddhism of Indian proscriptions against taking life played a major role in establishing an outcaste tradition in Japan. Nevertheless one must not overlook indigenous religious features of Japanese culture and the persistent psychological traits already present at the advent of Buddhism that made concepts of pollution and contamination particularly acceptable throughout Japanese cultural history.

The discussion of the history of Japanese outcaste status is introduced by a brief comparative overview of untouchability throughout the Far East. The material on Tibet, Korea, and India is derived, with minor exceptions, from an article by Herbert Passin, "Untouchability in the Far East." [1] This article has stood the test of time, although Passin is not completely accurate in stating that the outcaste phenomenon was absent in China; there is historical legal documentation to the contrary, as reported by Wolfram Eberhard [2] and Ch'u T'ung-tsu.[3] Passin's point that the cultural psychology of the Chinese did not well support the maintenance of outcaste status, however, remains generally valid.

The remainder of the chapter is devoted to a more detailed examination of the history of the outcaste phenomenon in Japan up until 1871. John Price has drawn most heavily on the outstanding work of Shigeaki Ninomiya who, in his too little known monograph, *An Inquiry Concerning the Origin, Development and Present Situation of*

---

[1] Passin (1955), pp. 27–47.
[2] Eberhard (1942), pp. 206–7.
[3] Ch'u T'ung-tsu (1947), pp. 173–174.

3

the Eta in Relation to the History of Social Classes in Japan, published in 1933,[4] had already made use of most of the relevant documents on the early history of Japan's pariah groups. Price has also included some new archeological evidence and other findings that appeared after Ninomiya's comprehensive report.

In this chapter the reader will become acquainted with various words used to describe the Japanese outcaste. Some general explanation is necessary concerning the conventions we have adopted in the present volume, as related to past and present usages within the Japanese language. The term *Eta,* to mean "outcaste," is the one most generally used in English translation and therefore is most familiar to the non-Japanese who have heard something about the subject of caste in Japan. At one time in Japanese history—during the Tokugawa period, preceding the emancipation of the outcastes in 1871—Eta was an officially recognized status term used in government documents. It no longer has such recognition today and in both writing and speech the term is offensive and pejorative. The Chinese characters used to write "eta" literally mean "full of filth." It is as pejorative as other terms such as *yotsu* ("four-legged") which makes direct reference to the supposedly subhuman attributes or polluted nature of the outcaste. The term *Hinin* (literally, "nonpeople"), also used during the Tokugawa period to officially designate a special type of outcaste status, is no longer used even in a pejorative way. In this volume when the terms Eta or Hinin are used historically as the proper name of a caste prior to or during the Tokugawa period, they will be capitalized. When used in later periods, to indicate expressed attitudes, these words as well as similar negative terms will appear in quotation marks.

There is no general usage of a neutral term acceptable to all. During the Meiji period, *shin-heimin* and *shin-hei* ("new commoner" or "new citizen") obtained some general usage but gradually became pejorative in reference and are rarely used today without such connotation. Following the development of the Levelers' Association after World War I, described in Chapter 2, the words *suiheisha* or *suihei* (literally "water level people") became a common way of designating the outcaste. This usage is still found occasionally but is no longer common.

More common today are the usages *tokushu-buraku, mikaihō-buraku* or simply *buraku* ("special communities" and "unliberated communities") and hence *burakumin* and *buraku-no-hito* ("people of special or unliberated communities"). Literally, the term "buraku" simply designates a hamlet or a rural community smaller than a village and is often used in this sense in Japan without any implication of outcaste status. One must therefore gain a sense of the term from the context

---

[4] Ninomiya (1933), pp. 47-154.

in which it is used. In the present volume we have adopted the convention throughout of referring to outcaste communities by the term Buraku capitalized and to the people as Burakumin. Whenever we use the term buraku uncapitalized we are using it in its more general sense.

There are other special terms, in some instances used by the government, by members of special organizations found within the outcaste communities, or sometimes by social scientists writing on the subject, that have special currency. These terms will be defined in context in special instances, but for the purpose of clarity we have not hesitated to change terms used by our collaborators and by Japanese writers so as to correspond to the conventions adopted here.

It is a mark of the covert nature of the Japanese outcaste problem that terms tend to become pejorative once they gain general usage. There may even be an objection on the part of some that the term Burakumin is gradually now coming to have a pejorative meaning.

Chapter 1

JOHN PRICE

A History of the Outcaste: Untouchability in Japan

OUTCASTE STATUS AND UNTOUCHABILITY IN ASIA

The caste phenomenon, principally that involving some sort of pariah group, has appeared throughout the Far East. Passin[1] in his general survey distinguishes between caste as hierarchical social structure peculiar to India and the severely segregated outcaste status involving some form of literal untouchability found in various Asian cultures. In the concluding chapters of this volume the position is taken that some concept of contamination is essential to the caste barrier itself. Hence, the untouchability of outcastes is a matter of degree. It does serve to distinguish specific outcaste groups whose socially defined degree of pollution makes them literally untouchable.

The Japanese Hinin, or "non-people"—itinerants, beggars, prostitutes, castoff commoners—were not "untouchable" as were the Eta, nor in the strictest terms were the Hinin considered as hopelessly polluted. They could gain commoner status under unusual conditions. Hence, in the sense in which we are considering caste, they were not true hereditary outcastes, although the lines could become blurred.[2]

Untouchability is related to the restrictive and prescriptive behavior that pertains to contact with or presence of polluted outcastes (or things associated with polluted outcastes). The code of prescriptive behavior is elaborated to protect the "normal" people. Not touching the special person is a common part of the prescribed behavior, but it is never the only prescription. Marriage between a normal person and

---

[1] Passin (1955), pp. 27–47.

[2] An American Negro, a true outcaste, can never become "white" if he has a known Negro ancestor, no matter how far removed; nor in Nazi Germany could a Jew become an "Aryan" if he had any "Jewish blood."

an untouchable, for example, is very much more polluting than simple touching.

There is a psychological and social parallel to untouchability at the opposite end of the social scale, where special qualities are attributed to extremely high status individuals. For example, in certain Pacific and African cultures the fear of their power and the need to protect high status people set off chiefs and kings as "untouchable" or "taboo." The nobility everywhere are accorded some deferential behavior or their "nobility" becomes simply a hollow title. Untouchability occurs when caste development is most extreme, so that there are barriers not only to intercaste movement in marriage but to intercaste association as well. (See fuller discussion, Chapter 16.)

There is some evidence that untouchability based on concepts of defilement occurred indigenously elsewhere in Asia, not only in India. Nevertheless, Indian culture has had considerable influence on the continued presence of such phenomena throughout Asia, with the influence of Hindu caste on neighboring peoples and the later spread of Buddhism and its proscriptions on the taking of life. Religious sanctions condemning groups with polluting occupations were reinforced historically by legal codification in several Asiatic cultures. The transmission of religious concepts of untouchability occurred in most instances without the introduction of the evolved Hindu caste system to which Buddhism itself was opposed.

In Tibet, Korea, and Japan the establishment and continuation of outcaste groups was much more pronounced than in China;[3] the emphasis on achieved status over hereditary status, and the general assimilative attitude of Chinese culture, seemed to stress personal superiority rather than considerations of race or blood as a basis of cultural inheritance. The Chinese considered pollution to be a temporary condition rather than a hereditary taint. Buddhist-inspired legal proscriptions concerning polluted groups had disappeared in the records by the eleventh century.[4]

Outcaste status without sanctioned untouchability beyond the prohibition of intermarriage occurred in Ceylon, a country more directly exposed to the more evolved caste stratification of India. In Burma, India's eastern neighbor, no Hindu type of caste system developed; nevertheless one did find pagoda slaves, or *para goon* who were both outcasted and untouchable. There is no evidence that untouchability in Burma was associated with the butchering of animals, an almost universal association elsewhere when outcastes and the Buddhist religion are found together.

---

[3] Eberhard documents legal sanctions in the Tang Dynasty related to Buddhist proscriptions on the butchering and eating of meat. Eberhard (1942), pp. 206–207.
[4] Wolfram Eberhard, 1965.

Passin points up some interesting parallels in the reports extant on untouchability in India, Tibet, Korea, and Japan. In each of these four Asian cultures, to the outcaste group is attributed an origin other than that of the majority. Thus an expression of ethnocentrism toward foreigners or outside races may have initially set these peoples apart. In India the untouchables are considered to be descendants of aboriginal tribes conquered by the Aryan invaders. In Tibet the *Ragyappa* are held to be an alien wandering tribe that settled down in their present location. In Korea the outcastes are supposedly descendant from "Tartars," and in Japan they are popularly held to come from various separate "races," including Koreans. However, popular theories are often after-the-fact rationalizations and must be carefully reviewed in the light of other evidence. Passin wrote, "These popular attributions express the feeling that the outcastes are so different from oneself that they *must* be a different race." [5] Whatever the popular attributions of their origins, all of these outcaste groups spoke the same language, had the same religion, and identified with the same culture as the surrounding majority population.

In each culture the untouchables were seen as inferior, and as so polluted that their very presence is a danger to normal people. Marriage, eating together, and social visiting between untouchables and members of normal society were disdained. In each culture they were rigidly isolated in ghettos, often actually outside the regular communities, with segregated cemeteries. In each culture evidences of luxury on the part of outcastes, such as expensive clothes, were illegal or severely frowned upon. This segregation from normal society was balanced by autonomy and solidarity within outcaste communities.

In each culture the outcastes were restricted to the despised and menial but essential occupations, usually centered around blood, death, and dirt. Occupation was a major method of distinguishing outcastes. Some outcastes in all the societies worked with dead animals, as in butchering, removing carcasses, or leather work. They are usually associated with removing dirt. And there were other relatively clean services that by analogy, accidental association, or monopoly came to belong to the outcastes, such as the making of willow baskets in Korea or sandals in Japan. There were, of course, some differences in occupation among the various cultures. Outcastes laundered for others in India, whereas they did not do so in the other cultures. In Burma the care of temples was an outcaste function, whereas in the other cultures they were generally kept away from temples. Also, there were distinctions between occupations of outcastes who live in their own settled communities and itinerant floaters in India (settled vs. beggars), Korea (*Paekchong* vs. *Chiain*), and Japan (Eta vs. Hinin).

[5] Passin (1955), pp. 27–47.

Elaborate etiquette was developed for business contacts: in both India and Japan outcastes had to come to the back door and were not permitted to enter the homes of the majority people. Except in the processes of butchering, outcastes could not handle foods to be eaten by ordinary people. In all four cultures hereditary hierarchy was important. In India, Japan, and Korea there were four basic, rigid castes or classes. In India and Japan the outcastes were technically outside and below the lowest caste, and in Korea they were a special part of the lowest class. All held outcaste status to be inevitable, immutable, and in some way deserved. Also, the concept of pollution was common to these four cultures—the magical, mechanistic, and aspiritual pollution that is resident in certain persons at birth or in certain things by their nature and that may flow out and contaminate other persons or things. Passin therefore suggests that untouchability was lacking as a continuing social dynamic in China because hierarchy there was more dependent—according to official ideology at least—on merit and less on heredity, and status was not held to be inevitable.

In India there are over fifty million untouchables, almost one out of every seven Indians. The caste system there apparently developed over the centuries as a product of relations among different tribal, religious, language, racial, and occupational groups. The practice of ranking social segments became increasingly elaborated in the social and religious concepts of India, particularly in Hinduism, where every person's position is ordained by karma, the endless chain of causation. One's behavior in one incarnation determines one's status in the next. At the bottom of the status system are those who carry on the despised services for the community.

The outcastes in Tibet are known as the Ragyappa and number over a thousand. They live in a segregated part of the southern outskirts of the holy inner circle, known as the Lingkor, in the capital city of Lhasa. They are paid to do their required tasks of disposing of corpses and clearing the carcasses of dead animals from the streets and public places. They have special rights for begging, they may be called on to search for escaped criminals, and criminals and vagabonds are often put in their charge and are made to live in their communities.

The principal outcaste groups of Korea are the Paekchong—slaughterers, butchers, and tanners; and the Chiain—petty criminals, prostitutes, diviners, beggars, itinerant peddlers, and those who practice similar "floating" occupations. Both of these groups are thought to be descended from a wandering alien group called the kolisiuchay of the Koryo Period (918–1329 A.D.). From the fifteenth century these outcastes were required to live in segregated communities. The Paekchong held monopolies in the despised occupations and were permitted to drive out non-outcaste competitors. They were not considered worthy of citizenship and thus were exempted from military service and military taxes. (In all four countries there seem to have been certain limited advantages to being an outcaste, and there were economic as well as ideological reasons for the maintenance of an outcaste group.)

The Hindu-Buddhist proscriptions against the killing of animals, in Korea as in other countries, apparently played a major role in setting off the Paekchong as untouchable. In the first of the Yi dynasty in 1392, the Paekchong, along with seven other "vile occupations," were designated as a special subdivision of the fourth or lowest class. The term "Paekchong" came to embrace both the Paekchong proper and the Chiain. In 1894 the outcastes were "liberated" by an official decree but, as in Japan and later in India, discrimination continued as before.

THE OUTCASTES IN JAPAN

The history of the outcaste in Japan, like that of low social classes generally, is poorly documented. The available descriptions were written primarily by an elite minority centered around the capital and the major towns; they do not faithfully record the culture of the countryside majority.

Since outcastes are ideologically outside normal society, they have either been systematically ignored or information concerning them has been distorted. During the Tokugawa period (1603–1868 A.D.) outcastes were often not listed in census tabulations, and when they were, they were often listed separately from "people." Some maps were made without outcaste settlements drawn in, and distances indicated or maps were even foreshortened to exclude these communities. After their emancipation in 1871, the outcastes were officially defined as commoners and then largely ignored for official purposes. It has been government policy to contend that there are no outcastes and hence no outcaste problem apart from that of general social welfare. Thus the outcastes, who in fact were maintained as outcastes, and who expanded in population and number of communities in the past century, are not distinguishable in most population data. It is only in the last fifty years, with the introduction of a scientific tradition, that Japanese outcaste culture has begun to receive full exploration and description.

Even the most recent interpretations of the history of outcaste culture are of questionable validity because they are so heavily biased by an interpretation of history in terms of a political variant of the Marxian dialectics of class struggle. Researchers in the Buraku Mondai Kenkyūjo (Buraku Problems Research Institute) have spent considerable time in refuting popularly held racial, religious, and occupational theories about the origin and social maintenance of the outcastes, only to substitute a somewhat dogmatic political theory. Even the claim that there are today three million outcastes seems to be advanced by the Buraku Mondai Kenkyūjo more for political purposes than for scholarly accuracy. Nevertheless, the abundant documentation this Institute is now producing will be invaluable to future researchers.

For over a thousand years it has been popularly held that certain low caste peoples are physically inferior to "ordinary" Japanese. Originally, this inferiority was attributed to the practice of defiling trades and the association with blood and death. By long association with supernatural or ritual impurities the very nature of a man was believed to change. This adverse change not only carried over to a man's descendants but was in a sense communicable. The simple presence of an outcaste or "untouchable" was slightly defiling. Today, with the germ theory of disease and a genetic basis for heredity, it is difficult to understand the nature of supernatural defilement.

In the past century, more "modern" rationalizations were added to the previous beliefs in supernatural defilement. In the Tokugawa period the outcastes were usually identifiable, at least within their local areas, by their residential communities, occupations, kinship ties, and often by such additional features as forms of dress, a patch of leather sewn on their kimono, hair tied together by straw, barefootedness, or deferential behavior. The dogma of ritually defiling trades was still a strong undercurrent, but local variations required additional explanations: whole outcaste communities had not practiced the defiling trades for centuries. Belief in outcaste physical deviance came to involve such things as meat in the diet, particular diseases, extreme inbreeding, and inherited abnormalities.

One of the most prevalent theories in the last century for the supposed physical inferiority of outcastes is that they are derived from an inferior race or an animal-like ethnic group.[6] Ideas of outcaste affinity to animals are seen in the old folklore. "One rib-bone is lacking"; "they have one dog's bone in them"; "they have distorted sexual organs"; "they have defective excretory systems"; and "they being animals, dirt does not stick to their feet when they walk barefooted." [7]

At least four theories have used the evidence of similar names to postulate the origin of the Eta. One theory held that a Philippine Negrito people, also called Eta, are ancestral to the Japanese Eta. Another theory is that the Eta are descended from a Hindu tribe called Weda. Ōe Taku[8] over forty years ago postulated that the Eta were descendants of a lost tribe of Hebrews, on the following similarity of

[6] We commonly find terms that associate outcastes with animals; *yotsu* ("four," i.e., less than five, a perfect number, or four legs, implying animals) is used metaphorically whereas *ningai* ("outside of the human") is unequivocal in meaning.

[7] Ninomiya (1933), pp. 47–154.

[8] Ōe (1919).

names: Hora, a village near Nara, has the tomb of an ancient culture hero, Emperor Jimmu, who was cared for by the local Eta; Hafurai, a people who were supposedly made subjects by Emperor Jimmu; Heburai, the Japanese pronunciation of Hebrew, and presumably with the term Hora, is a variant derivative from Hafurai.

In 1923 Kikuchi San-ya[9] presented the hypothesis that the Eta were closely related to the Orochon branch of the Tungus who live today in Sakhalin. The Orochon call themselves *etta*, and he infers that in Japan the name was modified to Eta and given a new derogatory meaning in the Chinese characters used. Kikuchi claimed that the Eta were distinct from the Japanese in that they have reddish and non-Mongolian eyes, prominent cheek bones, dolichocephalic heads, and short necks and stature. There is no sound evidence for any of the racial theories based only on the chance similarity of names.

A more popular racial view is that the Eta are descended from Koreans who came as early war captives or who were immigrants who practiced tanning and furriery. Often they are held to be descended from captives taken in a battle during the regency of the Empress Jingū (201–269 A.D.), but even the battle is not fully substantiated. Some slight credence could be given to a modified Korean descent theory for three reasons. First, over two thousand years ago southern Korea and western Japan were occupied by essentially the same race and culture. Distinctive variations of East Asian culture and the Mongoloid race have since emerged in Korea and Japan, but these differences today cannot be validly projected back much over 1,500 years. Second, Koreans did immigrate to Japan in the early historic periods as skilled tradesmen, although most of them were accorded high status, immunities, and privileges, and thus would not enter the lower classes. Third, with modern discrimination in housing, employment, and marriage in Japan against the Koreans, a few Koreans have married outcastes, moved into outcaste communities, and thus in social fact have become pariahs. However, the majority of Koreans who immigrated to Japan formed their own enclaves within the cities, and seem to have emerged as one of the new low class segments of Japanese society rather than a separate caste.

Taken as a whole, the outcastes are not descendant from Koreans, but are Japanese. In fact, the earliest outcaste communities are in the Kinki district, the very heartland of historic Japanese culture, rather than in the extreme west where we would expect to find more "Korean genes," or the extreme north, where more "Ainu genes" are present. The outcastes form a race only in the sense of an "invisible race," a race visible only to the eyes of members of a certain cultural tradition.

---

[9] Kikuchi (1923).

Outcaste status and attitudes about untouchability developed within medieval Japanese culture because of a complex set of economic, social, political, and ideological conditions. And once established, outcaste status has had great staying power. The formal rational explanations and protests on the parts of members of the majority society, or by the outcastes themselves, have had little effect on hastening change in outcaste history. The official emancipation proclamation and later liberation movements (see Chapters 2 and 3) are comprehensible as products of Japan's modern social revolution in general, but they have not resulted in any rapid shift in deeply rooted emotional attitudes toward outcaste individuals.

The outcastes in Japan today do not form any highly distinct, corporate, and separate subculture diffused throughout Japan. Rather, by residing in widely scattered communities, they reflect the regional and local variations of culture throughout the country. While the segregated character of their communities helps to foster and perpetuate some attributes of a separate subculture, the scattered character of the communities tends to weaken cross-community similarities.

Some of the diverse origins and past social positions are reflected in the variety of local and often colloquial names for outcastes. Most of these stress occupations,[10] but some indicate such things as the animal nature of outcastes, their inferior residential sites, their leaders, or are simply modern euphemisms.[11]

In the history of Japan there are thousands of somewhat distinct social groups that can be described as either classes, castes, guilds, or occupationally specialized communities. The outcastes constitute only a minor segment within this variety of segmented social groups, historically less than one percent of the total population, although rising in certain provinces at times to nearly five percent of the provincial population. Comprising about two percent of the total population today, they probably are a larger portion than ever before. During the past century the outcaste population increased seven times faster than Japanese society generally. This great increase was caused by "recruiting" from outside, by the redefinition of the outcaste segment, and by improved diet and health practices in the society as a whole. But since the proportion of outcastes in the total population is still low,

---

[10] *Hagi* (skinner), *kawata* (leather worker), *onbō* (cremator, funeral worker), *banta* (watchman for the bodies of criminals after execution), *shuku* (tomb watcher), *chasen* (tea whisk maker), *kojiki* (beggar), *doetta* (damn etta), and *kaito* (within the fence, i.e., a servant employed in a large establishment).

[11] *Yaban* (savage), *yotsu* (four, i.e., four legs), *ningai* (outside the human), *kawara mono* (river bank dweller), *yama no mono* (hill dweller), *danzaemon* (the name of an outcaste leader in nineteenth century Edo and a title after his death), *chōri* (police hand), *shin-heimin* (new common people), *ichibu kokumin* (minority people).

and since the outcastes live primarily in segregated communities confined mainly to western Japan, only a small percentage of the Japanese have any firsthand acquaintance with them.

The first fairly well-documented origins of caste in Japan can be traced to the development of occupational specializations in the ninth and tenth centuries. The geographical region of outcaste development was that of the Imperial capital, built in imitation of the capital of the Tang dynasty in China, where economic diversity and the vertical ranking of a social hierarchy were at their greatest. Japanese culture, under the influence of Buddhism brought in from China, depended on plant rather than animal foods and abhorred the ritual impurity of blood and death. Cattle were raised for plowing and other agricultural work rather than for their meat or milk. The growing popularity of Buddhism, with its strictures against taking life, helped to produce an outcaste segment in the society composed of those communities specializing in such occupations as slaughtering and processing of animal products. But Buddhism alone was not a sufficient cause for outcastism; it was only one of several forces. In fact, we find that some occupations were defined as outcaste that were only remotely connected with taking life, such as hawk tending for the elite (hawks were used in sport hunting) and burial-tomb tending.

Although outcaste groups appeared far beyond the capital region, the outcastes were invariably occupational specialists who operated within and for a small-scale local economy. They emerged as one functional segment of relatively closed corporate communities where economic interdependence and the inheritance of occupation and social position helped reinforce the endogamy required of a caste separate from normal society. Traditional occupational roles became spheres of monopoly as the outcastes formed guilds in the face of the economic competition and the increasingly severe discrimination of the fifteenth through nineteenth centuries. Concurrent with the growth of competition was the breakup of closed corporate communities, the growth of a national transport and trade network, and the ideological crystallization of class structure. In the Tokugawa period (1603–1868 A.D.) legally sanctioned caste and untouchability reached their height in Japan.

The social and economic functions that supported the existence of outcastes have largely disappeared in Japan's phenomenal post-Tokugawa modernization, and the hierarchical trends of Japanese traditional social organization and ideology were seriously weakened by this economic growth. Modern egalitarian ideologies, more in keeping with a socially mobile industrial society, have swept Japan. Since the outcastes have no distinctive physical traits and today possess few distinctive cultural traits, they can "pass" into the normal society once they are outside their home areas. Still, outcastism is disappearing at a seemingly slow pace. History describes the process; social science attempts to explain it (see Chapters 6 to 13).

OUTCASTE ORIGINS

Japanese culture, as distinct from earlier paleolithic cultures and the neolithic Jōmon culture, begins with the Yayoi period (350 B.C.–250 A.D.) and the introduction of rice agriculture into Japan from the continent. This highly productive irrigated field agriculture provided an economic surplus which, together with an increasingly complex social structure, greatly advanced the rate of cultural evolution in Japan. Some of the long-term trends of Japanese social structure have been the central position of the group rather than the individual, a strong hierarchy, the inheritance of occupation, and occupationally specialized communities. Group cooperation was required in sharing irrigation water in small valleys and in living in relatively compact villages arranged to keep most of the bottom lands free for agriculture. With population growth and an ensuing demand for cultivable land, kinship groups expanded, allied, and formed land-controlling chiefdoms in which loyalty and service to the group were essential.

Within these chiefdoms occupationally specialized communities developed as suppliers of specialty products and services to make each chiefdom economically and hence politically self-sufficient. This self-sufficiency was partially breached in the Tomb period (250–650) with the rise of a suzerain in the form of the Yamato clan, which became the Imperial lineage for the rest of Japanese history. However, in the Tomb period the local chiefdoms continued to gain in population and power, reflected in the great earthen burial mounds for which the period is named. Also, influences from the continent were felt, probably involving some migrations, and by later Tomb times mounted warriors extended the formation of confederations of chiefdoms much farther than in the Yayoi period. In the Tomb period we find the formation of aristocratic, common, and slave classes.[12]

In political terms the Nara period (650–794) marks the emergence of the Japanese archaic state which had a dogma of a centralized monopoly on the legitimate use of force. The Emperor, as head of the

---

[12] In reference to the period of transition between the Yayoi and Tomb cultures, a Chinese document, the *Wei Chih*, describes *Wa* or archaic Japanese as "a law-abiding people, fond of liquor, familiar with agriculture, versed in spinning and weaving and expert at fishing, living in a society of strict social differences which were indicated in part by tattooing or other facial and body markings. . . ." The *Wei Chih* credits the *Wa* with a considerable degree of political organization. They are said to have originally been divided into 100 tribes, varying in size from 1,000 to 70,000 households. Reischauer and Fairbank (1960).

Tennō uji or Imperial clan, had established a relatively large chiefdom in the Yamato area and extended varying degrees of political, military, and economic control into areas beyond his own chiefdom. At that time and for a few more centuries the Ainu had control of Hokkaido and northern Honshu.

Certain patrilineal clans called *uji-Kabane* were socially, politically, religiously, and economically, prominent. That is, the uji chieftainship for most purposes controlled its own chiefdom. With increasing size and complexity, the uji gained control of unrelated communities called *be* whose people were required to perform economic and other services. Although the records of the elite sometimes make it appear that the *be* were guilds or corporations in a sophisticated Chinese-like society, the *be* were essentially those farming communities that were in the chiefdom and outside the chief's lineage. Often, in addition to farming, and in some few cases even exclusively, the be carried on occupational specializations such as weaving, smithing, pottery, and leatherwork. Full-time professional craftsmen, usually referred to as *tomo-be*, were often located around the seats of government. All occupations tended to be hereditary for be communities as well as for be individuals.

Attached to some of the uji and be were a few *yakko*, who were slaves by conquest, crime, or debt, and could be bought and sold. Undoubtedly many Ainu were enslaved after battles. Occupationally the slaves were divided according to a modified Chinese system into tomb guards (*ryōko*), government cultivators (*kwankō*), temple and private servants (*kenin* or *yatsuko*), government slaves (*kunuhi*), and private slaves (*shinuhi*). The Taihō and Yōrō codes of the Nara period forbade intermarriage between freemen and slaves or between slaves of the first three categories and those of the latter two categories.

Slavery was nominally abolished in the Heian (794–1185) and later periods by governmental decrees, but there continued to be a body of semi-slaves such as serfs, bond servants, and indentured tenants. During the Kamakura period (1185–1392) there were tradesmen called *hitoakibito* engaged in buying and selling servants. In the Ashikaga period (1392–1603) children were kidnaped, bought, and sold to be raised as servants. In the Tokugawa period (1603–1868) decrees were passed to make this a capital offense and to limit the term of engagements of servants to ten years. Still, it has been only in the past century of great economic growth, with the development of real labor shortages, land reforms, and the spread of an ideology of egalitarianism, that serfdom has fully disappeared. The Nara slave caste, particularly the tomb guards and probably in some areas the private slaves, formed a significant part of the pool from which the outcastes were drawn in the Heian period. Without the continuing cheap labor market evidenced in serfdom the outcastes could not have been maintained through several centuries as a low occupational group. The background is one of precarious economic conditions which foster ingroup solidarity, dependency, low geographical mobility, and economic rigidity.

The operation of a "labor market" in early Japan had a different setting than that which has developed in Japan in the last few centuries. Early Japan was a socially segmented and stratified archaic state with weak integration of local areas. Each local area tended to be a closed corporate community with a multi-caste local exchange system, similar to the Hindu *jajmani* system. There was a complex of prescribed economic and other rights and obligations according to rank and occupation within the local social network. Every segment of local society had its roles and each segment had a vested interest in the operation of the system as a whole. Even the defiled, outcaste, or untouchable occupations were functionally significant in the local economy. Thus, various mechanisms such as the granting of monopolies, tax-free use of land, and sanctions for the outcaste leadership were created by the culture to insure the persistence of groups to carry out the defiled occupations.

Early native religious beliefs emphasized ritual pollution (*kegare*), avoidance (*imi*), and offerings for propitiation (*harai*) for association with blood and death. The slaughter of animals was associated with the agricultural ritual to insure sufficient rainfall. There is evidence that in pre-Nara times the common people would move away from their homes when there was a death in the family, and a new site would be selected for a capital at the death of a chief or an emperor. Childbirth, menstruation, diseases, wounds, dead bodies, and to some extent even simple physical dirtiness from soil or sweat were defiling, and those associated with them professionally, such as burial attendants for the elite, were considered of very low station. The ritual impurity that was inevitable in every station of life could be overcome by exorcism and cleansing ceremonies, by separating pregnant women from the household in parturition huts, and by having newlyweds live in nuptial huts. One name sometimes given to outcastes was *sanjo-no-mono,* "people of sanjō," believed to refer either to nomads who occupied abandoned parturition huts or to the special helpers at childbirth, whose occupation was considered unclean.

The Shinto concept of uncleanness as the greatest *tsumi* (things displeasing to the gods) contributed to the development of the Eta. Disease, wounds, death, and the necessary activities relating to death were regarded as causes of uncleanness, in addition to menstruation and childbirth. However, among the ancient Japanese meat was included in the diet and the flesh of animals, fishes, and birds was of-

fered to the gods as a sacrifice. The flesh of certain animals was prohibited as food (the ox, the horse, the dog, the monkey, the fowl), but
much was not (for example, the flesh of the deer, the rabbit, the pig).

The concept that the flesh of animals is unclean and displeasing to
the gods was firmly established only after the rise of Ryobu Shinto
in the early Nara period (710–784). This was the result of a fusion
between Shintoism and Buddhism, incorporating the Buddhist teaching of compassion to all beings and the Shinto idea of imi (avoidance).
Legislation was passed in the seventh and eighth and subsequent centuries forbidding hunting and slaughtering, though hunting and flesh-
eating continued well into the Tokugawa period. The ancient Shinto
idea of uncleanness was now attached to meat eating, and a minority
who continued to practice this ancient custom began to be despised.
We find that in 1683 eating the flesh of horse, cow, pig, goat, wild
boar, deer, monkey, bear, or antelope caused uncleanness for a hundred days.[13]

Since the Eta were held to be defiled, not only were they prohibited
from participating in the worship of the gods, but individuals coming
in contact with these defiled people were treated with disfavor, for
defilement was thought to be contagious. In early Japan the Eta were
indispensable as disposers of defiled objects in the precincts of the
Shinto temples.

Buddhism, which was introduced into Japan in the sixth century,
became widespread in the eighth and ninth centuries; it brought with
it a strong prohibition against disrupting the cycle of life and death
and proscribed the killing of animals and the eating of meat. Thus
Buddhism contributed to the separation of occupations associated with
animal slaughter and processing from the general body of commoner
and slave occupations. After the introduction of Buddhism animal
sacrifice was removed from the ritual for rain. However, there was
more than religious ideology behind abstaining from animal slaughter.
As early as 741 a governmental decree forbade the slaughter of horses
and cattle because "horses and cattle feed people by working hard and
they thus replace the work of people." [14] In this predominantly agricultural country meat was a minor source of food; animals were used
only after their natural death and then primarily for their hides. A
historical document dated 920 and referred to as the Ruiju Kokushi
states that "You should not kill cattle nor give them as a sacrifice." [15]

During the Heian period those be communities and slaves in occupations related to death and animal products tended to be forced outside the normal society. People in these occupations came to form the

---

[13] Ninomiya (1933), pp. 76–79.
[14] Ueda and Harada (1960).
[15] Hayashiya, et al. (eds.) (1962), p. 17.

main body of outcastes in Japan, but at the same time a number of occupations completely unrelated to animals or death were considered of very low station and were also treated as outcaste.

The *kakibe,* one of the categories of be groups of peasants and artisans not under the direct control of the Imperial clan, was divided into two segments. One of these segments was engaged in "degrading occupations" such as tomb-watching and caring for birds. One of the favorite sports of the elite at the time was falconry, and those who cared for the falcons were called *etori.* The first known written use of the term Eta, in the document *Chiri-Bukuro* of the middle of the thirteenth century, makes an explicit connection between Eta and etori: "Why should *kiyome* be called *eta? Eta* must have derived from *etori. . . . Eta* is a changed form of *etori.*" [16] "Kiyome" in this document refers to street sweepers, well diggers, and craftsmen controlled by the temple; and the kiyome were in fact called Eta. The same document indicates that poor priests, orphans, and beggars and criminals called Hinin (literally "non-human") were grouped with Eta in the same social category and that Eta were also called Hinin.[17] Until the middle of the sixteenth century the terms Eta and Hinin were rather loosely used.

There is evidence that many of the communities associated with building and guarding of tombs of the Tomb period became outcaste communities. We have already mentioned that one of the categories of slaves, the ryōko, were tomb guards. "In the Go-Kinai area many of the ancient Imperial and Noble tombs have, or had until recent times, an Eta community at their foot—telling of their functions as caretakers of the dead." [18]

The origin of the outcastes is traced to Kyoto in the ninth century by Ninomiya.[19] He reports that by custom Kyoto was the source of authority for them, with Eta chiefs going there to inquire into customary law to settle serious disputes. One of Ninomiya's sources claims that the first Eta villages were settled in Kojima (earlier Ishihara-no-Sato, now a part of the community of Kisshō-in) on the banks of the Katsura River and in another village to the northeast called Kakiage (earlier known as Sai-no-Sato). The earliest occupants of these villages were reported to have been cattle herders and disposers of the dead, but Ninomiya suggests that after the Department of Falconry was abolished under Buddhist pressure in 860, the etori, who had learned the skills of slaughter in gathering food for falcons and dogs, moved into these villages to serve as butchers or engaged in similar despised occupations.

[16] Ueda and Harada (1960), p. 47.
[17] Hayashiya (1962), pp. 19–20.
[18] Hall (1962), p. 526.
[19] Ninomiya (1933), p. 72.

Those following the low status occupations were forced by social pressures to gather in the same villages, invariably located on wasteland. It is usually inaccurate to say that one particular village is an Eta village because they slaughter animals there, and another is a Hinin village because the wandering outcastes live there. The variety of occupational groups represented in these outcaste communities is usually quite wide, and it is the rare outcaste community that is represented by only one occupation. Probably many of the etori (food gatherers) became tosha (butchers) who in time constituted the main stream of Eta. In addition, primarily from a segment of be-min (be people), came the tomo-be (professional artisans) who were tanners and leather workers. Also, the amabe (menial workers) and ukarebito (floating people) were an important part of the growing outcaste segment, as Ninomiya[20] points out.

THE OUTCASTES IN ASHIKAGA AND TOKUGAWA JAPAN

In the early large-scale colonization of Japan, Eta communities moved as an integral part of society.[21] As the sophisticated culture of the capital spread to the provinces, it fostered the growth of outcaste communities composed essentially of local people. However, in the later movements out of the Inland Sea region to northern Honshu and Hokkaido, migrant outcastes must have lost their identity as outcastes in the enforced equality of the frontier and war.

The Ashikaga (1392–1603) was a period of civil war in which social and geographical mobility increased sharply. Outcastes moved more freely than before, and there is abundant evidence that the Eta were often encouraged by the feudal lords (daimyō) to settle in their manors (shōen) to produce leather goods and perform other services. Whole families or even extended families would move. If individuals did move alone, they would retain their family and ancestral ties by re-

---

[20] Although not clearly differentiated legally or any other way until the Tokugawa period, it is useful to present Ninomiya's occupational classification of the outcastes for the Kamakura and Ashikaga periods. Ninomiya divided the Eta-Hinin caste of these periods into the following four categories. Each of these occupational groups had predecessors in early periods and a continuity into the Tokugawa period.

    (1) Butchers, tanners, and makers of leather goods. (This group, in the main, formed the Eta of the Tokugawa period.)
    (2) Dyers and manufacturers of bamboo articles.
    (3) Entertainers, prostitutes, and diviners. (This group formed the bulk of Hinin in the Tokugawa period and includes puppet show men, as well as some sweepers.)
    (4) Undertakers and caretakers of tombs.
Ninomiya (1933), pp. 74–76, 85–86.
[21] Hall (1962), p. 522.

peated visits, if possible, although the criminal nature of leaving a
feudal manor often prevented returning to it. A new settlement was
always a branch of the main village to which it attached itself.[22] Even
today about eighty percent of the outcaste villages are located in the
outskirts of the old castle towns.[23] Outcastes were allowed to use their
land as "squatters" and were not taxed, or taxed lightly on their produce or services. In view of the extremely heavy taxes on the agricul-
turalists to support a large military force, this was an effective way to
vie for the services of the outcastes.

Since the Eta developed around occupational specializations that
were taboo for non-Eta, they essentially held monopolies of their
trades. Given the general Japanese trends of inherited occupation, a
rigid socio-economic hierarchy, occupationally specialized communities, and ritual pollution, it was just this monopolistic character along
with a sedentary life that maintained the Eta as an outcaste group for
a thousand years. During the Ashikaga period the Eta were the most
fortunate of the pariah classes, that is, of the Eta-Hinin caste. They
held special skills and economic monopolies, owned property, and had
a stable community life; albeit this very stability assured their continuity as an outcaste population. The Hinin trades usually required
less skill, so that a person could move from one Hinin trade to another with relative ease. Also the Hinin were geographically more
mobile. They could move in and out of Eta or Hinin villages or take
up a respectable occupation in a commoner village and in time actually become a commoner. Written records and even laws from the
Tokugawa period maintain that the Eta are outcastes permanently by
inheritance whereas the Hinin are outcastes only by occupation and
social status. Yoshimune, the eighth *shōgun* or military chief of state,
and a great reformer for several years after 1716, demoted those who
attempted double suicide to Hinin status as a punishment. Through
the performance of *ashi arai* ("foot-washing") and the support of relatives, a commoner who had become a Hinin could become a commoner again within ten years, a thing also reported for Eta but extremely rare. This classification is after the fact that the Eta are in a
more permanent and thus more identifiable position.

In addition to simply slaughtering animals, butchering, and tanning
hides, Eta skills in working leather, bone, gut, and fur were in such
demand for the manufacture of saddles, armor, bowstrings, musical
instrument strings, and other goods that the competing military lords
vied for their services. Beyond the fully monopolistic occupations related to animals, several partial or local monopolies were developed by
the Eta and the Hinin. Primarily these were occupations that were

[22] Hall (1962), p. 525.
[23] Ninomiya (1933), p. 89.

considered degrading, such as village watchmen, public executioners, mortuary services, and the night-soil fertilizer trade. The Hinin were more often associated with the transient trades such as begging, prostitution, shooting gallery keepers, peep show men, monkey masters, dog trainers, snake charmers, jugglers, acrobats, and fox tamers. Criminals, who became Hinin simply by operating outside of normal society, were often banished to or even imprisoned in Eta communities.

The Eta and Hinin expanded their industries beyond the traditional degrading ones. Apparently by degrading an otherwise neutral occupation through their association with it and by using the standard strong-arm guild tactics of the feudal periods, they established new partial and localized monopolies in basket making, straw sandal and mat manufacture, tea whisk manufacture, weaving, and textile dying. In this period of relative affluence combined with a high demand for leather goods, the Eta almost fully absorbed into their caste and communities two occupational types: dyers and manufacturers of bamboo articles and undertakers and caretakers of tombs.

With this listing of occupations, it should be remembered that agriculture was never abandoned by the Eta or by any other outcaste group permanently settled on a piece of arable land. Be-like communities have continued from prehistoric times up to the present, and this combination of farming along with other occupations within the same community has been very common in Japan. While the head of the family may be a butcher, his wife and children are probably raising a sizable garden if a piece of land is available. The demands for Eta services in the feudal periods drew more individual Eta into the Eta monopolies, even though many of their communities remained predominantly agricultural. A 1920 survey of outcaste communities by the Ministry of Internal Affairs indicated that 49 percent of the households had farming occupations.[24]

The Eta migrants out of the Inland Sea region in the fifteenth through seventeenth centuries tended to retain their traditional occupations longer and so were more often identified as Eta by craft. Those who stayed behind more often emphasized the high status occupation of agriculture and were more easily identified by place of residence than by occupation. Since agriculture, particularly land ownership and control, holds a position of high status in the traditional sector of Japanese culture, of which the Eta are a part, an occupational emphasis on agriculture became an alternative to "passing" as non-Eta into the majority society.

The Ashikaga and Tokugawa pattern of outcaste migration shows up in eastern Honshu where the outcaste communities are usually found in more urban settings than in western Japan. This is consistent

---

[24] Cornell (1961), p. 286.

with the shift in the Inland Sea area to agriculture by the outcastes, mentioned above. Also, outcaste farmers could be more free and independent from daimyo control in the west than in the east. In the seventeenth century outcaste communities were located in semi-urban or urban settings in over two hundred fiefs and cities directly controlled by the Tokugawa military government. Relatively few outcaste communities developed in the northeast; those that did were more often located in castle towns, harbors, and commercial towns rather than in the rural districts. The Eta community in Sendai was founded when the daimyō Date Masamune constructed the castle town. The Eta had a monopoly on the leather work in the whole territory of the Sendai fief.

In the Tokugawa period the demand for Eta services continued to draw Eta to the castle towns where they received protection from the feudal lords. However, in the relative peace of this centralized feudal period, there was a rigid occupational status system even more complex than that of the Heian period. The noble and Imperial families along with the upper military formed an elite, while farmers, artisans, and merchants ranked below, with outcastes at the bottom.

In several ways the Eta caste is essentially a Tokugawa phenomenon, for it is in this period of some 250 years of internal peace that the Eta were pressured by legal and extra-legal forces into a distinct outcaste and untouchable segment of society. The critical monopolies of the Ashikaga period that were related to warfare, such as tanning and leatherwork, lost their importance in a time of peace, while the idea of the defiled nature of Eta had hardened. Additionally, the commercial development of the late Tokugawa period brought on a gradual loss of monopolies which helped to force many of the fast growing Eta population out of their traditional occupations. Judicial decisions and legislative decrees in the middle and later parts of the Tokugawa period [25] indicate the Eta were legally held as outcastes.

---

[25] Ninomiya wrote (1933, pp. 97–98):

The Tokugawa policy of maintaining the *status quo* of society was a severe blow to the Eta; for having been considered as the lowest of the classes and even lower than the Hinin, the Eta not only encountered bitter contempt from all sides but also suffered from various humiliating legal restrictions. Thus the Eta were required to marry Eta, and were not permitted to reside outside of the Eta villages; furthermore, they were forbidden to enter the service of commoners as servants. . . . The privilege of dressing the hair in conventional manner and of wearing *geta* was denied to . . . [them]. When approaching the home of a commoner, the Eta were required to take off their headgear and footwear before entering the courtyard; and they were not allowed to cross the threshold. Moreover, the privilege of sitting, eating, and smoking in company of the commoners was denied to them; and in court, the Eta were always seated in a lower position than that accorded to . . . [commoners].

There was a significant legal decision in 1859 (Passin, 1955, p. 35):

When an Eta youth was killed in a scuffle between Eta and non-Eta gangs,

Although the Tokugawa government policy was highly discriminatory, it did respect the customary bodies of self-government of the Eta and Hinin, and also took some action to stop the commercial invasion by commoners into the Eta monopolies.[26]

Outcastes in Edo

Edo (Tokyo) was never an important population center for outcastes. However, because the people of Edo were more literate than those in the rest of Japan, we know more about the outcastes of that city and can document some facts concerning their social organization. In 1800 there was only one Eta community in Edo. That community, with a population of 800–900, was located in Inai, later to be called Asakusa. A later report shows that there were about 4,000 Hinin (1,023 households) in Edo near the end of the Tokugawa period. A census in 1871 gave an all-Japan total of 280,311 Eta, 23,480 Hinin, and 79,095 miscellaneous outcastes. The 1920 survey showed Tokyo Prefecture to report only 7,658 outcastes, less than one percent of the official total of 829,675 listed for all Japan that year.

We will now present in some detail the various low status groups; for one can see in the Tokugawa period a hardening of caste dif-

---

Danzaemon, the Eta leader in the Kanto district, brought the case before . . . the city magistrate. After careful reflection, the magistrate delivered the now famous judgment: An Eta is worth 1/7 of an ordinary person. If you would have me punish the guilty party, let him kill six more of your fellows.

The following edict was issued in 1870 in the Wakayama feudatory (Donoghue, 1956, p. 43):

The morality of the Eta people is not good these years and they very often act viciously. Therefore, order them to abide by the following regulation:

(1) To walk at the edge of one side of the street and not to disturb passers-by, not only in the city, but also in their own community.

(2) Not to loiter except from sunrise to sunset, either in the city or in the suburbs. And also in their own communities, they are not to loiter arbitrarily during the night. On the holiday of Setsubun [holiday of the change of season] they are allowed to walk until five in the evening, but not later than that; on the last day of the year, not later than nine o'clock.

(3) They shall not eat or drink in the city.

(4) They shall not use umbrellas or headgear except in rainy weather.

(5) They shall not use any footgear, except sandals.

[26] In return for these monopolies, both the Eta and the Hinin owed some duty to the respective local governments. It was the duty of the former to act as executioners and to guard the bodies of criminals after execution. The latter, by order of the government, kept in custody the criminals who were very young or suffered from severe sickness, served as jailers and cooks for female criminals, acted as prison guards, transfixed the criminals with spears at crucifixion, and guarded the heads of criminals exhibited to the public. They also conducted a condemned man when he was carried around the city on horseback as a preliminary to execution, discharged the office of torturers in judicial trials, tattooed criminals, wielded the saw when heads were taken off with that instrument, and executed all the sentences pronounced against Christians. (Ninomiya, 1933, p. 102.)

ferentiation toward the more evolved caste system of Hindu India and
its segmentation of lowly occupations.

Non-Eta Low Class Groups

A detailed social classification of the lowest classes was constructed by Ishii[27] from Tokugawa records. He concluded that collectively the general population could be called *ryōmin* (good people),
differentiating them from the lowest groups, *senmin* (lowly people).

In the early Tokugawa period, between the ryōmin and senmin
stood an intermediate class of *gōmune* (and possibly the *kaburi kojiki*,
or vagrant beggars). Within the senmin Ishii listed five groups in
descending order of status: *shuku* (outcaste farmers), *chasen* (tea whisk
makers), *sarukai* (monkey breeders), Hinin and Eta. Depending on the
locality outside of the city of Edo, shuku, chasen, and sarukai might
be ryōmin instead of senmin, non-outcaste beggars and entertainers.

Gōmune status was not hereditary. In early Tokugawa times, before 1830, they were just lowly *chōnin* (merchants), but in the city of
Edo their occupations centered around begging, and begging was controlled by the Hinin chiefs. The gōmune could marry ordinary people
and they were tried for their crimes before ordinary courts, but their
occupational activities were sanctioned, controlled, and taxed by the
Hinin chiefs. Their begging was usually done in connection with some
kind of entertainment in front of houses, such as singing, dancing,
samisen playing, rope tricks, magic, story telling, and imitating bird
cries and animal barking. The gōmune themselves had subchiefs, rules
of conduct, and exclusive areas (*nawabari*) for operation. A license for
begging was required in specific areas of the city of Edo, for which a
fee was paid monthly to the gōmune chief. In the Tenpō Restoration
(1830) the gōmune were required to live in the Asakusa district of
Edo, a Hinin center, and from that time on they were considered to
be Hinin.

The shuku, especially in the Nara Prefecture area, were essentially
outcaste farmers who were segregated and not allowed to marry
ordinary farmers. In the Chūgoku area, centered around Nagoya, some
of them came under the control of Eta chiefs.

The status of chasen, the bamboo tea whisk makers, varied from one
locality to the next. In western Honshu their status seems to have been
particularly low; they were not allowed to mix with farmers, their
names were registered in a special part of the official records (under
mizu-nomi hyakushō, "farmers who just drink water" and eat no
food because they are so poor), they were required to sit in a lower

---

[27] Ishii (1960).

position than farmers on formal occasions, and in some places they
were controlled by Eta chiefs.

The sarukai put on monkey shows and received money for this
entertainment and, particularly in the Kyoto-Osaka area, for the luck
that monkey dancing brought to a household at important times. In
Edo they registered at the Eta chief's house, but they paid a fee to
Chōdayū, the sarukai chief who controlled the monkey dancing in Edo.
They married within sarukai groups.

One group of beggars is hard to classify but, since they were fallen
ryōmin, probably should be mentioned in connection with the
gōmune. These are the kaburi kojiki ("straw mat beggars") who were
essentially illegal beggars, but who formed a somewhat distinct subculture in Edo. They were scattered in sixteen districts in Edo, each
with a chief, and each beggar had a loosely fixed, unlicensed area in
which to work. Their chiefs or *oyabun* ("parent role"), collected a tax
from their *kobun* ("child role") on the first and fifteenth of every
month. They did not entertain as did the gōmune or Hinin but simply
stood in front of wealthy houses and begged. The kaburi kojiki chiefs
had houses with roofs of straw mats rather than tile or straw thatch,
while the ordinary kaburi kojiki dwelling was only a small shelter with
a standing frame of four bamboo poles and straw mats for walls and
roof.

Since the kaburi kojiki were not sanctioned by the Edo government,
many of them were regularly arrested and sent to prison in Asakusa
where they worked for the Hinin or escaped to become kaburi kojiki
again. When the kaburi kojiki committed some offense toward the
Eta or Hinin chiefs, when they raped the wives or daughters of their
fellow workers, when they begged by coercion, or when they looted a
burning house, they were either sent permanently out of Edo or
severely punished. Eta and Hinin chiefs had the faces of people who
were evicted from Edo drawn in likeness and these drawings were used
much as the police's "Wanted" poster is used today. Kaburi kojiki
could also be punished by being tied to a pole for three days: in the
summer in a dark room when the mosquitoes bite; in winter in the
river; in spring in the snow (if there was no snow, they were beaten);
and in the fall left without food.

The Hinin chief was called Zenshichi and lived in Asakusa. Zenshichi was in turn controlled by Danzaemon, the Eta chief. Under
Zenshichi there were ten subchiefs, each controlling one district of
Edo. In each of these ten districts there were further subdivisions
controlled by "camp heads" who in turn allotted specific areas for
begging and other Hinin activities to the people under them. Each
Hinin with an allotted area in Edo had a certificate that showed his
age, place of birth, address, date of issue, and the official stamp. Thus

the whole city was divided into exclusive districts for outcaste activities. In addition to the registered and controlled Hinin (*kakae* Hinin), there were some "wild Hinin" (*no* Hinin) who were not registered.

The Hinin took care of prisoners, their execution and burial. For all of these public enterprises the Edo government paid the Zenshichi, who in turn paid the employed Hinin. The private enterprises of Hinin in Edo centered around begging, scavenging, and professional celebrating or mourning (at childbirth, marriage, and death). A Hinin with a prosperous merchant in his assigned area who was celebrating a special occasion would put on his best clothes, go to the house, and with extreme politeness offer appropriate salutations and then protect the merchant's house by keeping the other beggars away. In return he would be given money, perhaps be allowed to collect old papers regularly and to help put out fires or do other emergency jobs for the chōnin for which there would be pay.

Used papers were sold to an agent who in turn peddled them to others for reuse. The Hinin were allowed to collect papers only in the daytime except on the last day of the year and at Setsubun (the eve of the beginning of spring), both general clean-up times. They were not allowed to beg with coercion or to put out fires unless asked by the house owner. The wives and daughters of Hinin sometimes wore women's umbrella-shaped hats and sang songs accompanied by the samisen. Because they were thrown money from the windows they were called *mado geisha* ("window-entertaining girls").

The typical Hinin house was reportedly eight *jō* in size (about twelve by twelve feet square), had a roof but no ceiling, and did not use *shōji* (paper screens) within the house. Hinin could wear only cotton, not silk. Those who were camp chiefs or district chiefs could wear *haori* (a type of jacket), but without an *obi* (sash) around it. The chiefs did not cut their hair and did not beg or play instruments in public, and had more freedom of movement than the other Hinin. Other Hinin could not wear haori, were required to cut their hair, could not go out at night, and were required to stay in their assigned areas.

If the Hinin broke the rules by stealing, using coercion, or leaving their assigned areas, they were subject to fixed penalties. The first time they left they were just scolded and told to stay. The second time they were tattooed on the upper arm, the third time around the left wrist, and the fourth time they were killed. These penalties were strengthened in 1790; the first time they were tattooed on the upper left arm, the second on the left wrist, and the third time they were killed. (Tattooing of criminals was a widespread practice in Japan.) Also, members of one class always had a somewhat residual right to

judge and execute members of the next lower class when there was a
clear breach of the law. Thus samurai did kill hyakushō and chōnin,
and all ryōmin could, with impunity, kill senmin when the latter had
committed a grave crime. However, the stories about samurai testing
a new sword by cutting off the head of a senmin appear to be un-
founded. Human heads were occasionally taken as trophies of battle
in Japan's history as a way to dishonor the dead man, but it was
considered to be a relatively honorable way to die. Decapitation was
not an appropriate way to kill outcastes.

Traditional Social Organization of the Eta

In the early 1600's the head of an Eta family with the family
name of Yano and a personal name of Danzaemon was the leader of
the Eta in Edo (Tokyo). His leadership and that of the successive
heads of the Yano family was sanctioned by the *bakufu*, the military
government of Japan based in Edo. During the Meiji Restoration the
family name was changed to Dan. However "Danzaemon" has been
used as a title and a term of reference for the successive outcaste leaders in Edo from Tokugawa into Meiji times.

The first Danzaemon lived in Nihonbashi Miya-machi and later
moved to Asakusa Torikoshi. In 1645, he moved to Asakusa Shin-
machi, now a western part of Imato-machi or a northern part of San-ya-
bori, where the Danzaemon Eta chief resided for over 250 years.
Shin-machi, near the Sumida River, became the major Eta enclave in
Edo. Around it were other social fringe sections such as Yoshiwara,
the famous prostitution district; Senju, a district where low class
transients stayed; and a district where low class people with incurable
diseases stayed (a kind of leper colony).

The large estate and mansion of Danzaemon was called Kako-i-uchi.
In the Kansei era (1789–1801) the land scale of Kako-i-uchi was about
12 acres (14,784 *tsubo*), and Danzaemon directly controlled 15 sarukai
households and 232 other "follower" (presumably all Eta) households
who lived either at Kako-i-uchi or in the vicinity. Danzaemon had
legal and taxing jurisdiction over the outcastes in Edo and in the
surrounding country, all of Kanhasshū (the eight fiefs of Kanto), all
of Izu, and parts of Kai, Tsuruga, and Mutsu.[28]

We have already mentioned his superior legal relationship over the
sarukai (Chōdayū) and Hinin leaders (Zenshichi). In the Kaei era
(1848–1854) the Danzaemon controlled some 6,000 households. By
1847 the size of his estate had been reduced to about 2.1 acres, but he
was still very wealthy. He led a life equal to a small feudal lord of the
time. Specifically, he was equal in wealth to a 3,000-*koku* (15,000

[28] Ishii (1960), appendix; and Kanzaki (1964), pp. 191–97.

bushels of rice) *hatamoto,* a high class warrior but considerably lower than a daimyō, who almost by definition drew over 10,000 koku each year. His income that year was 597 *ryō* in gold (one ryō was worth about 18 bushels of rice) and other smaller amounts in silver and copper. About 440 ryō were collected from ordinary Eta in the form of taxes and butcher's and leather worker's license fees.

The Danzaemon derived some income from the sale of drums, wicks, and other leather products made in a shop on his estate. He also held an official regional monopoly on the production and sale of leather goods. In return for the monopoly the Danzaemon presented leather goods of all kinds to the Tokugawa government. In the manufacture of candle wicks, Danzaemon selected fifteen villages a year to make them and gave instructions on how many to make. A wholesaler in his employ purchased the production of those villages and presented them for sale on one particular market day (*kinoene*) every other month.

Danzaemon arbitrated disputes between the outcastes in his control and punished those who broke laws pertaining to outcaste life and occupations. Conflicts between outcastes and ryōmin were handled by a ryōmin judiciary. Danzaemon's officers, who performed such duties as tax collecting and the enforcement of monopolies, were appointed once every five years upon advisement of a council of about 500 lesser outcaste leaders. A vote was taken by the council, but results of the vote were not made public and the Danzaemon used the results in arriving at a list of appointees.

The mansion of Danzaemon at the beginning of the Meiji era had a high wall, a large garden with a pond, and even included a shoe factory. The house itself had 14 major rooms and about 300 square yards (152 jō) of floor space. Danzaemon and the rest of the outcastes lost their monopolies with the Meiji Restoration, which ended the Tokugawa period and started the Meiji era. At the same time the outcastes were officially declared to be commoners. Danzaemon thus lost the basis of his economic and political powers, and the institution of a genuinely powerful outcaste leader completely vanished. There are, of course, many descendants of the various Danzaemon, and the Dan family tomb is still maintained at Asakusa Dairyūji. The thirteenth Danzaemon actually employed foreign technicians and built a shoe factory at Hachiba-chō, but it was a financial failure. The San-ya-bori Primary School was built on the former Danzaemon estate. This was later changed to the present Daitō Commercial High School.

Along with a wave of revolutionary reorganization in government and other spheres of life in the Meiji era, the terms Eta and Hinin were officially abolished and these people were henceforth to be treated on a par with the common people (*heimin*) in occupation and social standing. But the 383,000 outcastes enumerated in the census taken in 1871, the year of their supposed liberation, instead of disappearing as a distinct part of the Japanese population continued to live a segregated life stigmatized and branded by social customs. Not only did they not disappear but there has been in the past ninety years a proportionate expansion of their total population to the point where they have become one of modern Japan's major unresolved social problems.

..
SECTION II

*Attempts at Political
and Social Solutions
to the Outcaste Problem*

INTRODUCTION

The following chapters trace the more recent history of the outcastes, principally their self-conscious organization into a significant
political movement. Both similarities to and differences from the
political history of the American Negro since the Emanicipation are
noticeable. The time span is roughly the same. But whereas the integration activities of the Negro have been led by nonpolitical Negro
churches, recently joined by many sympathetic white churches, the
Japanese outcastes have been championed from the beginning by
organizations directly immersed in politics. Serious movements in
political directions have come much later in America. The history
of the Burakumin in this respect may possibly indicate something
about Negro actions in the future, despite the differences in the political climates of Japan and the United States.

In Japan the nonpolitical integrationist movements have become
rather pale shadows of the essentially Marxist leadership directing the
fight for political, economic, and social equality of the former outcaste.
With the collaboration of George Totten a large mass of documents
and publications were sifted to present the significant flow of events
recorded in Chapters 2 and 3. (Brief chronologies of the social protest
movements are appended to each chapter.)

The two chapters summarize what has been done through a political
approach to the outcaste problem. From the reports, it is obvious that
the political militance of some of the outcastes has resulted in governmental action, at least in the economic sphere. Here, it has made overt

31

discriminatory practices impossible. It is questionable, however, how radically this political action has changed social attitudes among the majority population.

The remaining chapter in this section presents an examination of what other social institutions that deal more directly with attitudes and values have done for the outcaste in Japan. The role taken by various religious denominations is briefly examined, and then the ways are discussed in which the school system and educational institutions generally have been used in an attempt to change prevailing social discrimination.

The role of the established religious institutions considerably differs from the role played by church groups in the United States. Whereas in America the major Negro leaders very often have a religious background, there is no such religious leadership in the resolution of discrimination in Japan. The history of religious activity in that country has often been the history of particular religious reformers who have in no way sparked social movements.

The influence of education has also taken a different course. Since the educational system in Japan is a nationally centralized one, up until the postwar period it was relatively easy to establish so-called integrated schools and to exhort teachers to help in ending discrimination. The results of this program will be examined below. After the war, with decentralization, there was an increase in the activity of some of the prefectures that added programs for changing attitudes about minority groups to the curriculum. There is as yet no evidence available concerning the efficacy of the program now established.

Chapter 2

GEORGE O. TOTTEN AND
HIROSHI WAGATSUMA

Emancipation: Growth and Transformation of a Political Movement

In April, 1869, a committee of feudal clan officials deliberated on how to rectify what was called by some "a national shame in foreign eyes" and "a flaw in the imperial rule." The subject of these meetings was the outcaste groups in newly modernized Japan.[1] During the next two years there were many suggestions about this problem. For example, it was recommended to the government that the Eta-Hinin status be abolished and that financial aid be given to initiate some industry through which outcastes could support themselves, such as the establishment of a leather industry and cattle raising in Hokkaido.

---

[1] A government auditor who had been much influenced by Western thought presented a plan for liberating the Eta-Hinin to the Kōgisho, a deliberative assembly that advised the government, composed of representatives of the 276 feudal clans. One delegate argued in favor of unconditional liberation for all these groups. Another suggested liberating and sending them to Hokkaido to help in opening up that new frontier.

Still another delegate considered the most immediate question to be revision of the system of measuring distances on roadways. The Tokugawa government had gone so far in attempting to ignore the very existence of outcaste communities that it had officially stipulated that road distances traversing them would not be counted in highway signs. For example, if an eleven-mile stretch of highway included one mile through or by an Eta village, the distance was officially posted as ten miles.

(Japanese historians are generally silent on the influence of the emancipation of serfs and slaves that was progressing contemporaneously in various countries. The American Civil War, 1861–1865, resulted in the emancipation of the slaves in the United States; the serfs in Russia were officially freed in 1861; in Colombia the slaves were given their freedom in 1862. Liberia had already been established in 1847 by the American Colonialization Society to settle ex-slaves in West Africa. The Japanese leaders could not have been totally unaware of these developments.)

Finally, a number of the leaders of these "special communities" submitted official petitions to the government, requesting emancipation.[2]

OFFICIAL EMANCIPATION (1871)

The Kōgisho (Lower House) finally recommended total liberation of the Eta-Hinin by an overwhelming vote of 172 to 29. In August, 1871, the government issued the Edict of Emancipation (Eta Kaihō Rei), Proclamation No. 61 of the Dajōkan (Council of State). Behind this edict was undoubtedly the government's desire to abolish the whole system of inherited status, caste, and privilege, except for the Imperial Family, for only thus could the new ruling groups give full and independent power to the new government they had created. (Eventually they were to establish a new aristocracy, but one that received its privileges in the post-Restoration dispensation.)

There was also an important economic reason for the edict. During the Edo period the land owned by the Eta communities, small and scattered as it was, had been designated as "tax-exempt land" (jōchi or nozokichi). In order for it to be included in the regular tax schedules, its owners had to be given the same status as other farmers.

Thus the interests of government policy rather than the welfare of the victims of discrimination brought about "emancipation." To have given it real social meaning, however, the Meiji government would have had to follow up with further administrative measures; at the time it was probably incapable of this because it lacked money and personnel, even if it had been sufficiently enlightened to desire to do so.

POST-EMANCIPATION DISCRIMINATION

Simple legislation was hardly sufficient to change social attitudes of discrimination built up over the centuries. In fact, these "new common people" (shin-heimin) lost the special privileges that the feudal society had accorded them—economic monopolies, for example, in butchering and leather work—without compensation. There was

---

[2] For instance, already in 1867, the Eta-Hinin of Watanabe Village in Settsu, the present Nishihama Buraku in Osaka (one of the three largest Tokusha Buraku in Japan, along with Shichijo in Kyoto and Fukushima in Hiroshima), when asking the government to emancipate them from their outcaste status, argued: "We are discriminated against as unclean people because we eat animal meat. However, those foreigners with whom Japan has recently entered into friendly relations also eat animal meat." Again in 1870, Genzaemon, head of Rendaiya Village in Yamashiro near Kyoto, also submitted an appeal for emancipation. See Buraku Mondai Kenkyūjo (Buraku Problems Research Institute), ed., *Buraku no Rekishi to Kaihō Undō* (1955), p. 129; also see Inoue (1959), p. 43. These two works have been relied on heavily in writing this chapter.

no longer any bar against the introduction of capital by non-Eta groups into the burgeoning leather goods industry; thus, majority Japanese took advantage of the skills the former Eta had developed over the years in this previously "polluting" type of work.[3] At the time of the Emancipation, people classified as Hinin could probably more readily melt into the majority population, for most of these had itinerant occupations. Most of the Eta, however, were tied to their local communities because their income was drawn from the network of social and financial relationships that traditionally supported these communities.

The Emancipation Edict was part of the process of abolishing all special feudal rights so that the new system of private ownership of land could be instituted. This culminated in the land survey of the Empire, completed by 1881. The people of the special communities— now usually referred to as Burakumin—were confirmed in their right to own the inferior farming areas to which they had earlier been relegated, or they remained tenants farming land owned by landlords. Over half of the former outcastes were engaged to some extent in agriculture. Others, in or near the cities, continued to butcher meat and tan hides, and some began to take over jobs generally considered undesirable or nonrewarding. Not only did the special communities lose their former monopolies, but they were required to pay taxes and enter military service for the prescribed term.

Because of the changes brought about after the Meiji Restoration, severe financial difficulties afflicted many of the ordinary people. Tensions and hostilities were often directed toward the former outcastes, who became scapegoats and butts of aggression for neighboring communities. In some instances, "eta hunts" (*eta-gari*), or "campaigns to exterminate the eta" (*eta-seibatsu*), developed. But financial difficulties were only a part of the problems and dislocations faced by the Japanese farmers. Many were suspicious of the new government and came to hate its policies of change, which they felt had been forced upon them. Some poorer farmers thought that emancipation of the Eta meant increased competition for land and feared that they would be dragged down to outcaste level. Many tended to blame the new government for any problem that arose. Frustration and anxiety among the commoners, especially in rural villages, broke out in a

---

[3] For instance, Danzaemon, the traditional leader of the Eta, emancipated by the Tokugawa government, after taking the new name of Dan Naoki, set up a factory in 1870 with special permission from the new Meiji government to produce shoes and to teach Burakumin Western techniques for making military footgear. To do so, he employed a foreign technician, hoping to help elevate his people economically, but the Edict of Emancipation deprived him of his privileged position. Non-Buraku competition and lack of capital caused him to fail. The company was saved by capital from Mitsui and survived purely as a business concern, without serving as a training ground for Burakumin industry. See Matsuda (1963), p. 48.

series of widespread rioting: during the ten years following the Restoration, over two hundred separate riots were recorded. Government office buildings, new schools, and police stations were attacked and burned, numerous government officials and policemen were killed or injured. Often, the "new common people" served as the most readily available victims for the rioters.

To illustrate, in January, 1872, a group of shin-heimin were attacked by angry farmers in Nara. Members of the former outcaste community had sent a formal notice to a neighboring village stating that, as they were now emancipated, they would no longer carry out their previous assignments of watching out for thieves, driving off beggars, and disposing of dead carcasses. The villagers felt they needed them for what were considered defiling, "dirty" jobs and asked them to continue, but the Burakumin remained steadfast in their refusal. In retaliation, the villagers refused the outcastes the use of the village-owned mountain sides to collect firewood. When three Burakumin were discovered trespassing on the hills, they apologized and escaped. A few days later, however, when two Burakumin ordered some *sake* at a shop, the storekeeper, in accordance with a new village decision, refused to serve them. Three more Burakumin joined the group, a quarrel ensued, and an angry crowd gathered. The frightened Burakumin fled to the house of the village leader, which was immediately surrounded. Fearful for his property, the village head acceded to the demand by the mob for the five Burakumin. Upon ejection, one was killed instantly, and three of the remaining four were killed later. Because the prefectural government had the mob leaders arrested, the infuriated villagers three months later raided the Burakumin community, burning most of the houses and beating many individuals. This time three of the mob leaders were sentenced to death and executed.

Another incident, known as the Mimasaka riot, again exemplifies a mob outbreak that culminated in an "eta hunt." On May 25, 1873, a farmer in Okayama Prefecture, long dissatisfied with the new government's policies, started the rumor that a stranger dressed in white was suspiciously wandering around trying to track down certain residents. The farmers gathered, armed with rifles and bamboo spears, and surrounded the house of the village head, demanding that he hand over the stranger who, they believed, had gone into his house. The village head insisted that there was no such person. Still unconvinced, the villagers broke into the house and searched for the stranger. Unable to find anyone, the mob moved on to a neighboring Buraku where they wrecked and burned fourteen houses. At the next village they destroyed the school building and a teacher's house. Then they split into two groups. One destroyed a school building and the home of the village head in an adjacent village, while the second group raided another Buraku. The groups merged at midnight and raided three more Buraku and set fire to the houses. Early in the morning the mob attacked a building of the prefectural government and also destroyed the nearby houses of the officers. The government recruited 300 ex-samurai for protection who started shooting and drove the mob away from the government buildings. The mob moved to other villages, destroying and setting fire to the houses of the village heads as they went. Many Buraku in the vicinity were raided. The mob increased in size, and on the fourth day, May 28, the whole district of Mimasaka became a scene of violence and destruction which lasted until June 1. Finally, 100 officials from the neighboring Okayama Prefecture, in addition to army troops from Osaka, arrived and subdued the riot. More than 400 individuals were arrested. According to official figures, 10 houses of government officials, 47 homes of village heads, 25 homes of policemen, 15 school buildings, and more than 300 Buraku homes were wrecked or burned. Eighteen Burakumin were reported dead and 11 badly injured. It was estimated that about 26,000 farmers joined the riot.

To be sure, outbursts against the Burakumin were only sporadic. Moreover, the attacks were rarely directed solely at the scapegoats, but included various symbols of state authority and local officials. Many ordinary farmers were simply afraid that the government policy was turning them into Burakumin.

The daily life of the new common people apparently was little changed for the better by emancipation. There was a constant fear of attack by aroused neighbors, and social discrimination continued in all aspects of life, including the new schools established to bring about universal education. Miyoshi Iheiji, one of the leaders of the early Buraku liberation movement, describes his experience at school:

When I entered junior high school in 1883, I was the first child from Sakamoto [a Buraku] and everyone was curious. . . . I was made to sit alone behind all the children in the class . . . nobody talked to me, nor wanted to sit by me. . . . A teacher of a physiology class asked me if it was true that we Burakumin did not defecate and urinate at the same time. . . . He also asked me who my ancestor was. I told him my ancestor was a general under Ōya Gyōbu Yoshitaka. He said that he had thought our ancestors were Koreans or Ainu. . . . I received the highest grades in my class, and when I was not present, the teacher told the class that it was to their shame to let an "eta" boy be the top student, and that they should study harder to excel an "eta." [4]

Despite legal emancipation, the Ministry of Justice in 1880 published *Zenkoku Minji Kanrei Ruishu (A Handbook of Japanese Cus-*

[4] *Buraku no Rekishi to Kaihō Undō* (1955), pp. 139–40.

38   EMANCIPATION

toms and Folkways) in which the Burakumin were described as "Eta
and hinin, the lowliest of all the people, almost resembling animals."
Such documents merely made overt the prevalent attitude of social
discrimination.

THE EARLY RECONCILIATION (YŪWA) MOVEMENT

Some advanced Burakumin, sensitive to the foreign philosophies
of liberalism, democratic rights, and socialism, attempted to apply
these ideas to a solution of their own problems. In 1902, a few Burakumin in Okayama Prefecture organized the Bisaku Heimin Kai (Bisaku
Common People's Association) to "attempt to overcome the cold and
harsh discrimination and mistreatment of Burakumin." Miyoshi Iheiji
became a central figure in this association. He urged the Burakumin
to unite and cooperate in improving their customs and manners, raising their moral standards, bettering themselves economically, and
educating themselves so as to achieve self-reliance and independence.
By so doing, they would influence the majority society to stop discrimination. The Bisaku Heimin Kai and other such associations, led
by middle class property owners in the Buraku, were significant because they arose from within the special communities and therefore
presaged the Burakumin movements that followed the First World
War.

Actually, these activities had little effect: discrimination continued
unabated. In 1902 in Wakayama, a monk of the Jōdo Shin sect of
Buddhism, encouraging people to donate money to charities, was
heard to say that since even worthless "eta" donate, those who were
really human should contribute more. In the same year a member of
the Diet, Ozaki Yukio, later to become a well-known figure in Japanese politics, objected to the simultaneous discussion of two bills by
remarking: "A combined discussion of the tax problem and naval
expansion is as incongruous as a son of a wealthy family walking
hand in hand with an 'eta' girl." Burakumin in Wakayama sent a
formal protest to Ozaki, demanding an apology. At the same time they
asked Prince Itō, the president of Ozaki's political party, to expel
Ozaki from the party. Both demands were ignored. At about this
time the District Court of Hiroshima approved the divorce of a non-
Buraku wife from her outcaste husband on the basis that "since
ancient times the 'eta' have been considered the lowliest racial segment, unequal to the general populace," and "according to tradition,
it is still normal for those who are not 'eta' to abhor marriage with
one." [5]

Heightened awareness of the continuing social discrimination finally

_____
[5] Fujitani (1960), pp. 21–52.

aroused Buraku leaders to action. In June, 1903, the inaugural meeting of the Dai Nippon Dōhō Yūwa Kai (Greater Japan Fraternal Conciliation Society) was held in Osaka, with 300 Burakumin from all parts of Japan present. They unanimously approved as objectives of the Society improvement of Burakumin moral training, customs and manners, general education, sanitary conditions, leadership, frugality and saving, and economic conditions.

This movement for "improvement" (*kaizen*) through self-help was in essence a call to lift the minority up to general Japanese standards in living conditions, employment, and education. It was fostered especially by leaders from the propertied class among the Burakumin— the well-to-do farmers and affluent merchants—located in the Kansai area, particularly in the cities of Osaka, Kyoto, and Kobe. (These Burakumin, while seeking social acceptance, could not extricate themselves from Buraku society without losing their economic base in the land and craft production-distribution networks.) Typical of the values inculcated in the name of self-improvement were those of the Meiji statesmen themselves: literacy, community cooperation, thrift, diligence, and cooperation with law-enforcement officials. These were intended to rectify what were considered the coarse, unruly habits of the common people and new commoners. Religion was also emphasized, particularly since the Burakumin, in general, were pious supporters of the Jōdo Shin sect. They advocated reverence for the Emperor, arguing that to practice discrimination was to ignore the Imperial will that all were to be equal in their loyalty to the Emperor.

Responding to an increase of literary output concerning the Burakumin problem and to the growth of political activities by outcastes and their sympathizers, the Ministry of Internal Affairs, in 1909, made a survey of Buraku with a view to helping them improve their economic and social conditions. According to the survey, the total number of Buraku was variously estimated at 4,324 and 5,532; another set the total population of Burakumin at 79,434.[6] These were highly unrealistic assessments that could only have served to avoid recognition of the extent of the problem. Nevertheless, in 1913, the Ministry of Internal Affairs helped Buraku leaders to organize the Teikoku Kōdō Kai (Imperial Path of Justice Association) to function as a central organization for the various self-improvement and conciliationist or integrationist groups and movements that had sprung up. The Prospectus of the Teikoku Kōdō Kai says in part:

After the coronation, our holiest and most benevolent Emperor issued the Charter Oath to sweep away all evil customs. Since then, each individual Japanese has been equal in his right and duty of loyalty and should not be

---

[6] *Buraku no Rekishi to Kaihō Undō* (1955), p. 164. Cf. other estimates reported in Chapter 5.

placed on different levels. And yet, not a few Japanese are still ignorant, stubborn, and old-fashioned. In their daily intercourse, they unashamedly forget the Imperial will and ignore the law of justice and humanity. . . . The reason for our establishing this Association is no other than our wish to observe the holy Imperial will of the late Emperor Meiji and carry it out in practice. . . .

They also published a journal called *Kōdō* (Path of Justice).

Those who joined this organization reflected an optimism, shared by the Meiji intelligentsia, that social barriers would vanish once the moral standards sanctioned by the majority had been adopted. By encouraging the well-to-do to donate money for schools, and by establishing new industries in the Buraku to absorb what was by now a sizable pool of underemployed labor, the more conservative business elite among the former outcastes seem to have used the "self-help" principle to arrest development of the militant, radical political sentiment that had already appeared among both the more intellectual and less propertied elements in the Buraku. These movements, when they did develop, spurned mere improvement in favor of real "emancipation" (*kaihō*), to be effected by "direct action." The emancipation movement arose because of the failure of self-improvement to make much of a dent in the continuing discrimination.[7]

The involvement of Japan in World War I on the side of the Allies deflected the government's attention from the emancipation movements of the increasingly organized Burakumin. At first, agitation diminished, but soon more leftist ideas, stimulated by the Russian Revolution, captured the imagination of many Japanese, including Burakumin intellectuals.

THE RICE RIOTS OF 1918 AND
THE SYMPATHETIC RECONCILIATION MOVEMENT

Inflation was spread generally throughout the world at the end of World War I. In Japan, the cost of living spiraled upward so that by 1918 prices had increased over those of 1914 by 130 percent. The income of the working class, by contrast, went up approximately 57 percent. The poor were hit especially by the increase in the price of rice, the principal staple of the Japanese diet, from 19 to 40 yen per *koku* (190.4 quarts). In the late summer of 1918, rice riots erupted

---

[7] For example, in 1914 army troops were quartered in a village in Okayama Prefecture, as was the general practice during maneuvers. A special Buraku, located in this village, was avoided by the troops, and it was not asked to billet them. The Burakumin protested to the village head and the governor of the Prefecture. In another village in 1916, the Hakata Newspaper in Kyushu printed some discriminatory comments on Burakumin, and about 300 angry Burakumin raided the newspaper office.

throughout Japan; people raided rice stores and destroyed police stations, demanding a decrease in price.

The first riot began in August, 1918, in a little fishing village in Toyama Prefecture on the Japanese sea coast and quickly spread to neighboring villages. Soon after, Burakumin rioted in Kyoto; they were joined by more Burakumin and the poor in general. The riots spread through almost all the cities in Japan (they were especially violent in Osaka, Kobe, Wakayama, Okayama, and Hiroshima), and from the cities, disturbances spread to the outlying farming and fishing villages. Coal miners also went on strike. In all of these riots the Burakumin were particularly active, often taking the initiative and leadership.[8]

These rice riots, eventually involving a great part of the total Japanese population, strongly influenced the development of the reconciliation movement. Up to this time its leaders emphasized self-improvement and tended to explain discrimination as the public reaction to the lower standards of Buraku life. After the riots, however, Buraku leaders demanded that the government assume greater responsibility, and emphasis shifted toward obtaining direct help for improving economic and social conditions in the Buraku.

In February, 1919, the first Dōjō Yūwa Taikai (Sympathetic Reconciliation Congress) was held, attended by delegates from both the Upper and Lower Houses of the Japanese Diet, government ministers, aristocrats, bureaucrats, and scholars, as well as by Burakumin leaders. After this historic meeting, the Buraku leaders decided to file a petition with the Ministries of Internal Affairs, War, Navy, and Education, asking for employment of Burakumin in government offices; discontinuation of the use of discriminatory words against Burakumin, such as "tokushu buraku," in official documents; complete abolition of discrimination within the army and navy; abolition of discrimination in public schools; economic programs for the improvement of Buraku conditions; and an annual governmental subsidy of more than one million yen for Buraku improvement.[9]

In 1920 the government, for the first time, appropriated 50,000 yen ($25,000) to improve the Buraku. Several organizations were formed jointly by the government and by Buraku leaders for the solution of outcaste problems. One of the implicit, if not explicit, purposes of

---

[8] A total of 8,185 individuals were arrested and sent to the public prosecutor's offices. Of these, 887 were identified as Burakumin. At that time the population of Japan was about 56 million, and the Burakumin were estimated at about one million. In other words, Burakumin, who comprised somewhat less than 2 percent of the total population, made up more than 10 percent of those arrested and tried. Although the poverty-stricken Burakumin were proportionately hurt most by the inflation, it is probable that they were more often arrested than non-Burakumin.

[9] Inoue (1959), pp. 95–96.

these government-sponsored organizations was to prevent Burakumin
from becoming more susceptible to revolutionary ideas, which were at
that time spreading throughout the working class.[10] In this, they were
not entirely successful; in 1919 and 1920 strikes broke out among
workers employed in the manufacture of leather goods, wooden clogs,
sandals, and toothbrushes.

THE SUIHEISHA

Revolutionary Optimism (1922–1925)

Several of the younger Buraku intellectuals had become increasingly influenced by Marxist theory and increasingly dissatisfied with
the patriarchal attitudes of government-sponsored reconciliationist organizations, as well as the self-debasing approach of many Buraku
leaders. They had sought advice from various socialist and Communist
leaders active in the labor, agrarian, and suffrage movements during
the postwar period of political unrest.[11] With their assistance, the
Burakumin began to organize their own group of activists.

In 1921, Sano Manabu, a Waseda University professor who became
a Marxist and Communist, wrote, "On the Emancipation of the
Tokushu Buraku," published in the magazine Kaihō (Emancipation).
He argued that the true emancipation of the Burakumin was possible
only through a general socialist revolution, and that they should therefore unite with the workers, who were likewise victims of capitalist
exploitation. This article strongly influenced young Buraku leaders.[12]

A similar line of thought was advocated by some socialist but non-
Communist members of the Buddhist clergy who helped to inspire
political organization in the special communities.[13] In spite of the fact

---

[10] Shortly after the first Sympathetic Reconciliation Congress, the great March 1
uprising (1919) in Korea occurred. Neither the Buraku leaders nor the government
was unaware of the similarity of the problem of discrimination and conciliation
between the domestic Burakumin and the Koreans in Korea and Japan. As a matter
of fact, a Japanese army officer who had taken part in subduing the Korean uprising explicitly drew the parallel at the second meeting of the Congress. Inoue (1959),
p. 96.
[11] They visited such people as Sakai Toshihiko, Yamakawa Hitoshi, Sano Manabu
(who helped to found the Communist Party in Japan but later turned away from
it) and Ōsugi Sakae (a famous anarchist who was murdered in 1923). Thus, it was
young Burakumin, influenced by socialist ideas, who forced the important socialist
thinkers to consider the Buraku question.
[12] It is interesting to note that Sano and most of the other young socialist Buraku
leaders at this time considered the Burakumin an oppressed national minority. Some
of them compared themselves to the Jewish people who were liberated by the Russian
Revolution. Most of them were influenced by President Wilson's ideas of national
self-determination, and they were also stimulated by the Korean independence struggle. For sources on this, see Inoue (1959), pp. 104–105.
[13] The forerunner of this movement in Nara was the Tsubame Kai (Swallows'
Club) formed about 1920 by Sakamoto Seiichirō (now—in 1964—a member of the

that they had traditionally been the recipients of charity by the clergy, the former outcastes now began to refuse it so as to learn self-reliance, and instead sought emancipation through political channels.[14]

A few young Buraku leaders in Nara Prefecture set up an office to establish a new "leveling" movement (*suihei undō*) for the purpose of removing all social and political distinctions and inequalities.[15] They published a small magazine, *Yoki Hi no tame ni* (*For a Better Day*), asking for the cooperation and participation of Buraku leaders in all parts of Japan.[16]

Neither the government nor the sympathetic reconciliationists liked this new movement with its obviously leftist orientation. It is reported that the Ministry of Internal Affairs sent a man to the Suiheisha (Levelers' Society) office who tried to bribe the leaders into changing their orientation. Militant, proud, and sensitive to what seemed to them to be the paternalistic, proprietary attitude of many of the majority society sympathizers and the more propertied Buraku elders, Suiheisha leaders proceeded with their plans, and on March 3, 1922, at Okazaki Park in Kyoto, held the inaugural convention of the National Levelers' (or Leveling) Society (or Association) (Zenkoku Suiheisha). About 2,000 representatives drawn from almost all the Buraku were present. Three items in the program were approved.

(1) We Tokushu Burakumin will attain complete emancipation by our own action.
(2) We Tokushu Burakumin demand economic and occupational freedom from the majority society and we shall obtain it.
(3) We Tokushu Burakumin will be conscious of human dignity and we shall march toward the full realization of human values.

Central Committee of the Buraku Kaihō Dōmei), Nishimitsu Mankichi, Komai Kisaku, and Yoneda Tomi (now Chairman of the Nara Prefecture Branch of the Buraku Kaihō Dōmei). The members of the Club wanted to "fly" away from Japan like swallows, to the South Seas, to find a better place to live. They studied the Malay language and obtained information on the Celebes and adjacent areas. They soon became convinced that the migration of Burakumin to other areas could be used for purposes of Japanese imperialism and dropped the idea. See Sakamoto (1961), pp. 34-43.

[14] For a brief account of socialist-Buddhist compatibility in Japan, see Totten (1960), p. 302.

[15] This name was selected in emulation of the organization of peasants and workers known as "levelers" that had played an active role in the democratization of England during the seventeenth century. "*Suihei*" literally means the "water level" or "horizon."

[16] Already a number of other independent organizations had been set up around the country and a number of young men of Buraku background had become active in social movements. For instance, in Fukuoka Prefecture, Matsumoto Jiichirō had set up a group; in Nishihama, a part of Osaka, Matsuta Kiichi and Iwano Shigeharu were studying Kropotkin, Furier, and Marx under Sakai Toshihiko. In Tokyo and Kyoto others were especially active.

The following declaration, borrowing from Marxist literature as well as from Christian and Buddhist writings,[17] was read aloud:

Tokushu Burakumin throughout the country, unite! Long-suffering brothers: In the past half century, the undertakings on our behalf by so many people and in such varied ways have failed to yield any favorable results. This failure was a divine punishment we incurred for permitting others as well as ourselves to debase our own human dignity. Previous movements, though seemingly motivated by compassion, actually corrupted many of our brothers. In the light of this, it is necessary for us to organize a new group movement by which we shall emancipate ourselves through promoting respect for human dignity.

Brothers! Our ancestors sought after and practiced liberty and equality. But they became the victims of a base, contemptible system developed by the ruling class. They became the manly martyrs of industry. As a reward for skinning animals, they were flayed alive. As a recompense for tearing out the hearts of animals, their own warm, human hearts were ripped out. They were spat upon with the spittle of ridicule. Yet all through these cursed nightmares, their blood, still proud to be human, did not dry up. Yes! Now we have come to the age when man, pulsing with this blood, is trying to become divine. The time has come for the victims of discrimination to hurl back labels of derision. The time has come when the martyrs' crown of thorns will be blessed. The time has come when we can be proud of being Eta.

We must never again insult our ancestors and profane our humanity by slavish words and cowardly acts. Knowing well the coldness and contempt of ordinary human society, we seek and will be profoundly thankful for the warmth and light of true humanity.

From this the Levelers' Society is born. Let there now be warmth and light among men![18]

The official flag of the Suiheisha was unfurled for the first time. It was black, emblazoned only with a round crown of thorns dyed blood red, an intentional symbol of the martyrdom of Christ. The flagpole was fashioned in the shape of a bamboo spear, symbolizing the militancy of the traditional peasant uprisings against injustice. Attendants at this meeting also decided on three concrete policies or courses of action: (1) to "denounce thoroughly and strictly those who insult us with derogatory words and deeds"; (2) to "publish a monthly periodi-

[17] Among words with religious connotations used were *batsu* (divine punishment), *junkyōsha* (martyr), *keikan* (crown of thorns), and *gongu raisan* (beseech and praise). The first sentence of the declaration is obviously modeled after the *Communist Manifesto*. Also, such words as *jiyū* (liberty), *byōdō* (equality), and *kaikyū seisaku* (policies favorable to the ruling class) carry Marxist connotations. An important reason for the religious words in the declaration is that its main author, Nishimitsu Mankichi, was the son of a Buddhist monk and had been strongly influenced by the teachings of Shinran, the founder of the Shin Sect. Nevertheless, his use of such words undoubtedly reflected the religious orientation of the mass of Burakumin at that time. See Nishimitsu (1961), pp. 34–44.
[18] Inoue (1959), pp. 107–08.

cal, *Suihei,* at the central office of the National Suiheisha for our unification and solidarity"; and (3) to "ask both the East and West Honganji Temples [of the Jōdo Shin Sect], of which the majority of Burakumin are parishioners, to express candidly their attitude toward our movement and then to decide on our own action depending on their reply."

"Thorough denunciation" (*tetteiteki kyūdan*) was the slogan that first epitomized the objective of the Suiheisha movement, an eye-for-an-eye retaliation against the discriminating majority society. When someone discriminated against Burakumin, members of the Suisheisha were to demand that the person apologize publicly by publishing a statement in a newspaper or by submitting a printed statement to the Levelers' Society for distribution. This policy was resolutely carried out. During 1922, 69 such cases were reported. A typical letter follows:

I have no words [good enough] to apologize to the Emperor and to all the members of the Suiheisha for my having neglected the Imperial Edict, issued by Emperor Meiji on August 28, 1871, for having used discriminatory language. I have been impressed by the kind lesson taught me by the honorable members of the Suiheisha and I would like to express here my appreciation.

I also strongly wish that those Japanese citizens who are poisoned by conventional, discriminatory attitudes like mine all be enlightened quickly. I hope they will realize that human beings are not to be patronized but respected. . . .[19]

Unfortunately not all discriminatory incidents ended in pretty apologies. Soon after the National Suiheisha was founded, the Nara Suiheisha decided to try this new tactic in order to change conditions at the Taisho Village Primary School, where discrimination was blatant. Buraku pupils were not allowed to sit with non-Buraku children, nor could they use the same lavatory. The task of cleaning classrooms after school was given only to Buraku children. Very few Buraku students were accepted into the upper school, even when they scored extremely well in entrance examinations. They had to use separate cups and pails at the school.

---

[19] This letter and the following example—from a prostitute—are from Inoue (1959), pp. 122–23:

To the Suiheisha . . . an astonishing number of proletarians are crying out from hunger and cold. Seventy thousand of our sisters throughout the country are cursing the red lanterns in the gay quarters. How could such a society be called healthy? It is a dark and sinister society. Yes, dark and sinister. "Let there now be warmth in the world and light among men!" The brave members of the Suiheisha are fighting on the battle front for emancipation. I was forgetting my own place when I addressed some of them with discriminatory words. I have now resolved to improve myself, thanks to the valuable ideas of the sympathetic and serious members of the Levelers' Society. . . .

Incidentally, women and young people were very active in the Suiheisha. In this respect the leveling movement resembled a national independence movement and differed from the labor and tenant farmer movements.

The Nara Prefectural Suiheisha leaders visited the school principal and asked him to abolish such discrimination, but the principal refused. Then the Suiheisha leaders held a Burakumin meeting in Kobayashi District and decided to demand the elimination of discriminatory treatment of Buraku children at the school, the punishment of a teacher who discriminated against Buraku children, and the punishment of those pupils who discriminated against Buraku classmates. Elected representatives, followed by more than a hundred Burakumin, visited the principal the next day and demanded that the above decisions be carried out; again the principal refused. A quarrel broke out between a district officer and the Burakumin, and the former was injured; the school principal, trying to stop the fight, had his clothes torn. A number of Burakumin were summoned to the police station for questioning, and eventually the teacher who had discriminated against the Buraku children was transferred to another school. Both the principal and the police chief soon resigned. Although the situation was scarcely solved and this was the first in a number of struggles, such victories gave heart to the new movement.[20]

The 1920's were a period of leftist radicalism in Japan, as in the rest of the world. In April, 1922, only a month after the inaugural meeting of the National Levelers' Society, the Japan Farmers' Union (Nihon Nōmin Kumiai), devoted to the interests of poor and tenant farmers, was organized, and two months later the Japanese Communist Party was officially though clandestinely formed.

Within a year following the inaugural meeting of the Levelers' Society, about 60 local branches, also called Suiheisha, were organized. Militant action by Burakumin against signs of discrimination spread rapidly. In 1923, the central office of the National Levelers' Society sent out a message urging Burakumin to attend the second national meeting. "The flag with a crown of thorns of the color of blood should be the symbol of our sufferings and martyrdom. Come and gather in front of an altar and mourn for the tens of millions of our ancestors groaning underground. Once we were lowly people (senmin). Now we are chosen people (senmin).[21] Three million beloved brothers, for a 'better day,' let us unite!"

On March 2 and 3, 1923, about 3,000 Burakumin attended the second national convention at Okazaki Park in Kyoto. It was there they decided to organize the Zenkoku Shōnen Shōjo Suiheisha (National Boys and Girls Levelers' Society) and Zenkoku Fujin Suiheisha (National Women's Levelers' Society). The Ministers of War and Navy were called upon to correct discrimination in the armed services. It was

---

[20] Kimura (1951), pp. 17–23.
[21] In Japanese, the written characters for "lowly" and "chosen" are different but are pronounced identically.

also decided to organize a branch of the leftist Japan Farmers' Union among the Burakumin to fight against exploitation by landlords. Another decision was to lodge a formal protest with the Tokugawa family, demanding an apology for the actions of their ancestors, the shoguns—for it was under their regime that the Eta-Hinin outcaste status had been so rigidly maintained from 1603 to 1868.

Soon after the convention an incident occurred that brought unfavorable publicity to the Suiheisha—not so much because of what happened but because the violence surrounding the incident was heavily emphasized in reports of it.

In 1923, in one area of the Nara Prefecture, discrimination against Burakumin was severe: they could not use public bath houses or barber shops, or rent houses in majority districts or work at the factories. On March 16, as a group of Burakumin was carrying a bridal trousseau, an old man made the four-finger sign at them. That evening, a committee from the Suiheisha chapter questioned the old man, while a leader of his village, a member of Kokusuikai (National Essence Association—an ultranationalist group), arrogantly offered to apologize for the man and demanded his release. The Suiheisha refused and the leader threatened a fight.

The representative of the Suiheisha visited the old man again two days later and found the ultranationalists joined by other groups, armed and waiting. Reinforcements from other chapters joined the Suiheisha group, and the two forces clashed. That evening, the youthful leader Kimura Kyōtarō with his comrades met with the leaders of the National Suiheisha and local chapters to discuss strategy; rumors of attack and spies were rampant. Buraku reinforcements from neighboring prefectures formed a "resolved-to-die group," for self-defense only, and arrived early on March 19.

By afternoon, more than 2,000 Burakumin had gathered; the Kokusuikai had also reinforced their numbers, and finally the Suiheisha forces moved toward their foe, the leaders first, escorted by the "resolved-to-die" group. Bells and bugles accompanied the march. The two "armies" finally confronted each other across a river; there was some shooting and some hand-to-hand combat with spears and swords.

The fighting was eventually stopped through negotiations by the police, but thirty-five members of the Suiheisha and only thirteen members of the Kokusuikai were prosecuted. And whereas twenty-five of the Levelers were sentenced to hard labor for six to fifteen months and ten were fined, only eight ultranationalists received hard labor sentences for six to eight months and only three were fined.[22]

After the second convention the Levelers' Society spread rapidly. In March a Kantō Suiheisha was organized, as well as new branches in

---

[22] Kimura (1951). See also Matsumoto (1948), pp. 48–53.

Kansai and Shikoku. On May Day, the Kyushu Suiheisha was set up with Matsumoto Jiichirō at its head. In 1923 over 300 branches had been formed in 24 prefectures. By 1925 the number had reached 703 branches—the high point in Suiheisha organization.

In November, 1923, the Zenkoku Suiheisha Seinen Dōmei (Youth Federation of the National Levelers' Society) was organized in Nishihama in Osaka by several men, including Kimura Kyōtarō, who had been deeply influenced by Marxism-Leninism. They planned to operate as a faction within the Society and bring it under Communist leadership. Consequently, when the third national convention of the Levelers' Society opened in Kyoto on March 3, 1924, the main point of debate was whether the Suiheisha was to become part of the proletarian movement or remain independent; the decision was postponed.

Meanwhile, the reconciliation or integration (yūwa) movements were not unaffected by the leveling movement. Perhaps the most important of them was the Dōaikai (Brotherly Love Society) of which Arima Yasunori was not only the founder but also the long-term president. Having received a liberal education abroad, he was receptive to the writings of socialists. With his aristocratic background he was able to secure as sponsors such prominent people as Baron Shibusawa Eiichi and Gotō Fumio, a Cabinet Minister. Though in the tradition of the reconciliationist movement, the Dōaikai was influenced by the leveling movement to the extent that it went beyond charity and called for the abolition of discrimination and social status. Arima later was elected to the Diet, and after inheriting his father's title of Count in 1927, he joined the House of Peers where he continued to present bills on behalf of the Suiheisha.

As the Suiheisha gained momentum and became more radical, the reconciliationists also attempted to move forward. In February, 1925, the various reconciliation movements were coordinated in the Zenkoku Yūwa Renmei (National Reconciliation League) brought into being by Arima. Later, the Ministry of Internal Affairs set up the Chūō Yūwa Jigyō Kyōkai (Central Society of Reconciliation Projects) headed by Hiranuma Kiichirō, then Vice President of the Privy Council and a supporter of Japan's traditional culture. By working through the more wealthy, propertied Buraku leaders, the government hoped to strengthen their position vis-à-vis the radical Suiheisha. In addition, local government officials made various attempts to establish anti-Suiheisha Burakumin organizations, but they were by and large unsuccessful.

International Dissension (1925–1930)

In its first three years the Levelers' Society attracted Burakumin leaders and intellectuals with a wide variety of ideological orientations:

serious supporters of the imputed Imperial opposition to discrimination; religious humanists drawing on the precepts of Christianity or Buddhism; and anarchists, social democrats, and Communists, who advocated various degrees of class struggle. Conflict among such diverse outlooks was bound to arise, especially as pressure was exerted by the moderate non-Buraku reconciliationists and the government authorities.

The fourth convention, meeting in Osaka in 1925, attracted over 1,000 observers. Matsumoto Jiichirō from Kyushu was unanimously elected the new Chairman. Under the prodding of the Youth Federation a proposal was made to reorganize the Suiheisha completely and shift the emphasis from tactics of "thorough denunciation" to "the class struggle of the proletariat." Democratic centralism was to be instituted and programs of action worked out in cooperation with militant proletarian organizations of all kinds of labor, agriculture, and the arts. The proposal did not pass, however, because of resistance from anarchists and those who advocated the independence of the Suiheisha, but it was indicative of the struggle going on within the organization.

The tempo of this struggle increased after the meeting. In September the Youth Federation dissolved itself and asked its members to join the Zen-Nihon Musan Seinen Dōmei (All-Japan Proletarian Youth Federation) that had been organized under Communist student inspiration. At the same time it was decided to continue as a reform group within the Suiheisha under the new name of Zenkoku Suiheisha Musansha Dōmei (Proletarian Federation of the National Levelers' Society), and to fight resolutely against all "reactionary" and "opportunist" elements within the Suiheisha. These young enthusiasts, still under the leadership of Takahashi Sadaki and Kimura Kyōtarō, saw the solution to the problem of status discrimination in the abolition of class differences through a proletarian revolution. Later on, the pro-Communist elements were to admit confusing status and class, but at that time the Proletarian Federation faction convinced many Burakumin that the causes of discrimination were embedded in the Emperor system, capitalism, and the aristocratic control of agriculture. Every tactic was to be used. Cooperation was to be sought on as broad a front as possible consistent with the maintenance of a high degree of militancy. And through "democratic centralism" the Suiheisha, like all other proletarian organizations, was to be made into an efficient, powerful, and responsive force.

In opposition to this tendency, the anarchists within the Suiheisha organized themselves under the name of Zenkoku Suiheisha Jiyū Renmei (Youth League of the National Levelers' Society). At a conference in October, 1925, they attacked the Proletarian Federation and shocked the whole leveling movement by exposing Takahashi Sadaki, its leader, as an "impostor," who had not really been born a Burakumin. So violent was the reaction to this that Takahashi was forced to retire from the leveling movement. Though Burakumin who tried to pass were not condemned, when an outsider became so devoted to equality and their cause that he falsely identified himself as such, the Burakumin reacted badly. Of course, Takahashi had defenders, and the question was complicated by the fact that he was attacked for political purposes, as a Bolshevik.

The entire socialist movement in Japan, from about 1919, had been split by the so-called *anaboru* controversy between the anarchists and the Bolsheviks. At this time the Communist influence was still increasing throughout the proletarian movement whereas anarchism had been declining from about 1921. In any case, the Youth League called for the "highest perfection of man," the independent "self-governance" of the Suiheisha, and opposition to doctrines incompatible with a genuine equalization movement. Everywhere, one of the main issues between the anarchists and Bolsheviks was organization, the former calling for decentralization and the latter for central control.

Those antagonisms seethed beneath the surface of the delayed fifth national convention, which convened on May 2 and 3, 1926. Although headquarters was now in the hands of the Proletarian Federation faction, its proposals for a militant new platform were met with a good deal of resistance. Since the last convention, a new manhood suffrage bill had passed the Diet, mainly because conservative leaders considered it a means of deflecting the growing tide of radicalism among the masses. Though it was ringed with various limitations and safeguards, the Marxists and social democrats saw it as a step in the direction of bourgeois democracy and planned to make use of it.

After the convention, the fissures widened. The anarchists were organized into the Zenkoku Suiheisha Kaihō Renmei (Emancipation League of the National Levelers' Society). The Proletarian Federationists moved toward political participation by forming the Zenkoku Suiheisha Rōdō Nōmintō Shiji Renmei (National Levelers' Society's League to Support the Labor Farmer Party) in 1926, after having moved steadily toward the left. Finally, the moderate Japan Levelers' Society was set up in January, 1927, retaining the original declaration, program, and constitution of the Suiheisha, though not abjuring moderate political activity. But while ideological controversy consumed much energy, real leadership could only be displayed in test cases. Here, dramatic action and publicity were perhaps more important than whether or not the right tactics were used.

The first case arose out of an attempt to end discrimination in the 24th Infantry Regiment stationed in Fukuoka, Kyushu. It had been traditional for army conscripts of Buraku background to be identified in their documents by the abbreviation "toku" (special) or by a red circle preceding the name. They were invariably assigned to shoe repairing and other such details and were rarely promoted. This situation had been taken up at the second Suiheisha convention in 1923, and a protest had been lodged with the Ministers of War and the Navy, without much effect. On the local level, the more radical elements of the Suiheisha, such as the Proletarian Federation, would accompany one of their inducted members up to the very gates of the camp, demonstrating with the Suiheisha banners. The next day the inductee would usually be locked in the stockade.

In January, 1926, several Buraku youths who were about to be inducted resolved to enter quietly but to protest the first overt act of discrimination, which occurred ten days later. The local Suiheisha protested, the Regiment responded negatively, and gradually tensions mounted. The Kyushu Suiheisha Federation and the Proletarian Federation youths began to mobilize class sentiment behind the case. Suiheisha representatives interviewed Buraku soldiers to gather factual information on incidents of discrimination, which they publicized at a series of meetings. They also requested permission to lecture to the soldiers to help overcome prejudice; this was first granted and then denied.

Discrimination continued, and the problem became more serious when the Regiment avoided quartering its soldiers on maneuvers in the nearest Buraku section of a village. The Suiheisha threatened that if the Regiment refused to act on the question of discrimination, it could expect Burakumin to refuse to join or aid any kind of military activity. They enlisted the support of the proletarian organizations; the nationally organized Japan Farmers' Union gave orders to its members to refuse to quarter troops. As the struggle developed, it gained much newspaper publicity, being reported abroad even in such journals as *The Nation* in the United States.

At this point the Japanese police acted. Before daylight on November 11, 1926, police searched Suiheisha leaders' homes in Fukuoka, Osaka, and Kumamoto. Ten arrests were made, including Matsumoto Jiichirō, now head of the National Suiheisha, and Kimura Kyōtarō, leader of the Proletarian Federation faction. The police claimed to have discovered dynamite and revolvers in Matsumoto's home, and hand grenades in the homes of other leaders. What was apparently a fabricated charge of a plot to blow up the Regiment's barracks brought to Matsumoto a sentence of hard labor for three years and six months, to eight others three years, and to one, three months. The case was appealed to the Supreme Court in October, 1928, in vain. Five of the ten became ill while in prison and died soon after having served

52 EMANCIPATION

their terms.[23] Burakumin struggles against military discrimination were going on at this time in a number of places throughout the country, but it took a stubborn character and a tough constitution to think of ways to defy military discipline and then survive the guard house and military prison.[24]

While Matsumoto was still battling the courts, the first general elections for the House of Representatives under the new franchise of manhood suffrage took place on February 20, 1928. The Suiheisha supplied three candidates for the Labor Farmer Party, including the defendant. Although none of them won, this marked a new departure into politics and the beginning of Matsumoto's political career, which will be discussed in the following chapter.[25]

But in 1928, the cabinet of Premier General Tanaka Giichi adopted drastic action against leftist movements throughout Japan. Mass arrests on May 15 resulted in the dissolution of the Labor Farmer Party, the most powerful leftist trade union, known as the Hyōgikai (Council), and the All-Japan Proletarian Youth Federation which the members of the Proletarian Federation of the National Levelers' Society had joined. Some twenty Suiheisha leaders were caught in these arrests. When the seventh national Suiheisha convention opened in late May, 1928, it seemed that almost half of those present were police. (The sixth convention, held in Hiroshima the year before, had been able to achieve little, divided as it was into the three factions: the Proletarian Federation, the Emancipation League, and the Japan Suiheisha. The League retained strength in the Tokyo area, the Federation controlled the headquarters and most other areas, whereas the moderate followers of Minami had dwindled considerably.) The seventh convention met in Kyoto where the movement had begun seven years before, and this year it reached its nadir. The anarchist League faction walked out, and the police dissolved it. Only 102 delegates were present, along with some 400 observers, compared with 2,000 when the organization was founded.

Reintegration and Disintegration (1930–1940)

By 1930, economic conditions, which had been deteriorating for some time became manifestly critical. Ever since the gold panic of 1927, Buraku living conditions had worsened. Small and medium enterprises reduced production or closed, many going into bankruptcy. By

---

[23] See Kimura (1951), pp. 17–23; and Matsumoto (1948), pp. 77–106.
[24] Kitahara Taisaku, a leader of the former Suiheisha and in the postwar period a leader in the Kaihō Dōmei, gives a dramatic account of his studied disobedience while in the army. See Kitahara and Kimura (1956), pp. 47–53.
[25] Also see Kyōchōkai (1929), pp. 484–85.

1930 three million people were jobless. As prices of silk and rice dropped precipitously, financial panic struck the farm villages. A complete crop failure hit Hokkaido and northeastern Japan in 1931; millions of farmers faced possible starvation.

The Burakumin especially suffered. Seventy percent of the leather factories in Tokyo and Kobe and 50 percent of those in Osaka had to curtail their operations. The price of leather goods dropped by half; footgear manufacturers were severely affected. Financial difficulty, frustration, and resentment among the general populace left people with little to think about except survival. In these circumstances, the obvious tactic for the Suiheisha was to join with other groups to demand that local and national government authorities take steps to do something about unemployment. It could also continue to seek out and expose instances of corruption in local government in cooperation with the proletarian political parties.

By the time the eighth national convention of the Suiheisha convened on November 4, 1929, a reconciliation with the anarchists had been effected, and the meeting took place in their stronghold of Nagoya. Some 156 delegates assembled, and the audience numbered about 2,000. The two major slogans called for unity and economic recovery. Mutual recriminations among the factions were almost totally absent. The membership of the National Suiheisha was now estimated by the police as 47,197 out of the 53,328 persons involved in the Buraku emancipation movement as a whole, which included some 398 separate organizations, counting the regional federations and local groups.

A big issue before the convention was discrimination in the armed forces. Matsumoto was in prison because of the Fukuoka Regiment incident. In March, it had been discovered that a military map listed a place called Eta Peak, and the convention lodged a protest against this. It went on to demand civil liberties for men in the armed services and the right to lecture on discrimination.

Economic struggles were also supported. Burakumin were asked to go out of their way to help in labor strikes by housing the strike leadership in a Buraku. In this way, many majority people could for the first time meet Burakumin, and mutual respect and cooperation were developing. Coordinated efforts sometimes resulted in gaining for the Burakumin the right to use publicly owned village land for hay and firewood.

Economic problems had become so pressing that the reconciliationist organizations also began to give them increasing attention. At the government-sponsored Zenkoku Yūwa Jigyō Kyōgikai (National Reconciliationist Projects Conference) held in May, 1929, the Ministry of Internal Affairs announced a policy of increased activity. (While the Suiheisha supported the idea of creating more facilities, it criticized the increase of local taxes on the Buraku to carry them out.) Figures on local Buraku conditions were being reported in greater detail in the organ of the Central Society for Reconciliationist Projects.

When the new school term began in September, 1930, in a typical protest, the local Suiheisha boycotted a primary school in a village in Okayama, protesting the segregation of Buraku children in the classroom. When 181 Buraku children were withdrawn from school, the leader's home was used as a temporary classroom for them and teachers were recruited for all subjects. But when the Emperor came to inspect troops on maneuvers, the school authorities asked the Buraku children to be present. Some were sent, but were beaten by bullies until the parents appeared with hoes and pitchforks. Some parents even managed to talk on discrimination in the classrooms, explicitly naming the Emperor as part of the hierarchical system that promoted discrimination. After this, the police intervened and the struggle spread to the whole of the Bisaku region. The result was a real victory—the end of classroom segregation, but at the cost of the arrest of a number of activists.

The ninth national convention of the Levelers' Society opened on December 5, 1930, in Osaka. Great care was taken to keep out provocateurs: over 130 delegates were recognized, but the number of observers was held down. Sources of discrimination were discussed anew, and the history of the Suiheisha reviewed. It was agreed that the economic basis for discrimination lay in the "semi-feudal" relationships prevailing in the landlord system, in small family enterprises, and in the system of cottage industry; the political basis lay in the hierarchical political structure of the Genrō, the Privy Council, the House of Peers, the General Staff, and the Military Command (the Emperor not being listed, as this would be illegal). There were slogans for Buraku solidarity; for freedom of speech, press, and assembly; and for recovery of the right to an ordinary livelihood. Tactics included not only school boycotts but also nonpayment of taxes and withdrawal from government-sponsored organizations (such as the Veterans' Association, Young Men's Association, and Fire Brigades).

The most pronounced tendency of the tenth national convention, which met in Sakurai-machi in Nara on December 10, 1931, was that favoring the merger of Buraku demands with the struggles conducted by other proletarian organizations. For instance, in Okayama and Fukuoka the Suiheisha had practically dissolved, and the active Burakumin were working instead in the tenant farmer unions. In Okayama an important struggle against discrimination was being waged, not in the name of the Suiheisha, but in the name of the National Farmers' Union.[26] In fact, Kyushu representatives formally proposed that the

---

[26] But in point of fact, only Burakumin were really involved. Inoue (1959), p. 158.

Suiheisha, which was merely a "status organization," should dissolve itself and merge into the various "class organizations." This issue was hotly debated, but a decision was postponed. Police estimated the strength of the Suiheisha as 43,300, about a thousand fewer than the previous year.[27] The Suiheisha continued to support proletarian parties other than the conservative Social Democratic Party, with which the remnants of the Japan Levelers' Society (now 2,464) continued to be affiliated. It also took a more moderate attitude toward government-sponsored improvements in facilities, and toward the work of the reconciliationist organizations.

During this time, some attempts were made by the government and the reconciliationist groups to improve Buraku conditions and thereby counteract the leftist tendencies of many of their leaders. A kind of civil rights bill for "the completion of integration" was jointly proposed by the Seiyūkai and the Minseitō, major conservative parties. Receiving support from the proletarian Diet members, it was passed unanimously. It was intended to improve local facilities to enable Burakumin to stabilize their livelihood and thereby improve their social position.

At a joint meeting of the various national reconciliationist organizations in June, 1930, a proposal was made to be forwarded to the Minister of Internal Affairs. It asked the government to "reinforce programs for vocational guidance and for relief work for the unemployed Burakumin," "make loans available to Burakumin," "improve Buraku industries," "protect the supplementary occupations engaged in by Burakumin," and to "set up a committee to survey the financial situation of the Buraku and to plan concrete methods for help." Inoue Kiyoshi points out that these measures were insufficient palliatives, that more fundamental policies were required, such as provision of land for landless Burakumin who could meet certain standards, reduction of the high rents for tenant farming, social security and unemployment compensation, or even some kind of minimum wage. Inoue, whatever his biases, is undoubtedly right in arguing that the reconciliationist organizations, because of their middle class character, were incapable of proposing such drastic measures.[28]

---

[27] Naimushō Keihōkyoku, *Shakai Undō no Jōkyō* (1931), pp. 9–10.

[28] Inoue (1959), pp. 139–40. The government, as mentioned above, first started appropriating money for Buraku improvement in 1920, and this was shortly followed by local grants-in-aid and the assignment to specific local government officials of responsibility for considering means to bring about Buraku improvement. The 50,000 yen appropriated in 1920 had been devoted to the Social Bureau of the Ministry of Internal Affairs for integrationist (*dōwa*) project. In the next two years, 210,000 yen each year was appropriated for improved public facilities in the local communities, such as neighborhood halls, nurseries, public baths, and night schools. The figures wavered around half a million yen annually: 490,000 yen in 1923 and

As noted earlier, with the trend toward growing participation by Burakumin in the various proletarian organizations, the governing council of the Kyushu Suiheisha Federation proposed at the tenth national convention that the Suiheisha disband and transfer the demands of the Burakumin to the agendas of the other, more broadly based, proletarian organizations. The theory behind this proposal was based on the "Political Thesis Draft" issued by the Japanese Communist Party in April, 1931, which saw Japan as on the threshold of a "proletarian revolution"; any status organization such as the Suiheisha would only hinder this denouement. The other document that contributed to this thinking was "The Task of Revolutionary Labor Unions in Japan," issued by the Profintern (Red Trade Union International), which assigned so many tasks to the trade unions that even the role of the Communist Party itself was almost usurped. According to this document, the unions should take upon themselves the elimination of all social prejudices dividing the toiling masses. Action on the dissolution proposal was postponed, and subsequent events caused its proponents to change their minds.

In the 1932 Thesis concerning the Japanese revolution, handed down by the Comintern, a new line was taken.[29] According to this, Japan had to undergo a "bourgeois democratic revolution" before a "proletarian revolution" was possible. A broad popular front was needed and there was no reason for not including a status organization. The questions were who the leaders of such organizations should be, how they should be oriented, and what tactics they should adopt. The obvious answer for these young activists was that the leadership belonged to the Comintern and its branch, the Japanese Communist Party. But the lack of initiative and leadership of the Party itself threw the problem to the Buraku leftists, who felt it was permissible for Burakumin to belong to Suiheisha organizations so long as they were oriented along class lines. Thus, the proposal to dissolve the Suiheisha was, for the time, abandoned.

This line of thinking gave new life to the leveling movement and

---

1924; 550,000 in 1925; 580,000 in 1926; 610,000 in 1927 and 1928; 650,000 in 1929; 580,000 in 1930; and 520,000 in 1931.

Then came the big jump to 1,970,000 yen in 1932; 2,370,000 in 1933; 1,790,000 in 1934; and 1,230,000 yen in 1935. Increasing inflation and the government's desire to quiet the home front after the Manchurian Incident were at work here, but the radical direction taken by the leveling movement was probably not without effect. In 1936, for the first time, a ten-year plan for conciliation work was set up, which was to involve some 55,800,000 yen; however, it was cut short by the war. In actuality these sums were insufficient to do more than scratch the surface of the problem of improving depressed conditions and opening up essential economic opportunities to down-trodden communities. See Harada (1963), pp. 7–11.

[29] For the texts of the 1931 and 1932 Theses, see Yamamoto and Arita (1950), pp. 215–20 and 252–92. Actually, the 1931 draft was unofficial.

animated the eleventh national convention of the Levelers' Society which met in Fukuoka on March 3, 1933. Some 158 delegates from the three metropolitan areas and eleven prefectures assembled amid an audience of over 2,000. The delegates expressed confidence in a new central committee and directed it to draft a new policy for the organization.

The new policy called upon the "six thousand" Buraku to cooperate with labor and farmer organizations through the new tactic of "Buraku committees." Such committees were to be formed at appropriate times to express concrete demands by the Buraku working people. They would fight for free clinics, maternity wards, and other health facilities; for funds for expanding businesses at low rates of interest or for public housing; for the building of roads, bridges, and sewers; and for various unemployment projects. In this way unorganized groups could be mobilized and majority neighbors benefited.

The question of how to apply this new strategy arose soon after the 1933 convention, when a case of discrimination occurred in a decision of the Takamatsu Regional Court in Kagawa Prefecture on Shikoku. Two half brothers and a friend met a cafe waitress who, unknown to her parents, had been visiting her friend in an effort to find a better job. The cafe owner had lent her father her future wages of 37 yen—a big sum for the poor—and she feared she would be tied to her job, which she found disagreeable. The younger half brother promised to raise the money if she would consent to marry him. This she did. The girl stayed for the night with her intended husband, returned home briefly, and then returned to her lover who had found a temporary room for them to stay in while he tried to raise the money. The father, unhappy at losing his daughter's wages, told the police that the girl had been abducted. He soon found her himself, and learned that the young men had hidden the fact that they were from a Buraku. The brothers were arrested and sentenced, the younger one for one year at hard labor and the older one for ten months. Both pleaded guilty to not having informed the girl that they were "special."

During the preliminary investigation, at the trial, and at the sentencing, the offending words "tokushu Burakumin" were used. The local Suiheisha unit realized that if this decision were allowed to stand, the Emancipation Edict of 1871 would in effect be nullified. The National Suiheisha Headquarters were asked for aid in organizing a campaign to denounce the trial and some leaders were sent to help. They found that a reconciliationist group, the Shōwakai, was trying to suppress publicity. After a couple of weeks they were expelled from the prefecture by the police at the behest of the court but another Suiheisha director was quietly sent. Manifestoes and pamphlets reporting the incident were distributed throughout the country. Every Buraku was asked to organize a struggle committee to denounce the trial and to publicize the case as broadly as possible.

Among Suiheisha leaders there was some discussion as to whether to label this a "class trial" or a "prejudiced judgment." It was decided that it would be easiest to rally the Burakumin on the basis of discrimination: during the struggle to reverse the decision, the Burakumin would come to realize that the government was against the poor. It is doubtful that as large a response would have been forthcoming if the leaders had not stressed the discrimination involved.

Direct protest to the top government ministers was one of the first steps taken. The Chairman, Matsumoto Jiichirō, led a delegation first to the Minister of Justice and then to the Ministry of Internal Affairs, protesting a verdict that made it a crime for a Burakumin not to publicly label himself a social outcaste. On August 28, the sixty-second anniversary of the Emancipation Edict, a huge protest meeting was held in Osaka. Some 126 representatives from 24 prefectures and more than 500 observers gathered, despite police intimidation. A planned petition march from Kyushu to Tokyo had to be canceled, but a group led by Matsumoto Jiichirō arrived in Tokyo on the 19th of October. Along the way they were welcomed by almost 200,000 people, and 47 speeches were made to an aggregate audience of some 163,000. Eleven other meetings were held.

In Tokyo they met with various government officials and presented the 50,000 signatures they had collected. The Socialist Masses' Party held two large receptions for them, as did various labor and consumer unions.[30] The campaign was almost immediately successful. In the following month the condemned men were released, the judge discharged, and the prosecutor removed. No "backlash" from the majority society followed the event; on the contrary, the Suiheisha leaders everywhere were subsequently treated with greater respect. This success provided the atmosphere of the twelfth national Suiheisha convention in Kyoto on April 3 and 4, 1934. Clearly, the earlier proposal to dissolve the Suiheisha had been proved wrong.

Following the meeting, the newest development concerned the question of discrimination in the arts. In 1934, the motion picture *Ai no Tenshoku* (*A Mission of Love*) and the novel *Nyonin Mandara* (*The Lady Mandala*), serialized in the newspaper *Asahi*, both expressed prejudicial conceptions of the Burakumin. As a result, the Suiheisha began the first of its "cultural" struggles. The Suiheisha's fight against military discrimination also assumed a new dimension with its attack against an article published in the *Yorozu Chōhō* (*Universal Morning*

---

[30] For the most detailed coverage of the Takamatsu trial and subsequent struggles, with relevant documents included, see Koyama (1934). While Inoue (1959), pp. 162–66, had access to several important documents, he evidently missed others.

Report) on November 23, 1934, by Lieutenant-General Satō Kiyokatsu,
entitled *Kijin to Eta (The Nobleman and the Eta)*.

The thirteenth convention of the Suiheisha was held in Osaka on
May 4 and 5, 1935, amid great enthusiasm. Discussion concerning the
use of denunciation tactics reached new levels of discernment. Each
case was to be considered on its own merits and its political significance evaluated so that it could be treated in such a way as to produce
integration with and understanding of the rest of society. It was also
decided that each Buraku committee should develop a program of its
own based on local conditions and experience as revealed in membership discussion and participation.

Greater political awareness also began to grow with broader political
participation. In the regular prefectural elections of September, 1935,
three Suiheisha leaders became candidates for the Fukuoka Prefectural
Assembly, and all three were elected. Then in the February, 1936,
general elections for the House of Representatives of the Imperial Diet,
Chairman Matsumoto Jiichirō—ex-prisoner, business owner, and
"social inferior" in view of the prejudiced—ran against four incum-
bents and one former Representative and won with 15,000 votes, of
which some estimated 9,000 were from majority areas. Militant and
proud of his origins, he took his place with other members of the
legislature.

With this political success behind, and with the leftist efforts to
create a "popular front" against fascism all over the world, the fourteenth national convention of the Suiheisha was held on March 3,
1937, in Tokyo. A new program was formulated: "We shall strive
through collective political, economic, and cultural struggles to protect and expand the rights of the oppressed Buraku masses toward
their complete emancipation." [31]

After this meeting came the April, 1937, general elections. Not only
was Matsumoto able to keep his seat, but the Socialist Masses' Party—
with which Matsumoto cooperated although he ran as an independent
—succeeded in electing 37 members, thereby becoming the third largest
party in the House of Representatives.

This atmosphere of optimism was shattered by the Japanese attack
on China, beginning with the Marco Polo Bridge Incident on July 7,
1937. As the country rallied behind the war effort, all organizations
were forced to reconsider their policies. The Central Committee decided to encourage Burakumin as Japanese citizens to participate
actively in the national mobilization for war. At the next meeting in

[31] Inoue considers this program a great advance. Previously the program had
called for a movement on the basis of class consciousness that had obscured the
meaning of the status character of the Burakumin. Also, the previous emphasis on
action by the Burakumin themselves had tended to isolate them. See Inoue (1959),
p. 170.

June, 1938, the position adopted, namely that discrimination contravened Emperor Meiji's Charter Oath and the Emancipation Edict, was the very policy the Imperial Path of Justice Association had espoused some thirty years earlier. The Central Committee decided on a new program—to understand the essential meaning of Japan as a Holy State, to contribute to Japanese prosperity, and to attempt the integration of the Japanese nation.

As the tempo of the war with China increased, the rigors of the controlled economy were most severely felt by Buraku industries. The leather industry, in particular, suffered severely. Although the demand for leather goods had increased with the war, the profits to be gained were monopolized by eight large-scale companies. Small home factories in the Buraku communities could obtain no raw materials except at a high cost. According to the available statistics there were an estimated 53,000 to 54,000 jobless in the Buraku in 1938 affecting 27 percent of the Buraku households.

In the spring of 1940, the formerly extreme left wing of the Suiheisha decided to appear to participate very actively in the war effort in order to gain some rapprochement with the military. This movement was not acceptable to the majority of the members, and the former leftists were expelled from the Suiheisha. This particular group dissolved itself toward the end of the year.

At the sixteenth national convention in Tokyo on August 28, 1940, it was proposed that the Suiheisha dissolve itself completely in order to concentrate whole-heartedly on the war effort, and that the Yamato (or Daiwa) Hōkoku Undō (Japan Patriotic Movement) be formed. Matsumoto Jiichirō, as the chairman of the Central Committee of the National Suiheisha, strongly opposed the dissolution. Other members of the Committee, who were being intimidated by the police, decided nevertheless on dissolution. At a meeting to support the Japan Patriotic Movement held in Osaka in May, 1941, Matsumoto criticized the Patriotic Movement and opposed dissolution of the Suiheisha, "even if I am left all alone." Many Suiheisha members supported him, and the meeting ended in confusion. The Suiheisha was never officially dissolved, but it became completely inactive.[32]

Matsumoto Jiichirō recounts how he was called to the Ministry of Internal Affairs in 1942 and warned that he would not be recommended by the Tōjō Cabinet as a candidate for the April, 1942, general election for the Diet unless he officially dissolved the National Suiheisha, but he replied that the organization had come into existence because of a natural need and could not go out of existence until that need disappeared.[33] Since the government was sure that Matsu-

[32] Inoue and Kitahara (1964).
[33] See Matsumoto (1948), pp. 204–07.

moto would be elected, he was finally given a recommendation and
elected. Thus he was a member of the Diet at the time of the sur-
render, when a totally new situation emerged.

SUMMARY

The leveling movement came into being a half century after
the "emancipation" of the Eta-Hinin. During the early years of the
Meiji Restoration, the "new commoners" found themselves scapegoats
for the frustrations and fears brought about by a rapidly changing
society. The Burakumin themselves were hesitant and leaderless in
dealing with their own untouchability, though a few made their way
upward by means of business astuteness or the new opportunities
opened by education, despite social discrimination. Philanthropists
and government officials were not entirely unaware of the situation,
but tended to view it through their own inherited set of prejudices.
The authorities dealt with the problem of outcaste status in terms of
crime prevention, sanitation, and emigration—if they dealt with it
at all; the philanthropists, in terms of creating social harmony (reconciliation) and of helping the Burakumin to help themselves. Even
many of the better-off Buraku leaders believed that if their people
would only be "clean" and dress and talk like good middle class
citizens, they would be accepted as such.

The First World War changed all this, for it brought a new flood
of revolutionary ideas from abroad, and it greatly increased the tempo
of industrialization within Japan, with its attendant social dislocations.
The great rice riots of 1918 exposed to the authorities and to the
Burakumin themselves the extent of their deprivation within Japanese
society, which continued to express contempt for them as unassimilated
inferiors. However, these riots also revealed their potential strength
upon taking direct action. It became clear to the more perceptive
leaders that positive, lasting results could be obtained only if this
activist potential were organized and led toward the attainment of
specific goals.

A conglomeration of ideas taken from such diverse philosophical
and ideological sources as Christian socialism, Buddhism, Marxism (in
the larger sense), Leninism, Kropotkinism, altruism, and self-determination were melded, and formed the platform from which the Suiheisha
movement was launched. From 1921 to 1925 the movement became
more intense and more revolutionary, with failures forgotten and
successes remembered. The conviction was born that "it is not we who
are at fault for being poor, dirty, and uneducated; it is the fault of
the majority society that has made us this way by discriminating
against us." The Suiheisha set out to change the attitude of the ma-

jority society by denouncing each case of overt prejudice and by demanding a public apology or some token of sincere repentance. When resistance was encountered, reactions on both sides often caused bloodshed. Even in situations not reaching such extremes, these tactics often tended to isolate the Burakumin and to turn their fight for emancipation into skirmishes against the majority society.

As Communist thinking spread within the Suiheisha, the more moderate elements became alienated and the anarchists to the extreme left fought against all authority, even organizational control within the Suiheisha. It was the Communist emphasis on class struggle that frightened the moderates who asked only for improvement of their status and who hoped to achieve ultimate harmony with national policies. The Communist argument, if not tactic, was to convince the leaders that the way to keep from becoming isolated and yet achieve results was to work through other organizations concerned with the eradication of poverty and with social revolution, such as the labor and tenant farmer unions. This point of view gained considerable support from about 1924 on, but the Communists carried their arguments so far by 1931 that they came to advocate the complete dissolution of the Suiheisha itself because it was a "status" organization. All effort, they argued, should be concentrated on proletarian organizations that were working for the proletarian revolution and a classless society.

The increasing radicalization of the Suiheisha movement and the growing economic difficulties accompanying the onset of the world depression motivated the non-Buraku reconciliationist organizations to more positive action for the eradication of overt prejudice in textbooks and elsewhere. These groups also compelled the government to double its spending on projects to improve public facilities in Buraku areas and to open economic opportunities and increase economic security coverage to categories that included Burakumin. Though far from adequate, this welfare trend continued into the wartime period after 1937.

In the early 1930's, pro-Communist elements in the Suiheisha began to realize that such powerful campaigns as the one conducted against discrimination in the 24th Infantry Regiment in Fukuoka, with all of its anti-militarist aspects, could not have succeeded without the special status appeal against prejudice. Consequently, they accepted the necessity for the Suiheisha's role as a status organization, but insisted that Buraku committees handle each situation on its own merits, work with other proletarian organizations, and keep leadership from the hands of reconciliationist leaders without alienating them.

After 1937, the Suiheisha, along with all other independent social movements, was drawn into the all-embracing national effort. However, it was the only such organization never to disband officially; its leadership was adroit enough to keep it from extinction.

While the Suiheisha, in representing a depressed minority, was in the mainstream of the proletarian movement as a whole, it was also characterized by a number of peculiarities. It was almost the only organization in which some progressive Buddhist influence was found, albeit to a minor extent—a fact that may evoke comparisons with the importance of religion to the Negroes and the Jews. It was the one in which women and children played a really important part. While it had no overseas affiliations, it recognized a kinship with the Koreans and the Taiwanese within the Japanese Empire, and with oppressed minorities everywhere.

CHRONOLOGY OF SOCIAL PROTEST MOVEMENTS FROM EMANCIPATION THROUGH WORLD WAR II

1867 Burakumin from the Osaka area presented to the Tokugawa Government a plea for emancipation.

1868 The Tokugawa Government declared the emancipation of Danzaemon, the Eta leader, and his sixty assistants for their service to the government.

1869 Katō Hiroyuki presented "A Proposition to Abolish the Eta-Hinin System" to the Kōgisho (the Lower House), a deliberative assembly that advised the new Meiji Government of the Emperor.

1871 Eta Kaihō Rei (Edict of Emancipation) declaring equality in status and occupation was issued by the new Meiji Government. Riots to oppose the Edict of Emancipation took place in several places in southwestern Japan.

1873 Twenty-nine Burakumin were killed or injured, 300 Buraku houses were destroyed by rural riots opposing emancipation.

1886 Sugiura Jūgō wrote *Hankai Yume Monogatari* (*Hankai's Dream Story*), a dream of the Burakumin's mass immigration to an island in the Pacific to establish a Utopian society.

1889 Nakae Chōmin discussed Buraku emancipation in the *Shinonome Shinbun* (*Dawn*) under the title, "The World of the New Commoners."

1895 A protest was made against discrimination and segregation at school in a village in Nara Prefecture.

1901   Yanase Keisuke published *Shakaigai no Shakai, Eta Hinin* (*The Eta Community, an Outcaste Society*).

1902   Controversy over discrimination by the Honganji temple school in Wakayama Prefecture.

A Buraku "improvement movement" called Bisaku Heimin-kai (Bisaku Commoners' Society) started in Okayama Prefecture.

A discriminatory decision was made by the Hiroshima court, which allowed divorce of a non-Buraku wife from her Buraku husband on the grounds that Burakumin were an inferior racial group.

1903   A meeting was held in Osaka to celebrate the formation of Dainippon Dōwa Yūwakai (Greater Japan Fraternal Conciliation Society).

1908   Shimazaki Tōson published his famous novel, *Hakai* (*Breach of Commandment*), dealing with a Buraku intellectual's tragic fate.

1912   Establishment of *Yamato Dōshikai* (Yamato Association of the Like-Minded) for the publication of a journal, *Meiji no Hikari* (*The Light of Meiji*).

1914   Establishment of Teikoku Kōdō Kai (Imperial Path of Justice Association) and publication of *Kōdō* (*The Imperial Path*).

1916   *Hakata Shinbun* (the Hakata Daily Newspaper) was raided by angry Burakumin for its insulting report about a Buraku in Fukuoka City.

There was controversy over the fact that an order to bivouac for soldiers was refused by the authorities in Okayama Prefecture because the majority of soldiers would have to be accommodated in a special Buraku.

1918   Many Burakumin led or participated in the rice riots.

1919   Demand for a wage increase was made by the Buraku clog thong producers and their craftsmen in Osaka.

The Buraku leather workers went on strike in Tokyo.

The Buraku shoemakers went on strike in Fukui City.

1920   A dispute over farm land broke out in Buraku in Aichi and Mie Prefectures.

1921   Sano Manabu's article, "Tokushu Buraku no Kaihō" ("The Emancipation of the Special Communities"), appeared in a new magazine, *Kaihō* (*Emancipation*).

1922   The foundation meeting of Zenkoku Suiheisha (National Levelers' Society) was held in Kyoto.

Government officials raided a Buraku in Oita Prefecture to remove their houses so that the Emperor might have a better view when traveling.

The National Levelers' Society declared that the Buraku temples and Burakumin belonging to the Honganji school would stop donations to the Honganji temples.

Branches of the Levelers' Society were established in Saitama, Mie, and Nara Prefectures.

Kimura Kyōtarō and other leaders were sued for acts of violence in a protest against discrimination at a primary school in Nara Prefecture.

The Levelers first published its official organ, Suihei (Leveling).

Kokui Dōmei (Black Robe Association) was established by the Shin Sect priests in Buraku to form a body independent from the regular Honganji Temple sect.

1923   The Levelers held their second convention in Kyoto. Zenkoku Fujin Suiheisha (National Women Levelers' Society) was established as an auxiliary.

An official statement was issued by the Ministry of Internal Affairs concerning Buraku improvement.

1924   Representatives of the Levelers' Society sent a letter to the American Ambassador protesting against the Anti-Japanese Immigration Law.

The Takasaki court in Saitama Prefecture was raided by outcastes for its adverse decision concerning Suiheisha's protest against the use of discriminatory words by non-Burakumin.

At its third general convention in Kyoto, the Levelers' Society decided that the Tokugawa Family should give up its princely title.

Matsumoto Jiichirō and others were arrested for planning the assassination of Prince Tokugawa Ietatsu (the Tokugawa Incident). Minami Umekichi and all other officials of the Levelers' Society resigned as a gesture of responsibility for the treachery and disunity among them concerning the Tokugawa Incident.

1925   The Levelers' Society held its fourth convention in Osaka and revised its constitution.

1926   The Levelers' Society held its fifth convention. An open split occurred between those opposing and those supporting Communism.

Yūwamondai Kenkyūkai (Study Group for Integration Problems) was opened in the Upper and the Lower House.

Zenkoku Suiheisha Rōnō Shiji Renmei (National Levelers' Society League to Support the Labor Farmer Party) was established by Zenkoku Suiheisha Musansha Dōmei (Proletarian Federation of the National Levelers' Society) and others.

Matsumoto Jiichirō and others were arrested for allegedly planning the dynamiting of the Fukuoka Army barracks as protest against discrimination in army regiments.

1927   A splinter society (Japan Levelers' Society) was established by Minami Umekichi and others.

Kitahara Taisaku made a direct appeal to the Emperor concerning the discrimination in the army when the Emperor was on an inspection tour of the regiment.

Zenkoku Suiheisha held its sixth convention, when it was split into three factions, namely, Zenkoku Suiheisha Musansha Dōmei (Proletarian Federation of the National Levelers' Society), Zenkoku Suiheisha Kaihō Renmei (Emancipation League of the National Levelers' Society), and Nihon Suiheisha (Japan Levelers' Society).

1928   Zenkoku Suiheisha put up Matsumoto Jiichirō, Nishimitsu Mankichi, and Miki Seijirō for the Labor Farmer Party at the first general election for the House of Representatives, but none of them won election. Matsumoto and others were sentenced as guilty of an attempted tyranny of the Fukuoka Army and imprisoned.

1929   At its eighth convention in Nagoya, Zenkoku Suiheisha discussed reunification.

1930   Numerous acts of discrimination at schools, in the army, and elsewhere were publicized by the Levelers' Society.

1931   At its tenth convention in Nara Prefecture, the representatives from the Kyushu district proposed to dissolve the Levelers' Society on the ground that it consisted of classes with different interests.

1933   At its eleventh convention in Fukuoka City, the Levelers' Society decided to fight against the "militaristic Emperor System."

The Buraku problem was taken up at the fifteenth May Day Assembly in Osaka.

A protest was made against the discriminatory decision by the Takamatsu court in the case of an intended marriage between a Buraku youth and a non-Buraku girl.

1934 At its twelfth convention in Kyoto, Zenkoku Suiheisha declared that the idea of dissolving itself would be an error.

1935 At its thirteenth convention in Osaka, Zenkoku Suiheisha decided to be more attentive to the social and political implications of discrimination.

1936 Zenkoku Suiheisha held its fourteenth convention in Tokyo. The Central Committee of Zenkoku Suiheisha decided to cooperate with the national policy in its "Program to Meet the National Crisis."

1938 Zenkoku Suiheisha held its fifteenth convention in Osaka.

1940 Zenkoku Suiheisha held its sixteenth and final convention in Tokyo. At its meeting in Tokyo, representatives of Zenkoku Suiheisha decided to dissolve Zenkoku Suiheisha and to support the Yamato Hōkoku Undō (Japan Patriotic Movement).

1941–
1945 No activities reported during the war years.

Chapter 3

HIROSHI WAGATSUMA

Postwar Political Militance

POSTWAR POLITICAL DEMOCRATIZATION AND THE BURAKUMIN

After Japan's defeat and the ensuing chaos, political parties soon reformed. The Peace Preservation Law, once used to arrest all liberal elements in Japan, was abolished and former Communist leaders were released from prison on October 10, 1945. Hailing the allied occupation as an "army of liberation," the Communist Party was officially re-established, and it made the emancipation of the oppressed Buraku a central issue, appealing to the outcastes to stand up and fight for their own liberation. A day after the formation of the Communist Party, the Japanese Socialist Party was formed.

When, in January, 1947, the former leaders of both the Leveling (Suiheisha) Movement and the Integrationist or Reconciliationist (Yūwa) Movement held a joint meeting, they broadcast a plea "to form voluntarily a strong unity . . . to establish firmly the great democratic revolution for the construction of a new Japan, and for the purpose of complete liberation of the oppressed Buraku population." This conference was followed by a series of meetings. One very large meeting was attended by representatives from the newly formed Progressive and Liberal parties, in addition to Socialist and Communist party officials. Japan's new parties, at least symbolically, indicated by their attendance their support of Buraku integration. Though for the Liberal and Progressive parties this support was a mere token, both the Socialist and Communist parties were to make "Buraku liberation" part of their continuing policy.[1]

---

[1] The more conservative parties usually indicated their interests under the words "reconciliation" or "integration" (Yūwa or Dōwa), whereas the Socialist and Communist parties talked of "liberation" or "emancipation" (Kaihō) when they discussed Buraku problems. For a study on the postwar Socialist movement, including its policies toward the Burakumin, see Cole, Totten, and Uehara (1966).

In the declaration issued at the February 20 conference, general agreement with the official American occupation policy was expressed. The prewar *zaibatsu* capitalists were attacked for monopolistic practices which injured small Buraku industries, there was strong support for the abolition of the aristocracy and other forms of privilege, and a hearty endorsement of an organized democratic front that was to cooperate in the construction of a democratized Japan. However, the conservative Liberal and Progressive parties were to interpret democracy as encouragement of the business and commercial segments of the population on a free enterprise basis, whereas the Socialist and Communist parties saw the future of Japanese democracy in a socialist state.

In November, 1946, the new Constitution of Japan was promulgated, taking effect the following May. Article 14 clearly stated that all citizens are equal under the law in political, economic, and social relationships, and that they are not to be discriminated against for reasons of race, belief, sex, social status, or family background. Thus, in democratic Japan under its new Constitution, the former outcastes at least legally, if not in fact, were to be free from any form of discriminatory practice.

In April, 1947, Matsumoto Jiichirō, who had been elected chairman of the reformed Buraku organization (at this time called the National Committee for Buraku Liberation—Buraku Kaihō Zenkoku Iinkai), ran as a member of the Socialist party for the House of Councilors, the new upper chamber of the reorganized Japanese Diet. He received over 400,000 votes, the fourth largest total of the votes cast. Nine other Burakumin were elected, either to the House of Councilors or to the House of Representatives for the first time. In the almost revolutionary atmosphere of the time, he was elected Vice President of the House of Councilors, thus shattering all precedent. In his new position, he would have been the first outcaste to enter the Imperial Palace in audience with the Emperor, but his militant attitudes against the status system made him reject all invitations to events at the Court. He demanded legislation reducing the budget of the Imperial household and asked that the Akasaka Detached Palace be turned over to the homeless evacuees returning from overseas. An emerging hero of the new democracy, he received great popular support.

In 1948, on January 21, Matsumoto shocked many by his refusal to bow in the traditional manner to the Emperor at the formal opening session of the second postwar Diet. This last incident appalled the Conservatives who wanted to marshal a vote of nonconfidence against him, but public opinion supported Matsumoto's gesture, and from the next Diet session on, the long tradition of formal obeisances in audiences with the Emperor were dropped from the parliamentary procedure. Matsumoto approached the Emperor directly, rather than walking sideways (like a crab) with head down in the traditional manner, and simply said to him, "We thank you for your coming." [2]

The Purge of Matsumoto

In January, 1949, Premier Yoshida maneuvered the American occupation into taking an act that was to disenchant members of the Buraku movement with American policies in Japan and to align them more solidly with the developing anti-American policies of the Socialist and Communist parties. Yoshida, a very conservative Japanese, was deeply incensed over the obeisance incident, and his cabinet managed to have Matsumoto added to the list of Japanese to be excluded from public service. It was alleged that he had acted as an official of the Japan Patriotic Society (Yamato or Daiwa Hōkoku Kai) during the war, and had therefore actively cooperated with the militarists against the United States. Matsumoto's name actually had appeared among the officials listed in a pamphlet by the society, but he had never consented formally to become an official, nor did he agree with the policies of this group. But Yoshida, by clever maneuvering, was to gain the support of General MacArthur. (In publishing a series of letters exchanged between Yoshida and MacArthur, a reporter for *Life* magazine exposed Yoshida.)[3]

---

[2] Inoue and Kitahara (1964).

[3] The most noteworthy letter reads as follows:

January 1, 1949

My dear General:

Mr. Jiichirō Matsumoto, Vice President of House of Councilors, was one of the so-called "recommendation candidates" in the general election of April, 1942, under the Tojo Government. As such, he should have been automatically purged years ago. But he was exempted because of the eminent role he had played as leader of the Suihei Movement for the emancipation of the ostracized class.

Now it has been discovered that Mr. Matsumoto had been always an influential member of the *Yamato Hōkoku Kai*, which, as you know, was designated in August last as an ultranationalistic organization falling under the Purge Directive. . . . Mr. Matsumoto is a prominent member of the Social Democratic Party. He is at the same time an avowed opponent of the Emperor system. In view of these facts some quarters may charge the government with a political motive which is entirely nonexistent. . . . My government, simply motivated legally, in fairness to all persons and in strict observance of the law, has decided to include Mr. Matsumoto among those designated for purge.

I trust this step of my government will meet with your approval.

Yours sincerely,
Shigeru Yoshida

Generals Whitney and MacArthur knew perfectly well what was behind the letters: a new election was coming up, and the Prime Minister wanted Matsumoto out of the way. But Mr. Yoshida had them in a difficult position. So, through General Whitney, the Supreme Commander avoided a written reply and orally advised the Prime Minister to wait until after the election. The Prime Minister accepted this advice—the dismissal of Matsumoto from the Diet was announced one hour after the polls had closed. Osborne (1950), pp. 127–39.

More than sixty trade unions, political parties, and other organizations, campaigned for the revocation of Matsumoto's purge.[4] Over one million signatures were obtained, including more than two-thirds of the members of both Houses. On March 15, 1950, the National Commiteee for Buraku Liberation issued a manifesto and organized a petition march, and representatives from all parts of Japan marched toward Tokyo, demanding an interview with the Prime Minister and the Minister of Justice. Some sat in front of the Diet Building, proclaiming a hunger strike.

The General Director of the American Civil Liberties Union, Roger Baldwin, wrote to his counterpart, Unno Shinkichi, of the Japanese Civil Liberties Society (Jiyū Jinken Kyōkai) to say that the evidence indicated that the purging of Matsumoto was a mistake, and that he favored a revocation. The delegate from the Soviet Union to the Allied Council for Japan also demanded Matsumoto's reinstatement. John Osborne wrote in *Life*:

But the pressure of Japanese public opinion gradually led to a lightening of the purge policy. On October 12 of this year, an appeal board composed of Japanese completed its review of 32,091 cases, and recommended 10,091 remissions. Prime Minister Yoshida approved 10,900 of them. The sole exception was Matsumoto. General MacArthur, in turn, approved, and received a warm note from the Prime Minister.[5]

On August 6, 1951, after two and a half years of continuing protest, the Yoshida Cabinet finally reinstated Matsumoto, among 13,000 others. But MacArthur's original acceptance of the purge probably solidified the anti-American orientation of the increasingly militant Buraku liberation movements. At the "People's meeting to welcome Matsumoto's return to the Democratic front," held in Kyoto, Tokyo,

---

[4] Principal among these organizations were the Japanese Socialist party, the Communist party, the Labor and Farmer party, the Congress of Industrial Unions of Japan, the Japanese Federation of Labor Unions, the League for the Protection of Democracy, the National Railway Company Labor Union, the Metal Industry Labor Union, and the Council of Democratic Women.

[5] This read:

October 12, 1950

My dear General,

I have just been informed through General Whitney that the decisions of the Public Office Qualification Appeal Board have been approved by you *in toto*, and I hasten to send you my sincere thanks for your prompt action.

I can well imagine the gratification and joy of the ten thousand more persons who have been granted special remission from the purge. To them it will mean a new lease on life. Restored to useful activities in their respective fields, they will now be able to contribute positively and abundantly to the task of national reconstruction.

This will be good news to all the families and friends of the released—news that will brighten many nooks and corners of Japan.

Yours sincerely,
Shigeru Yoshida

Osaka, and Fukuoka, Matsumoto cried, "For the sake of the nation's independence, for the sake of peace and democracy, for the sake of liberation of all the oppressed, we shall overthrow the reactionary powers of Japan and the United States." [6]

Although the anti-American and Marxian orientations of the Buraku liberation movement were apparent from the beginning, it was at the twelfth national meeting of the Buraku Liberation League held in 1957 that the movement was specifically defined as "the fight against monopolistic capitalism," and as an integral part of the "people's front of social democracy and national autonomy" under the leadership of the working class. In accordance with the Communist party's program, the movement was directed toward the fight with the present politico-economic system because ". . . Buraku discrimination exists . . . in order to suppress and exploit people. American imperialism, Japanese monopolistic capitalism and the government are maintaining feudalistic elements, including Buraku discrimination, in the society, as they found the feudalistic elements to be a very convenient means of domination and exploitation." Yamamoto points out three basic fallacies in such an orientation: (1) Buraku discrimination is not the product of feudalism, though the caste system was certainly made rigid during the Tokugawa period; (2) monopolistic capitalism is not maintaining feudalism but, rather, modernizing Japanese society in its effort to increase efficiency of productivity; (3) Burakumin are not exploited by monopolistic capitalism because most Burakumin are not employed by large enterprises—they are, rather, "excluded from capitalist exploitation." [7] Yamamoto also argues that although the Buraku Liberation League propagates the united action of *all* the Burakumin, the goal of their movement is actually the liberation of proletarian Burakumin only. The same criticism of the Liberation League's interpretation of Buraku was expressed by Naramoto Tatsuya, the director of the Buraku Problems Research Institute.[8]

THE POSTWAR ECONOMIC SITUATION

In the postwar chaos many Burakumin survived by the black marketeering of rice, meat, and leather.[9] The readjustment of industry that began in 1948 again produced great numbers of jobless people, and despite the Korean war boom, several millions remained out of work between 1949 and 1950. Needless to say, unemployment struck the Buraku hardest: in some areas, nearly all the employable indi-

[6] Inoue and Kitahara (1964).
[7] Yamamoto (1962).
[8] Naramoto (1961).
[9] Nakanishi (1960), pp. 183–227.

viduals had no work. In March 1950, for instance, in Nara Prefecture, 2,400 of the 3,000 individuals registering for governmental relief were from Buraku. In a Kyoto Buraku, whereas only 18 percent of the household heads were registered for relief work in 1940, the number had increased to almost 36 percent in 1951. In southwestern Japan as a whole, it was estimated that up to 70 percent of those registered for relief work were from Buraku. The severity of the situation stimulated the National Committee for Buraku Liberation (which was to become the Buraku Kaihō Dōmei, or Buraku Liberation or Emancipation League, in 1955) to militant action to resolve the economic problems of the Buraku.

In 1946, at the same time that the National Committee of Buraku Liberation was being organized, the Japan Farmer's Union (Nihon Nōmin Kumiai) was being rebuilt, and the Buraku farmers were organized into Union branches in each of their communities. In such prefectures as Ibaragi, Saitama, Nagano, Mie, Nara, Hyogo, and Fukuoka, Burakumin acted as core groups in campaigns directed against quota delivery of rice, land expropriation, and high farm rents. In Nagano and Okayama prefectures, they demanded the release of national forest lands previously used by the army for maneuvers, and the release of sites of war factories to landless farmers. In the earlier period, the Communist cells within Buraku and the local Japan Farmer's Union were more active in this than the National Committee for Buraku Liberation,[10] whose first activities were in education and in the establishment of work centers.

Buraku Organizations and Land Reform

A dramatic and influential effect of the American occupation was the liberal program of land reform established throughout Japan, which transferred the ownership of over three million acres from wealthy landowners to their former tenants. Eighty-seven percent of the total farm land was involved.

This vast program, however, at first ignored some of the particular problems of Buraku farmers. Tenant farmers who had been working less than three *tan* (about 0.7 of an acre) were excluded from the reform measures because it had been judged that such small-scale tillers could not possibly become successful owners, and 30 percent of the Buraku farmers could not meet this requirement. In Nara Prefecture, for instance, 70 percent of the land was turned over to former tenant farmers, but in one Buraku only slightly more than 50 percent of the total farm land fell to individual farmers, while 80 percent of the paddy land continued to be worked on a tenancy basis. The Buraku

---

[10] Nakanishi (1960).

organized and negotiated with the agricultural land commissions to revise the reform program so that it could be applied to tenants with more than two tan (approximately half an acre), or even, in some Buraku, to those with more than one. And some of these negotiations were successful: in Matsuzaka City in Mie, for example, farm ownership increased from slightly more than one-third of the households to 98 percent of the community.[11] Needless to say, owners of such small plots could not possibly eke out a living solely on farm activity; they had to supplement their farming with various other side jobs (see Chapter 6). Success in activities such as these demonstrated to the Burakumin the advisability of group action to alleviate their economic problems.

After the eighth national meeting of 1953, the Committee for Buraku Liberation increasingly directed its attention to what it termed "the struggle for improvement of economic situations within Buraku." Social or political incidents were often reformulated and used as pressure to resolve what the Committee felt to be basic, namely, that economic discrimination was not caused as much by intentionally discriminatory policies as by the government's refusal to consider the Burakumin as an invisible minority with special problems. The objectives of subsequent campaigns were the right of Burakumin to enter the village common for charcoal, grass, and firewood; government subsidies and loans for improvement of Buraku holdings in agriculture: in the cities; slum clearance and low rent public housing; improvement of sewerage and water supply; expansion of nurseries, clinics, work centers, and welfare programs; improvement in educational facilities and employment possibilities for Buraku youth; and loans to small-scale Buraku industries. With this increasing emphasis on the economic problems of discrimination, membership in the Liberation Committee continually increased. By 1955, over a thousand branches of the National Committee were to be found in 26 prefectures. Six hundred and fifty delegates and 1,800 observers attended the tenth national meeting held in Osaka in August of that year, where the official name was changed from the National Committee of Buraku Liberation to the Buraku Liberation League (Buraku Kaihō Dōmei). The need for fuller participation on a broader scale was stressed,[12] and a woman's auxiliary was organized and first met in March, 1956, in Kyoto, while another organization for Buraku youth was formed in July, 1957.

From the standpoint of the Kaihō Dōmei, Buraku problems were part of the failure of the entire Japanese nation to realize the objec-

---

[11] Nakanishi (1960).
[12] Nakanishi (1960).

tives of the new Japanese Constitution. As expressed by Kitahara, one of the Dōmei leaders:

Under the Japanese Constitution, Japan is supposed to have established a democratic society in which human rights for every citizen are to be respected and protected. Every Japanese is supposed to enjoy individual freedom and the right to attain a basic standard of life. However, in reality a large number of Japanese are exploited by the government and its capitalistic regime. When they try to stand up and protest, people are suppressed by police. . . . Burakumin, being the bottom strata of a hierarchical society headed by the Emperor, suffer the most from all kinds of defects and contradictions inherent in capitalistic society. Discrimination adds to their misery. They are refused the freedom of selecting their own domicile, their occupation, and of making a marriage according to their own choice.

For Burakumin, discrimination is not simply the result of something psychological. It is not the result of prejudice against Burakumin existing in the minds of the majority society members. The disadvantaged, backward living conditions, all kinds of negative qualities, and destitution within the Buraku, are a remnant of the former status discrimination suffered under feudalism. The Japanese government has neglected its duty to improve public health and social welfare for the protection of Japanese citizens generally. This failure is especially noted in the case of the Buraku. Public roads leading to Buraku are not paved, nor are they wide enough for the passage of vehicles of the fire department. In many places, the bulwarks on river banks protecting the area from flood are not continued around Buraku areas. Disaster always strikes Buraku the hardest. The government permits the unsanitary conditions and personal misery suffered within the Buraku to act as a compost for further vice, which in turn serves to aggravate the prejudice and discrimination felt against Burakumin on the part of majority Japanese. This vicious circle continues. It can only be stopped by active administrative measures on the part of the government to improve the basic conditions of Buraku life. The Buraku liberation movement, therefore, focuses its effort in a continuous fight to see that the government takes proper administrative measures.[13]

The concerted efforts of the Buraku organization to alleviate conditions may be illustrated by the following incident. In the late summer of 1953, the western coast of Honshu and northern Kyushu were badly hit by a major typhoon followed by winds and floods that caused considerable damage. Because of the unfavorable location of the Buraku, they were particularly hard hit. Under the leadership of the National Committee, the Buraku people campaigned actively to obtain government compensation, and as a result, in Honshu twelve and a half acres of village-owned land were released to them.[14] The move, made under

---

[13] Kitahara (1960), pp. 4–15.
[14] Nakanishi (1960).

pressure by the village office, was opposed by the majority farmers, but the National Committee stood firm and finally persuaded the village to recompense other farmers so that a new residential area could be built for the Buraku at the top of a well-situated hill.[15]

MILITANT PROTESTS
AGAINST SOCIAL DISCRIMINATION

The All Romance *Incident*

A historic case in setting the direction of the policy of the National Committee for Buraku Liberation occurred in October, 1951, with the publication of a short novel in *All Romance (Oru Romansu)*, a pulp magazine. The lurid story, entitled "Special Buraku," was written by one Sugiyama, an assistant public health instructor at the Kyoto City Health Department. He not only described the poverty and destitution of the Buraku but also lewd sexual activities in which Burakumin supposedly engaged.

The novel was claimed to be based on Sugiyama's own experiences in dealing with a Buraku in Kyoto. The setting was described as literally "hell on earth" (iki-jigoku), full of black marketeering, illegal *sake* brewing, crime, violence, and sex. For example, "In an open lot a number of children played, practically naked, their eyes filled with mucus, their faces and heads covered with boils." Again, "The internal organs of animals killed the day before are discarded in some corner, covered with black flies. One feels overcome by the stench." In another scene, he depicts a conversation in which a girl says she wants to become a prostitute to escape being a pariah. The reputation of this novel spread among the Burakumin, and Buraku communities in Kyoto seethed with resentment toward this obvious attempt at sensationalizing their plight. The National Committee protested against the writer and his responsible superior, the Mayor of Kyoto, who responded by immediately firing Sugiyama. But the National Committee continued to press the point that such writing was a symptom of the economic discrimination practiced against the Buraku in Kyoto by the authorities who ignored their obvious destitution. The Committee requested that officials in charge of various administrative districts mark on a map all sections of the city lacking public water supplies, sewage disposal, fire hydrants, and all areas with inadequate housing, high rates of tuberculosis, trachoma, and other public health problems, high absenteeism in the schools, and high concentrations of families on relief. The result was a vivid demonstration of Burakumin problems, since the marked areas fell entirely within the 18 Buraku in Kyoto and its environs. The Mayor and his officials, surprised and em-

---

[15] Inoue and Kitahara (1964).

barrassed, promised seriously to attempt to improve Buraku conditions.[16] The Kyoto City budget for 1954 for Buraku improvement was raised to 60 million yen, compared with 7.5 million for the previous year. By 1960, items for Buraku improvement totaled 103 million yen; by 1962, 300 million. Many wooden shacks have been replaced by low rent concrete apartments, and public toilets, sanitary water supplies, sewage disposals, new public bath houses, some community centers, and parks and nurseries for children have all been provided, the result of the furor stirred by the *All Romance* incident.[17]

The Nishikawa Affair

In the Nishikawa Affair the National Committee for Liberation was highly successful in using strike and boycott tactics to force a discriminatory prefectural assemblyman to resign. This case gained considerable attention in the Japanese press.

An assemblyman of Wakayama Prefecture named Nishikawa, a wealthy landowner from Kawakami Village, came from a family that had served under the Tokugawa regime as chief magistrates in the area. On February 27, 1952, he and other members of the prefectural assembly were invited to a celebration marking the opening of a mine. Coming late, Nishikawa found that a local assemblyman of outcaste background had been seated at a higher level than that left for him.[18] Nishikawa was further incensed when he learned that the same assemblyman had been invited to another political gathering whereas he had been passed over. He called the restaurant that was hosting the party and, becoming extremely irate, shouted, "Everybody is siding with the 'eta.'" He was overheard by two Buraku villagers seated near his party, who reprimanded him for the use of the word "eta." Still infuriated, he answered, "What's wrong with using the word 'eta'?"

News of this incident spread quickly and the National Committee organized a special protest committee in cooperation with other organizations, such as the Japanese National Civil Liberties Commission. Nishikawa's response was to defend discrimination. The enraged Burakumin at a meeting decided to demand that the prefectural assembly expel Nishikawa and at the same time promote special administrative effort to improve Buraku conditions. On March 20, the Wakayama Prefectural Assembly decided to investigate the incident,

---

[16] Tōjō (1959), pp. 160–70.

[17] Inoue (1962), pp. 27–35.

[18] At a sake party held on *tatami* mats in Japan, the ordering of seats is a subject of great concern. Usually the place of honor, for the guest of highest status, is at one end of a row of seats, and the closer the others to this position, the higher the status afforded.

and one week later the assemblymen unanimously advised Nishikawa to resign. Still defiant, he refused.

A protest campaign then spread throughout Wakayama Prefecture, with the local Socialist and Communist parties, labor unions, and the Congress of the United Front of Democratic Korean Residents of Japan (Zainichi Chōsenjin Minshu Tōitsu Sensen Kaigi), all joining the campaign. On April 16, the Struggle Committee ordered all children to stay home from school, but to counteract the effect of the boycott, the Wakayama Prefectural Education Commission closed all the high schools for three days. From April 19 on, the farmers refused to deliver their quota of rice and to pay their taxes. Fifty individuals moved into Kawakami Village and held a series of meetings with speeches in front of Nishikawa's estate. In addition, every day a few hundred Burakumin rode into the village and gathered in front of the Nishikawa house to shout further accusations. On April 21, more than 800 Burakumin assembled in front of the prefectural government building to demand that the government expel Nishikawa from the assembly and improve Buraku conditions. Finally, on April 27, when about 14,000 students from 57 schools were boycotting, the prefectural assembly accepted the demand of the special committee, promising that the administration would see to ameliorating Buraku conditions and that Nishikawa would be expelled from the assembly. On May 5, Nishikawa tendered his formal resignation.[19]

The Girard Affair: Burakumin Involvement in an American-Japanese Incident

Five years later another important affair occurred—the Girard case. In the considerable coverage given the affair in the American press, the American public remained in complete ignorance that the woman killed in a senseless act by an American soldier was a Burakumin; yet without understanding this facet of the case, the vehemence of the protest by leftist organizations and the indifference of a large majority of Japanese are incomprehensible. The situation nonetheless aroused emotions both in the United States and Japan concerning the possible jurisdiction of the Japanese courts over American military personnel.

In Sōmagahara Buraku in Gumma Prefecture, a large number of Buraku villagers were forced from their land by the construction of an American Army base. Having little other means of support, many of the former farmers collected the empty shells from the rifle range located on this base and sold them for scrap metal. The legal jurisdic-

---

[19] It is important to note that Nishikawa later ran in a by-election, and was re-elected to the assembly by a majority vote. Nishimoto (1960), p. 136.

tion of this particular range was not clearly defined, so the American Army authorities could not prevent the Burakumin from entering the range. On January 31, 1957, a Buraku housewife entered the range after military exercises had been completed. A remaining soldier, Girard, directed her to a nearby ditch full of shells, and said in pidgin Japanese, "Mamasan, daijobu, burasu, takusan-ne" (It's safe. Lots of brass [shells]). When the woman, Mrs. Sakai, went down into the ditch, Girard put an empty shell in a grenade-throwing mechanism on his rifle. Mrs. Sakai was warned by her friend that the soldier seemed to be aiming at her, and she started running. Fired from thirty feet away, the empty shell scored a direct hit, and the woman died on the spot. American Army authorities first announced that she had been killed by a stray bullet, but it was later established that Private Second Class Girard had shot her. A formal apology was sent from the American Embassy to the Japanese Ministry of Foreign Affairs.

The Buraku Kaihō Dōmei demanded that the soldier be tried in a Japanese court, since the incident took place while the soldier was off duty. After some controversy a United States-Japan joint committee finally decided that the soldier should be tried by a Japanese court. This became a sensitive issue in the American press, and there were numerous debates as to whether an American soldier should be subject to foreign jurisdiction. The Administration supported the State Department since any other position would have compromised the Japanese government, which was under fire from the left for permitting American military bases in Japan.

On May 18, Girard was indicted for murder at the Maebashi District Court. Girard's brother in the United States appealed to the Federal District Court in Washington, D.C., for a writ of habeas corpus; and the judgment of the court was that it was against the Constitution to hand to the Japanese an American soldier who was on duty. However, the Federal Supreme Court unanimously overruled the judgment of the District Court and supported the position taken by the American government. Girard was sentenced to three years in prison. However, under the very liberal Japanese interpretation of the sentence, which took into account the circumstances under which the crime was committed and the attitude of contrition and reform on the part of the guilty person, Girard was never sent to prison, but was released and immediately returned to the United States.[20]

The Liberation League used this incident to increase the vigor of the campaign against American military bases and against the United

---

[20] Girard was put under what is called *shikkō yūyo*, meaning postponement of execution of sentence. Technically he was to be on good behavior for a number of years. The Japanese description of the case can be found in Miyazawa *et al.* (1957), pp. 2–29.

States-Japan Security Treaty, which was being led by the Socialist and Communist parties.

There is evidence that a good deal of Buraku land was taken in establishing several other American bases,[21] but whether or not sites were deliberately selected by local authorities so that Burakumin would suffer displacement is not known. Whatever the basis of these decisions, the American military were probably in total ignorance of their involvement in a specific Japanese social problem. They were also unaware that the well organized Burakumin in these areas, supported by the Kaihō Dōmei and other organizations, have been the active core of leftist demonstrations against American military bases.

A Case of Re-education

One of the unique features of Japanese chess is that you can use the captured pieces of your enemy as part of your own force. The American Army capturing Japanese prisoners found a curious willingness to cooperate and, if necessary, even to join the American forces. In general, Japanese avoid irrevocable commitment to a particular political philosophy. It was part of the program of the Suiheisha movement of the 1920's to demand repentance; capitalizing on this characteristic they attempted, in their own terms, to "rehabilitate the prejudiced" and to show people the error of their ways. The following incident, which occurred in the winter of 1957, illustrates this. One could not readily find an American parallel.

Throughout that winter, influenza was widespread on the island of Shikoku, and the authorities decided to temporarily close Hiraoka Junior High School. Most of the students had already gone home, and a few of the teachers were drinking *sake* while chatting around the stove. A teacher named Shinkai drank too much and becoming red-faced and boisterous, he suddenly called to his colleague of outcaste background, saying, "Hey there, Mr. 'eta.' Come on over here." There was a general hush in the room, and the atmosphere became oppressively tense. Without answering, Mr. Yamazaki left the room; obviously upset, he revealed the incident to a few Buraku students. The students waited and questioning Shinkai, they asked him pointedly what he had meant by "eta." Shinkai promptly wrote the Chinese

---

[21] In addition to the Sōmagahara Base, Buraku land was taken for the establishment and expansion of the Etajima Naval Base in Hiroshima Prefecture, Itami Air Base in Hyogo Prefecture, and Itazuke Air Base in Fukuoka Prefecture. To protect their lands, Burakumin activity participated in campaigns against the establishment of American military bases in many other parts of Japan, as at the foot of Mt. Asama and Mt. Myogi in Nagano and Gumma Prefectures, in Aonogahara in Hyogo Prefecture, Nihonbara, Yokoi, Sangenya in Okayama Prefecture, and in Oshima in Wakayama Prefecture.

characters standing for "eta" on the ground and said, "The 'eta' are descendants of captured Koreans. If you don't want to be called 'eta,' you must study harder." The students asked him to repeat his remarks in front of their community. He agreed and accompanied the students to the Buraku where he continued to drink and make derogatory remarks. In the meantime, the parents of some of the students arrived and protested; upon being ignored, they had him arrested.

The next morning, people from the Buraku assembled, held a meeting, and formalized a series of demands. First, Shinkai must be fired instantly. Second, the school principal must take responsibility for the incident. Third, immediate action must be instituted to eliminate any discriminatory attitudes on the part of other teachers. Fourth, all teachers in the school should be made to understand the necessity of education toward the elimination of discrimination.

The Kochi Branch of the Kaihō Dōmei, when informed of the incident, also presented their demands. First, the responsibility of the prefectural superintendent of education for an incident of this nature must be clarified. Second, the prefectural board of education must immediately establish some concrete plan for further education to eliminate the vestiges of discrimination. Third, a research organization should be formed to determine the best means for establishing such a program.

Shinkai was indeed fired, but the school took no other measures in response to the demands either of the Buraku villagers or the Kaihō Dōmei. Angry at this neglect, the Buraku students decided to strike. They gathered at a nearby temple for a "teach in" to continue their studies on their own; a few teachers who went to the temple were much impressed by their conduct. In the evening of the same day, meetings were held which included, in addition to Buraku adults, students and six teachers from the school. Members of the village wanted to press a demand for dismissal of the members of the prefectural board of education, the school principal, and four teachers whose past behavior was deemed indicative of discriminatory attitudes. However, the students rejected this last idea; rather, what they wanted was to change their teachers' attitudes, as they put it, so the school would become a pleasant place to study.

The next day, another meeting was held by representatives of the Kaihō Dōmei, the Buraku parents, students, and a number of the teachers—this time attended by some members of the prefectural board of education. The decision of the meeting was to establish special education programs at the school for both teachers and students in an effort to eliminate further discrimination. On the same day, the majority students decided to request their Buraku classmates to call off their strike. Agreement was reached, and the students from the Buraku returned to school.

It was discovered later that as a result of his dismissal from school, Shinkai had become jobless and was faced with serious financial problems. The Buraku people decided to hire him as a calligraphy teacher for Buraku children. A Buraku woman proposed that Mr. Shinkai be sent to the Buraku Mondai Kenkyūjo (The Research Institute of Buraku Problems) in Kyoto on a fellowship from the prefectural government, and that after completing his study of Buraku problems, he be rehired by the school and placed in charge of education on eliminating discrimination. This idea was accepted by the prefectural government, and Shinkai went to Kyoto to be re-educated.[22]

THE GRAND MARCH OF LIBERATION

The fact that the movement for Burakumin emancipation has had a long history has been used to sustain and strengthen it. On August 28, 1961, on the 90th anniversary of the original emancipation ordinance that declared the Burakumin new citizens, a meeting was held in Osaka at which it was decided that a Grand March of Liberation should be organized in commemoration. Representatives of the Buraku were to present a petition to the national government as a culmination of the march that was to cover 1,200 kilometers, starting from Kyushu, proceeding across the long span of Honshu, and ending in Tokyo. Six thousand people gathered on September 11 to hear Matsumoto Jiichirō, now a Socialist party Diet member, speak concerning the danger of Japan's involvement in war as a result of joint American-Japanese policies. Thirteen individuals were chosen to walk the entire distance to Tokyo, to be accompanied through each prefecture en route by a delegation from that prefecture. The send-off was led by Matsumoto, riding in an open car and followed by women of the Kaihō Dōmei who held aloft a banner announcing "Fukuoka-Tokyo, 1,200 kilometers, The Great Petition March for Buraku Liberation." A group of sturdy young men came next, waving a flag with the traditional emblem of the old Suiheisha, the Crown of Thorns. Finally came the 13 chosen marchers, and 40 townsmen to accompany them as far as the Fukuoka border, all wearing red headbands (*hachimaki*) and *tasuki*, or red sashes.[23]

---

[22] This incident was reported in *Buraku* magazine (1957), No. 7, pp. 4–15.

[23] The *hachimaki*, or headband, was originally worn by warriors under their helmets, and became later a symbol of high spirits and great determination. The *tasuki*, or sash, was to tie long sleeves to the sides; it had a practical meaning when worn by the traditional kimono-clad warrior in a sword fight, or by housewives who need to keep their sleeves out of their work. However, since most of the marching Buraku representatives wore Western clothes, it was obvious that both

Sending off the marching troop were representatives of the Kaihō
Dōmei, members of the Socialist and Communist parties and of various labor unions, all waving red flags. Then followed groups of Diets-
men, prefectural assemblymen, and 400 representatives from adjacent
prefectures in Kyushu.

At each town, the troop was greeted by Buraku representatives and
large crowds. Demands for more liberal administration policies toward
the Burakumin were handed to the governors of prefectures and to
mayors and other dignitaries in towns along the way.[24]

In some places, the marchers divided into smaller groups, at each
place seeking to arouse the Buraku people in the adjoining areas. For
several days, they spread out among the large number of Buraku in
the Kansai District, to encourage groups in this area to unite behind
their campaign; in both Osaka and Kyoto, meetings drew large audiences. On October 2, a separate march organized in Nagano Prefecture also began moving toward Tokyo. On October 10, 1961, one hundred marchers from Kyushu and Nagano reached Shiba Park in
Tokyo, where 2,000 people had gathered to hear speeches and greetings by various leaders of the Kaihō Dōmei, labor unions, and the
leftist party.[25] Petitions were drawn up, to be given to the Prime
Minister and other cabinet members.

The petitions complained that although the Burakumin had been
officially liberated at the time of the Meiji Restoration, they were
still completely ignored and unassisted in adjusting to the new society.
They pointed out that the Meiji Government provided loans to former
warriors to help them start in agricultural and other occupations, but
that the net effects for the Burakumin were taxes, conscription, and
elimination of their previous monopolies in traditional occupations.
Farmers who lived in villages were still denied use of common lands
for the gathering of firewood to make charcoal and other necessities,
so that the excess population had moved to cities, there meeting with
discrimination in employment, education, and housing. The petitions
demanded that all these continuing inequities be rectified. They recorded that in 1958 a petition had been submitted to the Prime Min-

these items were used symbolically to indicate their spirit and determination. The
color red is obviously related to the red flag of the Communist front, and is used
as much by the Japanese Socialists as by the Communists.

[24] Buraku Henshūbu (Editorial Staff of *Buraku*) (1961a), No. 10, pp. 16–23; and
(1961b), No. 11, pp. 22–25.

[25] In spite of the emphasis placed by the Liberation League on the united front
with other labor organizations, there were as few as 100 participants from progressive parties and labor unions. This certainly reflects the lack of active concern for
Buraku problems on the part of regular progressive elements. This is shown in
other cases also. For instance, at the time of a famous strike at Miike mine in the
fall of 1959, in which 800 Buraku League members cooperated with the miners,
some union members called the newly appeared company union "tokushu buraku"
and caused angry protest from Buraku co-strikers. Yamamoto (1962, 1963).

ister's office to have a committee established to investigate Buraku problems and to have the various other ministries allocate funds from their budgets for related administrative measures. The 28th Special National Assembly of the Diet which was in session then, formally accepted the petition of the marchers.[26]

Kitahara Taisaku, one of the leaders of the Kaihō Dōmei, is very optimistic about the results of the Grand March.[27] According to him, the campaign had three major goals. The first was to demand of the central and local governments administrative measures to implement the abolition of discrimination and improve the economic and social conditions of the Buraku. Before the Grand March, the so-called "Administrative struggle" tended to be met by token budget raises, and focused solely on local governments. Kitahara believes that its dramatic value will help to secure more effective administrative measures.

A second objective of the campaign was to create greater cooperation among the organizations interested in the emancipation movement. Certainly the Socialist and Communist parties have been very much in evidence, but they have tried to link Buraku problems with international issues. Kaihō Dōmei leaders see the Buraku Liberation Movement as part of an extensive national campaign in the united front for the establishment of "peace, independence, and democracy." [28]

The third aspect of the campaign was to attempt directly to unify and strengthen the solidarity of the Burakumin. As of 1961, there were still only one-third of the supposed six thousand Buraku organized into the Kaihō Dōmei. The number of "organized" Buraku exceeded the "unorganized" in only a few of the prefectures, and in 10 out of the 48 prefectures (excluding Hokkaido, where there are no Burakumin) no Kaihō Dōmei branch exists.

The petitions submitted to the Diet were unanimously adopted by the National Assembly on October 20. The Prime Minister's office appointed a Deliberative Council for Buraku Assimilation, made up of the vice minister of all the relevant ministries, an editorial writer of the *Asahi News,* two university professors, the mayor of Himeji City, representatives from the Buraku Kaihō Dōmei, and representatives from a number of welfare organizations. It was decided that extensive research on Buraku living conditions should be carried out to form the basis of a future report.

---

[26] The complete petitions are reprinted in Buraku Henshūbu (1961c), No. 11, pp. 75–87.

[27] Kitahara (1961), pp. 10–18.

[28] Taniguchi (1961), pp. 4–7.

From the foregoing, it becomes apparent that the Japanese government has become sensitive to the organized pressure of the Buraku emancipation movement, and that overt discrimination is no longer legally tolerated. Government officials are aware that any indiscretion on their part will lead to organized retribution, which would compromise them politically. Whether the government's conciliatory attitude toward outcaste minority demands will result in large-scale ameliorative measures, however, remains to be seen. The Buraku Liberation League in its publications takes the view that it is having an important effect. Still, one must note that the general Japanese public is not aware of the Buraku liberation movement except during scattered dramatic incidents.

One indication that this apathy may be gradually giving way to more positive concern is the organization of study groups at many universities involving a significant number of students. But the outcaste is not yet a major social problem in bustling Tokyo, the industrial and intellectual center of Japan, with one-tenth of the population. The elite are more concerned with other issues. Whatever one's opinions concerning the advisability of linking the outcaste problem to the overall political positions of the leftist parties, the Japanese outcaste, by default, has nowhere else to go, for Japan's conservative parties have so far only with reluctance, paid any heed to this pressing national problem.

CHRONOLOGY OF POSTWAR
SOCIAL PROTEST MOVEMENTS

1946   Representatives of the former Zenkoku Suiheisha and Reconciliation Societies met to organize the Zenkoku Buraku Daihyōsha Kaigi (National Conference of Buraku Representatives). Buraku Kaihō Zenkoku Iinkai (National Committee for the Buraku Liberation) was established at the meeting of Zenkoku Buraku Daihyōsha Kaigi in Kyoto.

It was declared by the new National Constitution that all forms of discrimination based on social status should be fought and abolished.

1947   Tanaka Shōgetsu and four others from Buraku Kaihō Zenkoku Iinkai were elected to the House of Representatives and Matsumoto Jiichirō and another to the House of Councilors at the first general election after the war. Matsumoto was elected Vice Chairman of the House of Councilors.

General Headquarters of American Occupation advised the Diet to establish a special committee for Buraku problems.

1948   Matsumoto Jiichirō refused to bow in the traditional manner
        to the Emperor at the formal opening session of the second
        postwar Diet.
        Buraku Kaihō Zenkoku Iinkai held its third convention in
        Nara Prefecture.
        Buraku Mondai Kenkyūjo (Buraku Problems Research In-
        stitute) was established in Kyoto.

1949   Matsumoto Jiichirō was purged from public service. At its
        special meeting Buraku Kaihō Zenkoku Iinkai decided to
        protest the purge of Matsumoto.
        Buraku Mondai Kenkyūjo published its organ, *Buraku
        Mondai Kenkyū* (Study of Buraku Problems).

1950   Buraku Kaihō Zenkoku Iinkai held its fifth convention.

1951   Buraku Kaihō Zenkoku Iinkai held its sixth convention.
        Buraku Mondai Kenkyūjo became a corporative aggregate
        academic organization by permission of the Ministry of Edu-
        cation. Its organ, *Buraku Mondai Kenkyū,* was renamed
        Buraku.
        Matsumoto Jiichirō was reinstated and meetings were held
        in several places in celebration.
        Buraku Kaihō Zenkoku Iinkai held its seventh convention in
        Okayama.
        There took place in Kyoto a series of liberation movements
        sparked by the short novel by a Kyoto petty official describing
        the "filthy" aspects of Buraku life. This was called the *All
        Romance Incident.*

1952   There was an act of discrimination by a member of a prefec-
        tural assembly in Wakayama Prefecture and a protest cam-
        paign was held by Burakumin.
        Zen Nihon Dōwa Taisaku Kyōgikai (All Japan Council for
        Integration Programs) was held at the Honganji Temple in
        Tokyo.

1953   Buraku Kaihō Zenkoku Iinkai held its eighth convention in
        Hyogo Prefecture.
        From Buraku Kaihō Zenkoku Iinkai, Tanaka Orinosuke and
        three others were elected to the House of Representatives,
        and Matsumoto Jiichirō and three others to the House of
        Councilors. At the World Conference of Teachers held in
        Vienna, representatives from Japan made a report on "Edu-
        cation in Unemancipated Communities in Japan."

1954   Buraku Kaihō Zenkoku Iinkai held its ninth convention in Osaka.

1955   At its tenth convention, Buraku Kaihō Zenkoku Iinkai was renamed Buraku Kaihō Dōmei (Buraku Liberation League).

1956   Matsumoto Jiichirō left for Paris to attend the United Nations' Central Committee Meeting about social discrimination.
Buraku Kaihō Dōmei held its eleventh convention in Osaka. The serial article, "Buraku—The Appeal of Three Millions," was printed in the Osaka Edition of *Asahi Shinbun* (The Asahi Newspaper).

1957   A Buraku woman was killed by an American soldier, W. Girard, at Sōmagahara, Gumma Prefecture. Resulting legal procedures involved the question of Japanese jurisdiction over American military personnel.
At a school in Kochi Prefecture, a teacher insulted his Buraku-born colleague. His dismissal was sought and carried out.

1961   With the cooperation of the Socialist and Communist parties and the labor unions, "The Grand Petition March for the Accomplishment of Buraku Liberation" was made from Kyushu Island to Tokyo. The Petition was accepted by the 28th Special National Assembly of the Diet.

Chapter 4

HIROSHI WAGATSUMA

Non-Political Approaches: The Influences of Religion and Education

THE ROLE OF RELIGION

Buddhism and the Buraku Problem

During the Tokugawa period, Buddhism was the state religion of Japan; by law every citizen had to have some affiliation with a Buddhist temple. Even Shinto priests were required to receive their last requiem from a Buddhist monk. Buddhist monks and priests enjoyed much social prestige and their place in the status hierarchy was about equal to that of the warrior class. The government's support of the religion was certainly related to political and social control and it paid particular attention to the bureaucratic structure of the religious community. Temple monks who showed their loyalty to the government were helped to obtain high positions, while those who were critical or rebellious were suppressed and even banned. A rigidly hierarchical status structure was established among the temples, with head temples maintaining surveillance over subordinate branches. The Buddhist temple system during the Tokugawa period was a useful adjunct to the bureaucratic structure of Tokugawa Japan.

Although from the Kamakura period on one could find Buddhist writings on the idea of spiritual equality among people, Tokugawa Buddhism in no way opposed the official status structure of feudal society, including the segregation of its outcaste segments. A number of temples of the Zen and Jōdo sects became in effect family temples for the warrior classes, and excluded others not so highly placed. The Shin sect itself, to which the majority of the outcastes belonged, had a

88

fixed status system among its temples.[1] Temples in the outcaste community were called *Eta-Dera* and were treated separately. In those temples to which both outcastes and non-outcastes belonged, separate seats within the temples, *Eta-Za,* were set aside for the Eta of the community.

In the eighteenth century, the government decided to keep religious registries of the Buraku separate from those of the majority. The government also forced any temples in Buraku that were not already of the Shin sect to be officially put under their jurisdiction. These changes were made to simplify administrative procedures and thus to maintain more direct control over the Eta and Hinin. As a result, today almost all of the outcastes are traditional members of the Shin sect of Buddhism. Research in 1932[2] showed that 85 percent of the total outcaste population belonged to the Shin sect and 80 percent of this total (498 temples) belonged to the Nishi (Western) Honganji branch.[3] The only other significant grouping of outcastes is found in a small number of Nichiren sect temples in Nagano Prefecture.

Discrimination within the Shin sect continued after the Meiji Restoration despite a general reorganization of the complex system of branch and main temples in 1876. Although supposedly all branch temples were thereafter made equal, in reality this did not occur. The temples maintained their previous differential levels of prestige: the monks wore robes of different colors signifying the status hierarchy within their system, and the supreme pontiffs received both aristocratic titles from the Emperor and wives chosen from aristocratic families.

Generally speaking, the Meiji government was hostile to Buddhism because of their desire to westernize the state and also to justify the

---

[1] There is a legend that Saint Shinran, who founded the Shin sect in the beginning of the thirteenth century, spread his teaching among a group of "lowly" people, or untouchables, called "tsurumeso." They belonged to the Gion Shrine in Kyoto and, in addition to maintaining the shrine, they made and sold bows and arrows for it. (Their name, *tsurumeso*, is believed to be derived from the words *tsuru mese*, or "please buy bow-strings.") There is, however, no historical documentation of this legend. Actual conversion of a great number of outcaste people into the Shin sect was the result of the energetic missionary work of a priest named Rennyo (1415–1499) who is regarded as the "restorer" of the sect. Priests following Saint Rennyo also concerned themselves with mission work among outcastes. Certainly the teaching of this particular sect, which emphasizes the equality and fraternity among men, strongly appealed to the outcastes, together with the more general Buddhistic notion that good behavior in this world will give higher status in the next. See Satouchi (1957), pp. 215–97.

[2] Fujitani (1961), pp. 133–50.

[3] The Shin sect was split into two major factions or schools in 1619: the Honganji and the Ōtani. The central temples of these two schools are both called Honganji, or more precisely, Nishi (west) Honganji and Higashi (east) Honganji. Therefore, the schools are also referred to as the Nishi Honganji and the Higashi Honganji sects.

Emperor cult on the basis of the Shinto religion.[4] It neglected the organizational structure of Buddhism. Nevertheless, many new temples were built in the newly liberated Buraku during this period, some of which sought higher recognition within the traditional status system. It had been possible for temples with an ordinary membership to enhance the status of the temple by increasing the size of its donations to the central temple in Kyoto. In like manner, members of former outcaste communities sought now to gain some prestige by heavier contributions. But the Shin sect hierarchy remained unresponsive to the needs of their Buraku constituents. In April, 1899, at the time of the 400-year commemorative service for Saint Rennyo at a Shin sect temple, priests from Buraku were not given their proper seats at the service. This discriminatory incident aroused strong protest from the outcaste priests of the prefecture but nothing changed.[5]

Some of the integrationist activities of the 1910's and 1920's in many parts of Japan often aimed at renovation of the Shin sects, attempting to involve them in a drive to improve the general Buraku situation. Many of the propertied leaders from the Buraku who were active in these integrationist activities were at the same time supporters of religion and wanted to give their activities some spiritual backing. Their programs often referred directly to Buddhist ideas as well as to the Shin sect. Actually, no integration occurred and separate temple facilities were often maintained where outcastes and a majority group lived close together. Majority group temples never invited monks or parishioners from Buraku to their ceremonies, nor were Burakumin invited to participate in lectures or organizations of nearby majority temples. In the Buraku temples themselves, for the most part, the monks and priests were apathetic about integration. Many of them were old and preoccupied with donations to support the central Honganji temples in Kyoto. Magazines and journals published in this period by integrationist organizations often criticized the Shin sects and pointed out repeated incidents of corruption.

In the second decade of the twentieth century, priests from Buraku temples became more actively committed to the integrationist movement. For example, in December, 1911, about 300 Buraku priests in Hyogo Prefecture organized the Shinshū Wagō Kai (Shin Sect Harmony Association). The activities of this association were unclear, but seemed to center around lectures and general programs of "enlightenment." Soon after, the Kaizen Undō (Improvement Movement) was established with active participation by majority group Shin monks

---

[4] We have found no documentation concerning the attitude toward social discrimination held by any Shinto sects. Shinto today has no unified structure. Spokesmen of various shrines are not consulted nor do they seem to involve themselves in this social problem.

[5] Satouchi (1957), p. 282.

and some government officials. Participation in these enlightenment or integrationist movements by Shin priests or monks was mostly on an individual basis, and no active encouragement from the leaders of the Shin sect itself was received.

With the rise of the more militant Levelers' movement for Buraku liberation, a reform movement known as the Black Robe League arose among the younger priests. They demanded from the central temples the general abolition of status differentiation among monks and temples based on the amount of donation, and the elimination of such symbols of ranking as the assignment of different color robes. These young monks, refusing to conform to the system of color differences, wore the black robes from which the name of the league was derived.[6]

In response to the continuing criticism of leaders of the integrationist and Levelers' movements, Nishi Honganji issued an order in 1922 "to remove the old mistaken customs and notions and renew the church atmosphere," and "to consider everybody as a fellow-believer bound by Buddha's will, associate with everyone and appreciate the highest joy. . . ." In October, 1924, at Nishi Honganji, to which most of the Buraku temples belonged, the Ichijō Kai (Unity Association) was organized, and in March, 1926, at Higashi Honganji, the Shinshin Kai (True Body Association) was formed. Both these organizations aimed at preaching humanity and equality and contributing to the general improvement of the Buraku. Because of the lack of available reports and statistics, it is difficult to assess the effects of these organizations on discrimination. But several individuals affiliated with these groups came to dedicate their efforts to Buraku improvement. For instance, Sugimoto Shin-yu, the priest of Koenji Temple in Hyogo Prefecture (Nishi Honganji sect), spent his life helping Burakumin improve their education, community morale, and physical living conditions.[7]

In the Nishi Honganji, the Ichijō Kai, or Unity Association, was replaced by the "Committee for Social Education" in 1946, which in turn changed its name to the present Dōhō Kai (Brotherhood Association) in August, 1950. This Association has two purposes: one is to remove discriminatory prejudice among the majority (the "enlightenment campaign") mainly by encouraging lecture meetings at local temples and subsidizing the lecturer's expenses; the other by removing the feeling of inferiority among Burakumin themselves (the "campaign for awakening and self-improvement"). The Association selects "model districts" and, in addition to preaching, offers various welfare services, such as counseling, occupation and marriage guidance, recreational activities, sanitary facilities, and lessons in cooking, flower ar-

---

[6] Mori (1959), p. 229.
[7] Sugimoto and Onga (1961), pp. 28–34.

rangement, sewing, and tea ceremony. In the background of their activities is this attitude:

. . . one should not regard the discriminator and the discriminated as in
conflict. When a person "A" discriminates against a person "B," "B" may
become angry at "A" and tell him to apologize. "B" may even want to re-
taliate. "A" may pretend to be sorry for what he has done and apologize to
"B." In his mind, however, fear and suspicion toward "B" will increase and
a gap between "A" and "B" will be deepened and remain hidden. This is
not a solution. When a person is discriminated against and feels anger boil-
ing in himself, he must channel his emotion into a more constructive passion
for social improvement. Discrimination problems should not be taken up
only for the sake of those who are discriminated against. From the standpoint of Constitutional principles of democracy and of humanism, and particularly from the standpoint of our Sect which emphasized brotherhood, it
is wrong that people discriminate against people. . . . The Japanese have
long been confined within feudalism and received anti-democratic education. We have not been taught sufficiently that discrimination is wrong. Many
of us have been taught to discriminate. The discriminatory attitude is not
limited to those who express it overtly. Most of the people living in the
present society are not free from the discriminatory attitude. It is a kind of
social evil. The society as a whole should be responsible for a social evil. We
should not accuse an individual for his discriminatory behavior but we must
remove the social evil which makes an individual behave discriminat-
ingly. . . .[8]

Competitively, Higashi Honganji set up its own organization, the
Shinshin Kai, or the True Body Association of the Higashi Honganji.
Its name was later changed to Dōwa Kai, Integration Association, and
its activities were more or less similar to those of the Nishi Honganji.
But several years ago, as part of a general modernization movement,
the Integration Association was dissolved into a general campaign
called the Dōhō Undō, or Brotherhood Movement, which aims at
democratization and reform of the entire church system, strengthening
the solidarity of the membership. In the Sōka Gakkai, a politically
active offshoot of the Nichiren Sect of Buddhism, there is a great deal
of concern with reform of political and social institutions, but no
overt, direct program that explicitly addresses itself to Buraku problems.

In sum, the activities and outlook of Japanese religious sects suggest that they have been in no way comparable to the role of the
Christian church in the United States with respect to integration. As
a matter of fact, until very recently even Christianity in Japan has
been curiously uninvolved in the Buraku problem.

---

[8] Jōdo Shinshū Honganji-ha, Dōhō Kai (1959).

Christianity and the Buraku Problem

Christian activities with respect to the social problems of the Buraku were, until very recently, the work of individuals rather than of any organization within the Christian churches in Japan. In February, 1873, the longlasting ban on Christianity, which had existed for most of the Tokugawa period, was legally removed. Religious activity by missionaries quickly followed. A great deal of intellectual stimulus came from the ethics of Christianity, which to Japanese minds were often related to Western scientific accomplishments. But though many Japanese intellectuals phrased their concern with social reform in Japan in terms of Christian ethical principles, the evolving Christian leadership, both foreign and Japanese, mostly ignored the outcaste problem. There were a few individuals who did devote themselves to missionary work among the former outcastes.

In 1877, the Christian church, newly established in Hirosaki City of Aomori Prefecture, began its missionary activity in a local Buraku. An American missionary named Ing reported to his home church in the United States:

I would like to state something about the missionary work among the Eta. The place where these lowliest of people live is called Kazo-machi. I presume that the total population is about 2,000. Last Sunday evening I went to a lecture hall in the Eta community with Mr. Honda, Mr. Yamada, and others. Mr. Yamada, being acquainted with one of the Eta leaders, negotiated for obtaining this place for preaching. The audience was about 50 people who gathered in the evening, listened to the hymns and sermons.[9]

A well-known Christian leader, Abe Isoo, who was appointed minister to the Okayama church in 1887 also wrote of the Eta: "There was a Buraku named Takeda village nearby Okayama City. From that Buraku a family named Nakazuka legally joined the Okayama church where every Sunday morning Sunday School was held, and people were divided into many groups and listened to the sermon and lessons of the Bible. The role of instructor was given to elderly people among the church members. Mr. Nakazuka was one of them. Those who listened to the lesson by Mr. Nakazuka were mostly old men over sixty years. A few of them were former samurai. I felt strongly moved and touched when I saw this scene. As early as 1887, ex-samurai listened to the Bible lesson given by a Burakumin. This was only possible due to the virtue of Christianity." [10]

The more progressive members of the Christian church at this time

[9] Sumiya (1954), p. 67.
[10] Abe (1959), p. 63.

were preaching the equality of people before God, and in some instances tried to create a new relationship among the believers and to overcome forms of feudal status discrimination. In 1891, another famous Christian leader, Tomeoka Kosuke, was appointed chaplain at a prison in Hokkaido; during his three years' stay he made two discoveries that impressed him greatly. One was that as many as 70 or 80 percent of the total inmates had been committed when they were under fifteen years old; the other based on his inquiry into the background of about two thousand current or former prisoners, that the rate of delinquency and crime among members of Buraku background was four or five times higher than that among non-Burakumin. These discoveries led Tomeoka to devote himself to Buraku improvement and in 1897 he made a survey of the villages and towns for the Ministry of Internal Affairs and attempted to initiate Buraku improvements through the Ministry of Education.[11]

Another well-known Christian leader, Kagawa Toyohiko, moved into the slum areas of Kobe City in 1909, and dedicated himself to missionary work there until he moved to Tokyo in 1923. While working there he wrote about his experiences, and published *Hinmin Shinrino Kenkyū (Study of the Psychology of the Poor)* in 1916. In this book, in a chapter entitled "Eta Mura No Kenkyū" ("Study of Eta Villages"), we find that this famous Christian missionary was a victim of very strong feelings of prejudice and believed the myths about the separate origin of the Burakumin:

For instance, those [outcastes] living in the Nagata district of Kobe speak with a Chinese accent. The special people of Harima still preserve in their language Korean nouns. In the speech of the villagers of Minamino Buraku of Omi there is also the retention of Korean words. It is already clear from these facts, especially if one studies their skin, that . . . the Eta are a special race apart. This is a surprising fact, but I cannot help but believe that they are descendants of the Caucasian race [sic]. . . . They build their houses as if they were living in the stone age. The houses are built with coarse walls and no windows, no ventilation, and no room partitions. This is always true of their houses, wherever in Japan one might go. The structure is completely different from that of the Japanese houses. Some of their houses lack floors. As wood is always available to them they could build a wooden floor whenever they wanted to, but they are completely satisfied with the old way of living as in ancient times. They also continued the ancient custom of meat eating while everybody else was a vegetarian in the Tokugawa period. They kept on eating meat without hesitation. They have always been satisfied with lowly work of all kinds, that is to say, the work of slaves. . . . Nobody can deny that the Burakumin are a criminal race in the Japanese Empire. Minaminomura has a population of only 2,600. However, 305 of them are ex-convicts. I have heard that the rate of crime among Shinhemin

---

[11] Tomeoka (1963), p. 127.

in Wakayama Prefecture is three and a half times that of ordinary people. In short, they are a degenerate race, or slave race, or an obsolete, outdated ancient race of Japan.[12]

In another book written at about the same time, Kagawa has a chapter called, "In Regard to the Origin of Special Communities Within Hyogo Prefecture." He compiled a list classifying Buraku in the Prefecture according to the legendary origins of their inhabitants. Although from this list he admits to a variety of reported origins, it is clear that he thought the Burakumin in general definitely originated differently from the majority society. At the end of this chapter, he even mentions that there were certain *tokushu-min* or special people who have Ainu blood. Another possibility he suggests is that the Burakumin were of possible Negro origin.[13]

From this period almost up to the present, Christianity as a social movement has shown no organized interest in Buraku problems, though a few voices continued to be heard. In 1922, at the inaugural meeting of the national Suiheisha in Okazaki Park in Kyoto City, among the 2,000 excited participants was a young Christian named Takeda Kaneo who was to dedicate the next 30 years to mission activities among the Burakumin. In 1951, in his monthly journal, *Kyoseki (Shouting Stone)*, he wrote: "The Buraku problem is the most urgent and important social problem for Japan at the present. Unless those urged by Christian love dedicate their energy and soul to this problem the Buraku problem will never be solved." In 1952, in another journal, *Buraku Mondai to Seisho (Buraku Problems and the Bible)* he declared:

For the half century until now, for a long period of time, all kinds of political, economic, and social measures have been tried to improve the Buraku situation and to solve Buraku problems. They have always ignored the gospel of Christ and therefore failed to solve these problems. This point should be reflected upon calmly but severely. We believe that there is nothing so effective as the Bible and Christ's gospel contained in the Bible as a method of complete solution of Buraku problems.

In 1956, Takeda began a third journal, *Ōinaru Hikari (Great Light)*, still emphasizing the need for spiritual efforts to solve Buraku problems.

Another Christian figure who has been important in this respect is Nishimura Kan-ichi, the son of a most powerful *yakuza* (outlaw) leader. While still young, Nishimura went to the Philippines and in a rather wild setting heard what he believed to be God's call. Returning to Japan, he began missionary work in villages near Lake Biwa.

---

[12] Kagawa (1916), pp. 98–101.
[13] Kagawa (1920).

In 1938 he was appointed a voluntary civilian supervisor for boys under probation, thus meeting many juvenile delinquents:

As there were many Buraku children among delinquent boys I supervised, the more time I spent in casework, the more strongly I realized that the causes of these children's delinquency was often to be found in the backwardness of the Buraku situation, and the reason that Burakumin cannot solve such backwardness but keep reproducing discrimination was that those who ruled Japan created a social, economic and status discriminatory system to maintain their own power. The contemporary ruling class has taken it over and has no interest or sense of responsibility for Buraku liberation. In short, Japan's inferior politics contributes much to delinquency.[14]

In 1958 Mr. Nishimura was elected to the Lower House of Representatives from Shiga Prefecture and since then he has been attempting to move the government toward the improvement of the Buraku situation.[15]

Hiroshima was the first city in Japan where Christianity began to deal actively with Buraku problems after the war. In 1929, an American missionary, Weyman C. Huckabee, and his wife came to Hiroshima and established Ai Kōen (Garden of Loving Light). This nursery school was also used as a center for Sunday School and youth activities. When World War II began the Huckabees returned home, leaving Ai Kōen in the care of Hiroshima citizens. In the spring of 1948, another American, Mary Jones, went to teach English at Hiroshima Jo Gakuin, a girls' school and very soon became concerned with Buraku problems. She decided to help rebuild and re-establish Ai Kōen and turned her efforts toward the improvement of Buraku. In 1954 in Kyoto she, with Ito Kikuji of Doshisha University, helped to organize an association called the "Grain of Wheat" to provide educational fellowships for Buraku youth: in the following seven years, more than 40 young people were granted fellowships. She also met a young theological student, Higashioka Sanjii, and convinced him to devote himself to missionary work in Hiroshima. The women's club of the Methodist church to which she belonged financed a refurbishing of Ai Kōen, which became the Hiroshima Christian Social Center, run by Higashioka after Mary Jones returned to the United States.

The Fukushima Buraku in Hiroshima is one of the three largest in Japan. Higashioka himself is of Buraku origin and has experienced considerable discrimination within the Christian church. After he went to Fukushima, a Christian minister warned him it was a very dangerous place. He was also advised by one of the Christian church members not to marry a girl from this Buraku.

---

[14] Nishimura (1952).
[15] Matsuda, Masutani, and Kudō (1963), p. 134.

Under a more recent director, Lawrence Thompson, the Christian Social Center was operated on a professional basis, using social work methods both in individual case work and in group work. The case workers have been exploring the use of individual counseling in an attempt to resolve various problems related to child neglect and other interpersonal experiences. The emphasis has been on the center as a professional agency rather than as a meeting place for an academic discussion of outcaste problems; the community is being involved as much as possible in the work. Thompson is convinced that problems of the Buraku cannot be solved without some deepening of the sense of brotherhood which he believes to be the unique contribution of the Christian ethic.[16] This center has been instrumental in arousing the official attention of the United Church of Christ in Japan.

Higashioka and Mary Jones, in April, 1958, at a regional conference of the United Church of Christ in Japan, made a proposal that eventually sparked an important meeting at the Hiroshima Christian Social Center. Members of the Hiroshima Prefectural Committee of the Buraku Liberation League were in attendance along with professors from Hiroshima and Doshisha University. There was a statement of the responsibility of Protestantism toward the suffering of others, and a frank admission of the presence of discrimination within the Christian church itself. Financial assistance was considered necessary for the education of the outcaste children, since it was found that whereas the average rate of attendance at senior high school by those finishing junior high school was 80 percent for the prefecture as a whole, only 38 percent of the Buraku children went on to senior high school chiefly because of the poverty of outcaste parents. In the Fukushima Buraku neighborhood associations, self-improvement associations and social welfare associations began cooperating with one another to bring about improvement. A Fukushima hospital has been supported by cooperatives from the Fukushima Buraku and a modern building for the hospital was built in 1959. Hiroshima City has also been induced to build a concrete apartment building and a neighborhood center, a nursery clinic, and other neighborhood facilities for the large Buraku. Obviously, some church leaders have been instrumental in promoting a sense of initiative and accomplishment within this urban ghetto.

There is also some Japanese Christian missionary activity within the large Nishihama Buraku of Osaka. Three dedicated Christian ministers working for improvement in Osaka are Haneda Yutaka, Masutani Hisashi, and Matsuda Keiichi. These men have pooled their joint interests with those of Higashioka and Itō of Doshisha University in

---

[16] Thompson (1964).

an organization that is bringing Buraku problems to the attention of the organized Christian church. The activities of this group have received support from the United Church of Christ in Japan.

It is our impression that much of the thinking of these Christian activists runs along lines similar to that of the leftist-oriented Buraku Liberation League, cited in the previous chapter. They are concerned with the historical origins of the outcaste problem in the old feudal social structure of premodern Japan, and they look to further changes in the legal structure to bring about necessary improvements. They combine a basically Marxian understanding of Japanese social exploitation with a Christian humanism, believing that the Christian life should be free of prejudice and based on the equality of all people before God.[17] They stress, however, that the establishment of a socialist democracy as a means of political action is not sufficient for Buraku liberation. They believe that the problem cannot be solved until basic attitudes change. Although they do not use the sophisticated terminology of our final theoretical chapters, they do recognize the psychological problems as well as those of social structure. In assessing the role played by these religious activists it must be realized that they form a very small group, not representative of the main currents of thought among Japanese Christians nor of the official views of the Japanese United Church of Christ.

In 1962 the national meeting of the Christian conference for solution of Buraku problems was held in St. John's, the Japanese Anglican church in Osaka. Eighty representatives from various parts of Japan attended this meeting, and since then, not only in Osaka, Kyoto, Hiroshima, and the southwestern part of Japan, but also in Tokyo and surrounding areas, Christians actively interested in the outcastes have begun both social and evangelical activities among Burakumin, and have initiated concerted programs for education. We may note that the recent interest in the problems of the outcaste group in Japan among Protestant Christians is to some degree attributable to the activities in the United States concerning the Negro which reflect a general interest in minority problems.

The concern of the Catholic church in Japan is represented only by one individual, an American Catholic priest, the Reverend Francis Diffley, who has been engaged in social work for a number of years in one of the principal Buraku in Kyoto. Although other priests do have some contact with Burakumin, the outcastes are usually considered only in terms of their possible religious affiliation with the Catholic church. But under Father Diffley's direction, the work of Hope House, or Kibō no Ie, in Kyoto, has been strictly a social welfare program: proselyting is not a primary aim. The purpose is to demonstrate to the

---

[17] Matsuda, Masutani, and Kudo (1963), pp. 149–50.

Burakumin the concern of Christians with the brotherhood of all, regardless of origin. Father Diffley began his activities in the winter of 1959, initially working only with children. In the winter of 1960 new quarters were completed and the program expanded. There are now a dispensary, a credit union, social clubs, counseling services, and on a very small scale, a cottage industry center. The city has provided land, and a new two-story concrete structure is to be built containing a large meeting hall, a number of classrooms, a dispensary, a clubroom for teenagers, and offices for the credit union. Father Diffley's main purpose has been to develop some confidence among Burakumin through community action. He has established a board of consultants from the local community with whom he confers on every major decision. His job is a long-term proposition; overcoming initial suspicion was difficult. In the course of his work he has had to abandon many ideas that he initially held. He is personally convinced that change can only be brought about by having interested people live within the outcaste community itself, thus developing a true sense of belonging.[18]

THE USE OF THE SCHOOLS
IN BRINGING ABOUT SOCIAL CHANGE

There have been attempts to use education and educational facilities as a means of eliminating social discrimination in Japan. We have referred elsewhere to some of the problems, and will try here to summarize briefly the attempts of individuals within the school system to use such programs for solutions to the Buraku difficulties. The prewar history of educational programs can be divided roughly into three periods: the period of "sympathy education," Dōjō Kyōiku, 1884–1926; the "integration education" period, Yūwa Kyōiku, 1926–1936; and the "assimilation education" period, Dōwa Kyōiku, 1937–1949.[19]

Sympathy Education

In August, 1873, under the new Meiji government, a comprehensive system of universal education was established which was meant to be compulsory for all Japanese for at least four years. And though there was very strong discrimination in schools that contained both Buraku and non-Buraku children, separate schools for the outcastes were never advocated. Thus the official policy from the inception of the educational system in Japan was theoretically nondiscriminatory; what discrimination occurred was unofficial.

In the beginning, school attendance was quite low, particularly

---

[18] Diffley (1964).
[19] Morita (1960), pp. 5–48.

among outcaste children. Nevertheless, there was considerable interest in education: for instance, in 1873, in the Nishihama Buraku of Osaka with a population of over 5,000, a school was established by Buraku leaders themselves. During the following years even a few small private schools were founded in other Buraku which were later incorporated into the national public school system. But generally speaking, impoverished families could not afford education for their own children.

School teachers at this time came for the most part from the former samurai class and from the families of large landowners who were not given to hiding their prejudices concerning the outcastes. There were numerous instances of de facto exclusion of outcaste children from participation in school programs. In those Buraku that established schools a teacher recruitment problem immediately became severe, for few teachers were willing to teach in Buraku. Nevertheless, some young Japanese, influenced by democratic principles, and later by socialist policies volunteered for such activity. In many cases they were self-consciously motivated by the idea of educating outcastes to become leaders of their own groups. Articles were published by an active advocate of education, Nanbu Shigeto of Bukuoka Prefecture, that espoused education as a means of abolishing discrimination. His argument can be briefly summarized. Burakumin should occupy social positions equal to those of majority citizens, and should be encouraged to use their talents to become indispensable to society. To attain these objectives, the well educated should lead the Burakumin to develop from within and then benefit the entire Japanese society. The communities themselves should contribute financially to the education of such future leaders. The educated should travel widely about Japan, as living examples of accomplishment; this would help diminish prejudice against them and negate ideas of biological inferiority.

We have already noted the emphasis in some revisionist movements on programs of education to improve manners and customs, sanitation, and the like, to raise the status of the Buraku in the eyes of ordinary citizens. During this early period, the attitude of majority teachers who assisted in the development of Burakumin could be termed "sympathetic." They tried to indoctrinate generally held Japanese values, so that the children could become as hard working and as well mannered as the majority Japanese. It was believed that such education would naturally lead to a removal of discriminatory attitudes and practices.

Integration Education

In 1923, the Central Executive Committee of the Levelers' Association submitted to the Ministry of Education their opinion about the national educational program. As pacifists, they attacked the "morals education" at schools, claiming that education was "to teach children how to kill people," "to glorify so-called heroes and the brave who actually monopolized and abused the national polity," "to glorify murderous and savage wars," "to consider the exclusive discriminatory feudal tradition as part of the nation's value and virtue." They criticized the teaching of history in the schools as "admiration of the continuation of ugly warfare and struggle," and as "giving the wrong impression that only warriors are Japanese citizens." The Association therefore requested the Ministry to revise its educational programs to give a type of education that would lead to peace in a world where all the races and peoples could live together in harmony—a request which the Ministry of Education completely ignored. Nevertheless, as a reaction to the increased activities of the levelers' movement, the government did increase its budget for Buraku improvement, and government-sponsored integration organizations were formed in various parts of Japan. In these organizations, teachers were expected to play an important role.

In 1926, the directors of educational departments of prefectural governments met at the Ministry of Internal Affairs and were ordered to promote integration of the schools. The Ministry held such meetings in 1927, 1928, and 1929, and after 1932, the Minister himself attended. A Central Association of Integration Activities (Chūō Yūwa Jigyō Kyōkai) sent members to the normal schools for teachers in each prefecture and held other meetings emphasizing the importance of integration in the educational program. In 1933, the Research Committee for Integration Education (Yūwa Kyōiku Chōsa Iin-Kai) of the Ministry of Internal Affairs announced a general educational program for integration, emphasizing the following points: first, to cultivate respect for human rights; second, to clarify the origin of the Japanese race and cultivate a sense of the nation's racial unity; third, to exert efforts to abolish traditional discriminatory ideas and to cultivate the spirit of progress. The integration program was supposedly carried out at each school following these three basic principles.

According to the Committee's announcement, education for integration could be classified into three different elements. The first was training in discipline to emphasize the cooperative spirit of autonomous and self-dependent children—to observe public ethics, to maintain respectful attitudes toward public property and human dignity, and, above all, to demonstrate love and loyalty to the Emperor and the country. The second element was an emphasis on mutual sympathy and understanding to be expressed toward the outcaste children and their families by the majority society members. The third element in the program was curriculum education, in itself divided into three parts: intellectual education to cultivate clear reasoning about human dignity; emotional education to cultivate esthetic love of all people; and volitional education of the will so as to direct it toward cooperation with fellow citizens. One can find little to argue with in this program of the Ministry of Education; however, there is no evidence that it was actually implemented.

Assimilation Education

The government, although already under military control by 1938, had nevertheless remained active in educational efforts to eliminate discrimination against Burakumin. In August of that year, the Minister of Education, General Araki, issued an ordinance to prefectural governors, school principals, superintendents, presidents of colleges, and heads of religious groups, and requested their increased efforts to abolish discrimination through education because "Buraku discrimination within the nation is a national shame to Japan at a time when Japan is attempting to establish world peace and harmony." In 1940, at a National Meeting of the Integrationist Organizations (Zenkoku Yūwa Dantai Rengō Taikai) a report to the Ministry of Education emphasized, first, the establishment of a course particularly for integration at normal schools, youth schools, and teacher training institutions; second, assimilative integration in the training courses of youth schools; third, increased Yūwa integration on middle, high school, and college levels. In 1941, the Minister of Education started a training program of normal-school teachers, particularly for assimilation education, which lasted two years.

In 1940, a national campaign to support the imperial warfare was initiated. As the trend toward patriotism intensified, groups changed names, and, although the theme of assimilation continued, it was now formulated in the cause of patriotism. In 1941, the Central Association of Integration Activities reorganized itself, and its name changed to the Patriotic Assimilation Association (Dōwa Hōkoku Kai). With this change of name, what had previously been called the Yūwa Undo or Integration Movement became the Dōwa Undo or Assimilation Movement. From 1942, a lecture concerning Dōwa education became compulsory at each normal school.

In August, 1942, the Ministry announced *Kokomin Dōwa no Michi* (*The Path Toward National Assimilation*) as a general guide for assimilation education.[20] This little booklet states that the problem of discrimination is

---

[20] Mombu Shō Dōwa Kyōiku Kenkyū Kai (Ministry of Education, Research Association for Assimilation Education) (1942).

one of the defects and contradictions to be overcome as anti-state and anti-crisis at the time of the establishment of the new state. . . . Discriminatory ideas are deep-rooted in the mind of the nation, and in order to attempt their complete removal, reliance on the effect of general education is not sufficient and particular educational efforts aiming at the solution of this problem are necessary.

The basic purpose of Dōwa (assimilation) education as differentiated from previous Yūwa (integration) education was to be the increased emphasis on the solidarity and unity of the Japanese nation for the purpose of winning the war. While Yuwa emphasized primarily the humanity and fellowship of Buraku and non-Buraku children, Dōwa emphasized loyalty of both classes to the emperor and to the state. Dōwa, unlike Yūwa, stressed migration of Burakumin into Manchuria and their entrance into war industries and agricultural expansion. In short, the Dōwa movement aimed at the wartime mobilization of Burakumin by educational as well as other means. In 1945, at the end of the war, Dōwa Hōkoku Kai dissolved itself.

According to Morita, prewar programs for the elimination of discrimination should all be collectively called Yūwa education, to be differentiated from the postwar Dōwa education. Morita summarizes the major characteristics of prewar Yūwa education as follows: One, it always followed the policies and programs of the Ministries of Education and Internal Affairs. Two, it was always a governmental means of dealing with general Buraku problems, which were not treated in terms of "the basic contradictions of capitalism." Three, discrimination was understood only as a carryover of feudalistic traditions and was always attributed to the ignorance, selfishness, and lack of awareness of the Japanese. (The deeper roots of discrimination, from a leftist standpoint such as Morita's, lie directly in the capitalistic organization of society and the exploitation of the masses.) Four, training and discipline of Buraku children were emphasized so that such causes of discrimination as "untidy manners, bad speech, and lack of moral attitudes" could be removed. Five, teachers under such a program lacked spontaneity and sincerity; they passively received orders and methods from above.[21]

Japan's official attempt, through its centralized educational system, to eliminate discrimination by educational programs, was a much better organized program than anything that has yet appeared in the United States. The fact that it has not yet solved the problem of discrimination indicates that it is not simply a question of a rational approach. In our final chapters we will discuss why we believe that such a program cannot possibly get to the heart of discrimination.

---

[21] Morita (1960), pp. 45–46.

Postwar Assimilation Education

The new postwar constitution, developed under the American occupation, is in many respects a model document embodying democratic ideals of equality of human rights and peace among nations. The Japanese educational system was reorganized and decentralized. Previous authoritarian indoctrination stressing the individual's contribution to society for national objectives was rephrased in a philosophy of self-actualization. The new Japanese constitution became law on May 3, 1947. In the same year, the *Kyōiku Kihon Hō* (Fundamental Law of Education) was promulgated, emphasizing democratic education as a means of developing love of truth and peace. This Fundamental Law of Education became a reference point for postwar assimilation education, just as the new constitution became a reference point for political activities for Buraku liberation. Also, in 1951, the Japanese promulgated a Children's Charter emphasizing the rights of each child, guaranteeing his right to equality of education and opportunity. This Charter also has become a rallying point for assimilation education ideas.

Subsequently, there have been a number of statements by the Ministry of Education reaffirming basic human rights, but until 1959 implementation was minimal. The more progressive prefectural governments with large Buraku populations, however, were considerably more active.[22] In 1943, the Zenkoku Dōwa Kyōiku Kenkyū Kyōgi Kai (National Conference for Assimilation Education Research) was organized in Osaka. This was a federation of prefectural leagues of Dōwa Kyōiku Kenkyū Kai whose members were education committees, principals, and teachers. Prefectural and city educational commissions supported it financially. Research meetings were held and policy, programs, and plans of assimilation education were discussed, examined, criticized, and revised. In 1958 the purpose of assimilation education was defined as the cultivation and education of "an intelligent and active person who has complete understanding about the necessity to protect the rights and happiness of children, youth, and women suffering discrimination, poverty, and oppression, and to learn about the nature of discrimination and, as concrete critical knowledge, about the mechanisms of society which produce discrimination." To promote this it was held necessary "to understand that all Japanese peo-

---

[22] For instance, in Hyogo Prefecture with the largest Buraku population (about 200,000 individuals in 346 communities, or 5 percent of the total prefectural population), the Central Committee for Assimilation Education was organized as early as 1950 and published a guide book for teachers. The first textbook, *Nakayoshi Monogatari (Friendship Stories)*, was published in 1952; and in the next year the second volume was printed. Miura (1961), pp. 18–22.

ple carry the burden of social status discrimination and such a burden is doubled and tripled in the unliberated Buraku; and such discrimination is not only reflected in discriminatory words and deeds in non-Buraku people, but also in the fact that the Burakumin do not enjoy equal opportunity of education, freedom of choice of occupation, residence, marriage, and social intercourse." [23]

The definition of Dōwa Kyōiku was later revised to become "a part of national education which focuses its efforts on the basic contradiction of the contemporary society and aims at the realization of Buraku liberation, . . . because Japanese monopolistic capitalism subjugated to the United States of America makes use of feudalistic remnants of Japan, preserves Buraku, and creates and re-creates discrimination." The program of Dōwa education announced by the National Council of Assimilation Education Research shows that its aims are to produce people indoctrinated with Marxian understanding of society; people to work for socialist revolution. This was put side by side with humanistic appeals to brotherhood.

Another assimilation organization, the Nihon Kyōin Kumiai (Japanese Union of School Teachers) was also dominated by leftists. The Buraku is defined as "remnants of feudalistic system which was originally created by the feudal status system, later preserved by the modern political and economic structure, and preserved at present as one of the methods by which monopolistic capitalism exploits and oppresses the people." The purpose of assimilation education is "to rescue the Buraku children who are discriminated against . . . also to develop all the Japanese children in the intention and ability to be opposed to discrimination . . . and to fight for liberation of people from poverty and lack of human rights." [24]

Against such leftist programs, the Japanese government has been more recently trying some programs of its own. However, it was 1959 before the Ministry of Education appropriated a definite budget for assimilation education. For six or seven years before 1959, however, Dowa educational programs had been developing in some of the separate prefectures. For example, in Wakayama Prefecture in 1952 about 4.5 million yen was appropriated for assimilation education at school; and additional funds of 800,000 yen for adult education. Kyoto City appropriated 23.5 million yen in 1953, of which 3.7 million were allocated to educational programs. In many other prefectures, educational commissions were very actively concerned with Dōwa education. Booklets to guide education were published for use by teachers and others in these prefectures, and requests were sent from the prefectural governments to the national government for funds for this

[23] Tōjō (1960), pp. 49–98.
[24] Tōjō (1960), pp. 94–95.

activity. Since 1959 the national government has slowly been responding by yearly increasing the budget. In 1959, 950,000 yen were appropriated, about 5 million in 1960, and almost 21 million yen in 1963.
With these funds the Ministry of Education appointed primary and
junior high schools as models for Dōwa educational research. There
were compilations of educational materials, financial aid for the organization and establishment of meeting places, and research and
lectures on school education.

Yamamoto has been one of the most consistent critics of the government on the one hand, and leftist programs on the other.[25] He argues
that the various problems found in the schools in the cities of Kansai,
such as long absenteeism, truancy, delinquency, low scoring on I.Q.
tests, poor school records, should be the particular objectives of
assimilation education; that the obvious inferior performance of the
outcaste children in the schools compounds their inferiority feelings;
and that there is in these children a loss of interest in education that
prevents them from going beyond the primary grades and severely
handicaps them in obtaining employment. During its ten years of
history postwar assimilation education has not yet successfully solved
these problems. The real purpose of assimilation education should
not be the emphasis of Marxian understanding of capitalist society,
but emphasis on human dignity, which must start very early in the
school system. Yamamoto's statements are almost directly parallel with
recent expressions in the United States on the part of educators about
the problem of Negroes, Puerto Ricans, and Mexican-Americans in the
American school system.

Nishimoto of Kyoto Prefectural University defines Dōwa education
as "the democratic education for the removal of Buraku discrimination and, in this sense, for the liberation of Buraku." But he criticizes
the "optimistic" leftist standpoint and emphasizes that "simple change
of the external political system does not change human nature and
therefore does not lead to the removal of discrimination." He stresses
the importance of cultivating what he calls "the feeling of resistance"
(teikō-kan), that is, the strength of character that would protect Buraku
youth from either despair, or a defeatist desire to escape their status.[26]

Teachers' Attitudes Toward Buraku Problems

In research concerning teachers' attitudes the preponderant number were found to be fairly well informed on Buraku problems. The
following results were obtained by an opinion survey done with 357
teachers at 17 public primary schools in Kyoto by the Kyoto City Co-

---

[25] Yamamoto (1963).
[26] Nishimoto (1961), pp. 10–16.

ordinating Conference for Education for Assimilation in May, 1959.[27]
The majority of these teachers were fairly young, from 25 to 35 years
of age, and there was a roughly even distribution of males and females.
To the question, "How much are you concerned with Buraku problems?" 55.7 percent indicated that they were strongly concerned,
whereas only 3.2 percent said that they had no concern.

To the question asking why Buraku problems are problems of the
entire nation, 25.4 percent answered "I don't know." Of the remaining, the majority of 137 individuals explicitly stated that in a real
democratic society all forms of discrimination must be abolished. Fifty-
four said that human dignity requires a guarantee of the basic rights
of all in employment, education, and marriage. Further opinions
were to the effect that the existence of Buraku prevented the development of true democratic institutions (21); that Buraku difficulties
should be a political issue, to be solved by cooperation between governmental organizations and the Japanese nation as a whole (21); that
outcaste communities are often hotbeds of crime and other social
vices and a national campaign is needed to eliminate such communities (10); that the liberation of Buraku should be a premise to the
independence, freedom, and peace of the total Japanese nation (10).
Another question involved an incident: "This is an actual example of
what happened at school when a new swimming pool was built. At
the time of physical examination many children were discovered to
have trachoma and were forbidden to swim with other children. The
school principal had long neglected to take active measures to improve
the health of these poor children. The Buraku people of this school
told the principal that his attitude reflected basic discrimination
against Buraku children. Do you think it is going too far to accuse
the principal of such discrimination?"

The answers were as follows: 42.9 percent said that the principal
should not be accused; 32.2 percent that he deserved accusation; and
24.9 percent said, "I don't know." The reasons of the first group were:
Trachoma and Buraku discrimination are separate problems (44 individuals). The principal alone should not be held responsible for
trachoma; there are many other factors that interfere with the active
elimination of trachoma (19). Non-Buraku children also may have
trachoma. The principal may simply have lacked concern with hygiene
(33). Children with trachoma, Buraku or non-Buraku, should not be
allowed to swim with other children (38). Trachoma is not entirely
the principal's fault; the parents and teachers are also responsible (18).
Reasons of the second group were: Trachoma is prevalent among
Buraku children particularly and the principal's failure to take active

---

[27] Kyoto-shi Dōwa Kyōiku Renraku Kyōgi Kai (Kyoto City Coordinating Council
for Assimilation Education) (1959).

measures against it reflects his lack of concern with the betterment of Buraku (83). The principal has discriminatory feelings and lacks affection toward Buraku children (32).

In answer to the question, "What are the common and different aspects of Buraku problems in Japan when compared with Negro problems in the United States?" the following distribution occurred. One hundred and eighty-five individuals found both common aspects and differences (51.8 percent of the sample). Only common aspects were given by 20.7 percent; 7.8 percent gave only differences; 19.7 percent gave no answer. The common aspects pointed out were: both groups are victims of discrimination, their human rights are ignored, their living standards are low, they suffer from lack of freedom in marriage, employment, and other aspects of social life (206 individuals). Both groups lack knowledge and education, feel inferior, and are forced to live in an unsanitary environment (35 answers). Other scattered statements were made (18). The main differences described were: Negro problems in America are racial, involving two races, while Buraku problems in Japan are not, but rather are based on feudal caste segregated in occupations (207). (Today, only teachers who are themselves prejudiced still to a certain degree believe in the biological difference of the outcastes.)

Asked whether the special educational program is now necessary to help eliminate discrimination, 73.1 percent of the teachers answered positively, 15.9 percent negatively, and 11 percent did not know. The reasons given for special courses were: discrimination and prejudice are deeply rooted and true democracy has not yet permeated society (64 individuals); Japanese society does not sufficiently guarantee basic human rights, and special courses are necessary to supplement results of a more general education in democracy (79); Burakumin are Japanese and should not suffer from discrimination in occupation and marriage (30); true democracy will not be established unless Buraku problems are completely solved (30); a variety of reasons were given by the remaining 58 individuals.

Negative answers were backed by the following reasons: when democracy really prevails, people will respect others' rights and discrimination will no longer exist (34 individuals); discriminatory feelings exist in the society outside, but school children are not prejudiced (8); young people are free from discrimination; presenting this problem would have no good effect and might indirectly reflect the teacher's own discriminatory attitude (8); the remaining individuals gave uncategorizable answers.

When the teachers were asked whether or not they were now giving some special course for the elimination of discrimination, 64.7 percent indicated they were, 17.8 percent said they would like to but were unable to, 4.7 percent said they were not, and 3.8 percent said they did not want to. But only 19 percent of the teachers were willing to move to a primarily Buraku school; 21.8 percent would not; and the vast majority simply said they "didn't know." Lectures on Buraku problems had been attended by 84.7 percent of the teachers, and 71.4 percent said that they had read material on the subject. From this survey it is evident that three-fourths of the teachers seem to take a positive attitude toward helping resolve Buraku difficulties. They subscribe to the general notion that this problem is a carryover from the occupational segregation of the feudal period in Japan. However, opinion surveys of this kind do not reveal to what degree there is emotional commitment, or a genuine resolution of the residuals underlying former prejudices. In the United States many teachers who espouse an enlightened teaching program for Negro children nevertheless maintain a form of emotional distance from their Negro pupils because of unconscious attitudes. In our concluding chapters we discuss some of the irrational emotional factors that underlie caste attitudes and why they are not always amenable to conscious change.

SECTION III

Ethnographic Studies
of the Japanese Outcastes

INTRODUCTION

The following chapters present descriptive materials from a number of present-day studies by Japanese and American social scientists.

The first chapter is a general introduction, mainly from Japanese sources, concerning the distribution of outcaste communities in Japan. It affords a descriptive overview of the actual living conditions and occupational activities of the outcastes today.

A closer look is afforded by studies of individual communities—their social organization and their relation to their neighbors. In one way or another each of these ethnographic reports addresses itself to the question "Why do outcaste communities persist in the face of radical social and economic changes that are transforming Japan into one of the world's most progressive industrial societies?" The varied settings of these studies afford some contrasts and comparisons of these urban and rural ghettos.

These studies do not present an entirely consistent picture. The interaction patterns with the majority Japanese differ from place to place, as do the social conditions and modes of behavior within the Buraku. Though the caste lines remain drawn, there are wide variations in the degree and nature of contact.

Chapter 6, a descriptive report of urban Buraku based on the direct observations of Yuzuru Sasaki, illustrates the functioning of the social hierarchy within the urban outcaste structure. This report documents briefly some of the centripetal and centrifugal forces operating on

110

community organization. The differential social effects of life in a stable Buraku in contrast to a Buraku undergoing the effects of rapid mobility are also noted. The general system used by Lloyd Warner and his associates for rating social status or stratified social participation in American society was found relevant in understanding Japanese urban Buraku life.

The following chapters by Donoghue and Cornell contain cogent discussions of a number of issues on the basis of firsthand experience: what social mechanisms tend to keep Buraku life in relatively stable equilibrium; why Buraku communities do not dissolve as entities but tend to perpetuate some form of caste structure from within as well as in reaction to patterns of interaction imposed upon them by the majority Japanese.

The report of John Donoghue deals with a Buraku community in northeastern Japan that has remained specialized around the traditional occupations of the outcaste. Located on the outskirts of a city that originated around the headquarters of a local samurai in feudal times, it is typical of one kind of outcaste community.

John Cornell reports on another type of Buraku—one that has become a relatively progressive farming community. This community does not bear the stigma of ritually or aesthetically despised occupations. Superficially, members of this community function without much sign of overt tension in a number of political, economic-occupational, and even formal social settings with their farming neighbors, yet the stereotyped image of the outcaste is found in the surrounding majority population, and intermarriage with the majority is almost nonexistent.

It is characteristic of a society in which caste is operative to transfer caste attitudes to special groups who do not easily fit into the ordinary framework of the society. This inclusion of various sorts of socially marginal people, Hinin or "non-people," was described briefly in the historical section of this volume. The same transfer of caste to unassimilable outsiders still operates in rural Japan in many communities that were never actually classified as either Hinin or Eta. The transfer of caste feelings—hence caste-like behavior patterns—to special occupational groups supports further our contention that traditional Japan exhibits the characteristic social attitudes of a caste society as thoroughly as do those societies and cultures directly influenced by the Hindu religious culture of India.

The Chapter by Edward Norbeck touches briefly on a number of marginal groups and illustrates how informal behavior patterns are affected by community sanctions maintaining caste distances.

Finally, to illustrate the persistence of Japanese caste attitudes in spite of acculturation to American society, a study by a graduate student at the University of California is included that depicts the continuity of intra-community caste attitudes in Japanese immigrants.

Chapter 5

HIROSHI WAGATSUMA AND
GEORGE DE VOS

The Ecology of
Special Buraku

DISTRIBUTION OF BURAKU IN JAPAN

Outcaste communities are concentrated in the lands surrounding the Inland Sea, the ancient heartland of early Japanese culture (see endpaper maps). This is the birthplace of the Japanese nation, and most of the population resided here when the civilization of Tang China, including Buddhism, was introduced. Heavy secondary concentrations are found at the base of the Noto Peninsula (present-day Ishikawa and Toyama Prefectures) and in Gumma, Saitama, and Nagano Prefectures in central Honshu, areas which were colonized from the Inland Sea shortly after the introduction of Buddhism in the sixth century A.D. It is of considerable interest and importance that the map showing the Eta outcaste communities today and the map showing the relative distribution of Japan's total population in the early part of the tenth century present almost congruent patterns. Similar population densities are particularly noticeable in the areas immediately around the old capital cities Nara and Kyoto, the shores of the Inland Sea, in ancient Tsukushi (northwest Kyushu), and on the western Kanto Plain Conformity. They are also found throughout most of the Chūgoku Peninsula, including the old culture centers of Kibi (essentially modern Okayama Prefecture), the San-in region on the Japan Sea, at the base of the Noto Peninsula, and in interior Shinano Province in central Honshu, now Nagano Prefecture.

As discussed in Chapter 1, the Eta probably came into being as separate groups at an early date, originated in the areas surrounding the Inland Sea, and moved with early large-scale colonization as an integral part of the society. In the Yamato or Go-Kinai area many of the

113

ancient Imperial and Noble tombs have, or had until recently, an outcaste community at their foot—suggesting their ancient function as caretakers of the dead. In the later northward course of Japanese expansion into north Honshu and Hokkaido, such distinctions seem to have lost their force in the ready equality of frontier life and warfare with the retreating Ainu who inhabited these regions. However, around cities a few outcaste communities are still definable.

A number of clusters and isolated communities are found in peripheral areas which for the most part are the result of the later feudal period. These widespread secondary communities are generally situated at or near the sites of one-time castles or other fortifications. It would seem that these latter outcaste groups were imported by the ruling feudal lords to perform their traditional functions of disposing of the dead and of making military commodities, such as armor and bowstrings, as well as non-military products, such as the musical instruments and footwear essential to the culture of the time. These were made of leather, gut, hair, and bone. The present distribution of remaining leather worker's communities bears out this hypothesis.[1]

Outcaste communities seem typically to be located on the outskirts of the ordinary communities that they served. They were allotted the more undesirable sites—river banks, swamp areas, and the northern slopes of hills and mountains. Most rural farming Buraku still maintain generally unfavorable land.

Population Trends in Buraku

There is no certain way of knowing how many Burakumin there are in Japan today. Estimates vary, but there is general consensus that the proportion of outcastes in the total population is growing rather than diminishing. This rate of growth, occurring despite their official abolition as a definable group, is one of the remarkable phenomena of their long history. According to the estimates available, the size of the outcaste population has increased some four to ten times since 1870, while in the same period the Japanese population as a whole has about tripled (from 30 to almost 100 million).

Even before 1870, in the later Tokugawa period when discrimination was at its height, the number of outcastes was rapidly increasing. Ninomiya suggests as reasons for this rise: early marriages, consumption of meat which was plentiful because rejected by others, and the continual recruitment of new members from the majority society. "The ever-present stragglers of the upper estates filtered into the Eta villages either to seek a means of easy living or to hide their identity." [2]

---

[1] Hall (1962).
[2] Ninomiya (1933), p. 103.

The earliest published population survey of Kyoto, taken in 1715, showed 11 outcaste communities, 486 households, and a population of 2,064. A survey of Osaka in 1800 gave an outcaste population of 4,423 whereas in Tokyo in 1800 there was only one reported Eta community in Inai (later called Asakusa), with an estimated total population of 800–900.[3] The national census of 1871 gave a complete total of 281,311 Eta; 23,480 Hinin; and 79,095 miscellaneous outcastes (funeral workers, tomb watchers, and vagabonds). In 1920 the Social Welfare Bureau of the Ministry of Internal Affairs made a census giving some indication of their distribution at the time (Table 1), reporting on 4,890 outcaste communities and 155,370 households, for a population of 829,675.[4]

Much of the variation in average size noted in this report is probably due to the predominance of large urban communities in certain prefectures and the occurrence of many small rural communities in others. The averages are much higher in the more urban prefectures of Osaka (798.5), Aichi (with its city Nagoya, 364.6), Hyogo (with its city Kobe, 317.4), and Kyoto (314.8), compared with the national average of 169.7. In 1920 Tokyo reported relatively few outcastes and had an average Buraku size of 166.4 individuals. The proportion of outcastes in the population of Kobe is higher than in any other city in Japan, and the Burakumin population of Hyogo Prefecture, of which Kobe is the principal city, probably remains higher than that of all other prefectures except Fukuoka. In the 1920 survey Hyogo reported a population of 107,608 Burakumin.

In 1933 Ninomiya claimed that "The Eta people are increasing by at least 30,000 yearly. . . . In sixty years since Meiji IV (1871) the Eta have increased about 400 percent while the Japanese proper increased 80 percent . . ."[5] For the same period Smythe and Tsuzuki claim: "The natural increase of the Eta between 1870 and 1935 was 97 per 1,000 while that for the general population was 15 per 1,000."[6] Their estimates are based on a survey made by the Central Conciliation Society, an integrationist group that estimated 5,300 special communities, 195,540 houses, and 1,000,000 occupants.[7]

---

[3] Watanabe (1963), pp. 77–79.
[4] From this we can calculate that the average number of households per outcaste community was about 31.6, the average population per community was 169.7, and the average size of household was 5.3. Adapted from Ninomiya (1933), Appendix IV.
[5] Ninomiya (1933), p. 114.
[6] Smythe and Tsuzuki (1952), p. 114.
[7] According to another investigation in 1935 by the Central Integrationist Activity League (Chūō Yūwa Jigyō Kyōkai), there were 5,371 Buraku in 40 prefectures and two cities. One hundred sixty-seven Buraku were excluded from the list of communities identified in the government's 1920 investigation and 658 Buraku were added by the 1935 investigation. This difference may be largely due to the difference in the method of the investigation. Since they do not "exist" except unofficially, a

TABLE 1

GEOGRAPHIC DISTRIBUTION OF OUTCASTES ACCORDING TO THE 1920 CENSUS

Prefectures	Buraku Communities	Households	Population
Hyogo	339	18,547	107,608
Fukuoka	493	12,914	69,345
Osaka	60	9,773	47,909
Ehime	494	8,598	46,015
Okayama	297	8,806	42,895
Kyoto	134	8,515	42,179
Hiroshima	406	8,024	40,133
Mie	216	7,089	38,383
Wakayama	105	7,438	36,072
Kochi	70	5,477	33,353
Nara	71	6,427	32,678
Saitama	300	4,758	28,139
Shiga	65	4,882	25,819
Gumma	235	3,959	24,516
Tokushima	56	3,791	22,343
Yamaguchi	117	4,006	19,878
Nagano	288	3,200	19,263
Tottori	81	3,006	19,022
Shizuoka	55	2,304	14,476
Kumamoto	57	2,524	13,240
Tochigi	92	2,052	13,114
Kagawa	63	1,900	9,867
Toyama	200	1,444	8,242
Kagoshima	47	1,680	8,001
Tokyo	46	1,651	7,658
Oita	76	1,402	7,099
Aichi	19	1,365	6,927
Shimane	79	1,565	6,492
Kanagawa	33	932	5,712
Ishikawa	31	966	4,670
Gifu	23	928	4,634
Ibaragi	47	700	4,368
Niigata	32	580	2,929
Miyazaki	23	485	2,590
Chiba	22	474	2,588
Nagasaki	23	505	2,519
Saga	22	418	2,508
Fukui	5	478	2,318
Yamanashi	20	295	1,745
Fukushima	6	184	1,240
Yamagata	4	208	1,000
Aomori	1	37	286
Totals	4,890	155,370	829,675

According to the 1935 statistics published by the Ministry of Welfare, there were about 1,000,000 Burakumin in Japan, in about 190,000 households in 5,367 communities. Tōjō contends these figures are drastically low.[8] Another estimate at this time placed the actual figures from 2,000,000 to 2,500,000 in 5,500 communities.

In the fifteen years between 1920 and 1935 Tokyo, Kyoto, Saitama, and Kanagawa prefectures seemingly saw a decrease in the number of Buraku, while Okayama and 26 other prefectures saw an increase, suggesting a possible drift of Burakumin from agricultural to nonagricultural communities, contributing to a rise in the number of urban Buraku.

TABLE 2

DISTRIBUTION OF BURAKU POPULATION, 1935

District	Communities		Population	
Tohoku (Northeast)	9	(0%)	1	(0%)
Kanto (Large area around Tokyo)	835	(15%)	104	(10%)
Chubu (Mid Japan around Nagoya)	751	(15%)	75	(8%)
Kinki (Large area around Kyoto, Osaka, Kobe)	1,042	(19%)	438	(44%)
Chugoku (Southwest)	1,197	(22%)	147	(15%)
Shikoku	797	(15%)	122	(12%)
Kyushu	736	(14%)	112	(11%)
Total	5,367	(100%)	999	(100%)

SOURCE: Ministry of Welfare, 1935.

The current outcaste population estimates vary from one to three million. The higher figure seems to have been used for political purposes by the leftist outcaste leadership and has worked its way into the scientific literature as an established fact without solid evidence. According to governmental statistics (1962), in which one can naturally assume the actual number is underestimated, the Buraku population is 1,220,157 in 4,133 communities in 29 prefectures.[9] Yamamoto also assumes that the present Burakumin population within communities known as Buraku has been estimated to be approximately 1,500,000, and the total population, including all Burakumin residing outside the special communities, to be well over 2,000,000.[10]

new investigation may simply overlook some settlements. They disappear from ordinary view, according to Inoue (1954), when they are no longer subject to direct attention of special integrationist activities.

[8] Tōjō (1960), pp. 13–58.
[9] Chūō Seishōnen Mondai Kyōgikai (Central Committee on Youth Problems) (1962), p. 140.
[10] Yamamoto (1963), p. 204.

Even assuming a wide margin of error in the figures, the outcastes in 1871 seem to have constituted roughly 1 percent of the Japanese population while at present they comprise about 2 percent. That is, in spite of prejudice, the loss of their traditional monopolies and of former freedom from most of the feudal taxes, and despite new economic competition from machine-made, mass-produced leather goods and leather substitutes, the outcastes have doubled their proportion of the total population in less than one century. (There is no evidence as to whether outcaste fertility rates have actually been higher.) We would guess that the major reason for this increase would be involuntary recruitment from outside the outcaste population by a broadening of the definition of outcastes by the majority society. After their liberation during the Meiji period, the special communities must have continued to serve as one of the residential reservoirs for economically and socially deprived segments of the population, and such residence has been the prime criterion by which the majority society judges status. Intermarriage, as in the parallel Negro situation, usually results in the conversion of the couple and their children to Burakumin. Since color is no criterion of status, the definition of an outcaste is simply by association.

ENDOGAMY WITHIN BURAKU COMMUNITIES

There are strong tendencies toward geographical endogamy generally in Japan, but the outcastes have been limited to an extreme degree by local and occupational endogamy. For example, in 1868 in Nishinaka Buraku in Hyogo Prefecture, marriage within the Buraku made up 80.6 percent of the total number (175) of marriages. In an adjacent majority village, endogamy made up only 22.3 percent of the total number of marriages.[11] In Shin-machi, as reported by Donoghue, these patterns continue (see Chapter 7). A majority (62 percent) of the marriages there were found to be between residents of the community, and 79 percent between individuals of known outcaste occupation or status.

Couples having both parties born within the area comprised 55.4 percent of the cases, and in another 38 percent either husband or wife came from the area. A high degree of endogamy was also found in the community of Kajima in a recent study of communities near Osaka.[12] Those who moved into the community by marriage were from neighboring Buraku in the general Kansai area. In a second community, Sumiyoshi, of 288 families studied both husband and wife had been born in the community in 30 percent of the cases and either husband

---

[11] Mahara (1960b), pp. 131–80.
[12] Ōhashi (1962).

or wife in another 30 percent. In approximately 25 percent the husband or wife born in the community was married to a majority person who had moved in and identified himself with the community. Of the rest of the couples approximately 9 percent were both of non-Buraku origin and had moved in, and a small percentage (8 couples) were of Korean extraction.

The intermarriage between Buraku and majority individuals is found almost exclusively in the younger generation. These figures suggest that strict endogamy is progressively breaking down in this group; whereas less than 10 percent of the men over 50 had married non-Buraku wives, 38 percent of those under 30 have done so. Wives with majority husbands numbered less than 5 percent of those over 40, but close to 30 percent of those below 30.

For five years following 1945, in 127 Buraku communities in Kyoto Prefecture, there were 1,045 marriages, and Buraku endogamy, or marriage within the same Buraku, comprised 36 percent of the cases while intercommunity exogamy reached 65 percent. Exogamy most often means marriage between a member of one Buraku and a member of another, and thus marriage between different communities does not signify an increase of marriages between Burakumin and majority Japanese.

Suzuki, in a study of twelve Buraku communities in both urban and rural settings from six different prefectures, found that the number of cases in which a husband or wife is not an outcaste but has married into an outcaste community equals about 5 percent of the total urban population and 4.7 percent of the total rural Buraku population.[13] The number of cases of non-outcaste families or individuals equals approximately 8 percent of the total of 802 households studied in urban areas and less than 1 percent of the total of 381 households in rural areas. At the time of this study, only 13 percent of the total households in urban Buraku districts, compared with slightly over 5 percent of the rural Buraku, were found to be entirely or partially of non-outcaste background.

Besides those non-outcastes who married into the communities for personal reasons or moved there for the convenience of proximity to work, there are also those who, having failed in the majority society, have drifted into residence in a special community. Among the 73 households in these community samples in which neither husband nor wife nor unmarried household head is an outcaste, 38 are exempt from taxation because of their low income. An additional 20 households, 27 percent of the total non-outcaste people living within the sample outcaste communities, are paying a tax of less than 1,000 yen ($25) a year and are therefore in the lowest tax bracket in the Japanese tax sched-

---

[13] Suzuki (1953), pp. 369–80.

ule. Eleven of the twelve individuals classified as unmarried household heads are exempt from taxation because of lack of income. These data reveal the very low income of the non-outcaste people residing within outcaste communities and suggest that they may have been economically motivated to become Burakumin.

The rural-urban differences found in these recent studies suggest that the so-called Buraku areas of the city increasingly include a number of individuals who are not of Buraku origin.[14] And the rapidly increasing tempo of mobility in urban Japanese society may be breaking down the traditional gradual process whereby individuals become outcastes. The evidence seems to indicate, despite the general force of prejudice, an increasing trend toward mixed marriages. The younger generation of lower class Japanese may be breaking with family traditions preventing such marriages. But although there are cases of success in this kind of marriage, many unfortunate failures result from attempts to break the marriage taboo (see Chapter 12). One cannot discount the possibility that many of the present urban outcaste districts will become the socially disorganized quarters of the lowest strata of an urban proletariat (see Chapter 6).

OCCUPATION CHANGE WITHIN BURAKU

In contrast to the increase in population is a radical decrease in the number of outcastes performing the occupational roles that defined their status in the feudal Tokugawa period. A large number of Buraku do not include now a single member who practices a distinctively outcaste trade. Japanese culture has in recent years developed many new rationalizations for discrimination other than those specifically related to the traditional occupations. It would seem that the continuance of the outcastes in the future depends largely on the social persistence of the segregated Buraku (see Chapters 7 and 8). If the present industrial labor shortages increase we can expect to see more outcastes leave their communities. Part of this movement may simply be from a rural to an urban Buraku, and we do not yet know whether actual passing will increase under such conditions.

Since the emancipation in 1871, the most significant occupational trend has been toward agriculture. Around 1920 one village with 300 families of 1,900 people had the following occupational breakdown: 682 farming, 185 trade, 180 traveling players, 180 not reported, 97 day labor, 31 in industry.[15] Over thirty years ago Ninomiya claimed that fully one-half the Eta households engaged in agriculture.[16] The figures

[14] Suzuki (1953).
[15] Ninomiya (1933), Appendix III.
[16] Ninomiya (1933).

in Table 3 are from the Ministry of Internal Affairs 1920 survey of the Tokushu Buraku.[17]

TABLE 3

OCCUPATIONAL BREAKDOWN OF THE SPECIAL COMMUNITIES
COMPARED WITH THE NATION, 1920

Occupation	Buraku Households	Buraku Percentage	National Percentage
Farming	74,872	49	52
Manual labor	23,092	15 ⎫	8
Miscellaneous	20,583	13 ⎬	
Business	18,765	11	13
Artisans and manufacturing	13,358	9	19
Fishing	4,042	3	2
Government officials	174	0	6
Totals	154,886	100	100

SOURCE: Ministry of Internal Affairs, 1920.

The economic position of the Burakumin is poor when compared with the nation at large.[18] There are significant differences between the Buraku and the nation in the proportions of those engaged in manufacturing and governmental service. The low proportion of those engaged in service or government is related to the low level of education in the Buraku. Table 3 demonstrates the degree to which Burakumin are limited to selective occupations. The figures do not reveal, however, that those in agriculture have poorer land or are tenants. While only 10.8 percent of the farmers in the nation own less than five tan (approximately an acre), 66 percent of the Buraku farmers own less than five tan. The Buraku farmers must pay higher land tax to the landowner, and their land is usually located farther away from their residence, a great part of it in the hilly sections. The figures also do not reveal that manufacturing is limited to special types of handicraft. Discrimination in hiring policies by modern industry tended to discourage drift to urban occupations and the Burakumin have had to stay with their land in spite of its negative features. Buraku small handicrafters and even itinerant peddlers have been at the mercy of wholesalers from outside the Buraku.

---

[17] These figures exclude 484 households of the survey; they ignore the important distinction between landowner and tenant farmer by including both as "farming occupations"; and they do not single out the traditionally outcaste occupations. The outcaste tendency to move into the traditional field of agriculture has served to make their communities stable, identifiable, and persistent.

[18] Inoue (1960), pp. 63–70.

The occupational distribution of Burakumin according to a 1935 survey by the Ministry of Internal Affairs (Table 4) is misleading in

TABLE 4

OCCUPATIONAL DISTRIBUTION OF BURAKU PEOPLE, 1935

Occupation	Number of Households	Percent
Agriculture	123,100	64.0
Industry	19,000	10.0
Commerce	10,000	6.0
Fishing	5,700	3.0
Transportation	500	0.4
Labor	800	0.6
Miscellaneous	31,400	16.0
Totals	191,500	100.0

SOURCE: Ministry of Internal Affairs, 1935.

the large percentage of households classified under agriculture. Those who did not own any land, and those for whom agriculture was only one, sometimes minor, source of income were all classified under this category.

The small proportion of Buraku farmers who actually lived exclusively by farming is shown in Table 5. Their relatively low income is shown in Table 6.[19]

TABLE 5

DISTRIBUTION OF TYPES OF FARMERS, 1933

	Percent	
	Buraku	Non-Buraku
Those living exclusively on farming	45 ⎫ 100	73 ⎫ 100
Side-job farmers	55 ⎭	27 ⎭
Proprietor farmers	11 ⎫	31 ⎫
Proprietor-tenant farmers	37 ⎬ 100	43 ⎬ 100
Tenant farmers	52 ⎭	26 ⎭

Most of the Buraku communities located in rural areas and in agricultural settings cannot really be called farming villages.[20] For example, in Kobayashi Buraku, Nara Prefecture, only 140 out of 350 households own even the smallest section of land. The 1,500 indi-

[19] Material taken from Inoue (1960), pp. 74–82.
[20] Tōjō (1960).

TABLE 6

FARMERS' INCOMES, 1930

	Buraku	Non-Buraku
Income from farming	151 yen (49.7%)	499 yen (68.6%)
Income from other sources	153 yen (50.3%)	226 yen (31.4%)
Totals	304 yen (100.0%)	727 yen (100.0%)

viduals of this community are squeezed within 0.1 of a square kilometer (the highest population density in Japan), and they all eke out their livelihood by making plastic zōri (footgear). In Arabori Buraku in Nagano Prefecture, of a total of 150 households only 30 own about 1.47 acres each, another 70 own about 0.69 each, and the remaining 50 households own no land at all. The small amount of land owned by these Buraku households is of inferior quality, extending onto the arid lava located at the foot of the active volcano, Mount Asama, some of it two hours' walking distance from their community. The major occupation for the Buraku people in this community is trade in rabbits. And in Une Buraku in Okayama Prefecture, only 6 of the total 40 households are fully engaged in agriculture. Seventeen are partly farmers, and the rest all make and sell bamboo artcraft.

In Komano Buraku in Kochi Prefecture on the major island of Shikoku, for 92 households there is a total of only 2.2 acres of rice paddy and another 1.5 acres of dry fields, which cannot provide the villagers with sufficient vegetables. Burakumin in this community are therefore primarily engaged in small crafts. In other "agricultural" communities, outcastes make enough to survive by gathering empty shells from a nearby rifle range and selling them for scrap. In Nonaka,

TABLE 7

OCCUPATIONAL STRUCTURE OF NONAKA BURAKU

Occupation	Male	Female	Total
Agriculture	270	200	470
Illegal brewery	141	179	320
Day laborer	175	39	214
Unemployment relief	75	107	182
Sake peddler	64	75	139
Zōri weaver	—	86	86
Clothes peddler	52	18	70
Shoe repair	68	—	68
Pig raising	21	28	49
Zōri maker	37	—	37

a large Buraku on Shikoku Island, of about 1,000 households, only 27 percent are engaged in agriculture, while in neighboring majority districts, 67 percent of all households are agricultural. The land owned by Buraku farmers averages about 0.7 acre, whereas majority farmers in a neighboring area own about twice as much. Table 7 gives the occupational distribution of this Buraku.

The exclusion of the Burakumin from the occupation of their neighbors is not limited to agriculture. For example, many Buraku communities located among fishing villages find the fishing territory closed to them.

PRESENT-DAY URBAN OUTCASTE COMMUNITIES

Distribution of the outcastes among the nonrural populations of Japan reflects in rough fashion their occupational specializations in castle towns under feudalism. In the largest cities the present distribution differs greatly with location. Burakumin are concentrated in cities in southwest Japan; these have been investigated. The more recently developed cities on the eastern border of the Kanto Plain, Tokyo and Yokohama, have only a small number of outcastes while to the south, Nagoya, a former castle town, has a very large, stable Buraku. To illustrate distribution in the Kanto area as contrasted with that in the Kansai Plain we will briefly review some research material from both these areas.

Buraku Communities in Tokyo

Prior to the Great Earthquake of 1923 there were a few traditional, small special communities within the city of Tokyo. Of all the cities in Japan, Tokyo has the greatest amount of in-migration and internal mobility. Those traditional community patterns that did exist were somewhat disrupted by the Great Earthquake and fire and by the destruction of the city during World War II. These cataclysms caused the disintegration of the small Buraku districts and a dispersion of most of the Burakumin to majority lower class slum areas. Nevertheless, according to the careful research of Suzuki, there are still 13 identifiable small districts within the Tokyo city area with residents who are predominantly Burakumin and are descendants of the Eta of the Tokugawa period.[21] Suzuki estimates the total population of Burakumin in Tokyo between 20,000 and 30,000, with the majority still engaged in the footgear industry. Many commute to the Asakusa district, the largest trading center for shoes in Japan, which has a heavy concentration of small-scale establishments manufacturing sandals. In

---

[21] Suzuki (1953).

one of the 13 Burakumin districts described by Suzuki, two-fifths of the total of 1,200 households are on relief, 250 individuals are day laborers, 45 are street sweepers, 70 are rag-and-junk men, 28 are shoe-shiners, and over 100 individuals commute to Asakusa as shoemakers. A number of others work in shoe stores or as shoe repairmen in Tokyo. There are 23 Buraku on the western outskirts of greater Tokyo, outside the city. Most of the residents are poor farmers, supplementing their income by working as street sweepers, shoe repairmen, and butchers; a great many more are unemployed on relief.

Suzuki suggests that the descendants of Hinin were forced after the emancipation to move from one place to another and were joined by drifters of non-Hinin background, forming rag-picking communities, prostitute sections, and slum areas. These districts are not defined today as specifically of outcaste origin.

The Burakumin in Osaka

Ōhashi identifies 14 Buraku communities within the city of Osaka, many of them close to transportation facilities.[22] In one of these, Kajima, with about 1,500 people in over 360 households, 571 individuals in 140 households have been known to live in the area for several generations and are definitely identified as Burakumin. The background of the remainder, who have moved into the district in recent times, is not clearly defined. The district is severely overpopulated and most houses are dilapidated; residents are engaged in small home manufacturing or in peddling of brooms and dusters. The average income per household is under 24,000 yen, slightly more than 5,000 yen ($15) per individual a month. The Osaka working class generally makes about 31,000 yen per household or somewhat over 7,000 ($20) per individual.

The second community in Ōhashi's report is Sumiyoshi with 1,436 inhabitants. Many of its people are itinerant peddlers of fruit, vegetables, and fish, or are itinerant shoe repairmen. Their average income in 1959 was approximately 22,500 per household or between 5,000 and 6,000 yen per individual. The percentage of families on relief in this community is much higher than that of the majority population in Osaka.

POVERTY IN THE BURAKU

Government Relief and Welfare Programs

Burakumin rely heavily on government-supplied employment, consisting of various forms of unskilled labor on public work projects.

---

[22] Ōhashi (1962).

Table 8 shows the proportion of Burakumin registered for this type of relief work and the proportion of outcastes in the total population in seven prefectures. These statistics were collected in 1955.[23] On a national basis, in 1957 1.8 percent of the total population received social

TABLE 8

PROPORTION OF BURAKUMIN ON RELIEF IN SEVEN PREFECTURES, 1955

Prefecture	Estimated Proportion of Burakumin Registered for Relief Work	Estimated Proportion of Burakumin in Total Population of Prefecture
Kagawa-ken	30%	0.1%
Kochi-ken	70	5.9
Hyogo-ken (including Kobe)	45	5.7
Osaka-fu (including Osaka)	35	2.1
Kyoto-shi (including Kyoto)	60	2.7
Nara-ken (including Nara)	85	6.9
Mie-ken	70	3.5

welfare financial aid, according to the Livelihood Protection Law, but in Kyoto City 2.3 percent of the total received aid. The proportion of relief given to Burakumin in Kyoto was far higher than the national average. For instance, in Shichijō Buraku in Kyoto, 20.2 percent or 8.5 times the national average were aided, and in another, 15.5 percent or 11.2 times more than the average.

In Nishinomiya in Hyogo Prefecture, Mahara[24] reports that 1,152 households received this welfare in 1958. Of these households, 187 were in a Buraku; whereas only 1.1 percent of the population of the city received funds, 7.0 percent of the population of the Buraku were aided.

To illustrate the level of poverty of many outcastes we can use two sample budgets.[25] A widow, with one daughter of school age, is 41 years old, is registered for government labor for the unemployed, and receives from this 6,500 yen monthly (about $18). Each month rice costs her 1,400 yen and other food, 1,500 yen (a total of less than $10 a month); housing, 1,000; her child's education, 500 yen; and allowance, 300 yen. She has for miscellaneous use per month a residue of 1,800 yen—approximately $5.

In the morning she cooks two go of rice (under 700 calories), and rice gruel (700 calories). Her daughter eats part of the rice for breakfast and the rest for lunch. She herself eats no breakfast and eats part

[23] Mahara (1960a), p. 127.
[24] Mahara (1960a), pp. 129–30.
[25] Mahara (1960c), pp. 181–212.

of the gruel for lunch. For dinner, the two share the rest of the gruel, with a side dish costing about 30 yen (10 cents).

A scrap-iron buyer, or metal-scrap picker, living in a Buraku in Matsuzaka City in Mie Prefecture, has two children and a sick wife. His monthly income is about 6,500 yen (about $18). The monthly expenses for his family are shown in Table 9.

TABLE 9

MONTHLY EXPENSES OF A BURAKU FAMILY*

Item	Cost
Main food	2,775 yen
Other food	1,965
Seasoning	315
Cigarettes	30
Child expenses	80
Clothes	305
Bath	150
Barber	130
Sanitation	135
Utensils	35
Heat	355
Water	215
Electricity	153
Miscellaneous	375

* In addition to his income of 6,500 yen, the father received 813 yen from the government under the Livelihood Protection Law.

Government relief plays a vital role in Buraku communities. In Yahata, the largest Buraku in the Mie Prefecture, for example, 2,500 people, of 500 households, are squeezed onto land measuring 500 by 100 meters. People here have three sources of income that prevent them from becoming thieves. The first is unemployment relief work—unskilled labor provided by the government for those who are unemployed. Two hundred and fifty, or more than 26 percent of those who are in the appropriate age group, are registered for "getting a job." Legally, only one person from each household is allowed to register, and to increase their income many couples divorce and continue to live together. Work in addition to this relief is not permitted, but many outcastes here do find some supplementary income sources. Those who are on the relief work are considered the "wealthiest" people of the community.

A second source of income in this (Yahata) Buraku is provided by the government social welfare program, under the Livelihood Protection Law, to those who are destitute. About 130 households receive this money, and another 200 households receive supplements for medical, educational, and household expenses. In other words, about 25 percent of the total number of households are given some kind of welfare relief. The third source of income is the weaving of sashes for a local cottage industry. Minor sources of income include collecting rags, paper, and other kinds of material; peddling fruit and vegetables, and working on construction projects.

With this overview of distribution, population, and other features of the ecology of Buraku life in mind, let us turn toward the closer view that ethnographic studies provide.

Chapter 6

YUZURU SASAKI AND
GEORGE DE VOS

A Traditional Urban
Outcaste Community

DISTRIBUTION OF OUTCASTE DISTRICTS
IN KYOTO

There are nineteen districts in Kyoto (1964) that are officially
designated by the city office as "Dōwa Chiku" (district to be integrated); these the city has attempted to improve. All the stable outcaste communities with a long history are among the nineteen districts.
Several other relatively new outcaste communities have not been
officially identified, and their exact location and size is not easily determined.

The first Buraku area, well known as Takagamine, is in the north-
western part of Kyoto. The City Report of 1964 gives a population of
1,806 residents in 362 households but government statistics usually
underestimate, and the actual population is thought to be between
2,000 and 2,500 people. The second area, called Tanaka, is in the
northeast, not far from the confluence of the Kamo and the Takano
rivers; the official estimation here is 1,974 people in 410 households.
These two areas are made up almost exclusively of individuals of
outcaste background. The third area, located in Shishigatani, has 816
people in 165 households. The fourth, in east central Kyoto, is known
as Sanjō-ura where 1,793 people live in 351 households. The fifth, the
largest Buraku in Kyoto, Uchihama, with a population of 7,442 in
1,809 households, is east of the railway station. It is well known for its
traditional leather industry. Mixed with the original outcaste inhabitants is a sprinkling of Koreans, impoverished day laborers, garbage pickers of regular origin, and a group of migrants from the

129

northern Ryukyus. The sixth, a relatively new community, is Higashi
Iwamoto-chō, not officially identified as Dōwa Chiku. It lies to the
south of Uchihama and to the rear of the Kyoto station. The seventh
community, Yakata-machi, is also newly formed and not officially
identified. It is near Higashi Iwamoto-chō, and in both these new
districts about 70 percent of the total population is Burakumin, many
of whom migrated during and after the war. Today there is a large
influx of Koreans and non-outcaste lower class individuals, so that this
area is losing its specifically outcaste identity. The larger area, including Higashi Iwamoto-chō, the southern outskirts of Uchihama,
and Yakata-machi is often referred to as Eki-ura, the "back of the
tracks" of the Kyoto railroad station.[1] The entire district is becoming
more of a general lower class slum than a traditional Buraku district.
Higashi Iwamoto-chō is actually identified as a "slum district," need-
ing special programs. There are a dozen other communities on which
we have less precise information.[2]

Outcastes from each of these communities supposedly have definable
characteristics. The reason for and nature of these differences are
obscure.[3]

It is maintained by some informants that there is no ranking
or difference discernible among the various Kyoto Buraku, that there
is no basis for conflict among these communities, and that their
mutual sense of solidarity as outcaste groups prevents any manifestation of social gradation or conflict. Other evidence suggests that this
may not always be the case. There is a sense of disharmony between
the stable communities and those of greater in- or out-migration.
Obvious signs of tension appear between traditional inhabitants and
individuals who have entered more recently and settled near an
established Buraku.

---

[1] It is characteristic of Japanese cities to have a low status residential area to the
rear of the railroad station. The station fronts department stores, commercial businesses, and entertainment establishments. The railway station is a city center: public
transportation radiates out from the station front, and the main roads of the city
often converge there.

[2] Such communities include: Mibu (including Saiin), with the population of
1,236 in 248 households; Takeda, 2,730 in 591 households; Daigo, 1,007 in 213 households; Kuze, 1,154 in 195 households; Yamashina, 956 in 170 households; Kisshōin
with 478 people in 108 households; Toba with 263 in 48 households; Uzumasa
with 827 in 170 households; Matsuo with 421 in 78 households; Nassho with 305
in 55 households; and Yodo with 121 people in 23 households.

[3] One of the informants from Takagamine, for example, remembers that as a
child he was told by people of his own community that the people of Sanjō-ura
were rough and fearful. According to another informant, people of Saiin Buraku
are often referred to by other Burakumin as "sai no mekusari" (rotten eyed "sai"),
and people of Sanjō-ura Buraku are often called "sanjō no boro" (Sanjō people in
tatters).

DIFFERENCES BETWEEN A STABLE AND
A TRANSITIONAL COMMUNITY

A Transitional Community: Shin Buraku

Iwamoto-chō joins the southern outskirts of the older stable Buraku of Uchihama. It is often referred to as "Shin Buraku," that is, "the new Buraku." About 70 percent of the people here are of outcaste background. During and after the war, there was a large influx of outcastes from the Kansai area, the outsiders usually being called *iri-bito* (incomers) by neighboring Burakumin. In addition to outcastes, there are Koreans, some poor Japanese of non-Buraku background, and a mixed-marriage group which is not accepted by any of the other groups in the community. These become truly marginal in their social interactions.

Most individuals live in this new Buraku because of some financial duress. The population tends to remain mobile, for as soon as an individual's income increases, he is apt to leave. The community, therefore, is disorganized and without a tradition or character of its own, and residents sometimes try to avoid being classified as outcastes. For instance, with official recognition as Dōwa Chiku from the City Office, the community can obtain financial aid for physical improvements and social welfare services, though on a small scale. However, many avoid such aid because, it is believed, they are reluctant to be identified as Burakumin along with the people of neighboring Uchihama. In their attempt to deny their own identity, they have resorted to calling the people of Uchihama "eta," and have otherwise indicated that the residents of this traditional Buraku are beneath them. On the other hand, Uchihama residents consider those in the new area to be tough, rude, and criminal in nature. Even within the transitional community itself, tensions arise among groups who identify themselves with a particular block, and much name-calling occurs among blocks. Displacement of internalized self-hate takes the form of hostility toward others of Buraku status that can be somehow differentiated. Rather than concerted group action, people in this area tend to face their problems alone, without much social support or solidarity to bolster them.

People of this new area, although mostly destitute, spend much of their money on *shōchū*, a poor grade of brandy. Although some violence occurs as a result of heavy drinking, in general this neighborhood does not live up to the reputation of toughness and criminality ascribed to it by nearby Buraku. Neither is there any evidence that the disorganization in this community is focused particularly on youth or that it has resulted in organized gang behavior in adolescents.[4]

Fragile family ties and unregistered common-law marriages are common, and a wife may leave her home to join another man without incurring adverse social sanctions. Father Diffley, the Catholic priest who has worked many years in this district, believes that casual liaisons occur here more readily than among the lower class people without Buraku background. Wife beating is not unusual in Iwamoto-chō.[5]

In comparison with more stable Buraku communities, in- and out-mobility seems to contribute heavily to social and personal tensions and the fragile family relationships. More relaxed sexual attitudes are reported for other Buraku as well, but not to the same degree as in Iwamoto-chō. Here, the force of tradition is almost absent, whereas in the older Buraku with less mobility, community pressures remain sufficiently strong to discourage complete casualness in human relationships.

A Stable Buraku: Takagamine

Takagamine, behind one of the largest Zen Buddhist temple compounds in Kyoto, the Daitoku-ji, is closest to the Kyoto suburbs and is a good example of a well defined traditional outcaste community. There are approximately 500 households with a total population of between 2,000 and 2,500 people in Takagamine, almost all exclusively of outcaste background with very strong in-group feelings. They usually do not venture out of the community and in-migration and out-migration are minimal.

Most of the inhabitants work as unskilled laborers, a number working for the city as day laborers. They are often engaged on a temporary basis for street cleaning, garbage collecting, or collection and disposal of human waste from privies in those houses of Kyoto City that have no running water. Some members of the community become supervisors of work-gangs, and may be said to have what Lloyd Warner would call "upper lower class" status within this community.[6] The shoemakers, who work in groups under bosses, have a status somewhat below that of the supervisors of daily laborers.

---

[4] We have not been able to gather material documenting the actual presence of juvenile gangs in this area. None of our informants was familiar with such a phenomenon, and we presume if this phenomenon were of note, it would have come to our attention.

[5] Father Diffley believes the loose moral attitude is caused by the lack of opportunity to develop personal pride. Residents perceive themselves in a degraded role.

[6] Warner and Lunt (1941).

There are three general goods stores within the community that cater to the people's everyday needs, and their owners occupy a middle position in the lower class structure of the Buraku. The stores sell fried beef tripe, which is eaten as a between-meal snack. Regular butcher shops called *iremon-ya*, "a store which sells containers" (the word "container" is a slang expression used only by Burakumin of Kyoto to describe the internal organs or intestines of the cow), sell tripe raw. The eating of tripe, a traditional food for outcastes, is cited by majority people as repugnant behavior natural to Burakumin. On the other hand, merchants selling raw tripe occupy an upper position in the lower stratum of the prestige structure of the community.

There are two or three grocery stores in the community, several small shops selling inexpensive candy, and three tobacco shops. For some reason the tobacconists are accorded middle class social status. Merchants of the other food stores seem to be above butchers but are still within the upper part of the lower stratum of the community. Merchants in traditional Japanese society generally were considered of lower status than farmers, a traditional attitude that seems to be for the most part maintained today.

Grooming needs are met by a local barber shop and a public bath house. There are no laundries. One or perhaps two itinerant merchants sell children's clothes and inexpensive dresses and underwear for adults, but new clothes are usually bought outside the community. Proprietors of these establishments are accorded somewhat higher prestige than the proprietors of small food shops.

Some middle status individuals have professional charge of a nursery school or kindergarten; however, middle and upper status individuals within the community tend to send their children to a kindergarten outside. Almost every member of the community, including those who have moved out and are now more or less successfully passing, maintains strong religious affiliation with one of the two Buddhist temples in the Buraku.

Ten or twelve men are officials in the Kyoto city office; one is head of a government bureau and enjoys high social status, another is superintendent in a construction firm and has the equivalent of upper middle class status in the community. There are eight to ten ordinary city office employees, all with a high school education. Though we could obtain very little information about their experiences as workers, it seemed apparent that their motivation for attempting to pass may be strong.

A number of women are factory workers, and a smaller number are employees of small stores. If the husband works in a store or factory, generally the social status of the family is upper lower class. If, however, the father works as a day or construction laborer on an irregular basis, and his wife or daughter works as a factory hand, the family is considered of lower lower class position. This is also true if the father or head of household is dead or is an invalid.

Occupying a unique position within the community is an old high status family that still manufactures geta. This particular family headed the community until the death of the last head of the house when it declined financially. But although the present income seems to be limited, this family still enjoys the prestige of their previous status.

A few families within this community own land and rent out houses. These house and landowners occupy what might be called the "upper upper" social status within the community. Just below them are the five families who own shops outside the community, and perhaps also the head of the bureau in the city office.

Traditionally, the "upper class" families operating as oyakata (bosses) of groups of laborers have been in firm control of the important so-called Buraku industries and occupations, such as shoemaking, dyeing, the slaughtering of animals and handling of skins, and they also controlled the labor for crematories and burials. Another important Buraku industry is the collecting of various kinds of scrap materials—metal, leather, paper, cloth—called "kuzu" in Japanese. In one of the other special communities investigated in Kyoto is a wealthy family known as Kuzuya (the name of the occupation becoming the title of the family). The head of the family supervises 20 to 30 or more litter pickers, and provides them sleeping quarters, three meager meals a day, and big baskets to be carried on the shoulders for their work. The Kuzuya family sought to expand this hereditary occupation successfully, and becoming quite wealthy, continued to spend only a negligible part of its total income on its employees. They had considerable political control within the community and enjoyed the highest prestige.

DISTINGUISHING SOCIAL TRAITS WITHIN THE KYOTO BURAKU

Food

In contrast to what is reported concerning food habits of Burakumin elsewhere, the Kyoto Buraku as separate groups have tended to maintain certain eating patterns different from those of the majority community. People living within these Buraku have a long history and tradition of meat eating.

Since 1868 the consumption of meat as a means of improving the general diet has been encouraged by official government policies, and there is now widespread use of the usual cuts of meat throughout

Japan. But a distinguishing feature of the Burakumin's traditional meateating patterns was the preference for the internal organs—the liver, the kidney, the entrails, and the brain. In Buraku one can buy the livers and kidneys not only of cows but also of horses. Only since World War II have the Japanese generally, especially the younger people, taken to eating liver or kidney, and among the older Japanese there remains a strong feeling of revulsion toward the idea of eating any of the internal organs. The iremon-ya described above is unique to the Buraku.

Dress

Within the special community itself, dress is extremely informal, even careless. Even those who are fairly comfortable do not dress as well as outside people with the same income. One informant, a university graduate of outcaste background, said that a conscious distinction is made between dress inside and outside the community. There is a general feeling that Burakumin belong to one large family and when at home among family members one does not dress up. Children under six usually run about completely naked if the weather permits.

Another specific characteristic of dress within the Kyoto Buraku is the sandal, *setta zōri*. Why this particular type of sandal began to be used is unknown, but many outcastes were engaged in sandal-making at one time, and the use of this special sandal may date from that period. Many who formerly made sandals now make shoes, and it may be that shoes were considered an expensive or a less traditional Japanese product for outsiders. There is some feeling that the old sandal is part of tradition. Whatever the origin of the custom, in both Kyoto and Kobe many of the Burakumin adults wear setta zōri.[7]

Speech and Comportment

The speech patterns of Burakumin seem to be more informal than those of the general society. Informants familiar with the intricacies of the Kyoto and Kobe dialects say that there are distinctions between the language forms of the dialect used by the Burakumin and those of the regular lower class. To classify speech patterns requires subjective social judgments, but there are distinctive definable characteristics in vocabulary and in pronunciation.[8]

---

[7] There is some indication that the continued use of this form of zōri evokes some feeling of belonging and self-enhancement. One informant remembers that as a child he very much disliked seeing his own father walking in such zōri because he had become aware by that time that this was an easily identifiable characteristic of a Burakumin.

[8] Besides the general informal or ruder forms of language, some special words, like "kotchimae" or "iremon-ya," mentioned before, are used only among Burakumin. In

Although there are economic differences among members of the urban Buraku, special culture patterns are shared by all. Individuals of the wealthier families may learn to comport themselves in a style acceptable to the outer society, but they are very much aware of the ordinary standards of speech, dress, and comportment of the entire community. This sharing of distinct patterns within the community helps maintain a strong sense of ingroup social solidarity.

Within the Buraku it is very difficult for individuals with higher incomes to isolate their children from the rest of the community. The pattern, observable in the outside society where middle or upper class individuals, through separation of residence and educational facilities are able to isolate their children from the "unacceptable" and therefore encourage them to develop certain modes of comportment, does not function successfully within the Buraku. Although children are sometimes sent outside to school, the community's speech patterns and modes of behavior are generally shared whatever the economic means of the family. Emotional alienation occurs in individuals who decide to pass. But they can easily reassume old language patterns and other gestures of communication spontaneously since they have had ample firsthand experience growing up with peers within the community.[9]

Takagamine and a few other Buraku the word "shirakoi" is used for mischievous and outcastes rarely realize that this word is not used in majority society. Some non-Buraku informants indicated that sometimes pronunciation of certain words is different. For instance, in Kyoto, the sound "zazizuzezo" tends to be pronounced by Buraku people as "rarirurero." Instead of saying "yukuzo" (I will go), Buraku people tend to say "yukuro."

[9] For instance, one of our informants, a government officer in the correctional field who is successfully passing, told us of his intention to live in a Buraku in order to "know better the delinquent children of the community." In answer to our question on how he would disclose his hidden identity (background) to the outcastes so he would be accepted as a boarder in some house, he said, "I would say that although I am now boarding at atchimae-person's house, I feel uncomfortable. The use of the single word 'atchimae' would be enough to disclose my background to Buraku people."

1. The ghetto persists within the changing city.

2. Modern sanitation stops short here.

3. Ghetto streets are the children's playground.

4. Passing time with a smoke or a snack.

5. A Buraku home.

6. Jizo san's shrine guards this house.

7. Growing up six to a room.

8. A snack of fried tripe.

9. Daily laborers having lunch.

10. Jobless youth killing time by gambling.

11. A working mother and her child.

12. Stretching leather for drying.

13. A traditional occupation: making sandals of straw.

14. Making the modern leather shoe.

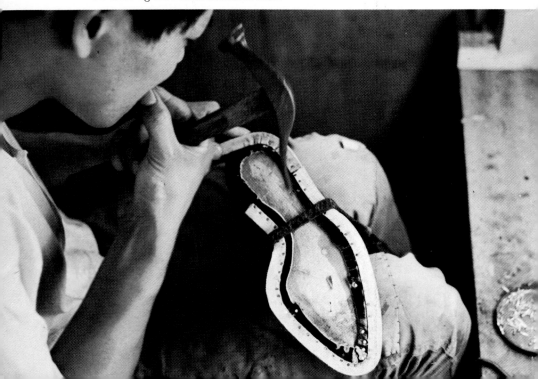

15. Plastic shoes are now a Buraku industry.

16. Bleaching leather in the river.

17. Drying leather in the sun.

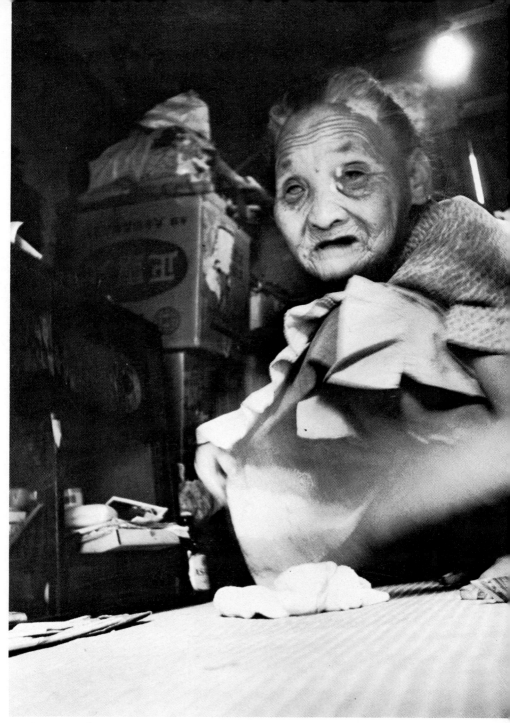
18. Three afflictions: age, trachoma, and outcaste status.

19. The mark of oppression persists within the changing culture.

Chapter 7

JOHN DONOGHUE

The Social Persistence
of an Outcaste Group

This chapter summarizes field research in which the major objective was to determine some of the factors contributing to the social persistence of Shin-machi—an outcaste community located on the outskirts of Toyoda City[1] in the Tōhoku District of northeast Japan. The following description and analysis is directed to the two questions: Why do the outcastes remain a distinct subgroup in Japanese society? Why do Burakumin remain in overpopulated substandard communities, rather than migrate to large cities where their pariah stigma may be lost?

Let us summarize some of the points made in earlier chapters. The outcastes are not racially distinct nor do they have major overt cultural characteristics that might differentiate them from the majority society. They are not required to live in segregated villages, and the hierarchical social structure of the feudal period no longer exists. Moreover, Buddhist religious taboos against the taking of life and Shinto conceptions of pollution associated with blood, dirt, and death, both of which contributed to the early formation and development of the Eta, have undergone essential modifications. Most Japanese people now eat meat, and majority butchers, tanners, and shoemakers, occupations formerly held only by Eta, are found throughout the nation. The primary distinguishing feature of the outcaste is residence in a socially segregated and isolated community. What follows focuses specifically upon the dynamics of intergroup and interpersonal relations, and upon the socioeconomic organization that influences the social persistence of this community.

At present, the special communities, traditionally located on river

---

[1] All place names in this chapter are pseudonyms. The nature of the community and its relationship to the majority society makes this necessary.

banks and other marginal lands, maintain a perceptible distinctness because of substandard, slum-like dwellings and serious overpopulation. Although many of the Burakumin are employed in the customary Eta occupations of butchering, leather and fur processing, begging, and other menial tasks, the largest percentage are farmers, fishermen, and unskilled laborers. They are further differentiated from the majority by an income far below the national average, and by their tendency toward local and caste endogamy.

ATTITUDES OF NON-BURAKUMIN IN TOYODA

A great deal of misunderstanding concerning the Eta exists in Toyoda in the Tōhoku District of northeast Japan. Most citizens prefer to avoid the subject of the Burakumin even in conversation. Most informants, although unaware of the location of Shin-machi, are familiar with the term *Shin-machi-nin* (people of Shin-machi), which is applied to the outcastes of Toyoda. Few city residents have ever been to Shin-machi and most have never knowingly met an outcaste. Buraku dwellers do not affect the lives of the Toyoda people, and do not constitute a recognized social problem. This lack of concern, however, in no way diminishes the attitudes of prejudice and hostility; rather, it propagates ignorance, obscurity, and even mystery. Four of the most general attitudes held by Toyoda informants toward the pariah caste are offered below.

Disgust is the most widely held and commonly verbalized attitude. Individuals who are unwilling even to discuss the outcastes distort their faces and exclaim, *kitanai* (dirty). These feelings are sometimes manifested more directly. For example, after one of the customers in a small wine shop noticed blood on the hands and shirt sleeves of a young outcaste he shouted disparagingly at him and was joined by several others: "You are dirty, you animal killer! Look at the blood all over you! You are a filthy *yaban* (barbarian, savage)!"

Fear is another commonly found attitude of the Toyoda people. Outcastes are considered dangerous and capable of inflicting bodily harm. There are exaggerated stories of physical prowess and fighting skill and they are likened to the gangsters and hoodlums portrayed in American films. There is also the fear that surrounds the unknown. Burakumin are believed by some to be sinister characters with evil powers, and mothers sometimes frighten their children with gruesome tales of the "eta" bogey-man. It is said, too, that the outcastes are afflicted with such contagious diseases as syphilis, gonorrhea, tuberculosis, and leprosy.

Because the Burakumin and their village are forbidden, the attitude of *erotic curiosity* prompts such questions as: "Do the 'eta' look different? Are the women really beautiful? Are they rough, like gangsters? Do they actually speak a different language? What kind of food do they eat?" Many wonder if Buraku girls are "better" than ordinary women, some young males have erotic desires for outcaste women, and restaurant hostesses often joke about an imputed enlargement or distortion of the genitals of the male "eta."

The spread of the final attitude, which might be termed *objectivity*, seems to be increasing steadily among the younger generation, but it has the fewest adherents in Toyoda. This attitude is not widespread because it depends primarily on observation.[2] "Look at the 'eta' and their houses—they *are* dirty, they have dirty occupations and they are diseased." "The 'eta' always marry each other, so their strain is weak. They are an exclusive, intimate group that rejects outsiders and any form of aid." "I feel sorry for the 'eta' because of their lowly position, but I will have nothing to do with them until they learn to live like other Japanese, that is, give up their occupations, marry outside their small community, clean up their villages, homes, and themselves, and drop their hostile clannish attitudes." Such beliefs are based less on legend than others but, as with dominant Negro-white relations in the United States, they operate as a self-fulfilling prophecy in maintaining the outcaste status.[3]

The beliefs and myths of the Toyoda citizenry preserve majority group exclusiveness by associating the Burakumin with violations of some of the most fundamental and sacred Japanese values—those centering around purity, lineage, and health. The following are two of many popular legends heard in the city.

A young man met a beautiful girl in a restaurant. After a short courtship they were married against the wishes of the boy's parents. They lived happily for awhile, but when their children were born idiots with spotted complexions, it was discovered that the girl was a Burakumin.

It was customary prior to the turn of the century for Burakumin to wash the bodies of deceased commoners in return for an offering of *sake* but after the outcastes began to realize their emancipation, they frequently requested money for their services. Sometimes the demands were exorbitant. When the sum was refused, the Burakumin would threaten the family by vowing to drink the water used in bathing the body. The people were usually frightened into relenting to the Burakumin demands.

---

[2] Such viewpoints exist, as Merton states in another context, not as prejudice or prejudgment, "but as the irresistible product of observation. The facts of the case permit no other conclusion." Merton (1949), p. 182.

[3] Merton (1949); Myrdal (1944); MacIver (1948).

The general theme of the first story is the unhappiness of anyone who marries an outcaste, and the physical and mental deformity of the offspring. This is probably the most widespread myth, as it is employed by parents to discourage children from affairs that might result in a "love marriage." Even the most informed Japanese balk at the thought of marriage to an outcaste because of the popular notion of their "weak strain" from long intermarriage. The second legend illustrates the supposed barbaric quality of the Burakumin; not only were they mercenary, but they profaned the sacred, defiled the dead, and imbibed the impure and dirty.

SHIN-MACHI

Shin-machi's 347 inhabitants are housed in 43 dwellings, some including as many as ten households, located on a narrow dead-end road on the southeastern edge of Toyoda. Several relatively new houses dot the village, but the majority are old and dilapidated. Windows are covered with newspapers, and holes in the roofs are patched haphazardly with cardboard and paper held in place by large stones.

Family genealogies indicate only 18 surnames in Shin-machi, and seven of these account for the majority of the 78 households. Sixty-two percent of the marriages are between residents of the community, and 79 percent between individuals with Eta occupations and status. Thus, almost every individual is either consanguineously or affinally related to every other individual. Adoptions are frequent, especially between siblings, and illegitimacy is common; few families have no illegitimate births recorded in the city registration book (koseki).

The traditional outcaste occupations support 30 percent of the households. Another 35 percent are day laborers or claim no occupation. The remainder are dependent upon menial, low-income occupations such as begging, rag collecting, knife-grinding, peddling small confectioneries at festivals, and collecting food and clothing left at graves after certain religious festivals. Only four residents hold jobs that might be construed as ordinary occupations.

Analysis of the social and economic structure of Shin-machi reveals two clearly defined status groupings, with marked differences in prestige, power, attitudes toward outcaste status, and systems of interpersonal relations. Individuals generally identify themselves with the group to which they objectively belong (in terms of occupation, wealth, education, house type, and kinship orientation), and they are rated by others as belonging to one group or the other. The terms "upper class" and "lower class" are used here to differentiate them. (The Burakumin themselves make the distinction between "the people down there" and "the people up there," which are not altogether accurate references to the geographical location of lower and upper class dwellings.)

The upper class is composed of 13 households with a total of 75 members, 46 female and 29 male. The residences, many of which are clustered in one section of the village, are typical modern Japanese houses, each owned by its occupant. The heads of the households are usually literate, and several have reached high school. Upper class children have attended school regularly since the end of the war, and most will probably finish high school. Constituted authority in Shin-machi is vested in the upper class, with the headman and his assistant being members of this group.

There is a high degree of occupational stability in this class. All of the trades have been practiced in the households for at least three generations and, typically, a household has only a single occupation, such as drum-maker or shoemaker. In some instances, however, secondary income may be supplied by the employment of unmarried sons and daughters in wine factories and in offices outside the community.

The lower class has a total of 272 persons, 137 males and 135 females, residing in 65 households. The makeshift lower class dwellings, none of which is owned by the occupants, are overcrowded and poorly heated and lighted, thus sharply differentiating them from the upper class houses. Only two lower class individuals have completed the third grade. Though recent educational reforms have tended to increase the school attendance of lower class children, it still remains sporadic, primarily because of inadequate clothing, irregular diet, and prolonged illnesses. Also, ridicule by both teachers and students in the public schools reduces incentives for education; postwar hostility against Buraku children in schools is apparently directed at lower class students, who are distinguished by shabby clothing and dirty appearance.

In contrast to the upper class, the low-income occupations of the lower class are marked by diversity and irregularity. Of those interviewed, 43 of the families receive the major part of their incomes from fur cleaning and processing (12), day labor (17), begging (4), peddling (7), and relief (3). Another ten families claim no employment. Since these jobs are seasonal and part-time, lower class families are generally supported by more than one occupation.

The class division is a fairly recent phenomenon in Shin-machi. Prior to the depression of the 1930's, the Burakumin had been a rather homogeneous and economically prosperous group. Although overt discrimination had been more severe, the monopoly in the fur and leather crafts had assured them an adequate income. During the depression, however, many of the outcastes, especially the animal slaughterers and fur workers, suffered a marked decline in income. The demand for leather goods declined, the prices of traditional handicraft were depressed, and opportunities for outside employment were virtually eliminated. Few Burakumin starved during this crisis, partly because of their reliance upon the meat from slaughtered animals, but many were reduced to begging. Some sold all personal belongings, including houses, household equipment, and clothing.

The demand for fur goods never again reached a pre-depression level, so the majority of those engaged in the fur business have not been able to regain their former living standard. But all outcastes were not equally affected by the depression and many have since become prosperous, so that there are now two sharply differentiated groups, the relatively wealthy and the poor.

At the outset of the research in Shin-machi, it was believed that all the residents were forced to remain in the outcaste community because of the discrimination and prejudice of the larger society. But as our study progressed, it became increasingly apparent that the problem was not simply the relationship of the outcaste group to the larger society, but also relationships within the Buraku. Although the Burakumin are despised and discriminated against, the attitudes, beliefs, and fears of the outsiders do not fully explain the persistence of the community. In response to the external forces and outcaste subordination, Shin-machi has developed internally a distinct socio-religious identity and unity, and a strong set of social, economic, and psychological restraints upon individual mobility.

Community Organization and Social Solidarity

Although Shin-machi is a subdivision of Toyoda City, it is the only district that elects its own headman, holds town meetings, and maintains liaison with the municipal government. These are extralegal functions, not provided for in the postwar city charter. However, they indicate that both the city officials and the Burakumin recognize the "special" (tokushu) character of Shin-machi. They also tend to stimulate community identity and cohesiveness by directly involving community members in local Buraku problems.

The village headman (sonchō) and his assistants (secretary, treasurer, fire and health commissioners, and shrine attendant) handle disciplinary matters within the community, cases of discrimination by outsiders, and such issues as the raising of money for special purposes, collecting taxes, and arranging religious festivals. General meetings, held in the village shrine and attended by at least one member of each household, are called by the headman to discuss village problems and, if possible, to reach decisions by agreement among the villagers.

In addition to sounding out opinion and disseminating information, the town meetings reinforce community solidarity. Few issues are settled at any meeting, but individuals become involved in the problems of the whole community. The town meetings generate feelings of belonging primarily because the problems are unique to the community and, in most instances, directly related to outcaste status. Except for religious celebrations, these meetings are the only occasions when all members of the community assemble for business and entertainment. Large quantities of *sake* are consumed, and status differences and special interests are subordinated to the greater general interest.

The pattern of social control that has developed in Shin-machi is related to its system of self-government. The Burakumin, particularly those at the apex of the power structure, are intent upon concealing from outsiders every aspect of their mores, especially those believed to violate or differ from majority Japanese standards. Stringent controls are therefore exerted upon community members to restrict relationships with the majority society. Public disturbances, lawbreaking, or any behavior that might bring disrepute to the Buraku are discouraged by ostracism, ridicule, and criticism, and even by threats or acts of violence. A person who discusses community affairs with an outsider is treated as a "fink" with pressures comparable to those employed by criminal groups and juvenile gangs in America. These measures obviously stimulate ingroup exclusiveness and set the Burakumin off as a closed subgroup.

Religious affairs also function to integrate the community. These observances, like all public community activities, are held at the Shinto shrine in the center of the Shin-machi graveyard, and are presided over by the headman. Religious celebrations are of two kinds: Buddhist festivals to commemorate the dead, and Shinto or shrine festivals in honor of the local tutelary deities. While the themes differ, the rites are identical, and the overall unifying symbols are those of common ancestry, common territory, and common problems.

On Buddhist holidays the close kinship ties among the members of the community are made explicit by the homage rendered to common ancestors. These bonds are reinforced by community decoration of the graves, and prayers and speeches at the shrine make constant reference to relationships between the behavior of the living and expectations of the dead. Perhaps the most dramatic suggestion of kinship unity occurs during the spiritual interaction between the old men of the village and their common ancestors through a medium at the celebration of *Higan* (a Buddhist holiday commemorating the dead).

At the Shinto festivals, major emphasis is on cooperation and community welfare. The headman reviews past accomplishments and failures of the community, suggests ways to bring about greater realization of community goals, and asks the gods for their protection and good will. The principal concern is the continued well-being of the Buraku.

In every speech and in every prayer mention is made of the community in its relation to the world outside. Some are pleas for greater cleanliness in the village, or for curtailing the slaughter of dogs; others center on the outcaste's low position in Japanese society, or on the cruelty of the world as signified by a particular instance of discrimination. Some orations invoke the intercession of the gods for the attainment of economic success, for the marriage of daughters, and for less discrimination by majority society members. Clearly, the shrine and its gods are the locus of community identification; the religious rites express a system of relationships that differentiate this group from those surrounding it, and give it a distinct socioreligious identity and unity.

During the drinking sprees accompanying the festivals, conversation invariably turns to the common enemy, the outsider. Occupations and poverty, family difficulties and poor living quarters, are all discussed in the context of relationships with the majority. All the fears and hopes expressed in the ceremonials are reiterated in conversation at the sake parties. Songs are often sung in a secret traditional Eta vocabulary (a kind of Japanese pig-Latin used frequently when outsiders are present) with an enthusiasm that reflects the intensity of the individual's identification with the community. The subordinate relationship of the community to the larger society, then, is an essential aspect of the social and religious life of Shin-machi, and it is an important mechanism for maintaining social solidarity.

Social Organization and Patterns of Stability and Mobility

Individual members of Shin-machi are torn between the desire to emigrate and so lose outcaste identity, and the desire to remain in the community, thereby assuring a degree of social and economic security. Since the Eta emancipation in 1871, and probably before, individuals have passed into the larger society. However, the opportunities for leaving the Buraku have become greater since World War II, and this has intensified the ambivalence about remaining in the community. Remaining in the community has so far been the stronger sentiment, and the community has even increased in population from 310 in 1920 to 347 in 1954. A brief analysis of the socioeconomic organization of the two classes may reveal some of the factors underlying this situation.

Upper Class Burakumin

The household is the basic social and economic unit of the upper class. Each household is ideally composed of a man and wife, their eldest son and his wife, and unmarried children. The eldest son inherits the family property, debts, obligations, and occupation. He is also obligated to support his aged parents and to maintain the lineage, and at the death of the head of the household he is bound indefinitely to the residence and trade of his father.

Junior sons in the upper class are encouraged to migrate and seek employment in one of the larger cities. This accomplished, all obligations between the migrant and his family are terminated by mutual consent. When such emigration occurs, outcaste identity presumably is lost and the individual may be assimilated into the general population. Although the position of the younger sons appears advantageous insofar as it enables them to escape the outcaste stigma, considerable anxiety results from the situations into which they are thrust. Outside the community, migrants live in constant fear of discovery, and the consequences for those detected in their attempts to pass are usually disastrous. Several disillusioned persons have returned to Shin-machi after such failures; breakup of marriage, loss of family and job, and sometimes suicide, result from detection in an attempt to pass.

However, one of the greatest sources of frustration for the émigré stems from the still undeveloped wage-earning economy, combined with the pressure of overpopulation. Employment opportunity in Japan is still largely regulated by kinship affiliation and its extension —"The society is no more than an organization of families." [4] The migrant outcaste has no family connections; he has no sponsor and no reference in the society outside his community. Furthermore, in order to lose his stigma it is almost essential that he move to the urban centers, the major underemployment areas of the country into which a vast number of persons from rural areas flow daily.

The social and economic factors that arouse anxiety in the junior sons also tend to reduce mobility aspirations of the eldest sons, whose duty is to remain in the community. Those of upper class families are highly skilled craftsmen as a result of years of apprenticeship in the family trade. If they remain in the community, as they must in order to practice the inherited occupation, they are assured a degree of economic security. The choice therefore lies between abandoning a means of livelihood in order to erase the degradation of caste, and remaining

---

[4] Stoetzel (1955), p. 57.

a low-status Burakumin with an assured means of subsistence. The psychological dilemma is never solved.

The precarious economic balance in the upper class depends upon the regular out-migration of junior sons. The household economy is unable to support an additional individual or family, and the over-crowded housing conditions in Shin-machi make it impossible to shelter new members. Moreover, the Buraku occupational monopolies are so marginal that the addition of a single competitor would seri-ously depress individual incomes. Although mass production in the leather industries has reduced the market for handicrafts, the Shin-machi tradesmen still have a steady if limited outlet for their goods; if these conditions remain unaltered, the upper class Burakumin are assured a regular and relatively high income. The system of out-migra-tion may therefore be viewed as a conscious attempt by the craftsmen to limit competition from junior sons who are potentially new mem-bers of the guild. Consequently, both the guild and the separate families have a vested interest in maintaining the continual flow of individuals from the community.

The upper class attitude toward the elevation of outcaste status also bears upon the emigration pattern. The intensity of their desire to erase all caste barriers cannot be overemphasized. They believe that they have acquired the material symbols and social skills necessary for recognition as members of the Japanese middle class but that they remain in the community because of family obligations, because of the order of their birth. Their interest and effort is focused upon raising the collective status of the Buraku. Members of this class believe that the outcaste stereotype held by the majority society will be modified by changes in the condition of the community. And as the deplorable physical environment of Shin-machi results in part from large population and low income, Buraku leaders feel that a stable population is a major factor in the status enhancement of the whole community. The notion of total caste mobility does not spring from a deep-rooted sympathy with the Burakumin and their problems, but has developed because the leaders feel that they will be able to enhance their own status only by elevation of the entire cast.

The fervor with which the upper class now seeks social and economic equality has coincided in general with the rising educational standard and the decrease in direct discrimination. Prior to World War II, the aspiration of community leaders of Shin-machi was predominantly for simple acceptance by the majority; the role the outcastes were destined to play in the society was conceived as immutable. With the return of the war veterans, the character of the upper class and the pattern of community leadership underwent significant changes. The young returnees were literate, optimistic, and experienced. They were unable to accept the inferior outcaste status based upon tradition, ignorance, and prejudice; rather, they felt that the majority society must eventually regard them as equals.

The recent decrease in the incidence of overt and direct hostility toward the Burakumin has tended to reinforce the new upper class beliefs, since it appears that majority attitudes are now shifting toward greater tolerance. This apparent trend has impressed upper class members with the proximity of their goal of equality, but psychological anxiety has been magnified because the actual status of the Burakumin has not changed significantly, and there are still sporadic cases of discrimination and outgroup hostility.

In order to facilitate changes in majority attitudes, upper class leaders have instituted an improvement program designed to eliminate conditions within Shin-machi believed to be at variance with the prevailing standards of the larger society. Specific improvement is sought in the dirty physical appearance of the community, and in the "barbarian" behavior of certain Shin-machi residents. The former is difficult to eradicate because it is largely a consequence of inadequate housing and overpopulation. However, periodic inspections are made by the health and sanitation officers, and suggestions offered for the improved use of existing facilities. Communitywide cleanup days are held several times a year; and such practices as killing animals within the community and littering the area with garbage are discouraged.

The upper class Burakumin are at least partially aware of the outsiders' conception of them as immoral, criminal, irresponsible, and alcoholic, and they are also aware that such accusations are sometimes justified. There is promotion of such Japanese virtues as maintenance of family obligations, honesty in business dealings, moderation in drinking, and interest in child welfare. Failure to conform evokes gossip, ridicule, and condemnation.

Obviously, the specific improvements desired by the upper class require alterations in the living conditions and behavior of the lower class. But by and large, this class does not act in accordance with the new rules, thereby evoking hatred and disgust from their "superiors," attitudes similar to those expressed by outsiders toward the outcaste. In fact, upper class Burakumin often refer to members of the lower class as "those barbarians," "those dirty people," "beggars," and "Hinin."

Lower Class Burakumin

The social and economic life of the lower class is dominated by the fur and leather processing industry and regulated by a system of

fictive kinship relationships: nearly two-thirds of the lower class households receive a proportion of their income from this industry. One
wealthy and powerful individual, himself an outcaste, has an absolute
monopoly in it, including the allocation of employment and the ownership of all lower class houses—the homes of his employees.

In this Buraku one finds a type of social-occupation-power relationship between this man and his tenants which is in effect a traditional
set of diffuse reciprocal obligations known as the *oyabun-kobun* system, long an essential feature of the socioeconomic life of the lower
class. Knowledge of this system is crucial to the understanding of
community persistence.

The oyabun-kobun (literally, father role—child role) is a system
"in which persons not usually related by close ties of kinship enter
into a compact to assume obligations of a diffuse nature similar to
those ascribed to members of one's immediate family." [5] It is a ritual
kinship generally established by a special rite of passage. Members
address one another by familial terms. Although it satisfies many of
its members' needs, its primary function is the ordering of economic
relationships. It operates in many spheres and on various levels in
Japanese society, and there are a number of variations in its form,
duration, and specific functions.

In Shin-machi the oyabun-kobun institution regulates two interrelated aspects of economic organization: landlord-tenant and employer-
employee relationships. During the depression, a representative of a
large Tokyo fur company loaned money to a number of Shin-machi
inhabitants, as well as to the Toyoda butcher shop proprietors. In
time, the borrowers became hopelessly indebted and were forced to
sell their homes and businesses to their creditor, and a group of
Burakumin thus became dependents of the new landlord, who required them to work for him to pay the high rents he exacted.
Through his financial control over the local butchers he demanded
the hides of all animals slaughtered in the Toyoda area. He now owns
the large leather and fur stores in Toyoda as retail outlets.

By incurring obligations (*on*) to the oyabun, the followers are
pledged to his service; in return, he assumes responsibility for their
support. Because of his control over the supply of hides, his readily
available labor force, and his system of distribution, the oyabun gradually forces the smaller independent furriers into the organization. At
present, all but one of the furriers in the community are his employees,
and he allocates the amount and kind of work done by each. Except
for a few wealthy individuals, all are financially dependent upon him.

The oyabun is the most revered man in the community and there
are innumerable stories of his kindness and generosity. He continues

---

[5] Ishino (1953), pp. 695–707.

to aid the poor with favors and loans, and thereby reinforces his dominant position. The patron is committed to aid impoverished families, to assign jobs to clients in proportion to need, and to assure a certain minimum income to the families under his protection. Because of his wealth and record of generosity, he has created a kind of economic security for the lower class.

The obligations that characterize the oyabun-kobun relationship are a powerful deterrent to mobility, especially when reinforced by financial indebtedness. The oyabun is outside the community class structure because he does not participate in community affairs, and because he is not considered a member of Shin-machi by other members of the community. However, he lives on the periphery of the Buraku, and is regarded by Burakumin and non-Burakumin alike as an outcaste.

The obligation of the patron to assure his followers subsistence is an incentive for individuals to remain in the community. Although several lower class families must resort to begging, and others may occasionally go hungry, it is believed that no one will starve in Shin-machi as long as the oyabun-kobun system exists. The people have faith that any crisis can be met by resort to the patron's benevolence and there is also the possibility that some may gain more than mere subsistence. In addition to the opportunity for at least limited mobility within the occupational hierarchy, there are other possible advantages, such as loans for house repair, clothes, tools, and in one case, the initial investment in a confectionery and wine shop.

Although economic considerations are the major factors inhibiting lower class movement from Shin-machi, the same cultural and psychological conditions exist as those discussed in the preceding chapter. A large percentage of lower class Burakumin would be unable to pass into the larger society because they lack the ability properly to handle social relationships and speech forms outside the community.

Since the Japanese language is a highly respected art and an index of social class, people are most conscious of the variations in dialects and of the kinds of individuals who use them. Upper class urban dwellers, for example, use standard forms, while rural inhabitants speak local dialects, which immediately mark them as rustics. The lower class Burakumin in Shin-machi have a distinctive dialect similar to that spoken in isolated communities in the mountains nearby. They are also distinctive because they are illiterate in a society in which literacy and learning are valued skills. Additionally, their knowledge of correct Japanese behavior is insufficient. Since the way in which interpersonal relations are conducted indicates an individual's background, lower class outcastes are often branded as curious, different, or barbarous. The Burakumin are conscious of differences between themselves and outsiders and tend to withdraw from situations that might demand social interaction with majority people.[6] Members of the lower class generally regard themselves as truly inferior, believing that their position in Japanese society is predetermined and immutable.[7]

Outcaste status for lower class Burakumin is a matter of indifference and acceptance, except when specific questions are asked about it. In general, they are willing to discuss Eta problems, and are even flattered that outsiders will deign to speak to them. Similar questions about the Buraku could never be asked of upper class members, who vigorously deny that there is any difference between themselves and the majority and resent insinuations that such distinctions exist.

Intra-Group Relations: A Summary

In part as a result of the differences among outcastes in their attitudes toward their own status, hostility developed between the classes; the net effect of this has been to increase community solidarity by intensifying intra-group interaction. It has been suggested that members of both groups are constrained to remain in Shin-machi. However, the upper class is mobility oriented while the lower class is characterized by status acceptance and indifference. The upper class is committed to improving conditions in Shin-machi in order to raise the collective status of the Buraku, a program that requires total commu-

---

[6] An example is afforded by the following experience told to me:

A young man left the community to look for employment in Hokkaido, where there is little discrimination against Burakumin. Upon his arrival, he became lonesome because he had no place to go and had no acquaintances in the city. In an attempt to ward off solitude he stepped into a cabaret, but as he pushed open the doors, the hostesses began to laugh. Embarrassed, he immediately returned to Shin-machi. The young man claimed that "the girls laughed at me because they knew where I came from." (Obviously the girls would be unable to distinguish him from any other stranger.)

[7] The following excerpts from an interview with a lower class Burakumin convey this self-image clearly:

Q. Are you the same as common people (heimin)?
A. No. We kill animals. We are dirty, and some people think we are not human.
Q. Do you think you are not human?
A. (long pause, and then) I don't know.
Q. Are the common people better than you?
A. Oh, yes!
Q. Why?
A. They do not kill animals. They do not live here (in the Buraku). They are good people.
Q. Do you think you or your children will ever leave this district or change occupations?
A. No, we are new common people (shin-heimin).
Q. Do you think outsiders will ever come to this village and treat you as friends?
A. No, people on the outside don't like us. Things haven't changed for a hundred years.
Q. Do you believe this is right or fair?
A. (long pause) I don't know; we are bad people, and we are dirty.

nity participation. Since they are not mobile, persons of the lower class either do not comprehend or are unable to respond to the upper class innovations. This refusal or inability to conform to the standards dictated by the community leaders has separated the two groups. Members of the upper class feel disgust, hatred, and embarrassment because of lower class indifference, while lower class members believe that upper class policies are unnecessarily restrictive and unwarranted. If this situation were to exist in a society where both groups were really readily mobile, the differing orientations would either stimulate serious conflict or be eliminated altogether. But since both segments of this community are predisposed toward spatial immobility, the latent conflict is partially channeled into solidarity behavior.

The mechanisms described earlier for maintaining Buraku secrets have been designed and implemented by the upper class, and are directed specifically at the lower class. Cleanup days, sanitary inspections, town meetings, and religious ceremonials are also intended to educate the lower class to upper class conventions. These events, sanctions, and regulations require a high degree of interest and participation by the upper class. Therefore, leadership which might otherwise be directed away from the community and toward tasks more directly relevant to individual or class mobility is oriented toward the internal affairs of the community. Although the motivations of the dominant group spring from a desire for individual status enhancement, the consequence of these drives is to solidify the community by focusing social action on problems of an intra-community nature. The integration thus achieved functions to maintain Burakumin as a distinct and unified subgroup of the larger Japanese society.

CONCLUSION

The social persistence of Shin-machi is determined by a variety of conditions governing both the internal and external social relationships maintained by Burakumin. A sanctioning system exists that is intended to conceal from outsiders many of the physical and social characteristics of the community. These controls engender exclusiveness and prohibit intercourse with members of the majority society.

The socioreligious organization, which is oriented toward the social problems of the underprivileged minority, stimulates ingroup unity and identity. The regular system of Japanese social relations, with its emphasis on obligation, loyalty, and duty, discourages migration.

True mobility aspirations have been inhibited by negative self-concepts, poor education, and the maintenance of traditional occupations. Because of vested economic interests in Shin-machi, the community leaders are oriented toward caste mobility, and are therefore predisposed to remain in the community, and to emphasize stability and unity. Although tensions have developed between the two classes within the Buraku, mutual hostility actually serves to increase the intensity of social interaction among community members.

We conclude therefore that the persistence of the outcaste in contemporary Japan cannot be explained simply by the discriminatory attitudes and prejudices of the majority. Attitudes toward self, the traditional system of Japanese social and economic relations, and the internal structure and organization of the Buraku itself are all essential in maintaining this continuity.

Economically marginal groups in Japan, such as the outcastes of Shin-machi, are often bound internally by close-knit systems of social and economic relationships and characterized by the prevalence of protective, hierarchical, and kinship-oriented institutions such as the oyabun-kobun system and the extended family. These traditional Japanese tendencies, which may develop as adjustments to precarious social and economic conditions, foster ingroup solidarity, dependency, and socioeconomic rigidity. However, a decline has been noted in the importance of "feudal" socioeconomic institutions that has been caused by the recent prosperity.[8] It is possible that if the employment capacity of the economy is expanded, the outcastes may gradually disappear as a distinctive subgroup of the society. But if they continue to remain an economically underprivileged group, they may also remain dependent upon "feudal," protective institutions and continue to reside in Buraku despite possible changes for the better in the majority society's attitude toward them.

[8] Ishino and Bennett (1953).

Chapter 8

JOHN CORNELL

Buraku Relations and Attitudes in a Progressive Farming Community

The following report is derived from field work carried out in Japan from 1957 through 1958.[1] It is focused on four principal issues: how an outcaste farming community is formally and informally related to its adjacent communities economically, politically, and socially; how the majority (or *ippan* Japanese, as they are termed in this area by the Burakumin) view their Burakumin neighbors; how the Burakumin view their own living conditions as a de facto caste community; and how living within an outcaste community generates forces of social cohesion that maintain the community and give it continuity while its leaders seek to liberate it from the disadvantages of its special social status.

Buraku in the same prefecture under quite similar ecological conditions can vary widely in their social isolation and internal cohesion. Nevertheless, a detailed description of one of three types of concentrations found in the vicinity of Okayama City on the Inland Sea in southwestern Japan reveals features common to many outcaste communities. The obvious differences from the communities described in the previous chapters are attributable to the progressive outlook found in the Okayama area.

Okayama City itself contains three distinguishable districts of outcaste concentration. These urban districts (called *chiku*) are less clearly

[1] Adapted in part from the paper, "Outcaste Relations in a Japanese Village," that appeared in the *American Anthropologist*, Vol. 63, No. 2, 1961, and from a subsequent report, "Individual Mobility and Group Membership: The Case of the Burakumin," prepared for the Second Conference on Modern Japan—Changes in Japanese Social Structure—held at Bermuda, on January 19-25, 1963. Basic field research was supported by a Fulbright Research Award through the Chair of Sociology, Kyoto University, 1957-1958, and an American Philosophical Society grant-in-aid.

delineated than Buraku in the suburbs, which remain basically agrarian; movement in and out of the chiku is prompted more often by needs of shelter than by concern with social status. The Burakumin of the largest of these, Mikado, have gradually infiltrated surrounding ippan areas since the war. While certain key features of their special status survive for those remaining (one finds there, for instance, the only outcaste Buddhist temple in this part of southern Okayama Prefecture), it lacks the cohesiveness found in the Buraku outside the city, and it is difficult to construe this to be a community in the same sense as a rural Buraku. It may be assumed that resident families live largely independent of any lasting commitment to the minority community and that members of these family units are often less secure and more oriented toward passing than in the typical nonurban Buraku.

In the Okayama hinterland, greater physical isolation brings about a different type of mobility. Assimilative mobility is rare since geographic Buraku boundaries are well delineated; hence outcastes more commonly move between established Buraku than from the Buraku into undifferentiated areas. Marriages tend to be between Buraku units. Since movement is difficult or impossible to conceal in the rural areas, it is not as frequently attempted. Majority group anxieties about residential infiltration and possible mixing in other ways do not approach the same level as in the urban milieu.

The nonurban Buraku of Matsuzaki, the subject of this chapter,[2] illustrates that lateral movement by itself, when Buraku limits are clearly delineated and maintained, is not a source of inter-caste tension. In the last two or three decades Matsuzaki families have been moving directly across the physical barrier of the Sasagase River into the ippan area of Nakahara. At this point six Burakumin families live in Nakahara, and are no longer administratively part of Matsuzaki. Since this newly resettled group is yet a bit distant from the nearest ippan houses, relations are formally amicable though not intimate: the Burakumin are not excluded from public functions such as a summer outing or the annual party for the fire brigade where participation is based on legal place of residence and not on kinship or identification with an informal neighborhood group. For functions of the latter sort the Nakahara settlers keep their ties with Matsuzaki.

Matsuzaki is especially attractive to the large migratory segment of landless Burakumin in the Bizen area. There is a steady flow of in-migrating surplus laborers from outlying places in search of more stable employment. The drift is from outlying communities where job

<hr>

[2] Matsuzaki was intensively studied by the writer and by sociologists under Yamamoto Noboru of the Sociological Research Center, Osaka Metropolitan University from October, 1957, to January, 1959. Other reports on this field work by the writer may be found in various publications by Yamamoto.

opportunities are relatively scarce, to the urban environs where work is far more readily available, and where it is easier for the unstable, landless, undereducated mass of the Burakumin to support themselves than in the economically more primitive hinterland. Matsuzaki frequently serves as a way station both for those simply moving between Buraku and for those on their way out of caste status.

The economic advantages of Matsuzaki's position near Okayama—within the urban frame but not formally part of the city—is offset by its comparatively impermeable caste isolation. Here and elsewhere in the prefecture the special community is an integral part of the local economy, and its working population is divided between farm and factory work in about the same proportions as in neighboring ordinary communities. But even though one finds that minority and majority persons work regularly together, there is nevertheless little lowering of the physical and social barriers between their home communities.[3]

For contrast, one can observe in this vicinity an even more socially closed Buraku that deviates in no immediately obvious way from its ordinary neighbors, and in particular lacks a slum element that so often is the rationalization for discriminatory attitudes. East Horen is a static unit of eleven households, located several kilometers west of Okayama and adjacent to Niiike, the community made famous in anthropological literature by the volume *Village Japan*.[4] Like Niiike, it consists mostly of moderately prosperous farmers. Being far from trade or industry, Horen people endeavor to raise themselves to the level of the ippan half of their community (known as West Horen) by exploiting their chief asset, their farmland. But the social gulf between the two Horens remains great although the inhabitants are formally courteous and correct to one another. Only the children fraternize; adults associate exclusively in affairs of the entire community and in dealing with higher administrative echelons.

In Niiike, however, the gulf is more properly a chasm, perhaps because both sides are very familiar with each other. Horen outcastes have always worked only as farm laborers in Niiike. Because of Horen's physical compactness and small, static population, old attitudinal barriers are convenient to maintain; there is no particularly pressing reason to lower them—in fact, it is easy to find in the mischievousness of East Horen children fresh behavioral justification for separation. What all such Buraku communities have in common, whether urban, crowded Matsuzaki, or striving, prosperous, but stiffly

---

[3] Yamamoto also worked in three Buraku in Kumayama in the Wake district of eastern Okayama (see especially Yamamoto, *Sabetsu Ishiki to Shinriteki Kinchō* . . . (1959a). In addition to the places herein noted, Cornell made surveys of Buraku in Gonai Village in the Kojima Peninsula and in the vicinity of Takamatsu City.

[4] Beardsley, Hall, and Ward (1959).

rejected East Horen, is the unacknowledged but impenetrable shield of status isolation.

MATSUZAKI, AN URBAN-ORIENTED FARM BURAKU

Okayama City and its environs is on one perimeter of one of the oldest settled alluvial plains of the Inland Sea. On the outskirts of Okayama to the southwest are a series of hamlets or Buraku, both in the paddy-carpeted green valley and on the hills that bind it on all sides but the south. Spreading out into surrounding valleys from the City center one finds settlements characterized by a transitional economy. Occupations in this area are about equally divided between farming and salary or wage employment. These hamlets make up what is called Yokoi village (incorporated into the newly created town of Tsudaka in 1959). At the time of this research the village was comprised of six *ku* or administrative districts. Matsuzaki, the outcaste community, the largest of the hamlets on the valley floor, was historically a separate ku, and continues to be so today even after the recent administrative changes.

In the Yokoi hamlets one finds an occupational dichotomy between peasant farmers oriented toward rural life and workers who commute daily from the village. Matsuzaki similarly has resident farmers and workers in the Okayama labor market, as well as a special group of local merchants serving the outcaste community. Its population remains fairly stable, ranging between 800 and 1,000 persons. Its past can be traced with certainty only to the early nineteenth century, when 36 households were recorded, but we can be reasonably sure that it was originally settled not long after the Bizen Feudatory (*Han*) was established at Okayama early in the sixteenth century.

Unlike the other old and populous hamlets of this area, Matsuzaki is not traditionally associated with farmlands largely owned and tilled by its people. Rather, its farmers, who have usually been tenants in the past, work lands in districts formerly owned by and still identified with other communities. The residential pattern of Matsuzaki, a dense, compact mass arranged on a grid of alleys and paths, shows that it is the largest Buraku in the prefecture, with a population that exceeds 20 percent of the Yokoi total. Such concentration, coupled with crowded living conditions and many petty shopkeepers, mark the outcaste residential area off from ordinary communities in the same village.[5]

Conspicuous size is in part a direct cause of the special character

---

[5] Anyone familiar with the place knows that the people in this densely populated hamlet are—to use the current euphemism—*mikaihō* (unemancipated).

and social complexity of this community; a pressure for living space and a variety of local commercial services give life here a distinctly urban flavor. All of this part of Yokoi is subject to intensive urban influences, but conditions in Matsuzaki are due to a local demand for urban facilities created by a high concentration of people with a limited agrarian base.

Though precise statistics are lacking, the outcaste hamlet has undergone at least two periods of extreme population growth. The first is in the late 1920's and early 1930's when the community received subsidies as part of one of the many nationally sponsored slum clearance and resettlement programs which were then the main instruments of the government's policy to eliminate the outcaste problem, mainly by removing the most glaring problem of overconcentration. The second population spurt came after World War II, and by all accounts this was the greater; it is quite possible that the number of households in Matsuzaki doubled between 1945 and 1958. Even for outcaste communities this was unusual growth, which can be attributed to the peculiar economic attraction to the sizable job market of the Okayama metropolis. On the whole, outcaste communities tend to be relatively larger than neighboring ordinary communities, and in this case special circumstances aggravated this basic tendency. By contrast, neighboring communities in Yokoi appear to have suffered a population decline from about the end of World War I.

The economic basis of the community is not very different from that of the rest of the immediate area; farming is the main employment of about 40 percent of the households and nearly all the rest have at least some land. The role of agriculture is greater than in adjacent ordinary areas; even the very nearly landless are able to obtain a bit of government land in the now unused military rifle range within a few minutes' walk from their homes. Many who cultivate only such minuscule plots are also involved in farming by participation in labor exchange arrangements. The more substantial outcaste farmers devote a greater portion of their household's energies to it than do ordinary farmers in the same area: land-holding and technical improvements have developed rapidly, whereas in nearby communities the trend is toward outside wage employment, leaving farming to the women and to hired help. As important as the economic advantages of full time farming is the social opportunity it affords the outcaste for better status in his own and the outside communities.

As noted in preceding chapters, the most accepted Japanese theory indicates that occupational differentiation was a fundamental cause of the rise of caste-like groups in the eighth and ninth centuries. Certain demeaning and ritually contaminating occupations, which until the end of the Tokugawa era were legally recognized as monopolies of the

Eta, are still the basic industry of scattered outcaste communities. Noboru Yamamoto, a leading Japanese authority, suggests that Eta communities in the Tokugawa era were typically at least self-sufficient in agriculture.[6] Thus, the exclusive specialties from which the outcastes derive their notorious reputation were part time and secondary even then, but were important social criteria for distinguishing them occupationally. An oral tradition survives among villagers that the primary caste specialty of the Matsuzaki outcastes was to serve in the police organization known as the *banta* for the Bizen daimiate, which had jurisdiction over this area. No living resident could be found though who had personal recollection of this fact. There are villagers who recall a private slaughterhouse in the vicinity of Matsuzaki until early in the second decade of this century; the dread and avoidance of those engaged in slaughtering and butchering of animals, a monopoly of the old Eta, are still vividly remembered after these many years by ordinary informants who grew up in neighboring communities.

Modern secondary occupations of Yokoi outcastes, often the major source of income of poorer households, are generally of two kinds: peddling and construction labor. Most of the adult population at one time engages in itinerant selling of goldfish and flowers. While there is no special opprobrium for these vocations nationally in Japan, they do bear the outcaste stigma in Yokoi and are shunned by majority and even by well-to-do outcaste households. Both peddling and construction work normally mean employment outside the village, which reduces the occasions for contact between outcaste and ordinary villagers while at work. Female flower sellers, for instance, go from door to door in Okayama, returning only after the day is almost over. Men are often away from the village for days or even weeks selling goldfish or working on construction projects in distant metropolitan centers.

As Yokoi becomes an increasingly mixed economy and a blend of traditional and modern Japanese culture, the intensity of relations within the village tends to decline. However, contacts between the city and adjacent farming villages are becoming more intense. Orientation to the city for supplies, services, and recreation is a feature of life everywhere in Yokoi; traffic into Okayama is facilitated by a paved highway and frequent bus service. Movement within the village has appreciably declined and local school children and itinerant tradesmen make up the only sizable daily flow between communities. Movement between Matsuzaki and points outside the village is considerably greater than for any other community, not only because of its very large population but because a larger proportion of its people have outside business each day.

---

[6] Yamamoto, personal communication, 1958.

RELATIONS BETWEEN MATSUZAKI AND NEIGHBORING COMMUNITIES

Cooperation in Agricultural Activities

It is in agricultural matters that the village nexus retains its great importance. In any of its hamlets farmers would be severely handicapped without the cooperation of other villagers. In most secondary, nonfarming occupations intercommunity solidarity is neither essential, nor particularly desired. But in each Buraku of Yokoi the nucleus group is made up of those households that support themselves by farming alone; few nonfarmers, even if well off and respected personally, rank as high as the old and substantial farming families.

All the important village-wide cooperative groups are concerned directly with some form of agriculture. These quasi-legal organizations operate as part of the formal structure of the political village and draw their membership from all residents who share the same vocational interests. Cooperative associations are the chief coordinating bodies of village agriculture, and intercommunity relations channeled through them are close, continuous, and inevitable. Most of these relations take the form of periodic meetings of representatives of the farming households of each community, and outcaste farmers are represented in the same proportion as those from other communities. Additionally, in relations within the formal structure of the village, the principle of civil equality is carefully observed; however, outcaste community representatives are always individuals who, save for their social background, are comparable in means and demeanor to other, ordinary villagers.

Matsuzaki farmers also share ownership of and responsibility for three important irrigation systems serving paddy areas also worked by farmers of adjacent Buraku. These irrigation associations are mainly coordinating bodies whose affairs directly concern only a supervisory representative from each community. In-village matters between Buraku touch comparatively few persons in each, usually only the elected officials or those active in public service.

In addition to relationships within the formal village framework, there exist bonds between individual farmers that override the principles of representation by community. Some younger Matsuzaki men who farm full time belong to a society of progressive farmers in which they are brought into frequent close contact with ordinary villagers of like interests. Members of this society meet to discuss mutual farm problems; they occasionally travel together, sometimes on overnight trips, to experimental farms. Yet personal acquaintances and friendships that develop in this way are not extended to the families of the

individuals concerned, and have no visible moderating effect on the
distance separating their communities.

Even when an adult informant was well acquainted from childhood
with someone of Matsuzaki, it was usually an age-group friendship
formed in school or in the Youth Association (Seinendan) and did
not remain active after assumption of adult responsibilities. Those
associations with Burakumin adults reported from formal contexts,
much of the time in meetings on village business through the *yakuba*
or the agricultural cooperative, never seem to warm to the point of
frequent visiting at each other's homes. This isolation is partly due to
a general tendency to deemphasize inter-hamlet contacts in favor of
going directly into the city for marketing, employment, and recreation.

Political Relationships

Village assemblymen in Japan are by law chosen at large, but in
fact they tend to be nominated by one or more local communities; in
Yokoi this practice has a special meaning. There is a continuous power
struggle between the outcastes and the rest of the electorate. Village
assembly candidates are nominated by caucus in their home areas and
voted into office by acclamation. This is possible because of an implicit understanding that there will be no more candidates than numbers of seats to fill. Thus the number of seats held by outcastes is determined in advance by compromise between political factions, and
in the special community there is clear pressure on the voter to cast
his ballot only for his own kind. As for the mayoral office, such are
the realities of the power balance in the village that, despite the relatively greater voting strength of the outcaste community, it cannot by
itself muster a plurality for its own candidate and cannot expect any
significant number of votes from any other section of the electorate.

Politics, like agriculture, acts as a counterforce to the trend of urban
orientation. On the whole, politics in Yokoi is not very spirited and
partisanship is not intense except when the outcaste faction is vitally
concerned. There is an exceptional degree of solidarity among the
residents of Matsuzaki, and the Buraku invariably closes ranks in the
face of external threats. Village politics provide the main way in
which threats to outcaste group security and community survival can
be met and resisted. Outcaste leaders are more than just heads of
affluent farming households with a permanent stake in the community.
Of equal importance is their office in the local chapter of the "Emancipation League" (kaihō dōmei). Some of the most prosperous outcaste
farmers are, in fact, at odds with the leadership or at least politically
apathetic, and the most powerful figure in the community is a non-
farmer whose power is derived almost entirely from the fact that he is

the head of the village Emancipation League and is prominent in out-caste politics in the prefecture.

The League serves as a kind of "shadow government" in the Buraku, its leaders being simultaneously village assemblymen, and its members consisting of all the people of the community. The peculiar dual role of these leaders is most obvious to the rest of the village when there is a local issue that incites the League to action. In 1953, a complex problem concerning the amalgamation of Yokoi with Okayama City arose. The crux of the question was the disposition of the former military rifle range that had been taken over as farmland by many poor outcaste families while remaining nominally property of the national government. As part of the city, the range would revert to the use of the national defense forces; since many outcaste families faced eviction from their tiny subsistence farms, a delegation marched to the village office to demand, under threat of violence, that the assembly reject the planned union with Okayama. The proposed union was ultimately abandoned.[7]

Although outcastes are a political minority in Yokoi, they have suc-ceeded in obtaining veto power over policy that concerns any large segment of their group. The result is paradoxical: the contradictory combination of civil equality and social inequality induces a state of political equilibrium at times of crisis. The Yokoi outcastes' ultimate weapon, force, is unconventional for Japan.

General Social Relationships

Informal contacts with outcastes are ostensibly harmonious in Yokoi wherever villagers come together, as in the schools and shops and in casual encounters in the fields or in dwelling areas. Unlike the practice in many places with large outcaste populations there is no attempt to avoid the outcaste settlement area when the route leads through it, though the casual passerby never seems to loiter. Evidence of tension is rarely demonstrated, but real attitudes are difficult to perceive. Overt incidents of discrimination against outcastes, which appeared with considerable frequency in the Japanese press, are al-most unknown in Yokoi at the present time.

As in most Japanese villages, there are several officially sponsored organizations based on age, sex, and role in the household. Member-ship in such groups is nominally individual; but division of these societies into community chapters limits opportunities for regular con-tact with members of other communities mostly to the elected officers

---

[7] Apparently relinquishing all prospects for joining the city, the village merged with the next adjacent farming village to the north in February, 1959, becoming part of a new "town"—Tsudaka-chō.

of each community group. Adding to the effect of their segmented structure is the obvious decline in the functional importance of these organizations in recent years, a national trend that is aggravated by the extreme occupational heterogeneity in the village.

Although the barriers to marriage and the formation of other familial connections with ordinary people have become important issues in presenting the outcaste problem to the Japanese public, they present no difficulty in Yokoi. The marriage barrier has never been breached and neither outcastes nor majority folk seriously challenge it. However, mixed marriages are not uncommon when a spouse is chosen from outside the village area; these so-called integrated marriages (*dōwa-kekkon*) amount to over 10 percent of the unions registered in Matsuzaki. As a rule, only poor outcastes of nonfarming households marry ordinary people, whom they met and wedded while living in some distant place. In such unions it is likely that both spouses recognized that caste lines were crossed. The attitude in the village toward mixed marriages is uncompromisingly negative; it is assumed that the ordinary spouse in each case was little better than an outcaste, that he had become socially degraded previous to the marriage. Stories in which families are broken or a spouse commits suicide in consequence of the sudden discovery that he is married to an outcaste are steady fare in the Japanese press; these are presented to the public as a major current evil of the outcaste problem. Yokoi villagers look pityingly on any such reported mixed union in which the majority spouse is of at least average economic background, but are indifferent to those in which the non-outcaste is a *rumpen* (rootless) proletarian or a Korean. To the villagers, the tragedy involved in the cases in which families are broken by the outcaste issue is the resulting social degradation rather than the disruption of the marriage. Strong emotional attachment which is often the basis for a mixed married is not regarded as justification for disregarding obligations to maintain family status or strictures against marrying across caste lines.

ATTITUDES OF THE IPPAN VILLAGERS
TOWARD THE MATSUZAKI BURAKUMIN

Okayama is reputed to be a progressive prefecture in its treatment of Burakumin and similar outcaste-like people; the prefecture was the scene of the earliest demonstrations against the rigid Tokugawa restrictions on the Buraku caste and of the first organized efforts to achieve social equality. In Sudaka town and in the hamlets of Yokoi there has been a special effort to educate the public to accept outcastes as equals. A school curriculum designed to instill this attitude in children has been used for years. In spite of educational programs focused on improving the formal and informal channels of communication and contact between members of Matsuzaki and the surrounding area there is still covert evidence of social attitudes based on the traditional stereotypes found in other regions of Japan. The Burakumin of Matsuzaki remain essentially a group apart.

Most usually the rationale behind this "apartheid" is expressed— if at all—in terms of Burakumin being "different," "strange" in an uncomplimentary sense, or because they are devious or "shrewd." Virtually no informant, not even very candid ones, can say exactly why he feels so, except that this complex seems to arise from a variety of cognitive bases, never just one. It is very common for a genuinely cooperative informant to voice the thought, "It's very difficult to explain"; then he will go on to cite things in Burakumin behavior he does not admire.

Only in the immediate vicinity of the outcaste community are directly unfavorable comments heard about Matsuzaki as a whole. The incidence of directly critical responses recedes abruptly beyond the area of the village of Yokoi itself. The more respected and generally the younger an ordinary villager is the more guarded he is in speaking about the Matsuzaki people. There is a significant difference noticeable between the generations; the oldest persons of ordinary background living near the outcaste community are the least restrained in expressing their disdain. The most discriminatory remarks were made by some aged individuals who had spent part of their lives in the United States; they spontaneously equated their feelings about the Matsuzaki outcastes with anti-Semitism, which they had come to know during the time spent in the United States.

In the writer's own interviews of ordinary informants, unvarnished denigration of the outcaste community was relatively rare and certainly difficult to elicit. Repeated attempts to lead innocuously into such expression of opinion were met with guarded reticence. However, allusions to the character of individual outcastes were somewhat less rare and, as a rule, came spontaneously. For example, a young wife ran away from her husband's house in Matsuzaki, and within a few hours the gossip had spread widely through other communities and was being discussed quite freely without the inhibitions which usually accompany references to the outcaste Buraku. It would seem that this choice tidbit was being treated just as if there were nothing special about the persons involved, yet the manner in which it was discussed conveyed the impression that this type of loose behavior was to be expected among outcastes.

Ordinary villagers express their feeling in terms of particular acts attributed to the local outcaste element without giving thought to the more basic social problem. For example, the fact that a number of

Burakumin live from hand to mouth is not taken into account in explaining their notorious criminal record. They are usually blamed when things disappear in nearby communities. A particularly common complaint is that outcastes steal firewood, which is one of the scarcest of local commodities; only the more prosperous farming communities have access to adequate woodlots. Though such theft might be justified by the acute inadequacy of wooded stands, the need of the offenders is not considered in making these accusations. Neither is the possibility that some ordinary person in need of fuel may have committed the theft.

Quite the opposite sort of attention appears in envious references to the apparent wealth of outcaste farmers, who have built many more grape hothouses than their ordinary neighbors have been financially able to do. Guarded, as usual, but strongly implied in some of these references, is that capital for the buildings did not come from honest sources—that is, probably from postwar black-marketing.

Welfare and public works programs for the exclusive benefit of residents of the special community are criticized, in the sense that slum clearance, a public bath, or a public crematory assisted by public funds represents undeserved preferential treatment.[8]

In spite of the formal and informal contact, it is obvious that the ordinary Japanese of Yokoi tend not to discriminate between the individual and the community. The pattern of responses of Yokoi villagers referring to Matsuzaki was impressively consistent. When pressed to expand at length regarding the quality of "strangeness" or difference, regular attitudes toward individuals were not clearly or consistently developed but tended to rely on a characterization of the entire Buraku unit; the image was based on the behavior of some of the lower class members of Matsuzaki. Observers were prone to think of "everyone over there" as rough in speech, crude or brutal in relations with each other, quarrelsome, highly sensitive to insult, born traders, and more "cohesive" than ordinary villagers.

People in this area are very much aware of the standard historical explanations of the origins of the outcaste group, of the descent of contemporary Burakumin from the old Eta. They speak, as a rule, of a Korean provenience originally, yet they differentiate Burakumin from modern Koreans living in Japan, noting that while Koreans are bad, they are not as bad nor as "dirty" (*kitanai*, which can mean ritually unclean) as the outcastes. Generally, however, such language is avoided in Yokoi when specifically directed toward Matsuzaki, and

---

[8] The community bathhouse, built with public money before the war, and the crematory erected in the spring of 1958 by public subsidy, are officially described as open to anyone, but their location in the Matsuzaki settlement and their operation by officials of this Buraku makes them in practice nearly exclusively outcaste facilities.

covert feelings are disguised in complaints of offenses against good taste and society that could be leveled against anyone.

Dietary practices are one of the most resistant kinds of popular dislike of Burakumin in Japan. But in Matsuzaki the only visible peculiarity is the cheap quality of the food. An occasional peddler of tripe visits only a few regular customers; most people either do not have the money for food so different from the daily fare or now consciously reject it as associated with "eta." Some Japanese will still refuse food from a Burakumin, though this occurs more rarely than in the past. In an incident related by a prefectural official of a school, children happily shared tidbits of the lunch of a generous fellow until they learned he was from the Buraku, whereupon all pointedly refused to take any more from him.

Incredible as many of the beliefs are, there is often an indisputable ring of authenticity to them, especially if one has been alerted to expect strange, mysterious, or antisocial acts from Buraku people at an early, impressionable age. In studies by Yamamoto[9] and myself of the age and manner of first exposure of school children in places with stable communities of Burakumin to elements of their image, we found that the young were already aware of the meaning of this social difference and were alerted to the potential difficulties in contacts with Burakumin by the second or third grade level.

The tendency to view outcaste behavior with suspicion, if not outright distrust, is exacerbated by stringent taboos on open discussion of them. It therefore becomes virtually impossible to verify or refute opinions by objective means. Although the average person who seeks to be objective is not rationally disposed to accept such tales, he remains emotionally incapable of ignoring them, so strongly do they pervade the social atmosphere of the neighboring communities.

BURAKUMIN OPINION ON
THEIR STATUS AND LIVING CONDITIONS

Among the residents of Matsuzaki the old feudal notion that they are innately inferior is not consciously held. One gains the impression, nevertheless, that a large percentage of the outcaste community at the present time remains incapable of understanding explicitly the connection between their conditions of life and the social-historical circumstance that their leaders and organizations, such as the Emancipation League, are struggling to alleviate. Relatively few outcastes think in terms of status equality or abstract principles. Few recognize that the very presence of an outcaste community among

---

[9] This problem is discussed by Yamamoto in an unpublished MS (1959b), pp. 51–78.

other hamlets is a continuous latent source of tension. Such individuals prefer to see their grievances in the context of the broad
social problems that are unresolvable until they have been totally
assimilated.

Locally, complaints against specific abuses are rare, and responses of
Matsuzaki outcastes to a questionnaire strongly suggest that consciousness of directly discriminatory attitudes on the part of ordinary
villagers is not an important factor in outcaste relations in the immediate vicinity. Some 29 percent (36 of 124) of the respondents think
they have been subjected to specific discriminatory acts, largely in the
form of uncomplimentary references to their status; less than half of
these instances occurred in the village, and most of the rest took place
during elementary schooling. Furthermore, most respondents (about
69 percent) are convinced that there is no longer need to tell the
children about discrimination against their kind; this may reflect a
feeling that as a result of improvements in living standards in Matsuzaki there is now no difference between the majority and themselves.
The outcastes interviewed are predominantly of the opinion that the
root causes of their social differentiation are their living conditions,
substandard speech, and reputation for rough manners. Attitudes,
then, seem to cluster about the image of their community in comparison with others in the village, rather than about individual reactions
perceived to be prejudicial to their group.

A semantic limitation intrudes upon, and perhaps confuses, the
interpretation of these data: the term sabetsu (discrimination) has
come to have a very precise, stereotyped meaning in reference to the
outcaste group. It is generally applied to overt, emotional, and always hostile acts by ordinary Japanese against outcastes. The structural forms by which Yokoi outcastes are set apart from the rest seem
not to fall within the compass of this meaning of the term, and
Matsuzaki respondents may not perceive the organizational distinctions of heir Buraku as caste discrimination.

There is a diversity of attitudes concerning the broader problem of
how best to achieve final assimilation into the mass of society. The
prevailing attitude of the outcastes is that by dissipating some of the
most obvious "trace" features of their status, such as special occupations, obnoxious behavior, and heavy drinking and pugnacity, they
will be accepted as equals by other Japanese. This view is encouraged
by the Emancipation League, but at the same time 43 percent of the
respondents do not support the aims of the national and regional
outcaste leadership who advocate vigorous reform programs (only
33 percent support them). More seem to prefer to avoid trouble by
letting matters solve themselves gradually and spontaneously. Their
leaders take the opposite, actionist position, and have been able to

arouse considerable support for even fairly violent action against policies that threaten outcaste economic welfare. In sum, the view in Matsuzaki seems to be that shared by ordinary informants: discrimination, or sabetsu, has been conquered; hostility against their status is no longer sanctioned as respectable nor, in fact, does it effectively persist. Yet there is some evidence that this rejection of discrimination as a factor in village relations is only pretended, and discriminatory feeling secretly continues strong.

The Burakumin of Matsuzaki need not be too conscious of prejudice as long as they continue to live within their own community structure. The evidence we elicited might suggest that remaining within the community is a protection for many against what they might experience should they seek to leave.[10]

Acceptance in ippan society probably is greater in urban than in rural areas, but in actual conduct and planning of life the Burakumin investigated demonstrate a decided reluctance to strive for this supposed better life. Although very few respondents are conscious of having experienced sabetsu personally (in seven studies at hand, negative replies average over 70 percent), one can agree with the evaluation of a schoolman in my own study in Okayama that only the intelligent, those comparative few with initiative of their own, truly want to get out. Again, for instance, we find that in a Buraku in the city of Nara some 77 percent of 331 interviewed confessed they would rather stay.[11]

In the countryside, where the opportunities for association with ippan persons are ordinarily fewer and the Buraku is patently more distinctive, there is—even just at the edge of a city—perhaps less realization of the stresses and loss of security that living like ippan

---

[10] There have been research efforts in a number of Buraku to test the general level of satisfaction with living conditions. Studying urban Burakumin in Hiroshima in 1951, Suzuki (1952, pp. 142–70) found that of 82 householders chosen randomly from the rationing list, more than half (61 percent) preferred to live in their Buraku. When asked "If you were to live elsewhere, can you think of any sort of undesirable conditions you might face?," most thought of the personal hardships this would entail.

"Personal relationships would be difficult."

"I would face discrimination."

"Because I am a shoemaker, everyone would know of my Buraku origin."

"It would be hard to get acquainted and people wouldn't help me out."

And so on.

In a companion study of a Buraku in urban Saitama Prefecture, Suzuki (1953, pp. 381–94) shows that outcastes feel strong attachment to their place; some 82 percent of 97 respondents desired to continue to live in the district rather than face the prospect of strained personal relations with ippan neighbors and co-workers. Living inside is not considered a happy fate, yet outside is imagined to be emotionally worse. This is primarily because of the belief that ippan will be at least cold—if not openly hostile—to them. This opinion of itself would seem to have become a minority "self-fulfilling prophecy" for which the proof of experience is only incidental to the fact that it fits their image of the other life.

[11] Nara-ken Minsei Rōdōbu (1953), pp. 60–61.

can bring. Living just at the edge of the city, Matsuzaki residents agree that Buraku life is easier.

When the interviewer asked why, he got more unequivocally positive responses from the majority favoring the status quo than from the minority who preferred the outside. While some of the former showed singular complacency, the bulk of them stressed the emotional and economic security the Buraku affords. A little over 59 percent of those queried stated that they intend to continue living in the Buraku, content there or not.

So far as personal aspirations are concerned, many have permanently cast their lot with the Buraku who feel little satisfaction with it. Should conditions permit successful departure, Matsuzaki respondents strongly desire to leave (by just over 70 percent).[12] Yamamoto sums up the results of these conflicting sentiments: "Most believe that it is better to dress poorly, eat poorly, live with relatives, do any sort of work, but still be able to live; and to be able to avoid the feeling of inferiority in being known as someone from the Buraku." [13]

Assimilationist attitudes of Matsuzaki people were also probed. Above 67 percent favored intermarriage with majority society whenever possible;[14] but at least 80 percent said that they had never considered such marriage for themselves.[15] This approximates the same response Yamamoto got to the same point in four other Buraku in central Japan.[16] Affirmative respondents in Matsuzaki expressed marked idealism, and defended the principle of intermarriage.

"It is only natural because we are the same human beings."

"It will lessen discriminatory feeling."

"All men are equal."

"(It is a good idea) in order to avoid consanguineous marriages."

"(Through intermarriage) discrimination will disappear spontaneously. However, it cannot be done at present."

"Whatever our ancestry, discrimination will disappear by mingling of bloods."

"There will be much more chance for 'love' marriage."

On the other hand, respondents who disapproved did so basically for reasons of personal security.

"There's no need to feel restraint if (one marries) within the Buraku."

[12] Yamamoto (1959a), p. 47.
[13] Yamamoto (1959a), p. 46.
[14] This survey was conducted by Yamamoto Noboru and the staff of the Sociological Research Center, Osaka Metropolitan University in December, 1958, and January, 1959. Some of its results have been published in Yamamoto (1959a) and Cornell (1961); most of the following material is appearing for the first time.
[15] Yamamoto (1959a), p. 47.
[16] Yamamoto (1959a).

"I still can't help feeling inferior (with outsiders)."

"Both sides get along better (by not intermarrying)."

"I would feel ill at ease toward people in the Buraku (were I to marry an ippan person)."

The sense of these reactions is reluctance to take the step while favoring it in principle; intermarriage is seen as a desirable, though distant, objective. Matsuzaki respondents' image of Buraku society is a mixture of pride in some moral standards that are higher than comparable ippan values and embarrassment in others that are lower.

In a point-for-point comparison of the Burakumin with their normal neighbors on a series of 20 value aspects (see note 14), significant divergences were found on 14 of the points. Table 1 is a simplified presentation of the points on which the Burakumin self-image differ sharply from the ippan image. There are few differences in matters

TABLE 1

BURAKUMIN RATINGS OF THEMSELVES COMPARED WITH
THEIR RATINGS OF IPPAN NEIGHBORS

	Percentage Rating on Specific Traits (N = 125)		
	Burakumin	Ippan	No Clear Difference*
Positive values on which Burakumin rated themselves higher			
1. More cooperative with neighbors	89.6	0.0	10.4
2. Work harder	87.2	0.8	12.0
3. More respectful to ancestral dead	55.0	4.0	41.0
4. Generally more cooperative in collective enterprises	48.0	9.6	42.4
5. More deferential toward persons of status	37.6	8.8	53.6
6. More other-oriented than self-oriented	32.0	21.0	47.0
7. More filial	28.0	5.6	66.4
8. Prefer arranged to love marriage	19.2	2.4	78.4
Positive values on which Burakumin rated Ippan higher			
9. More standard speech habits	8.0	53.6	38.4
10. Better reared and educated	2.4	46.4	51.2
11. Daily lives more rationally planned	3.2	31.2	65.6
12. Better, more tastefully dressed	13.6	23.2	63.2
13. More hygienic habits	13.6	20.8	65.6
14. Observe proper relations between the sexes better	4.0	16.8	79.2

* A large number of ambiguous or ambivalent responses ("both about the same") are combined in the third column.

of family (*iegara*) and lineage loyalty, nor is there appreciable difference in the relative position of the spouses in the household. No discrepancy is seen in deference to authority in the Buraku and village levels.

Pointed differences do occur with respect to form of marriage; Matsuzaki thinks of itself as adhering somewhat more closely to the conservative *miai* (arranged marriage) pattern (in actuality, incidence of *renai*—"love"—marriages is higher among them). In contrast, they recognize as a moral flaw their propensity to coarse and even violent behavior. The Burakumin regard their stealing and reputation for acts provoking fear in others as another serious character flaw.[17] Equally as serious, in their eyes, is their association with occupations that are not only different but which are regarded as morally unclean (*kitanai*).

In summary, we can see that not only are there hazards, real or imaginary, for the Burakumin in associating with the majority world, but the psychological burden would seem to be a serious deterrent to the individual venturing alone into outside society. He has a sense of loyalty to his group which, though widely deprecated on moral grounds, he feels has many moral virtues worthy of his respect.

The individual often sees the Buraku as affording no more than a tolerable life condition. Most of its residents appear to accept the premise that life therein can never be happy. One of the younger, firmly committed leaders of the Matsuzaki community, for instance, observed that "everyone hates the place." He could, however, see nothing to be done about this short of moving everybody out, and this, he commented, would be a prohibitively costly undertaking. The only immediate solution is to improve living conditions inside.

Similar discontent is reflected in answers to the question: "If conditions permitted, do you think that in general it would be better to leave the Buraku and live among ordinary people?" Some 71 percent prefer to leave, while about 13.5 percent reject the idea.

Resentment is never against any specific feature of the community; complaints about the limitations of the minority role refer to the whole entity construed as a complete, if miniature, social universe. Its coercion is felt most keenly in the lack of economic opportunity, in the relatively humble—even dishonorable—occupations the Buraku imposes. A sense of personal helplessness is mirrored in statements bearing on wage employment in unmistakably Burakumin "trace" callings, those which in the vicinity involve none but Burakumin. Because these do offer a better livelihood than farming, which, though respectable, is often marginal, many persons are unhappily drawn into their orbit.

The occupational structure of Matsuzaki is very complex. While

---

[17] See Yamamoto (1959a), p. 53, Table 12.

classic "untouchable" callings have now almost disappeared, residual discrimination has by analogy adhered to any menial work that becomes economically popular among Burakumin. Today, such activities are mostly those associated with a floating labor force. Seasonal peddling, the commodity varying with the time of year, and construction labor under labor contractors include the more important ones. Embarrassment in being identified with these occupations is softened somewhat by going away where the minority connection is unknown. Even so, employment in these lines usually depends on some sort of collective organization based in the Buraku. Purchasing and sorting flowers, for instance, is frequently done cooperatively through a group of neighbors; hiring of young men for construction jobs, usually in one of the large cities, always occurs through arrangement with a local labor recruiter. The most marginal segment of the outcastes, therefore, is dependent on the community to exploit their only marketable asset —themselves.

We can no more than selectively explore the range of social and economic dependency relationships of the individual to the community. Whether he works as a farmer or a shopkeeper within the community or whether he normally works as a peddler or laborer outside, he is a member of certain social structures of the Buraku. These comprise his meaningful dependency attachments, and the most meaningful of these are larger collectivities than the family, such as class, informal neighborhood groupings, instrumental voluntary associations, and the politically influential chapter of the Kaihō Dōmei.

SOCIAL COHESION AND
PATTERNS OF GROUP PARTICIPATION

The commitment of the outcaste to the Buraku and his rationalization for preferring the security of its in-group relationships as against the ambivalent attractions of the ordinary society is discussed elsewhere in this volume. Better than most contemporary Buraku, Matsuzaki represents what the community means as the focus of caste to the individual, for its location in the suburban fringe of a sprawling urban center brings together features of both the self-contained rural Buraku and the widespread lateral mobility induced by urbanization and industrialization.

As a minority member each Burakumin normally finds his most meaningful dependency relationships to the group through his community, and this dependency is expressed more powerfully in some ways than others. We shall limit ourselves to examining the special forms of cohesion within the Buraku in the case of Matsuzaki, stressing particularly the integrative role of the leadership elite who through strong identification with group advancement make an adjustment that satisfies achievement and power needs within the community in a way not possible by individualistic passing into the majority society.

It is evident that over the past century, in Matsuzaki as elsewhere in Japan, social relationships have shifted from *gemeinschaft* types, such as family and lineage (*kabu*) to those of *gesellschaft*, emphasizing a rational means-ends orientation around particular economic, political, or social problems. More than a century ago, probably no one resided in the Buraku unless he belonged to one of its five great lineages. The authority of these kabu or "stocks" faded slowly; even as late as 25 to 30 years back a newcomer's position in the community is said to have been insecure if he were accepted into a kabu. Today the influence of the kabu has shrunk to a vague recollection of common descent and a weak feeling of kindredship indifferently maintained by rites to an ancestral god (*ujigami*). Comparatively few continue to keep the festival days of the god, many do not know the location of its shrine, and some younger persons are not aware that their family ever had a kabu relationship. Modern kabu relationships also show curious deviations from the descent-group norm; for example, we find that sometimes one derives kabu affiliation from the wife's side when the couple resides in a house belonging to her kin, while his children by a former wife belong to the kabu of his parents. Insofar as they survive in the present day, kabu seem to be assuming the character of units of common residence instead of common descent.

Kabu-uchi (kabu members) help each other by allocating functions within the group incidental to conducting death rites and disposal of the dead; the kabu may act defensively to protect a member in trouble with the law. But, as one older informant put it, "kabu-uchi help each other but they are not so important as 'relatives' [*shinzoku*]. Unlike blood relatives or neighbors, they do not offer mutual aid in everyday life."

Rules of inheritance in Matsuzaki are generally weaker than in neighboring ippan communities. Primogeniture tends to be modified by the principle that the parents live with the son they get along with best or who most needs their continuing support after marriage. One form this takes may be termed ultimogeniture, that is, a younger son inherits the house and the largest share of whatever farmland there is. Or it may result in a reverse sort of branching, the parents and a younger son breaking away to establish a new household, leaving the eldest in possession. Reasons given by informants for this practice are couched mainly in interpersonal, rather than clearly economic terms; for instance, the parents seek to avoid in-law tensions with the first son's wife, which is frequently cited as a very worrisome family problem. If a younger son has financial difficulties because he inherits so little property, the parents find it easy to move in with him adding their earning power to his. Since the total amount of land available for division in most cases is quite small, economic consequences of fission are minor as compared to interpersonal relations when the parental unit breaks up.

In default of strong family ties, one turns to association with friends of similar interests and to close neighbors, especially those whose houses face the same narrow section of alley. In the most crowded, indigent slum neighborhoods, among the most meaningful relationships of daily life appear to be those of the neighborhood, taking the form of frequent visiting and casual loitering in chattering groups in the alley; where a neighbor operates a tiny street stall, there may be found spontaneous work bees and knots of baby-sitters. In the solitary neighborhoods (where family continuity is correspondingly lowest) people are ambiguous about connections with true kin but express a positive preference for intimate neighbors, whom they think of as "our relatives."

As an agricultural community, Matsuzaki has a formal structure of instrumental associations, such as the *fujinkai* (women's association), the *seinendan* (youth association), the *nōgyō-iin* (agricultural liaison committee), and the *PTA-kai* (school P.T.A.). Because of their sponsorship by national groups they will continue, although they enjoy no great amount of popular support.

On the other hand, truly voluntary associations provide active, popular community relations. Predominantly, these are the type known as *kō* (in the vernacular, *kōai*). Membership in them is often hereditary. Most kō operate basically as religious ceremonial groups, offshoots of popular Buddhism. Other kō combine a financial purpose with pietism; the *Ise-kō,* for example, is a mutual aid society which provides travel expenses for pilgrims to Ise. The familiar *tanomoshi-kō* is the only one that is completely secular, serving as a cooperative credit society. There are reputed to be 20–30 of these in existence, with 30–60 members apiece. Each such ko meets one or more times a month to bid for loans from a common fund. This style of kō has a particularly weighty effect on community solidarity; unlike the religious ceremonial kō, however, participation in them is largely limited to families who are able to bear the 300, 500, or 1,000 yen contribution required at each bidding session. Families most affected are of at least the middle stratum of the Buraku.

The poorer, indigent families lack the means to join kō, but turn instead for support to the more informal assistance of neighbors and kin. They also rely on the tolerant attitude of village authorities toward squatter's rights on unused public lands adjacent to the settlement, and they reap the most benefit from public welfare and work programs.

For all residents of the Buraku, but especially for those who are dependent on nonagrarian pursuits, the fact that Matsuzaki is favored by special public subsidies as a special community is an important stimulus to its collective solidarity. Originally intended to offset the inequality of Burakumin living standards, they have become a permanent part of the fiscal structure of the community. In our survey, a majority of the sample (53.6 percent) enthusiastically approved continuation of these subsidies, while only a small dissenting group (15.2 percent) saw it as a way of aggravating sabetsu. When equally needy normal communities in the village do not receive such subsidies, it is recognized by these few that a feedback of jealousy and resentment may result. Overwhelmingly, though, the bad effects of preferential treatment are felt to be morally offset by the proportionately more desperate needs of Burakumin. Not even these dissenters doubt the justice of the Buraku receiving this open charity; withal, they leave little doubt that the dogma of poverty occupies a central position in the Burakumin self-image.

Buraku Solidarity and the Kaihō Dōmei

Irrespective of family and lineage, occupation, or personal aspirations, physical presence in the community exposes an individual to serious collective pressures to conform; and the points of conformity are to be found in the articles of faith of kaihō dogma that are preached and enforced by the Kaihō Dōmei. The moral and social pressure of the kaihō cause probably contributes significantly to the effectiveness of Dōmei control in Matsuzaki, and position in the Dōmei is one of the primary areas into which individual ambition and initiative is easily channeled and sublimated. (Another area is the practice of modern agriculture.)

The presence of a chapter of the Dōmei organization in Matsuzaki was approved by a majority who regarded it as the only effective advocate of their minority cause and the single best means of uniting them in the struggle for kaihō. Yet there were more who approved of its goals than of its methods; a common complaint was that it is too radical, too much given to violence. Some also felt that the very aggressiveness of the Dōmei tends to heighten discrimination by publicizing and reviving hostility at a time when they are supposedly ceasing to be a serious problem. In Matsuzaki there has been some disillusionment with its head-on approach because of the tensions and hostility caused a few years ago when it vigorously attacked the proposed merger of the village with Okayama City. The motives in this case were fear of losing the privilege of cultivating public lands under a lenient village administration and the probability that incorporation into the city would deprive the Buraku of its balance of power position in village decision-making.

The leader (*kuchō*) of Matsuzaki and its village councilors (*sonkaigiin*) are also officers of the local Dōmei. Very few respondents alluded to this fact. Some adverse comments were obtained about one or two councilors using their position for personal profit, but the consensus is that these are the best men for the jobs. The criterion of unselfish public service is the key to the selection of leaders. Outstripping all others in popularity is the headman himself, who is the chief of the Buraku Dōmei and, in fact, an important prefectural functionary of this organization.

This central figure is surrounded by a small and close group of intelligent, usually better educated and more worldly younger men who hold effective control in the community. Such individuals may be thought of as an elite. However, as one of these men remarked, the elite are in no sense the headman's *kobun* (henchmen); they are united by mutual concern for the kaihō movement. While men of this sort might be expected to attempt private escape by passing, once committed either economically, socially, or both, such persons are bound more tightly to the community than the average. There is a paradox here: those who are leaders, either for or against the kaihō movement, are by personality and intellect more susceptible to the lures of individuation within the larger society; but where the issues of kaihō enter, they are morally bound to work with the group.

Individuation Among the Leadership Elite

The average person in Matsuzaki appears to shun individualistic goals. This type comprises the mentally inert, usually economically harassed bulk of the community. These residents have almost no concept of their social dilemma as Burakumin, nor of what they personally might do to overcome it, beyond the immediately personal problems of getting along day by day.[18]

The elite, though, are mainly a group apart in thought and action. There are actually two types in the community, both aware of the broader social implications of their status: at the one extreme are the kaihō leaders and at the other its chief opponents. From these come the most rational, self-assertive, and aggressive members of the community; they are usually qualified to become an official of the Buraku, but whether they do or not depends upon their position on kaihō. Let

[18] As one informant said, "They are like frogs in a well who think that the whole universe is the water in which they live" (*i-no-naka no kawazu taikai wo shirazu*).

us think of these as the "pro-Dōmei" and "anti-Dōmei" factions. The pro-Dōmei elite provides Matsuzaki with most of its effective leaders through the activities of the Dōmei, and these form a shadow government, apart from their official functions at the village and Buraku levels. The smaller anti-Dōmei faction comprises the only real independent voice raised against the stewardship of the Dōmei.

Politics and public service through the Dōmei is one of the principal ways an individual can serve his own purposes; he acquires prestige and power through his close identification with the Buraku and all it represents. It can be argued that public service in the political field is not the most logical way to exercise personal ambition, and particularly not in a special community where solidarity compacts are especially strong. Yet in Matsuzaki there seems to be a need for the concentration of power in a prestigious few. In the past, the power concentration lay with the entrepreneur-dealers who traded in special Buraku products, or in powerful landlords; but now there is a coterie of political actionists who ride the Dōmei to power. In prewar days there existed here what amounted to an oyabun or "boss" but since the war no single leader has attained this role.

The Dōmei is not an obtrusive feature of the Buraku structure; unless there is some overt crisis in relations with the ippan segment of the village it is normally quiescent. But its influence through the dual or shadow role of its officers, as elected public officials, can be felt at all times.

It seems probable that a new set of values, of a secular, rational character, has come to hold sway in the past several years, during almost the same period in which the Dōmei has enjoyed a return to postwar power. Leaders exhort against acts of conspicuous waste in private spending for funerals, weddings, and the like, and the habits of gambling and drinking. Family planning, economizing through community sponsorship of periodic Buddhist memorial services for the dead, and community services primarily for the underprivileged have gained in value. For example, even those who have baths at home are pressured toward patronizing the community bathhouse. Sanctioned norms in the community, then, tend to favor the viewpoint of the Dōmei, and their most vocal advocates are its leaders.

Influential people are found principally among the 60 to 70 substantial farmers (claiming agriculture as their only gainful occupation) of the Buraku's upper class. These individuals also form the nucleus of the so-called *sengo-ha* (postwar generation) clique of progressive farmers. A core group of these young men began as early as 1948 to participate in a village "Good Farming Society" (Kō Nō Kai). Attracted by the society's interest in experimental farming methods that could increase output, they were the main agents in bringing about a minor agricultural revolution. Through their pioneering interest the possibilities of hothouse cultivation of grapes captured the imagination of fellow farmers, many of whom, thanks to the Land Reform, were landowners for the first time. By 1954, their efforts in converting former *hatake* to hothouse use had induced about half the community's full-time farming families to build hothouses of their own on borrowed capital.

Agriculture has generally declined in the postwar economy of Yokoi village, but in Matsuzaki not only has the Land Reform provided many former tenants with land of their own, but the impact of this redistribution on the livelihood of each household has been still more revolutionary.[19] Farmland, previously transmitted to heirs only as a customary tenancy right, now has become private property. The post-Reform cultivator is free to vary the use of a specific plot in order to take advantage of new agricultural technology and the changing demand for agricultural products. There has been a decided movement away from the established sequence of summer paddy rice and winter wheat or barley to dry-field growing of special or luxury crops, including grapes, melons, and strawberries.

As a vehicle of private ambition and advancement, modern scientific agriculture has no rival today in Matsuzaki. The Buraku elite, nearly all farmers of this stamp, exhibit more independence of action, more initiative, and more individualistic motives in farming activities than in any other pursuit. The potential economic advantage of modern farming is felt to be high, and it is recognized that the collective efforts of this small group of elite young men have made possible both the new techniques of luxury crop production and the capital to convert fields to hothouse and truck-farming uses. This clique has a strong sense of collective obligation to the whole farming element of the community. They feel they should encourage adoption of these new agricultural practices as well as to help arrange loans for others.[20] Alert

---

[19] Total land in cultivator ownership in Matsuzaki was a little more than doubled by the Land Reform, from approximately 54 to 108 acres.

[20] Such leaders feel their obligation to the group stops at getting new producers started and working together to process and market the crops. The minute details of grape culture, for instance, how to correctly trim leaves and buds, the effects of weather changes on the plants, when to spray, how much fertilizer to apply, and the like, are matters the individual producer must learn for himself through experience and by careful record-keeping. The usual feeling is that these are competitive secrets (*hiden*) with which the clever, resourceful person may outstrip his fellows without social disapproval. A rather forceful illustration of this occurred during my study in Yokoi. Led by a ranking member of the sengo-ha clique, who is a village councilor and an officer of the Dōmei, a few of the most progressive farmers asked that I help them master a difficult new production "trick"; it was a secret process of quick-freezing muscat grapes so they might be kept in a fresh condition for up to six months beyond the harvest when, of course, prices could be expected to rise to a peak. This spokesman pointed out that it was rumored that such a process was currently in use in the United States. I was asked to seek in-

to the more competitive new lines of agriculture, they search for a technical breakthrough in any untried but promisingly lucrative field.

Such enterprise is not characteristic of all the independent farming class. Typically it seems to result when dependence on full-time farming is combined with above average education and relative youthfulness. The pull of individuation on the Burakumin is largely confined to achieving minimal freedoms. Unless he is able to pass, at best a risky business for all but the most highly qualified in terms of native ability and education, he cannot expect to realize these freedoms himself. They may be desirable objectives, but there exists a great discrepancy between these idealized minimal goals and those he knows are reasonably attainable. The limited occupational mobility of Japanese society puts a premium on complete personal freedom for anyone; the younger son, the marginal cultivator, or any other who is tenuously committed to the community incurs a liability of insecurity. But the economically unstable Burakumin resident is freer to move from one outcaste Buraku to another, freer to seek romantic attractions, and freer to achieve the highly valued ideal of intermarriage with an ippan person.

The Burakumin elite, on the other hand, can rarely afford such freedoms. His obligations to the community and the caste militate against the minimal freedom of relative physical mobility. He is more a prisoner of his caste than his less-favored proletarian fellow who, lacking an adequate land base and the family position requisite for leadership, is allowed greater flexibility in making critical life choices. Inheritance patterns also favor the economically less secure individual; inheritance practices are least consistent and loosest at the lower social strata, more consistent, tightly lineal, and prescribed at the highest stratum.

This commitment causes the elite member to channel and modify his personal striving for economic advantage in line with the restraints of Buraku life. Modern agriculture, as we have seen, is a major area of private ambition. Another area more closely keyed to total, or lifetime, commitment to the community is leadership under the banner of kaihō actionist policy. While here motives of personal achievement are closely related to general values of Japanese individuation—recognition gained through personal effort, maximum freedom from group control, and increased reliance on firm, rational approaches to

formation from the Department of Agriculture and other sources in this country. My American sources did send helpful information but it turned out that, as of 1958, the quick-freeze process had been tried only experimentally with mixed results. The technical papers sent me were eventually translated and placed into the hands of the Matsuzaki growers. The knowledge that a grower in the northern part of Yokoi had already mastered the secret, which he was said to be guarding closely in order to capitalize on off-season demand, prompted this somewhat dramatic request for technical assistance.

situations—the elite's efforts to realize these values is in fact intensified by collective orientation toward the Dōmei organization.

The elite who make up the nucleus of the Dōmei would seem to represent the crystallization of the hopes and goals of the larger universe of Buraku residents. Or, to put it in another way, what the elite want and what they do would seem to set the tone of individuation as it is visualized and permitted within the restraints of outcaste society.

CONCLUSIONS AND DISCUSSION

Recent research in the Okayama area suggests that the modern descendants of the Eta are not easily distinguishable as a separate Japanese subculture, for communities of outcastes articulate with society in a manner that does not deviate basically from the normal patterns of the area. Residents of such communities all over Japan do make up the largest of the native minorities but, unlike most minorities, they are as fully integrated as any other segment of Japanese society, although in certain unique ways. The ways of life of any local group of outcastes are very similar to the culture of the locality. The validity of this point becomes greater with the passing into disrepute of traditional caste occupational monopolies.

One of the most difficult and yet most vital problems in studies of modern outcaste groups is to determine the actual components of the outcaste complex: the sets of values and socioeconomic features that may be used to characterize "outcasteism" anywhere in Japan. However, there is no effort in this chapter to approach the problem in such a broad perspective.

A need for basic empirical data, primarily a need for more direct study of communities, has prompted most of the increased research interest in the outcastes since World War II. This is a radically new approach for social research in Japan because of the previous stringent taboo on field studies of outcastes per se which previously prevailed among Japanese social scientists. In reviewing recent studies, interest seems to center on two levels. The first is associated with the "outcaste problem." Among the Japanese, public understanding of the meaning of "outcaste" is confined mostly to this horizon since few have direct knowledge of the Burakumin and how they live. On this level modern heirs of the old Eta status and its stigma are viewed by their sympathizers as a downtrodden minority whose persistence into the present age constitutes a pressing national issue to be debated in terms of flagrant social injustice.

The other level of study is concerned with local segments of outcaste society—the so-called "special" communities. Studies at this level present a sharp contrast to the work of earlier scholars whose interests

were largely historical and folkloristic. The method of the new research has been broadly that of "social research"; the hazards of field
relationships for the native that lie in the intensive and personal methods of anthropology are probably responsible for the fact that this type
of research is left largely to a few foreign students.[21]

Research problems are palpably different in the macrocosm of
national issues and the microcosm of the community. In the former,
attention turns heavily to institutional relations, to concerns of social
and economic way by which the emancipation can be practically implemented. These concerns are popularly expressed in exhortative
catchwords such as "emancipation" (kaihō) and "integration" (dōwa).
Today these have become rallying points in a struggle for equality
under the aegis of national and regional action organizations within
the structure of the National Emancipation League, which has been
likened to the American N.A.A.C.P. Objective detachment is rare at
this level. Reform issues roughly divide their partisans between two
major courses: the indirect approach inspired by a national policy of
subsidizing projects to improve living conditions in outcaste communities and to encourage better career opportunities; and the direct
approach of the Emancipation League, which is committed to sweeping social changes through political means.

Factionalism among the outcastes themselves, which stems from the
same polar disagreement as to the means of alleviating the problem,
suggests that Burakumin political unity on the national level is more
a desired state than a realized condition. Although the direct action
forces probably have an overall majority, their local strength varies
from pervasive influence in such an area as Wakayama Prefecture to
very moderate support in rural parts of Okayama Prefecture.

At the local level, however, internal affairs and relations with non-
outcaste communities are not normally met in terms of these divergent
opinions; here there is mainly a high echelon policy struggle over how
best to allay discrimination and segregation. Outcaste relations in the
village are more dependent on fitting Eta status traditions to particular local conditions and on the presence of a well established outcaste
element set apart by residential restrictions.

From our studies it is apparent that a latent state of tension exists
in Yokoi Village because of the presence of the people of Matsuzaki
Buraku. This state is heightened by the cohesive character of the outcaste community itself and by a developed minority group consciousness, at least among the leadership of this community. This tension is

[21] The only published reports of direct field studies are by Donoghue (1957) and
a preliminary statement of field conditions in another area by Cornell (1960). Important reviews of current outcaste conditions based on some field experience, and
which are anthropological in character, are Smythe (1952) and Passin (1955).

normally checked by the formal village structures that regulate contact and cooperation among the Buraku of the village. Relations of outcastes with ordinary Japanese outside the village cannot be affected by these purely local controls, but they also seem to be unresponsive to the forces of social reform that are working at the national level. The effectiveness of these intra-village restraints on the outcastes is dependent upon the existence of a distinct community entity; they are dependent to a much less extent upon genealogical descent and caste origin. Thus, a resident of the special community is treated locally as an outcaste regardless of family background. At the local level, the village Emancipation League has the same aims as the regional and national bodies, but in the village it has only brought about a social and political stalemate.

Historically and logically there have been two major approaches to studies of the relations of the outcaste minority to the majority in Japan. The first, represented by "tension" studies, resulted in a series of inquiries into prominent nexuses of tension in Japanese life; papers on outcaste groups stressed attitudes and other interpersonal responses.[22] In this and later work by Japanese, the unit of study has been a group equivalent to a community, but national and political as much as sociological references were used to interpret these phenomena.

The less favored approach is that of a structural analysis of the outcaste community unit and of its formal relation with immediately adjacent sectors of the whole society. Donoghue, in his chapter in this volume, saliently recognizes that the persistence of segregation in "special" communities can reasonably be explained in terms of internal factors, most of which are responses to the immediately contiguous milieu of ordinary society. My position is in basic agreement: discriminatory attitudes, "self-fulfilling" biases, and inter-group tensions are made to flow within and to support the local system of minority-majority relations by mechanisms within the Buraku or those that directly connect it to majority communities. Superficial observation of interpersonal relations in Yokoi does not provide prima facie evidence of the degree to which discrimination survives and of the extent of the isolation and deprecation of the outcaste. No discrimination occurs in the village except by direct reference to the spatially defined segment which is the Buraku.

Research at the community level suggests strongly that efforts at reform through a uniform program administered from the national level cannot be successful when applied to variant sets of local conditions. It is a matter of largely historical and philosophical interest that outcaste social position seems to have received much of its char-

---

[22] Nihon Jimbun Kagakukai (1953).

acter, if not its impetus, from the disavowed ideology of ritual impurity related to certain positions and occupations. It is equally irrelevant to the study of the community microcosm to think of it in terms of a minority whose distinctive social handicaps are based solely on economic hardship and relative lack of opportunity in modern industrial Japan. This is very close to the position taken both by the government and its social welfare programs and by the outcaste leadership itself: that given the same economic opportunities as everyone else, Burakumin can rise from their low caste position spontaneously. This is to explain the effect in terms of its cause, for the characteristic poverty and underemployment of outcastes throughout Japan seems to be symptomatic of conditions arising out of residential segregation. When this is coupled with the relative immobility of Japanese society, the phenomena inherent in outcaste status tend to be perpetuated.

A formula for the emancipation of Burakumin that will work in all the several thousands of their communities in Japan is probably nonexistent. It is better to understand that each community contains its own accommodation to the outcaste status and therefore to the nationwide problem of emancipation. Primarily it is because of the restriction of certain families thought to be predominantly of Eta extraction to traditional communities that caste difference and segregation in Japan are today known and preserved.

Chapter 9

EDWARD NORBECK

Little-Known Minority Groups of Japan

The indigenous population of Japan has long included many small minority groups other than the Eta-Hinin, the Koreans, and the Ainu.[1] These groups are socially distinct from the Eta and Hinin but share with them various circumstances and characteristics that put them outside the majority population. Although generally fading, some of the groups persist today.

The definition of caste is applicable to these peoples. Until their dissolution as distinct social groups began, all appear to have been endogamous. When intermarriage did occur, it was principally between members of similar minority groups. All practiced distinctive occupations, sometimes multiple, and little social mobility was possible. The general population commonly regarded them as social inferiors similar to, though less base than the Eta.

Information on most of these groups is scanty, especially concerning their present conditions of life; this is not surprising as they have long been few in number and lacking in national importance. Data on the number of people who are currently members of the groups are not available, but the total is probably not more than thirty or forty thousand persons, a figure that indicates a sharp reduction during the past century. Although comprising only a tiny and shrinking part of the Japanese population, these non-Eta minority groups provide valuable information on social and racial prejudice. They may also be interestingly compared with the Eta, whose history is generally similar but who will probably be much more persistent.

[1] I am indebted to Habara Matakichi, Ishizuka Takatoshi, Noguchi Takenori, and Ōtō Tokihiko for useful information given in personal communications, verbal and written. I am also thankful to Harumi Befu and Mimi Cohen for their aid in the preparation of this paper.

Virtually no data in European languages are available on these minorities. Relevant published writings by Japanese scholars are fairly abundant, but they tend to be brief, fragmentary, and to present little information on contemporary circumstances. The data given in this chapter are drawn principally from the Japanese accounts, field research by the author in 1950–1951 and 1958–1959, and oral and written communications with Japanese scholars. Despite many gaps, materials at hand are adequate for a general account and some observations relating to problems of minority groups in other parts of the world.

For convenience, non-Eta minority groups will be described under a simple classification that embraces most groups, although definitive histories or ethnographies cannot be given. Local names and dialectic variants of names for these peoples are abundant but the English classification here refers to occupational specialties: migrant marine fisherfolk; woodworkers; hunters; ironworkers; riverine migrants; quasi-religious itinerants; miscellaneous groups in secular occupations.

HISTORICAL OCCUPATIONS OF MINORITIES

Migrant Marine Fisherfolk

Excluding the Eta-Hinin, the largest surviving group with minority status consists of marine fishermen who until recently were migrants who lived on their boats. Japanese scholars conventionally refer to these people as *Ebune* (houseboat), a term used principally in Kyushu. Dialect variants are *Efune* and *Embu*. In Oita Prefecture, similar peoples are called Shā, but in the Inland Sea area, no generic term for these people exists; they are known by the name of their communities ("the people of Toyota") or by their fishing techniques.

These fisherfolk are distributed most heavily along the warm, southern seacoast of Japan, where they live in organized communities. The greatest concentration is found on the coast and islands of the Inland Sea, and only a very few communities exist on the coasts of northern Honshu and Hokkaido. These scattered communities do not form a united people: there may be friendly relations among adjacent communities and among those that work brings together, but the fisherfolk of any given area are probably unaware even of the existence of many distant settlements of similar people.

An account published in 1941[2] lists 48 communities of "Ebune-like" peoples throughout the nation. Most of these are buraku or hamlets, small administrative subdivisions of villages, towns, or small cities. The largest of the communities, Yoshiwa-chō, a part of the city of Onomichi in Hiroshima Prefecture, then consisted of 480 households,

---

[2] Yoshida (1941), pp. 181–207.

and was much larger than the average settlement. Only 130 of the 480 were "pure" boat dwellers and the remaining families lived at least part of the time on land and supported themselves chiefly by fishing, marine transporting of goods, and peddling dried fish, seaweed, and other commodities.

This listing of 48 communities appears to fall far short of the total number of segregated groups of fisherfolk: information provided in 1959 by a Japanese scholar indicates a much larger figure.[3] At this time, ten communities of Ebune were reported for the Nagasaki area,[4] and the number of "Ebune-like" communities in the Inland Sea area was estimated at about 100. (Most of these people had by this time taken up life on land, although their livelihood was still drawn principally from maritime activities like those of Yoshiwa-chō.) If we add the small unknown number of similar communities still existing in other parts of Japan, the total figure appears fairly substantial. However, the communities probably average fewer than 200 persons.

Although there is local variation in the culture of these communities, some traits are reported to be generally characteristic. Until recent years, these peoples derived their livelihood principally from fishing, most commonly by hook and line or other simple techniques. In the Nagasaki area, for example, spearing is still the technique that is primarily used. Both fishing grounds and fishing methods in offshore Japan are firmly regulated by law. Before becoming settled land dwellers, the people followed a fixed cycle of movement from a home base. In many groups, it was the women's task to peddle the catch, transporting the fish in buckets or baskets placed on the head, and to sell them to land-dwelling people along established routes, where certain houses of farmers and tradesmen served as commercial inns (yado) for the peddlers. Social relations with people outside their own group were limited principally to economic transactions, and, until very recent years, these transactions took the form of barter. Except for occasional brief lodging in established yado along the routes, boats served as dwellings.

Inheritance was by ultimogeniture. When an elder son married, his parents secured for themselves and their remaining dependent children a new boat and new fishing equipment, giving the old to the son. The youngest son cared for his parents in their old age and, on their death, inherited their boat and other property.

Various other customs of the migrant fisherfolk are distinct from those of the land-dwelling Japanese. Young men and women chose their own mates, and married early. Certain ancient customs continued, though abandoned by the general population, in the nineteenth cen-

[3] Noguchi, personal communication, 1959.
[4] Noguchi (1958), pp. 27–32.

tury, customs such as the staining of women's teeth; coming-of-age ceremonies for both males and females; the practice of changing given
names, routinely for young men during adolescence and for both sexes
any time that misfortunes were suffered; *yobai* (night visiting), on
the part of unmarried young men who slept at night with single
girls if their presence aboard the boat of the girls' parents was not
detected; throwing night soil at a new bride; and various magical-
religious techniques of curing illnesses.

Women were economically important, held high status, and controlled household finances. In fact, the status of women is said formerly to have been higher than that of men, and only female children were adopted by prospective parents.[5] Various Japanese scholars
have noted similarities between the culture of the Japanese boat
dwellers and the *Tammin*, the boat dwellers of Coastal China.

The foregoing descriptions refer to customs that are disappearing
or have already disappeared in most communities. A tendency toward
settled life on land became pronounced during the early twentieth
century. Since the end of World War II, the number of people living
on boats has decreased greatly, and other customs of the former migrants have been abandoned. Among the factors that have brought
about these changes are the dwindling supply of fish in Japanese
waters and the increasing competition from ordinary fishermen employing more efficient techniques. Compulsory education and restrictions on movement during the war years also inhibited migratory life.
Marine transport of goods in powered craft became a common occupation, and peddling came to include canned fish and various other
foods not produced by the fisherfolk. Improved economic conditions
resulting from the new occupations permitted purchase of houses on
land where, for a time, school children and old people were left while
able-bodied adults moved about to fish, a practice still followed by
people of some communities. Most of the present members of this
minority group probably now live settled lives on land and, as time
passes, turn increasingly to land employment.

The communities have not disappeared, however. They remain geographically distinct, and their members continue to be regarded by
their neighbors as social inferiors.

Woodworkers

As with the fishermen, only a small and specialized part of Japanese woodworkers have held the status of a minority group. These
are former migrants who manufactured on the lathe and offered for
sale small objects of wood—bowls, trays, and wooden dolls (*kokeshi*).

---

[5] Yoshida (1941).

Known most commonly as *Kijiya,* they were also called *Kijishi, Kijikuri, Kijihiki, Rokuroshi, Rokurohiki,* and *Hikimonoshi,* all of which terms refer to their occupation.

In former times, the Kijiya were concentrated principally in central and southern Japan, the most populous part of the nation. Many Kijiya are said to have come from a single village, Higashi-Oguramura in Shiga Prefecture, and to bear the surname of Ogura. Kijiya moved about in small groups of a few families, getting from the mountains the wood with which to make their wares. Contact was maintained between geographically separated groups by means of two shrines, each of which claimed to be the place of enshrinement of the legendary princely ancestor of the Kijiya. Officials of the shrines traveled through the country, meeting the dispersed Kijiya and collecting contributions from them. Through these shrine officials, the Kijiya received licenses or official permission to gather wood and to pursue their occupations. A document written in 1872 records 1,536 families of Kijiya under the control of one of these shrines.[6]

The Kijiya were forced to abandon migratory life soon after the beginning of the Meiji era (1868), when the right to secure wood was taken from them. Many became woodworkers in urban furniture and lacquerware factories, and others became farmers and charcoal makers. Several small communities of Kijiya were reported to exist in Fukushima Prefecture in 1939,[7] of which only a few households still engaged in their traditional occupation. It seems doubtful that any communities composed solely of Kijiya exist today, although a few individuals and families continue to be known by this name.

Hunters

In former times the mountains of Japan harbored a number of communities of professional hunters and their families. These people were called *Matagi,* a word that may be derived from a dialect word meaning "hunting." They were sometimes called *Yamadachi,* which is said to be the hunters' term for themselves. For several centuries these communities have been restricted to northern Honshu, and most of the writings on the Matagi refer to settlements in Akita and Aomori prefectures. Although the hunters moved about in the course of their work and were probably once migratory, the bulk of our information describes fixed communities, from which the men moved widely to hunt and sell their game and other products.

The chief product of the hunters was at first animal hides which

---

[6] Makino (1938), pp. 306–58.
[7] Yamaguchi (1939), pp. 10–27.

were used for clothing and the decline of the Matagi began many centuries ago when textiles began to replace the hides. The number of animals decreased as farmers invaded hunting lands, and after the introduction of Buddhism the demand for game was sharply curtailed by the religious injunction against eating meat. Matagi were at times employed to kill wild animals that destroyed crops. Males traveled through the nation part of the year selling bear livers which were highly valued as medicine, and hides of the animals they had shot. In recent times, some Matagi have added to their wares medicines prepared from purchased ingredients and hides imported from China. But by the middle of the nineteenth century most Matagi had been driven to take up other occupations and had become absorbed by the general population. At the same time, hunters were again briefly useful as skilled marksmen. Licensed to use guns in a land where guns were denied to commoners, they were recruited to guard the coast after European ships began to appear in Japanese waters.

Three communities of Matagi, subsisting by a combination of agriculture and their traditional occupation, were reported in Akita Prefecture in the 1930's,[8] and they appear to continue to exist today. A few also probably live in Aomori Prefecture.

The hunters have piqued the curiosity of both scholars and laymen in Japan because of their unusual mode of livelihood and distinctive customs. The living Matagi have frequently been the subject of articles in the popular press of Japan as surviving relics of the ancient past. Many popular writings have concerned their techniques of hunting bears, associated taboos and unusual supernaturalistic beliefs and practices, and their use of a secret vocabulary.

Ironworkers

Japan has always had specialists in iron metallurgy that appear to have been socially distinguished from other people. These were specialists who smelted iron sands and produced objects of iron and steel. (Iron metallurgists are distinct from blacksmiths, who, although they once constituted a despised occupational class, are not discussed here for lack of adequate information.) At one time they were migratory, ranging through Japan wherever iron sands were available; but they took to settled life around the fourteenth century as their technical skills became more elaborate, requiring equipment and facilities that were not portable. As production grew, many subspecialties developed, but all persons directly engaged in the production of iron and steel who lived in segregated communities were customarily called

---

[8] Mutō (1933), pp. 81–92.

Tatara (or *Tatarashi*), a term that has been given various etymologies referring to iron metallurgy. Communities of Tatara were concentrated in central Japan where iron sands were abundant.

As producers of iron and of steel of fine quality, the Tatara were encouraged and protected by feudal lords. They lived in communities that were rigidly closed to outsiders, sometimes enclosed by fences with guards at the entrances. Life within this community was highly organized, and many regulations and sanctions governed behavior. Their occupation became hereditary and, according to their own rules, no member was allowed to forsake his occupation and take up residence in the outside world.

Neighboring farmers sometimes served the Tatara as temporary or part-time employees in unskilled capacities, but social life was rigidly restricted to members of their own and other Tatara settlements. Though outsiders were sometimes eager to have iron produced in their area because of the economic advantages it offered, relations between the Tatara and their neighbors were usually cool and sometimes hostile. Farmers complained because the manufacture of the charcoal necessary for smelting denuded the mountains and caused floods, and the collecting and washing of iron sands caused sedimentation that was injurious to the streams and to the rice fields. Many disputes and law suits arose over these issues. One of the largest of the law suits, filed in 1845, suggests that Tatara communities were once numerous. About 30 iron-smelting communities on the upper reaches of the Kawabe River were sued for damages by farming communities along lower reaches, principally in Bitchū Province which used water from the river.[9]

After the opening of Japan to the West during the second half of the nineteenth century, imported steel and Western techniques of metallurgy rendered the methods of the Tatara obsolete. By the early 1920's the communities had ceased to exist. A few were revived in the 1930's after the Japanese invasion of the Asiatic mainland began, and a handful continued to exist until the end of World War II. Although the name Tatara lingers today for some residents of a few communities of Shimane and Tottori prefectures, they are essentially extinct as a separate social group.[10]

Riverine Migrants

Japan has long had groups of landless wanderers who followed the courses of rivers in their seasonal movements. In historic times

---

[9] Matsuo (1931).

[10] Ishizuka, personal communication, 1959.

their habitat has been principally central and southwestern Japan. Most accounts refer to these people as *Sanka*, although numerous variant names are also reported including *Mitsukuri, Minaoshi, Oge, Pon, Ponsu, Ponsuke, Shokenshi, Kenshi, Iwayasa, Seishi, Seburi, Jiryōji, Buriuchi, Agari, Noai, Kanjin, Temba,* and *Kawara-kojiji,* names that usually indicate the means by which the people gained their living. But we cannot be sure that all of these names refer to a single people and moreover, we do not know whether Sanka is their own term for themselves or a term used by ordinary Japanese to refer to them; they themselves do not voluntarily admit to being Sanka.[11] The multiplicity of names seems to be in part a reflection of multiple and seasonally variable occupations. The etymology of the word Sanka is unclear and it is written with Chinese characters in several different ways. The various characters suggest these meanings: a wandering people; people whose dwellings are in the mountains; mountain people who steal; and people who live in caves in the mountains.

Although the Sanka have been romanticized by modern Japanese novelists in a manner resembling various European writers on the Gypsies, they are little known. Secretive and suspicious of outsiders, they kept to themselves and avoided unnecessary contact with other people. They traveled in small groups of a few families and moved toward the mountains in the summer and toward the warmer climate of the lowlands and the seacoast in the winter. Large groups came together for weddings and important religious ceremonies.

Dwellings of the Sanka are reported as crude, improvised shelters and caves hidden from the casual eye, and sometimes as cheap inns. Their livelihood was gained from minor skills and such petty tasks as catching fish in streams; retrieving and selling lost objects found in streams; making brushes, brooms, baskets, and straw sandals that were peddled from door to door; and mending straw raincoats. Some groups called Sanka were beggars and others were diviners who diagnosed illness and cured by prayer or magical techniques. Still others sold talismans and medicines. There is no clear line between them and various other peoples, especially migrants following quasi-religious occupations; it seems probable that the name Sanka has been applied locally to almost any uneducated, impoverished, and homeless wanderers. Like the Gypsies of the Western world, the Japanese Sanka and similar roving peoples were said to derive their livelihood in part from petty thievery.

As with the other minority groups under discussion, the industrialization and modernization of Japan made the traditional occupations

---

[11] Yanagida (1911–1912).

of these people obsolete or difficult to follow and in many other ways
strongly discouraged migratory life. At the turn of the twentieth century many thousands were called Sanka: an account published in
1911[12] reports a hearsay figure of thirteen or fourteen thousand around
Osaka alone. People known as Sanka still exist, but few of them appear
to be migrants. Most have lost their identity, and the number of persons now given this name is probably very small.

Quasi-Religious Itinerants

During medieval times and perhaps much earlier, the Japanese
population included numerous named groups of impoverished people
whose livelihood was gained from various petty tasks connected in
some manner with Buddhist and Shinto beliefs and customs. Historic
accounts record a profusion of names for these groups which, for convenience and for lack of detailed information concerning them, have
here been placed under a single heading. Among the names are
*Shōmonji, Kugutsu, Kairaishi, Ebisukaki, Ebisumawashi, Dekoma-
washi, Itaka, Kuchiyose, Daikokumai, Ichiko, Yamaneko, Ommyōji,
Hijiri, Saruhiki,* and *Manzai.* No clear picture may be derived of the
antiquity, numbers, or relationships of the various groups, and it is
uncertain which of these names refer to organized social communities.
The distinctions are unclear between these heterogeneous peoples, the
Sanka, the Hinin and, particularly, the Eta. This is not surprising
since the modern Eta appear to represent a composite of people with
diverse cultural backgrounds. The earliest substantial account of the
Eta to appear in the English language includes "Nomads" as one of
the largest components of the Eta communities near Kobe.[13] Yet many
Japanese accounts refer to peoples bearing the various names cited
above as distinct from the Eta and Hinin.

Occupations followed by these groups were numerous and change-
able. Some were religious mendicants who chanted sutras in exchange
for food. Others were shamans, diviners, faithhealers, tellers of myths
and tales, musicians and performers of religious dances, peddlers of
talismans, and performers of ceremonies of purification. Sometimes
their livelihood was derived in part from secular work such as basketry
and the manufacture and peddling of other household objects and
footwear. As the centuries passed, the performers of music, dance, and
other quasi-religious forms of entertainment came to be wholly secular
entertainers—singers, dancers, actors, and puppeteers. Others adopted
small secular handicrafts as a means of gaining a livelihood. Most or

[12] Yanagida (1911–1912).
[13] Ninomiya (1933), pp. 47–154.

all groups were once wanderers, but some took to settled life as circumstances made continued wandering difficult.

Among the minority groups discussed here, those following quasi-religious occupations were the first to disappear through blending with the general population, merging with the Eta, or becoming identified by other names. It is improbable that any organized communities of people bearing any of these names exist today.

Miscellaneous Groups in Secular Occupations

For lack of adequate information, I shall mention only in passing certain groups of Eta-like peoples who derived their living from secular occupations. Some of these were probably descendants of earlier peoples engaged in quasi-religious occupations. They lived in settled communities and earned their livings as undertakers, midwives, guardians of prisoners, executioners, and makers and sellers of bamboo articles. Names given to peoples of this kind include *Ombō, Tōnai, Hachi, Shuku,* and *Sagari.*

Although most of these groups appear to have merged with the Eta or otherwise to have vanished, it is probable that a few communities of people bearing these names continue to exist.

RELATIONS WITH MAJORITY JAPANESE

Japanese accounts make it clear that the general population regarded all of the forenamed groups as social inferiors with whom no person should mingle socially except when making use of the services they provided. Prejudicial attitudes appear to have ranged from mild feelings against some groups to extreme hostility toward others, only slightly less strong than that directed against the Eta. Above all, marriage with members of these groups was to be avoided. Popular ideas, discredited by scholars, "explained" various of the minority groups as racially different from other Japanese—descendants of the Ainu. of the primitive Orochon of eastern Siberia, or of Koreans.

For lack of information, it is not possible to rate the groups according to the degree of prejudice that ordinary people felt against them. In modern times the ordinary Japanese citizen seldom came into contact with many of these groups. It seems certain, however, that none was thought to be as low as the Eta. Even groups living near Buraku and engaged in similar defiling occupations were regarded as somewhat above the outcastes. Unlike the Eta, the members of these minorities seem to have suffered from little or no discriminatory legislation. Their position of social inferiority does not appear to have been supported by special sumptuary laws denying them privileges held by commoners. One may assume, however, that they were the subjects of considerable informal discrimination.

Writings by Japanese scholars indicate that prejudice against these peoples has greatly weakened during the last century. This trend reflects in part, of course, the dwindling of the minority groups themselves. Since most of them today are only small remnants unknown to the nation as a whole, it seems reasonable to think that lingering attitudes of prejudice are local rather than national. Wherever recognized communities remain, some measure of local discrimination also appears to remain. For example, although de facto communities of Tatara are now a thing of the past, in the regions of Shimane and Tottori prefectures where known descendants of the Tatara live, marriage with them is still generally avoided.[14] This is interesting since the Tatara seem to have been looked upon by their neighbors as only slightly inferior and they often took neighboring farmers into their employ. The alienation of the Tatara seems to have been due in part to disputes arising from the damage their smelting operations caused.

Information on social discrimination is fullest for the Ebune and similar fisherfolk. The Ebune of Nagasaki Prefecture continue to live in separate communities and to be regarded as less than ordinary. Marriage among them is reported to be principally endogamous with the general exception that Ebune women sometimes marry mineworkers, whose social status is not greatly superior to theirs.[15] It is also reported that several Ebune men married non-Ebune women while in military service during World War II.[16] Unaware of the social positions of their husbands and affinal relatives, the women were deeply distressed when they were brought to their home communities after the war.

Discriminatory attitudes toward the "special" fisherfolk appear to remain strong in the Inland Sea, where most of these people are concentrated. The following account of a community of special fisherfolk in this area is drawn from personal observation by the author during 1950–51 and a brief visit in 1959.

The Sokobiki of Hama Buraku

The hamlet of Hama, administratively a part of Kojima City in Okayama Prefecture, is a small community of about 20 households

---

[14] Ishizuka, personal communication, 1959.
[15] Noguchi (1958).
[16] Noguchi, personal communication, 1959.

composed almost entirely of fishermen and their families. Locally they are called Sokobiki, a term meaning "bottom trawling," the technique of fishing used by these people. Although poor, they are not destitute, and a few families are well-to-do by local standards. Their dwellings, clothing, and standard of living are on the average only slightly inferior to those of their neighbors and social superiors, who are principally farmers and fishermen. Some Sokobiki continued into the 1950's to peddle dried fish in neighboring communities, an occupation that was held in low esteem.

The Sokobiki derive their livelihoods by honest means, and they cause no social disturbances. Their children attend the same public schools as those of their neighbors. Sokobiki men belong to the local fishermen's cooperative, through which they sell their catches, and they and their women participate in the Parent Teachers' Association and other associations that bring them in touch with outside people. They attend Shinto shrines and Buddhist temples in common with their neighbors. The head of one Sokobiki household served for several years as a member of the city council, an elective position, and he is highly regarded for his intelligence and administrative talents.

The hamlet of Hama is separated physically from its nearest neighboring community only by a narrow street, barely wide enough to allow the passage of a small automobile, yet the social separation between its inhabitants and their neighbors seems unbridgeable. Social relations with the Sokobiki are limited to the necessary—economic affairs, events connected with the school or urban administration, and the like. These are all smooth, so that the casual observer notes only cordial relations. Beneath the surface, however, attitudes of prejudice toward the Sokobiki are generally strong. They are said to be only slightly above the Eta. No self-respecting person would marry a Sokobiki. The rare intermarriages that have occurred have been between Sokobiki men and outside women "led astray by money." The term Sokobiki itself is so derogatory that it is not ordinarily used in public, and its use before a member of the Sokobiki group would constitute the most terrible insult. In other areas of Japan, this word means only a technique of netting fish.

Inquiry as to the reason for this prejudice yields various answers. Some people, the elderly and least educated, say that they are of a different race, but attempt no identification of the race. Sokobiki are said to be inferior because they are strangers and newcomers who took to settled life in the community less than three centuries ago. They are also said to be extremely vulgar and immoral, tending toward blackmarketeering and other petty crimes, and sexual promiscuity— charges that are not substantiated. Their children are described as less studious in school than other children, receiving poorer grades and excelling only in athletics—charges that are indeed true. A few express the opinion that the position of the Sokobiki is largely a heritage of the past and that little about their present circumstances warrants the contempt they receive.

An idea of the position held locally by the group may be gained from the following incident, observed by the author. My wife and I then lived as guests of a middle-aged widow, sharing domestic life with her and her teen-age son. Our relations with the widow Matsui were very friendly, and she concealed from us little about her own life or community affairs. Although known as somewhat progressive in her attitudes, she was a highly respected member of her community, with a well deserved reputation for intelligence.

One day the widow saw through the opened shutters a woman with a basket on her head walking up the path to the house. Mrs. Matsui admitted her with a warm greeting, using in address the given name O-toku. She was introduced to me in proper fashion by her surname and invited to join us for a cup of tea. An animated discussion between the two women soon followed, with O-toku now and then asking me polite questions about life in the United States. After some minutes, Mrs. Matsui noticed through the shutters two women of her own community coming up the path. Breaking off the conversation, she suddenly closed the shutters and ushered O-toku into the next room, closing the doors behind her.

Mrs. Matsui then admitted the two women, and chatted and drank tea with them for about thirty minutes. When they left, the widow readmitted O-toku to the room and, after a moment, said in a laughing voice, "It wasn't necessary to go into the closet." O-toku, also laughing, resumed her earlier seat and conversation began anew. After some minutes, the guest prepared to go. Mrs. Matsui then bought from her a small quantity of dried fish, and O-toku, expressing in farewell hearty wishes for the well-being of Mrs. Matsui and her relatives, left.

Mrs. Matsui explained that O-toku was a Sokobiki from Hama whom she had known from early childhood. The two had become fast friends during their first years of school and, despite the discouragement of friendships of this sort, they had managed secretly to maintain their bonds through the years. For over two decades, O-toku had come to Mrs. Matsui's community to peddle dried fish. When it was possible on these occasions, the women enjoyed each other's company and informed each other of their domestic affairs. But these intimate meetings had to be secret: "My house, as you know, is placed so that people cannot easily see who comes and goes. If those two women knew that I had been serving tea to O-toku and treating her as a friend, life would be hard for me here."

THE BASIS OF PREJUDICE

Examination of the circumstances of life of these various minority groups reveals a number of characteristics presently or formerly held in common that appear to have contributed to their low social status. All derived their living from specialized occupations that served in varying measure to set them apart from other people. Only a few groups, such as the undertakers, practiced despised occupations, but the specialties of others were minor skills that generally secured only a bare livelihood. The outstanding exception is the Tatara, who, after their skill in metallurgy became well developed, were for a time relatively affluent. Prejudicial attitudes toward them appear to have been mild, and to have derived in part from contention over the damage caused by their work.

Poverty was the general rule. Clinging to their traditional occupations long after changed economic conditions of the nation as a whole had made them unprofitable, most of the groups grew poorer as the centuries passed. Among some groups, extreme poverty appears to have led to petty theft as an habitual practice, and this undoubtedly lowered their social status still further. We may note, however, that these peoples generally made their livings in legitimate if not prestigious ways.

All groups, including the Tatara, seem once to have been migrants, landless and lacking substantial property, who were looked upon by the general population with the suspicion accorded to impoverished strangers. It seems probably that among woodworkers using the lathe only those who were migrants were considered markedly inferior. In some areas *Ji-kiji* (settled woodworkers) were distinguished from *Watari-kiji* (migratory woodworkers) in this way. A community of Miyagi Pefecture (Shichigashuku-mura) visited by the author in 1959 contained several families called Kijiya who earned their livings chiefly by making wooden dolls. They were regarded as ordinary if poor citizens and were said "always" to have been so regarded and "always" to have lived in the community. It is worth noting that communities of ordinary fishermen have long engaged in techniques of fishing identical to those followed by some groups of special fishermen, but they have no histories of having once been migratory.

Occupations pursued by some of the minority groups had a religious significance that in one way or another served to place them at a social disadvantage. Some were in fact religious specialists, and these are reported to have been well regarded in ancient times: begging was once regarded as a religious act that cured illnesses and conferred other supernatural benefits. But changing ideas of religion made mendicancy and other religious specialties undesirable. Many groups then became secular entertainers, a circumstance that lowered their social positions. Others, whose work was connected with death, funerals, and childbirth, were given religious significance of another sort. Belief in supernaturalism imputed to them a condition of dangerous pollution and they were for this reason avoided.

For the minority groups that have persisted the longest and about which we have the fullest information—the special fisherfolk, woodworkers, and ironworkers—no evidence exists to suggest that supernaturalistic beliefs held by the population at large contributed importantly to the formation of attitudes of prejudice. But both Matagi and probably Sanka continued to kill animals and to eat meat, practices that may have lowered their positions after Buddhist prohibitions of these practices became general. No clear evidence suggests, however, that these people were regarded, like the Eta, as being supernaturally defiled by their occupations. (The Tatara themselves seemed to have regarded their work as having religious significance, but this appears to have been a rationalization of their own that gave them self-esteem —and doubtless reinforced their attitude of exclusiveness.)

Social isolation of these groups was not due solely to avoidance of them by the general population. Partly as a result of awareness of their low social positions, the minority groups followed a behavior pattern common to minority groups elsewhere in the world. Secrecy about their own affairs and avoidance of their social superiors were characteristic as were common religions and myths of noble or exalted ancestry. Social solidarity and a strong ingroup feeling seem to have been well developed among the fisherfolk, woodworkers, hunters, and ironworkers. (For most of the remaining groups, data on this subject are scanty or lacking.) Though for centuries these peoples were wanderers, they appear to have come together in large groups at fixed intervals, thus reinforcing social ties. Distinctive customs that were often related to their occupations, dialectic differences, and, for some groups, secret vocabularies, also served both to unite them and to set them apart from the general population. To what extent members of these groups accepted the prejudice of their neighbors and looked down upon themselves is uncertain. Information on this matter is available only on the special fishermen, who were said to despise themselves.[17] Discrimination against the minority group fishermen increased after they moved to the land, where they were thrown into constant

---

[17] Yoshida (1941).

contact with outsiders through their changed occupations, children's schooling, and other necessary activities.[18] The same thing probably happened to other groups when they took to settled life; at least consciousness of their low position may well have grown because of the constant reminder provided by the actions of their neighbors.

As we have noted, many of the circumstances discussed here apply also to Burakumin, but one important factor relates to religion. Before Buddhism became well established in Japan, many small occupational groups engaging in petty handicrafts existed. These held low social status but were not pariahs. Buddhist beliefs concerning the taking of life, contact with death, and the eating of meat that encouraged the formation of the "untouchable" Eta did not apply to the work of the fisherfolk, woodworkers, and ironworkers. If they did apply to the hunters, this probably never led to strong feelings of prejudice because their numbers had already become small. Some prejudice arising from, or reinforced by, religious beliefs appears to have applied to those in semi-religious occupations, small groups geographically close to the Eta, and those who took up occupations followed by the Eta. These, we may note, were the first of the non-Eta minority groups to disappear, probably in large part through merging with the outcastes.

Circumstances of the outcastes also differed in other significant respects. They were the first to settle in permanent communities, and their population soon became far larger than that of all other minority groups combined. The intense prejudice directed toward them and the discrimination from which they suffered appear to have fostered among them greater solidarity than existed among the non-Eta groups. Only the Burakumin became nationally organized to combat discrimination. These various circumstances brought the outcastes to the attention of Japanese citizens throughout the nation, including those in areas where no outcastes lived, and appear to have contributed to their continuity as a minority group.

Today, the special fishermen make up the only non-Eta minority of any size, and they are more properly described as a number of groups with common occupations. The woodworkers and ironworkers have scattered and their descendants have lost their special identities through employment in modern occupations and the anonymity of urban life. The Matagi have become museum specimens. Other groups we have discussed are extinct or exist today only as tiny remnants. The special fishermen were favored for survival because they alone engaged in an occupation that provided a livelihood through the centuries and is not yet wholly obsolete. Although now principally land dwellers,

[18] Noguchi (1958).

their adjustment to changed economic conditions was accomplished through retention of many ties with their former maritime life and residence in separate communities. It seems probable that despite the weakening of discriminatory attitudes, their internal solidarity and visibility will serve to maintain them for many years to come as local minority groups.

Chapter 10

HIROSHI ITO

Japan's Outcastes in the United States

Oddly enough, there are virtually no references to the outcaste problem in any of the numerous articles and studies reporting on the Japanese in the United States that have appeared over the years in various scholarly and popular publications. The present study[1] should make it abundantly clear that caste prejudice and its attendant problems were not shed by the emigrants as they left Yokohama, Osaka, or Kobe for the United States. One purpose of this report is to fill a gap in the substantive literature on the Japanese-American ethnic group. The second major aim is to uncover the mechanisms and consequences of this particular prejudice and to examine and perhaps refine some points of general sociological knowledge, especially those derived from earlier American ethnic group studies.

THE PROBLEM OF COLLECTING MATERIAL

It was known that the subject of the Japanese outcaste was a delicate one, and some difficulty in locating and obtaining the direct personal cooperation of outcaste individuals had been anticipated.

---

[1] This working paper was originally prepared in 1952 under the supervision of Leonard Broom while the writer was a Sigmund Livingston Memorial Fellow at The University of California, Los Angeles.

This chapter is the only work available documenting the continuity of caste attitudes by Japanese immigrants within the United States. We have been unable to locate any copies of a similar unpublished study which is supposed to exist, done by someone using a pseudonym, on outcaste relations in Hawaii. This chapter has been included with only slight modifications and deletions from the original, which was not intended by the author for publication in this form. (Note by G. D. V. and H. W.)

Before long, however, it became clear that the magnitude of the problem had been grossly underestimated.

Attempts at Field Work in Southern California

In my investigation I approached two Nisei (American-born Japanese) men who were reputed to have outcaste origins. One was a college graduate whom I had met as a student; though we were not intimate, I regarded him as a friend. The other, an able and attractive person who had been a prominent student leader in his high school days, was a closer friend.

In both instances there was an immediate negative reaction when the subject of the Eta[2] was broached. Their demeanor was grim and strained. The college graduate at first professed total ignorance of the outcaste problem, but a few minutes later, in response to my request for advice on how to approach one of the reputed outcaste Issei (literally, first or immigrant generation), he revealed that he knew the Issei personally and believed that he would eject from his house, if not kill, any person who dared to make an overt reference to the Eta.

Plans to approach reputedly Eta persons with direct reference to the outcaste problem were immediately abandoned. It was decided that the subject of the inquiry should be hidden as much as possible. Only the most discreet and responsible majority Japanese with whom I was personally acquainted were confidentially consulted for information and further leads. This method of selection of informants made interviews and reinterviews necessarily difficult and often exasperatingly circuitous.

In most instances an informant, under persistent prodding, would relate some details of a specific case of outcaste rejection (for example, breakup of a proposed mixed marriage). However, the informant would refuse to identify the individuals or families involved or to provide enough detail to permit a guess as to their identity. In short, there appeared to exist powerful sanctions against publicly identifying outcaste individuals or families.

Those known to be "busybodies" in the Japanese community were at first avoided, but later some effort was made to tap such sources.

---

[2] In the United States there is no substitute word like Burakumin that is used in a neutral way to discuss the problem. The original pejorative word remains in use since more neutral words would not be understood. This makes dispassionate discussion almost impossible. We have used the word outcaste in the text in several places where Ito has used the word Eta in accord with our general policies in editing this volume. (Note by G. D. V. and H. W.)

To minimize the risk of having the research itself become a subject of gossip in the community, thereby further complicating the field work, interviews with such individuals were conducted as if the research objectives were a generalized study of changes in the social participation patterns of the total Japanese population in the Los Angeles area. Questions concerning the Eta were supposed to be only incidental, springing from the innocuous curiosity of the investigator.

In the course of these interviews thirty-six families were more or less reliably identified as outcastes. Under the circumstances, positive rather than suspected identification of an outcaste constituted a major methodological problem, for unless the individual himself was the source of knowledge, there was little assurance that objective knowledge, rather than gossip, was operating. Only one case of self-identification of outcaste membership was found.

The only other verification that appeared possible, and that only partially, depended on the knowledge and memory of non-outcaste persons familiar with the geographical origins of suspects. That is to say, if the home hamlet of an individual were known and that hamlet was an outcaste Buraku, then a non-outcaste individual familiar with that area can make a rather positive identification. But such persons were particularly prone to be close-mouthed, and with good reason, since a public informer of an outcaste's identity could be easily traced. A more serious shortcoming in the technique of identification by geographical origin is the fact that the specific hamlet must be known, for many villages and towns are socially heterogeneous; that is, the outcastes were distributed in special segregated hamlets within villages that also contained other, non-outcaste hamlets.

It is believed, however, that these inherent difficulties did not vitiate the value of the research. A primary objective was the discovery of the effects of group rejection rather than the effects of actual outcaste origin. Therefore, in this sense, the Eta group includes suspects as well as those positively identified as outcastes.

After a list of families was obtained, a questionnaire was to be sent, followed by a direct interview in the home. Because of the difficulties just described, the original interview schedule, which contained direct reference to the Eta problem, was revised so as to mask the real objective. In order to reduce the interviewing period and the problems of initial rapport, the schedule was mailed in advance to the interviewees with a covering letter. One hundred and twenty schedules and letters were sent out, 20 to reputedly outcaste families and 100 to randomly selected non-outcaste families from prefectural groups who would be familiar with the outcaste problem. Unhappily, a month of calling at the various selected family homes netted such a limited number of completed schedules that this whole venture had to be abandoned.

The only practical course left open was to gather data on the outcaste group from selected non-outcaste informants. This was done, using some 28 informants, however not without doubts regarding the validity and reliability of the data so collected. I attempted continuously to view the information in the light of my subjective assessment of the particular informant's reliability and perspicacity, but it is clear that the findings reported below must properly be regarded as extremely tentative. Of course, the theoretical considerations based on those findings should be considered to be hypotheses.

Field Work in the Sacramento Area

There is widespread belief among Japanese-Americans that a community known as Fornia in the delta region of California harbored, at least in the prewar period, the largest group of outcastes in the United States. Two trips were made to this area, the first in the spring and the second in the summer of 1951, or, around the midpoint and near the end of the field research phase of the study.

On the first occasion, the few days available were spent in reaching and working with the non-outcaste informants in the area suggested to us by one of the primary informants in Los Angeles. One of the most productive was a long-time resident and socially active Issei businessman who has served for many years as the local correspondent and representative of a major Japanese vernacular newspaper published in San Francisco. He was able to arrange a meeting at his home of six other non-outcaste Issei whom he considered to have wide knowledge of the Japanese in the delta region and the ability to discuss the Eta problem objectively.

Another almost equally productive informant was the priest of the Buddhist temple that now serves all the Japanese Buddhists in and around the area. Though discreet about family identities, he was able to provide revealing information on the outcastes, especially marriage and religious participation patterns of those in his congregation.

On the second trip, a large amount of valuable data on the outcastes of the prewar Fornia area was gathered. Four very productive hours were spent with long-time Fornia residents, a non-outcaste man and his wife, who were among the small number of non-outcastes apparently trusted and liked by the Eta in the area. The remaining three hours were spent with a retired Issei couple, also long-time residents; they did not associate closely with the outcastes as did the other couple.

OUTCASTE AND NON-OUTCASTE EMIGRATION FROM JAPAN TO THE UNITED STATES

Of the total Japanese immigrant population in southern California in 1920, 23 percent were from Hiroshima Prefecture.[3] The next largest prefectural groups, Wakayama and Okayama, each constituted 10 percent of the total, or less than half the Hiroshima contingent. There were only three other groups whose respective numbers claimed more than 5 percent of the total—Fukuoka (7 percent), Kumamoto (6 percent), and Yamaguchi (5.5 percent).

Although these proportions probably do not strictly reflect the total Japanese immigrant population in the United States, they do indicate that the Japanese population here does not constitute a geographically representative sample of the population of Japan, but is heavily biased in favor of southwestern Japan, especially the areas surrounding the Inland Sea. In addition, earlier studies indicate that the Japanese immigrants in the United States may be characterized as having been drawn in large part from the lower, though not the lowest, economic and social strata of the rural sectors of Japan.

Now, the best estimate of the size of the outcaste population in Japan in 1920 indicates that this group comprised approximately 2.5 percent of the total national population. But the available data on their distribution by prefectures show that although outcastes were to be found in all but two of the prefectures on the three main islands of Japan (Honshu, Shikoku, and Kyushu), they were in largest numbers in the Inland Sea region (see Chapter 5).

Given these factors, one would expect, by a crude application of the push-pull theory of migration, that the outcastes would emigrate at a relatively higher rate than the non-outcastes. One would therefore expect this group in the United States to comprise *considerably more* than 2.5 percent of the total Japanese immigrant population here.

It was found, however, that only ten of the more than forty Japa-

---

[3] The figures on prefectural origins of the total Japanese population in southern California in 1920 were obtained from a printed pamphlet loaned to the investigator by the late Mr. Honko Matsumoto, an old resident of Los Angeles. This pamphlet presents the findings of a family-to-family survey of the Japanese residents of southern California conducted in 1920 by the local Japanese Association with the blessings of the local Japanese Consulate. Mr. Matsumoto participated in the survey as one of the staff members. Kenjin-kai (prefectural associations) membership figures are available, but these are generally inadequate for the present purpose. It is known that many who are eligible for membership are not members. At the same time, there is no detailed knowledge of the differential proportions of prefectural people who do or do not join the respective associations.

nese prefectures in which outcastes live in Japan are represented in the supposed outcaste population in the United States, whereas all prefectures are represented here by non-outcastes. Those prefectural groups among which outcastes are alleged to be present in the United States are Hiroshima, Wakayama, Okayama, Fukuoka, Kumamoto, Yamaguchi, Kakoshima, Mie, Kochi, and Fukui. Furthermore, the collated estimates of the informants put the proportion of the outcastes in all but one of those prefectural groups at only about 1 percent. While the one prefectural group exceptional in this connection constituted only a small proportion of the total Japanese population in southern California in 1920, it is the understanding of the informants contacted that most of them are outcastes. Indeed, the informants were unable to refer the investigator to a single family of that prefectural origin that was positively *not* outcaste.

Similar findings turned up in the Fornia area. Fewer than 10 percent from the indicated prefecture were judged to be non-outcastes. When Fornia was most heavily populated, in the early 1930's, the total number of Japanese was about 1,800. Some 15 to 20 percent of this number, or 270 to 360 persons were thought to be outcastes. And it is estimated that 90 percent of this population was from the exceptional prefecture.

The finding that only ten prefectures are represented in the immigrant outcaste group, whereas all prefectures are represented in the immigrant non-outcaste group, makes it doubtful that the simple inclusion of an economic variable will suffice as an explanation. It appears likely that some differential treatment owing to administrative decisions was involved. Much control over the administrative implementation of emigration policy was held at local levels. It may well be that some local or prefectural officers took it upon themselves to block the emigration of the outcastes in their respective jurisdictions, believing that such individuals would prove to be shameful representatives of the Japanese people abroad.

Characteristics of Outcastes and Non-Outcastes at Time of Immigration

What information could be gathered on the differences in cultural, occupational, religious, and educational backgrounds and age and economic status between the outcastes and non-outcastes at the time of their emigration indicates that the two groups were very similar in most respects. Both groups generally came from a rural environment and from families of relatively low economic status. Most were Buddhists or Shintoists. Those few who had adopted the Christian faith prior to emigration seem not to have been of outcaste extraction. In our sample, the mean age of the outcaste group is lower and the outcastes are generally judged to be a bit more educated. The outcaste group seems to have emigrated somewhat later. If this is actually so, it explains the lower mean age and the higher educational attainment since an increase in compulsory public school education was taking place in Japan during the period of emigration to the United States.

COMPARATIVE ACCULTURATION
BY OUTCASTE AND NON-OUTCASTE JAPANESE

It seems clear that Japanese of outcaste extraction have avoided public identification with any minority status among Japanese immigrants, as indicated by the lack of any open identification of themselves or by the lack of any open struggle for the acceptance of their group.

Occupational Distribution and
Economic Status in American Society

The outcastes in the United States tend to avoid economic activity that is historically associated with Eta—butchering, shoe repairing, and others requiring the handling of meat or animal products. On this basis one would assume that in the United States they would seek occupations unrelated to outcaste status. They would also tend to avoid occupations or businesses that would ordinarily increase the possibilities of explicit rejection, for example, those that depend on non-outcaste Japanese patrons, such as Japanese restaurants.

The findings concerning the occupational distribution of outcastes are very clearly in line with the expectations. Large numbers of the prewar Japanese ethnic population became owners and workers of small businesses catering to other local ethnic groups. In the major areas of outcaste concentrations, there were no instances of outcaste merchants. None of the Japanese undertakers, cobblers, or, interestingly enough, butchers who were checked were seriously suspected of being outcastes.

In the thirties, a considerable number of Japanese families ventured into commercial hog raising in the environs of Los Angeles, and only two of these families were identified as outcastes. An overwhelming majority of the outcaste families were in vegetable and fruit farming, either as operators on leased land or as laborers. In the Fornia farming area, the major money crop was a specialty fruit and so the outcastes, as well as other Japanese and non-Japanese farmers there, were closely identified with that crop.

In prewar Southern California, a majority of the identifiable outcaste families were engaged in various forms of truck farming. Those in urban centers seem to have had the same occupational distribution as non-outcaste Japanese urbanites except, of course, in the particular respects noted above.

A number of non-outcastes are given to describing the outcaste group as a whole as shrewd, miserly, and individually and collectively wealthy. There appears to be some objective basis for such a contention, because the values of the holdings of a few of the more successful outcaste farmers are very high by the ethnic group standards. Nonetheless, with the data at hand, it is impossible to compare the objective relative economic status of the outcaste with the non-outcaste group. We can only note that the collated opinions of informants place the outcaste slightly above the non-outcaste with regard to mean economic status and mean amounts of expenditures for ceremonial and ritual purposes.

General Orientation to American Society

When this study was formulated it was hypothesized that the outcastes as compared to the non-outcastes would tend to be more positively oriented to white Americans and less positively or perhaps negatively oriented to Japanese. Rapid acculturation would be to their advantage.

However, adequate assessment of this speculation was not possible because of the difficulties in the search for outcaste families. Our data on outcaste behavior refer almost entirely to those who have not lost direct touch with the non-outcaste group. The methodological difficulties arise, of course, because by avoiding the non-outcaste group and rejecting its norms, those outcastes who may have been drawn to the dominant American group are effectively hidden or at least not readily available for study.

Nonetheless, the findings reported below are significant in that they show that some of the immigrant outcastes have chosen as their behavioral reference the high prestige elements of the Japanese society rather than the American society they have entered. It cannot be said, however, that this choice has entirely precluded the white American as a reference group.

The following kinds of behavior were chosen as the dimensions along which to compare the outcaste and non-outcaste:

A. Positive orientation to American Society.
    1. Participation in American sociocultural leisure activities, such as watching competitive, amateur American sports; attending movies; listening to popular music; ballroom dancing; informal dinner parties; bridge and poker playing.

2. Affiliation with one of the Christian religions.
3. American school education.
4. Use of American dress, food, etiquette, and language.
5. Relocation to the midwestern and eastern United States from the various assembly and relocation centers during World War II; active participation in the American war effort.
B. Negative orientation, or continued reference to the Japanese.
1. Participation in such Japanese sociocultural activities as *ikebana* (flower arrangement), *odori* (traditional dance), *shibai* (theatrical drama), *shigin* (recitation of Chinese poems), *kembu* (dancing with a sword, accompanied by shigin), *tanka* (traditional short poems), all of which have been associated historically with high ascribed status; watching Japanese movies; Japanese forms of sports and athletic competition such as *jūdō* and *kendō*.
2. Affiliation with one of the Buddhist or Shinto religious sects.
3. Formal Japanese language education for Nisei in the United States and in Japan.
4. Use of Japanese dress, food, etiquette, and language.
5. Voluntary segregation, that is, requested or otherwise accomplished transfer to the Tule Lake segregation camp during the war; Issei repatriation and Nisei expatriation during or following World War II.

Indices of Positive Acculturation

Positive orientation to American society as measured in the foregoing terms can be said to characterize the American-born Nisei but not the immigrant Issei. All the leisure time activities mentioned seem to be enjoyed by an overwhelming majority of the Nisei, but Issei generally frown on them, both for themselves and for their offspring. As fas as could be determined, the outcastes and non-outcastes of the first and second generations are not noticeably different in this respect.

Affiliation with one or another of the Christian religious groups, though more frequent in the Nisei group, is found among the Issei. Here, however, the evidence is that the outcastes are under-represented; only a very few of them belong to the various Japanese Christian congregations.

In terms of the levels attained by both Issei and Nisei outcastes and non-outcastes, American school education does not seem to be differentiating. Earlier investigations have shown the Issei to be quite low and the Nisei particularly high in levels attained. This appears to be true for both the outcastes and the non-outcastes.

In the matter of food, etiquette, and language, the Issei of both groups are in large measure "un-American." Even with respect to dress, they are prone to be conservative and somewhat out of fashion. The majority of Nisei, though irretrievably wedded to a diet in which steamed polished rice plays a large part, are otherwise quite American. Outcaste and non-outcaste Nisei are generally undifferentiated here, but there is shaky evidence that the former are slightly more concerned with strict propriety of dress and social convention, and are more given to conspicuous consumption.

No positive evidence concerning differential outcaste and non-outcaste rates of relocation or active participation in the American war effort emerged in the course of the study. However, in the next section more findings relevant to this area are presented.

Persistence of Japanese Traits

Negative orientation to American society, or rather, the alternative mode of adaptation represented by behavior with positive reference to the Japanese values and forms, is of course more characteristic of the Issei than the Nisei. Furthermore, both the outcaste Issei and Nisei, by comparison to their non-outcaste counterparts, appear to be significantly more frequently associated with these values. The number of outcastes participating in Japanese activities is not large in absolute terms, but the percentage of the total outcaste population who participate is much larger than the percentage of non-outcaste participants. For example, the outcastes are judged by many instructors of "high culture" activities to be much more active in their fields of interest than the "ordinary" Japanese. It is noted that the outcastes are especially fond of shigin and kembu.[4] They are, in addition, more faithful spectators at Japanese painting and ikebana exhibits, at programs of classical dances and drama, and at Japanese movies.

As in Japan, the outcastes are characteristically affiliated with the Shinshu sect of Buddhism. The outcaste members are reported by

---

[4] One may speculate that the shigin and kembu serve, especially for the outcastes, as ideal vehicles for a psychologically satisfying symbolic expression of otherwise blocked aggressions. For one thing, the shigin is a form of ballad that very often deals with the brilliant and courageous exploits of samurai heroes. Anyone who has witnessed a performance will understand when the shigin singer is described, inadequately to be sure, as "a mass of dynamic tension, with some strained noises." Much tension is generated and released during a single performance, for by the end, the performer is often flushed and perspiring from the effort apparently required. Physiologically, his condition may be compared to that commonly associated with the rage reaction. Kembu seems to serve as a formalized or stylized dance interpretation of shigin works, in which a single performer, typically a boy or a young man dressed in simple samurai costume, poses, stalks, and leaps about on the stage while brandishing a gleaming samurai sword. His movements are coordinated with the performance of the shigin singer who usually stands or sits at one of the front corners of the stage.

priests to be somewhat better Buddhists than the non-outcastes, observing their religious duties and obligations.

No data were uncovered concerning the extent to which outcaste and non-outcaste Issei sent their children to Japan for formal educational training. However, according to teachers of Nisei and Sansei (third generation) at Japanese language schools in the ethnic communities, it seems that outcaste children were slightly more conscientious than non-outcastes in their language studies, and were somewhat less reluctant to participate in student programs, oratorical contests, and the like, in which demonstrated ability and achievement were the criteria of success. On the other hand, parents of outcaste students were less inclined and in some cases refused to participate actively in parents' associations. However, informants were quick to point out that outcaste parents were by no means less concerned with their children's welfare.

It is popularly believed that outcastes are more prone to mental disorders and certain physical diseases, especially trachoma, but there is no evidence to support this. Another belief popular among the less informed of the "regular" Issei is that the outcaste is filthy in his person and in his home. Thus, when a non-outcaste comes across an unkempt non-outcaste household, he is prone to think that the family is living "like outcastes." And, no doubt, when confronted with a clean outcaste home, he believes this "exception" proves the rule. The findings, on the contrary, show that in residence, food, Japanese etiquette, and language usage, the outcastes are generally indistinguishable from others and, indeed, in some respects are somewhat superior. For example, the consensus of the informants was, despite a number of dissents, that outcastes can be depended on more than non-outcastes to follow Japanese social conventions concerning greetings, gift exchanges, and so forth. Outcaste children are often spoken of by non-outcaste Issei as "good, well-behaved, conscientious, and patient."

Surprisingly, the informants agreed that the outcastes in their respective ethnic communities are on the whole more fair-skinned and less hirsute than the non-outcastes, and that outcaste females are on the average more attractive.

One customary Japanese practice is often obviously ignored by the outcastes when non-outcastes are involved. This is the serving of freshly brewed green tea and some condiments to guests. Some of the informants, patently not trusted completely by the outcastes, report that they have never been served tea, though beer and soft drinks have been offered and accepted. Other informants who enjoy closer relationships with outcastes have had no such experience, and some even eat with the outcaste family if the latter happens to be dining at the time of the visit. Both groups of informants explain the breach of custom in terms of outcaste reluctance to embarrass a visitor who may believe in the ritual impurity of anything prepared by outcaste hands.

Big parties featuring special Japanese culinary efforts and amateur entertainment programs were frequently held ostensibly for memorial purposes, at private outcaste homes in the prewar Fornia area. Such parties, which included dozens of families, were almost invariably exclusively ingroup except for the local priest. In a few instances, when three or four of the more respected and trusted non-outcaste community leaders were invited, they were seated by themselves at the head of the long festive board: imported sake was given to them and their food was served on special trays. Outcaste wedding ceremonies, funerals, and parties, however, are closely restricted.

In what appears to be close to the limiting case, though in a converse situation, some outcastes who had to call regularly on a non-outcaste for business reasons would refuse to enter the house and would conduct their business through the doorway or outside. Others, though persuaded to enter, would decline to share the same table and would state their business while squatting on their heels next to the wall.

The return of relatively small numbers of outcaste families following the war to the prewar areas of concentration, especially to the Fornia area, gives rise to some interesting questions. Informants agree that those who did return had some worthwhile property to return to, especially farm land that had increased in value during the war. Many families, however, went from the relocation centers to communities in the Midwest and the East, and it may well be that many decided to escape intra-ethnic community life. It seems likely that some returned to the West Coast, but probably sought the anonymity of the larger metropolitan areas, such as Los Angeles, San Francisco, Sacramento, and Seattle. However, there is good evidence that a disproportionate number of outcaste families were among those who went to the evacuee segregation center at Tule Lake, and then to Japan after the war. Of a cluster of six families who lived in a major outcaste concentration in the Fornia area, five are reported to have gone on to Japan; many other former residents in the area are reputed to have repatriated. For legally adult Nisei members of such families, the move entailed a renunciation of American citizenship and amounted to irrevocable expatriation.

Data on the outcastes of prewar Los Angeles, equally fragmentary though they are, indicate that the phenomenon of outcaste repatriation is not unique to the Fornia area. One may speculate that the motivation of these outcastes is not unlike the motivation of those who are now taking part in the "high culture" activities within the Japanese ethnic enclaves in the United States, that is, their need for recognition by those they consider "significant others."

SOCIAL AND PSYCHOLOGICAL CHARACTERISTICS OF OUTCASTES IN THE UNITED STATES

Self-Consciousness and Sensitivity

Earlier studies have found that marked self-consciousness and sensitivity are characteristic of minority group members having ambiguous social positions in modern America. Should the dynamics underlying such a situation be applicable in the case of the outcaste in the United States, they might be expected to be about twice as self-conscious and sensitive as the non-outcaste Japanese. Not only are the outcastes "marginal" with respect to the dominant American society but they are also marginal to the Japanese ethnic society of which they are nominally full members.

The data bearing on this aspect of the problem, while admittedly derived in large part from impressionistic accounts supplied by non-outcaste informants, are in line with the expectations. The outcastes are judged to be as a whole more suspicious and cautious in interpersonal situations and more sensitive to real or suspected slights. In the Sacramento area, a certain shopkeeper suffered for months the economic ill effects of an outcaste group boycott of his store brought on by a single unintentional slight to one of his regular outcaste customers. Often, even the friendly overtures of non-outcastes are met by rebuffs. In fact, it appears that intimate friendships between an outcaste and non-outcaste are very rare. In the few instances found where a "normal" Japanese could count one outcaste among his close friends, he was close to other outcaste individuals as well.

Primary and Secondary Group Contact and Formation

A major general finding of the study was that whereas non-outcaste primary groups frequently cut across prefectural lines, outcaste individuals almost invariably establish a primary type of relationship only with other outcastes from the same prefecture. Correlatively, those contacts made and maintained by outcastes with non-outcaste individuals or groups, whether for economic, recreational, or religious reasons, are almost invariably of a very segmental or a secondary group character. As noted above, attempts by non-outcastes to enlarge the area and bases of contact are usually immediately checked by the outcastes. Here, as in the case of self-consciousness and sensitivity, the motivational explanation probably lies in the need to minimize the threat to psychic security posed by the possible discovery of outcaste identity and subsequent explicit rejection.

As might be expected from the general overt denial of outcaste affiliation, there is an absence among the outcastes of the formal, publicly recognized organizations that are found in great numbers among the other Japanese. Similarly, the high degree of intra-outcaste cohesion is to be found only within relatively small, prefecturally homogeneous groups.

The old feeling has obviously persisted; it appears that among all Japanese, for one to be publicly labeled as Eta is to be damned, or more properly, intolerably shamed. Efforts by members of the outcaste group in the United States to alleviate their situation are marked, not by joining in the endeavor to neutralize the pre-Meiji social definition of outcaste membership, but rather by hiding the fact of outcaste identity. Or, should this fact already be public knowledge, efforts seem to be directed toward minimizing the possibility of explicit, overt rejection.

In the 1920's, a prominent non-outcaste newspaperman in the Japanese community in Los Angeles took it upon himself to work for the social emancipation of the outcaste by publishing a paper reporting the efforts and successes of the Suiheisha, the outcaste protest organization that mushroomed in that decade in Japan (see Chapter 2). In a recent interview, the publisher recalled that although the paper was published for nearly a year, there was only one individual who came to him and revealed his outcaste identity. This person, a resident of a farming community in Imperial Valley in California, had mistakenly assumed the publisher to be an exceptionally courageous but foolish outcaste. None of those who were already known to be outcastes even acknowledged the publisher's efforts. Some families who are rather widely known in the community to be of the outcaste group are almost certainly aware that they are so identified. But, as opposed to overt, covert identification appears to constitute a tolerable, if painful, burden.

Militant or Organized Aggressive Reactions

In contrast to Japan, militant reaction on the part of the outcastes is almost completely absent in the history of the Japanese ethnic group in the United States. No overall outcaste organization has ever appeared here. Furthermore, if any of the outcastes here did contribute to the organized and widespread protest movement that appeared in Japan in the twenties, non-outcastes do not know of it.

Earlier studies have found that militancy is not characteristic of the most deprived and oppressed groups, and that there is a maximum hostility if frustration of a group (a) violates normal, morally justifiable expectations, (b) is felt to be unnecessary or avoidable, and (c) is perceived as a threat to the sense of status.

While some forms of rejection, such as restrictions on intermarriage, are traditional and still sanctioned as "legitimate," though in opposition to official Japanese policy since 1871, overt and public anti-outcaste discrimination is not so sanctioned, informally or otherwise. Public mention of an individual's outcaste identity therefore violates the normal, morally justifiable expectations.

The particular circumstances of the two instances of militant reaction that were uncovered in the course of this study may be described in terms of the preceding formulation. In both cases overt, public reference was made to the identities of the outcastes involved indicating that such identification constitutes sufficient reason for militant reaction.

The earlier instance took place in the 1910's when discrimination against Japanese was high in California. Among the legislative actions taken by the legislature was one that severely restricted the farm land tenure rights of the Japanese alien farmer. Under this external threat to the immigrant group as a whole, the outcastes and the non-outcastes worked together to form corporations through which land could be purchased. In one of the parties held to celebrate the successful establishment of such a corporation, an ordinary participant, slightly tipsy, overtly referred to the Eta identities of some of the others. The transgressor of "proper" behavior was set upon by the outcaste members of the corporation and rather severely beaten. The existence of the corporation itself was also severely threatened until the necessary reintegration was attained by means of a public apology by the transgressor.

The later instance of militant outcaste reaction took place in the mid-twenties in the Fresno area of California. The attractive daughter of a non-outcaste owner-operator of one of the small shops in a town was sought by a number of suitors, among whom were a few outcastes. One suitor, in an attempt to reduce competition, had published in the local Japanese paper an anonymous article in which the families of certain of the suitors were clearly identified, though not by name, as Eta. This provoked the immediate and intense antagonism of most of the outcastes in the town, which led to an en masse physical attack by the group on the newspaper office during which much damage was done. The group was also bent on killing the publisher but widely respected Japanese notables from outside the area were able to restore peace. The publisher soon left the area for good.

Anomic Behavior: Delinquency, Crime, and Suicide

One would expect, on general principles, that outcastes would exhibit more of the symptoms of anomie than non-outcastes, because they enjoy only nominal equality of status within the ethnic group, regardless of achievement (see Chapter 13). However, despite persistent questioning of informants on this matter, only one reasonably clear case of anomic behavior was uncovered. This concerned a Nisei with outcaste origins who, though known to have been exceptionally energetic and able through his high school years, is, in his early thirties, a listless pool hall loafer. None of the some eleven instances of suicide which were uncovered in the course of the study could reasonably be related to the outcaste question.

Briefly, it seems that only a proportionately small part of the overall low rate of delinquency and crime found in the Japanese ethnic group in the United States is to be attributed to the outcaste subgroup. The evidence is rather that the outcastes, somewhat like the American lower middle class, deviate from the norms of the larger society not in the direction of "innovation" but of "ritualism." [5]

Internal Cohesion and Solidarity

According to the reports of the non-outcaste informants, the supposed outcastes tend to "stick closely together." In many social or economic activities in which the non-outcaste usually participates more or less independently of other families, the outcaste family is noted either to participate in close conjunction with other outcastes or not at all. For example, when an outcaste individual attends Buddhist ceremonies, he is usually in the company of other outcastes.

There is also evidence of a higher degree of economic interdependence, especially with regard to collective or cooperative financing. However, the difference between the outcaste and non-outcaste in this respect does not seem to be great. One noticeable difference is that within the outcaste group there is less reluctance to provide direct inter-loans of money as compared to the non-outcastes.

---

[5] Merton's typology and formulation of the modes of adaptation of individuals differently placed in a given social structure has proved useful. "Innovation" and "ritualism" are taken from his typology. (Merton, 1949, pp. 125–49.)

Personal attributes of high positive value in Japanese culture appear to be stressed even more by the outcastes than by the non-outcastes. For example, outcaste children are generally praised by non-outcaste Issei for their obedience and their use of correct social appropriate honorific language in varying situations. Those non-outcastes who have had sustained contact with outcaste individuals contend that the latter are on the whole more trustworthy, honest, patient, and diligent than the non-outcastes, despite the popular stereotype. The evidence is that within the outcaste group, there is at the conscious level a fierce pride in individual worth, combined with the belief that the ordinary Japanese in the United States is a pitiful and inferior person. Nonetheless, this conscious self-conception as well as this assessment of the non-outcaste is never publicly expressed.

Enforcement by the non-outcaste of outcaste endogamy has been by far the most obvious and frequently operating mechanism of outcaste rejection.[6] There appears to have been a rather substantial number of instances over the years in which incipient courtships were blocked, proposed marriages called off, or even accomplished marriages annulled in the name of maintaining family purity on the part of the non-outcaste families involved. At the same time, however, there seems to be developing within the outcaste group a corollary to the non-outcaste position, namely, an attitude of superiority manifested by, among other ways, an active encouragement of Nisei outcaste endogamy. In some respects, outcaste Issei are more difficult than non-outcastes in the matter of approving marriage partners for their offspring.

Intra-Ethnic Group Power Structure:
Ethnic Group Leadership

Seemingly driven by the structural conditions of the larger American society, Issei in one of the large number of Japanese ethnic enclaves have sought prestige and status in terms of relative position in their respective enclaves. This probably helps account for the many formal organizations to be found in the Japanese communities and for the proliferation of offices that usually characterizes such organizations. The outcastes, in their struggle for status, would therefore be expected to vie actively for high position in the ethnic group power structure as defined by formal organizational leadership. Here again, however, they are conspicuous by their absence. Of dozens of past and present ethnic group leaders reviewed, only one, the president of the Japanese association of one of the larger enclaves in Southern Cali-

---

[6] See the section Marriage and Family Patterns for the details of this aspect of rejection.

fornia, was known to be an outcaste. A few others have served on the lay governing board of two major Buddhist temples, but not as chairmen.

The situation has little or nothing to do with the objective abilities of the outcastes.[7] There was one case uncovered in which an able outcaste person tried to win the presidency of the Japanese association in a major community in Imperial Valley, California. His lack of success was reportedly due to a whispering campaign concerning his outcaste identity, instigated by the opposition. However, there is abundant evidence that the deterrents to outcaste participation in the hierarchy of ethnic group leadership lie not so much in the negative attitudes of the ordinary Japanese as in the general reluctance of the outcastes themselves. There have been a number of instances in which responsible non-outcastes in an organization have appealed to prominent outcaste members to assume formal leadership positions; in all such reported instances, the outcastes have refused.[8] The threat to psychic security is probably the major determinant of this behavior.

MARRIAGE AND FAMILY PATTERNS

Enforcement of outcaste endogamy by the ordinary Japanese has been by far the most obvious and ubiquitous mechanism of outcaste rejection. Presumably because of the great importance placed on family status in Japanese culture, the marriage situation was a uniquely critical one in which inquiry into genealogy had to be expected and tolerated. For this very reason some of the pressure for outcaste endogamy probably derives from within the outcaste group itself.

Many Japanese parents have explicitly kept their children from associating with those of known or suspected outcaste parents to reduce the possibility of having to deal with an "impossible alliance." There are undoubtedly a large number of instances where intergroup friendships have been stopped early to prevent serious involvement. There have been at least two and probably several more cases of annulments of intermarriages when the previously hidden outcaste origin of a partner was revealed. Further, there are hundreds of instances of the

---

[7] Indeed, as rated by such indices as economic status, the outcastes as a whole appear to be superior to the non-outcastes. And, as mentioned earlier in another connection, while the outcastes are slightly younger, as a whole they are slightly better educated.

[8] Some non-outcastes, especially those envious of the relative affluence of many outcastes, would probably argue that the outcaste who refuses to assume leadership positions is merely acting in terms of his selfish economic interest, for it is customary in most organizations for the leader to lead the members in contributions to the organization's coffers. There is no evidence of this, however. And more significant is the finding that for similar religious or other services, outcastes are relatively more generous than non-outcastes.

breaking up of a proposed marriage, because the discreet investigations of the invaluable "go-between" had turned up the hitherto
hidden outcaste identity of one of the parties involved. As a result,
marriage is often difficult for the outcaste individual. Fragmentary
reports indicate that among them marriage rates are slightly lower,
age at marriage slightly higher, and marriages between cousins are less
rare.

A non-outcaste Issei who has frequently served in the capacity of a
baishakunin or *nakōdo* (go-between) reveals that as a general rule go-
betweens never introduce people of marriageable age if one of the two
is known or rumored to be outcaste. Should intelligence available in
the local community be inadequate, the go-between has recourse to a
special family investigation service that has its main office in Tokyo
and branch representation in all sections of Japan. A striking finding
in the Fornia area was that neither of the two major informants interviewed could recall even a single case of intermarriage in prewar years,
among either the Nisei or the Issei in the area. Third-hand information in a few cases of mixed marriages has been received since the end
of the war by informants.

In virtually all cases of a disruption of a proposed alliance because
of the origins of one of the two involved, some reason other than that
of outcaste status is more or less publicly provided. Oddly, the significant opposition to a proposed intergroup alliance frequently comes
not from the parents of the non-outcaste but from their relatives, who
see the alliance as a major threat to the subsequent marriageability of
their offspring.

Nonetheless, the number of mixed marriages has been increasing
over the years. Romantic attachments between an outcaste and an
ordinary Japanese, which in earlier times were usually terminated by
the parents of the latter, now often lead to marriage, though frequently in the face of considerable family opposition. Of the two
parents, the mother is characteristically more concerned, sometimes
suffering some form of nervous breakdown. The Issei father often
points out the threat which intermarriage poses to the mental well-
being of the mother.

Ritual and Ceremonial Aspects

In the past, engagements were usually formally announced at a
dinner party held in a restaurant in the Japanese community or at the
home of one of the betrotheds and attended by relatives and close
friends of both families. The ubiquitous baishakunin characteristically
served as master of ceremonies.

The wedding ceremony, held at a temple or church, was followed later in the afternoon or evening by an extravagant dinner reception at a restaurant, and guests went prepared for several hours of speeches, dining, drinking and listening to and participating in amateur entertainment in which ribald songs were featured.

Such forms appear to have been common to both outcastes and ordinary Japanese.[9] However, guest selection, invitation, and attendance are reported to be different for the two groups. Whereas in ordinary marriages invitations are sent more or less freely, the outcastes were much more restrictive. For them, weddings are almost exclusively ingroup affairs; very few non-outcaste persons are invited to attend. Some informants complain that they have not been invited to the weddings of young people whom they have known since birth. It is perhaps significant that non-outcaste community leaders in the Florin area are reported to have made a special point of attending weddings of outcaste people in their respective communities regardless of whether or not they received formal invitations.

Some of the outcaste groups have been noted on the whole to be slightly more ostentatious and extravagant in such ritual matters as weddings and funerals, although the data on this point reveal exceptions.

Filial and In-Law Relations

Although many Issei lament the disregard for filial piety exhibited by the average Nisei, the informants are generally agreed that outcaste children are surprisingly free from this defect. Also, the extended outcaste families appear generally to be more closely knit than the others.

In all instances of mixed marriages discovered in the course of the investigation, the relationship of the couple with their outcaste in-laws was reputed to be especially harmonious; in most, their relations with the other in-laws tended characteristically to be strained. In general, then, while ordinary Japanese persons rarely penetrate the primary outcaste groups, once admitted, they are warmly received.

SUMMARY: OUTCASTE GROUP REJECTION IN THE UNITED STATES

Japanese with outcaste origins have met with severe discrimination throughout much of Japanese history, and their social rejection has apparently played a significant part in emigration patterns. How-

---

[9] As the Issei era wanes and the Nisei comes into its own, these practices are being abandoned in favor of receptions held at the temple or church immediately following the ceremony during which guests stand around genteelly sipping insipid punch and nibbling at thin slices of wedding cake.

ever, rejection has persisted for those who emigrated to the United States.

Although these outcastes have not publicly identified themselves with the outcaste protest movement in Japan, and instead have attempted to improve their disprivileged lot by masking the fact of their social identity, they have not been entirely successful. First of all, there were many ordinary Japanese immigrants already familiar with the social identities of one or more outcaste immigrant families. Such persons appear to have passed on this knowledge, albeit surreptitiously, to other non-outcastes in order to bolster their own tenuous sense of status. In addition, because the traditional customs were followed, thorough investigations were made of the social histories of all families in proposed marriage situations. The outcaste identities of a considerable number of families were thus revealed.

A rather large number of outcaste families are obviously aware that their identities are public knowledge in the Japanese ethnic community. For this group, there is a maximum concern to keep this knowledge from being expressed explicitly in public. Two instances of militant and violent reaction on the part of the outcastes were set off by just such events. Possibly because of the threat of such reactions, regular Japanese have taken and continue to take considerable care to refer to the "eta" only covertly.

Outcaste intra-ethnic group behavior is generally characterized by greater caution and sensitivity in interpersonal relations. They exhibit more internal cohesion than the non-outcastes, although the considerations deriving from the decision to mask their identity appear to have precluded the formation of formal organizations among them.

Primary group relationships only rarely extend beyond the bounds of a particular prefectural outcaste group. Contacts with non-outcastes from the given prefecture and with persons from other prefectures are almost invariably of a most segmental kind. Efforts on the part of some non-outcastes to develop the contact into something more are resisted. Those few friendships that cross the line are marked by great mutual trust and confidence.

Contrary to expectations, anomic behavior does not appear to be prevalent in the outcaste group. Rather, what deviations were noted tended to be in the direction of overconformity to certain of the norms of Japanese society.

The members of this group have resisted any effort to gain positions of prestige in the formal leadership structure of the overall ethnic group. The deterrent has probably been that such direct competition with ordinary Japanese for social prestige would increase the possibilities for overt rejection. But rather than by-passing the rejecting group and acting wholly with reference to the values and norms of modern

American society, the outcastes are apparently driven to seek ethnic group respect and acceptance by engaging in Japanese "high culture" activities. This gains support from the finding that the rates for wartime segregation and war and postwar Issei repatriation and Nisei expatriation tended to be higher for the outcaste than for the ordinary Japanese.

The primary mechanism of outcaste rejection has been the reluctance on the part of the ordinary Japanese to enter into marriage with the outcastes. In cases of mixed marriages, the relations of the husband and wife with their non-outcaste in-laws tend to be limited and strained.

Those occupations historically associated with the outcastes and those otherwise debased in Japanese society, while widely found in the Japanese ethnic group, are avoided by the outcaste members of the group. Also avoided are occupations and businesses that increase the possibility of explicit rejection by ordinary Japanese.

It should be made clear that most of the findings reported on the foregoing pages refer to the Issei segment of the Japanese ethnic population in the United States. It appears most likely that active outcaste rejection is less frequent on the part of ordinary Nisei and will become even rarer in the future. Further, by the time the Sansei or third generation Japanese achieve majority it would be surprising if even the term Eta were to be found outside of the few Japanese historical societies that may emerge in that generation of Japanese-Americans. [10]

---

[10] One cannot conclude that acculturation to American ways has completely removed intra-ethnic prejudice among the American-born Japanese. Several years ago co-author Wagatsuma was told by a young woman who was a temporary student at the University of Chicago that on two different occasions when being dated by American-born Japanese young men she was informed in the course of a first evening together that her escort was of "proper" non-Eta background. The young woman, from Tokyo, was somewhat unfamiliar with the outcaste problem in her own country and was mystified by American-born Japanese raising the issue with her in the United States.

SECTION IV

Psychological Perspectives

INTRODUCTION

The following three chapters comprise an exploration of the general and specific consequences to the individual of a social situation in which assimilation from a socially despised minority group is blocked by strong social prejudice.

In exploring the effects of Burakumin minority status on some aspects of personality development we relate our data to five ordering concepts, which permit us to demonstrate how growing up in a Buraku differentially affects the Burakumin child and, by creating a subcultural distance, functions to separate him from the majority society. These concepts are: differential socialization experience, differential role expectancies, social self-identity, selectivity of reference group, and selective permeability. Chapter 11 is focused on the first three of these concepts; Chapters 12 and 13 on the other two. Chapter 11 expands upon these concepts from the subjective standpoint of the inner experiences of an outcaste, problems of self-discovery, self-hatred, and the ruptures that occur in his affectional ties.

The next two chapters approach these social psychological problems from the viewpoint of social belonging and tendencies toward conformity and deviancy with respect to the majority society.

Chapter 11, "Socialization, Social Self-Perception, and Burakumin Status," examines the socialization experiences of the Burakumin as they may be different from those of ordinary Japanese. We come to the conclusion that the influence of social discrimination on self-image is of central importance among the Burakumin as it is among other minority groups elsewhere.

Chapter 12, "Group Solidarity and Individual Mobility," examines the social and individual defense mechanisms operating within the community that keep an individual a Burakumin and prevent his assimilation into majority society. In Chapter 12, we consider how social identity functions in the Buraku community from the standpoint of social solidarity within the outcaste reference group, as well as from the standpoint of the psychological and social barriers to "passing." The previous chapters on rural Buraku communities by Donoghue and Cornell have described some of the social processes that integrate and maintain the outcaste community. This chapter is supplementary in that we examine the processes of group solidarity related to psychological defense mechanisms which make "passing" so difficult for the "Invisible Race." Finally, this chapter examines the personal effects of discrimination in inter-caste love relationships.

Chapter 13, "Minority Status and Attitudes Toward Authority," examines how members of minority group communities defend themselves against what are perceived as agencies of a hostile majority society. Social role expectations of the adult Burakumin in many instances do not tend to induce as strong a conformist identification with prevailing social authority as is found in middle class Japanese. In this chapter we seek to understand the respects in which social discrimination induces some form of social deviancy and lack of respect for constituted authority.

If we were to generalize from Negro or Mexican-American experience, we would anticipate that, having experienced generations of social discrimination, the Burakumin in addition to participating in radical political activities would manifest various forms of socially deviant behavior to a greater extent than the majority population. First, we would anticipate a high incidence of apathy with regard to education or to public health and sanitary activities initiated by governmental authority. Secondly, we would anticipate some deviousness and dependent opportunism with respect to welfare programs. Third, we would anticipate a higher incidence of antisocial attitudes expressed in delinquent or criminal behavior. The evidence from Japan supports these hypotheses. In sum, the Burakumin group identity serves to make the Burakumin somewhat "impermeable" to ordinary social authority.

Some Ordering Concepts

Differential Socialization Experiences.—Differences in experiences during socialization within a complex culture lead to "modal" variations between groups and subgroups.[1] Under the general concept of differential socialization, one can discuss how the nature of cultural

---

[1] Kardiner (1939). For reasons well delineated by Linton we prefer the term modal personality to basic personality without, however, rejecting most of Kardiner's formulations.

values, concepts of adult roles within the family, child-rearing practices, and so forth, influence the development of modal personalities in distinct class, caste, or ethnic groups. The word "modal" implies that culture patterns deeply influence the prevalence of certain forms of ego defense or control mechanisms and patterns of interpersonal interaction within one group as compared to another. Certain forms of childhood experiences within particular cultural settings predispose the adult to select certain modes of coping with his experiences. Members of any one such group can easily reach negative conclusions concerning another group on grounds that they seem to behave or respond "unnaturally" or "immorally."

The concept of differential socialization and of possible resultant modalities in personality traits is necessary to understand why individuals of any one group or social segment of a complex society feel some degree of strangeness or cultural distance in relating to those of another. While wide range of variation in personality mechanisms is found in even the most isolated societies, nevertheless, the astute observer of any specific group notes certain modalities in behavior characteristically used in coping with life situations as psychologically more available for the given group than for others comparatively observed.

Differential Role Expectancies.—Social roles are perhaps best understood as modalities of behavior reinforced by formal or informal sanctions and expectancies. At every stage within a culture, starting with infancy, behavior is thus oriented. Expectancies are fairly uniform within simple societies, but in more complex societies, they may be highly dissimilar, thus helping to distinguish among social or subculture segments. For example, parents within a particular class or caste segment may differ widely as to the degree of impulse control or responsibility expected of an individual defined as a grade-school boy or a so-called adolescent.[2] What is expected of a mature adult or an aged grandparent may depend on the status position of the family within a culture. These expectancies either become internalized as part of the self or are selectively resisted, depending upon the permeability of the individual to various reference groups (see concepts four and five below), or upon the degree of motivation of the individual toward conformity or deviancy. In a complex society, conflicts occur when inducements toward social mobility within a class hierarchy and other problems such as acculturation expose the developing individuals to a series of alternative expectations of role behavior.

---

[2] The Japanese, from his earliest years, is expected to depend more on the *family* social roles, which are well defined traditionally in *family* terms, and is less encouraged to define social roles in *individual* terms. In American society, concerned with individual achievement, what is termed "independence training" starts very early in comparison with the Japanese.

Social role expectancies are turned toward the individual from infancy. This concept of social role expectancies is, therefore, intimately related to the nature of differential socialization experiences.[3] The concept "role expectancies" has more often been used in discussing adult social roles than in discussing those of the infant, but there is no reason for this limitation. In this sense, attitudes taken toward toilet training and masturbation, for example, are closely related to what is expected both from the child and from the future adult.

Social Self-Identity.—The concept "social self-identity," or ego-identity, has been used by Erik Erikson[4] as a bridge between the psychoanalytic framework and that of sociology. He points out the importance of the period between adolescence and young adulthood in modern society, for it is then that definitive decisions about future life roles have to be made. As one moves from simple, rigid societies with few alternate adult roles, to more complex, segmented societies, this period becomes increasingly important. For Erikson, the self- or the social self-identity is not an addition of various roles but a unique integration of roles which encompasses certain elements of self-perception that, properly speaking, cannot be related to roles at all. As demonstrated below, this concept has particular relevance for those problems of self-acceptance and self-hatred that are related to minority status.

Selectivity of Reference Group.—"Reference group" is a concept taken from social psychology[5] and is particularly useful in understanding some of the stresses and conflicts experienced by the Burakumin both intra-psychically and inter-personally. The individual's standards, attitudes, and status aspirations stem from and are related to certain groups—the individual's reference groups. Usually these are groups of which he is an actual member—*membership groups.* When they are not, the discrepancy between the two—for example, if an individual actually lives in one group but aspires to belong to or is made to relate himself to another—causes tension.

Social psychologists sometimes neglect to emphasize the internalization process in relation to reference groups. One can look at superego formation as an early manifestation of the internalization of the reference groups represented by primary family and religious ideology. We relate this concept to our discussion of social solidarity and the appearance of ingroup or we-group identifications and outgroup or they-group hostilities. We also relate the concept to, but at the same time maintain some distinction from, the psychoanalytic interpreta-

---

[3] See Whiting and Child (1954).
[4] Erikson (1950) and (1959), pp. 1–171.
[5] See Sherif (1948) and Shibutani (1961).

226 PSYCHOLOGICAL PERSPECTIVES

tion of superego. The more sociologically oriented theories emphasize the actual groups to which an individual refers rather than the operation of internalized processes. In addition to what has been inflexibly internalized as early superego, the individual is continually ordering his behavior in terms of a primary reference group and he or others are continually judging this behavior in accordance with the norms and standards of this group. (At critical stages of development the individual shifts from one reference group to another and numerous conflicts can occur when the reference groups have conflicting expectancies and sanctions.)

The first reference group is the primary family or parental image, psychologically speaking. These images are internalized and become part of the ego structure and part of the moral and superego structure of the individual. As the individual becomes more aware of the outside world, however, peers become a very important source of social activity, and begin to influence the standards and norms of the individual and his behavior. Depending upon the relative rigidity of earlier internalization, the individual will more or less take cues from his most immediate, important primary group relationships. Internalized standards of behavior learned in the family, set up in a formal sense in many societies by the religious orientation of the family, will determine how permeable the person is to his peer groups, and will help the individual select among the alternate peer groups available to him.[6]

All sorts of conflicts between the role expectations of one group and another are possible, especially in hierarchical societies that have become increasingly mobile with social change. Our examination of the Burakumin will show particularly poignant examples of individuals caught between social directives and a confused concern as to what group they are to relate to. Individuation is never a complete process, and one understands a good deal of personality integration as well as social integration in terms of the group to which an individual feels he most belongs.

Selective Permeability.—A final concept that is developed herein for analyzing the material on the Japanese outcastes is that of relative or "selective permeability." This concept emphasizes the mechanisms within the ego that are concerned with selective cognitive perception and interpretation of the outer social reality. With this concept we attempt to relate certain structural components of personality to the concept of reference group. In an analogy borrowed from biology we may say that the ego is a membrane that selectively allows certain experiences to penetrate and become an integral part of the total self.

---

[6] Chapter 14 expands this examination of the reference group specifically in respect to the development of socially deviant attitudes.

This concept is especially important in understanding cultural distance created between different culture or subculture groups. In a sense the most important reference group is the one that can penetrate the individual's experience the most readily. In a well-functioning culturally conditioned ego, ideas that are hostile or contradictory will not be allowed to come in where they are directly in opposition to those of the primary reference group. Potentially disruptive, inconsistent, or discordant elements are protectively kept out so that they do not upset the viable homeostasis of the living structure.

There is a prevalent misconception that difference in the cultural modes of living themselves cause lack of understanding between individuals. We would say that it is not the differences in behavior that cause misunderstanding, but the need to preserve protective barriers between individuals and groups. This is particularly noticeable where caste or class discriminations are made by one segment of a population against the other. Differences are emphasized as a barrier to the assimilation process, or they are used selectively in a defensive way to enable the individual to maintain his integrity when rejected.

GEORGE DE VOS AND
HIROSHI WAGATSUMA

Socialization, Self-Perception, and Burakumin Status

DIFFERENTIAL SOCIALIZATION WITHIN THE BURAKU

The Burakumin are considered to be somewhat impulsive and volatile in their behavior patterns, an impression sometimes related to a perception of the Burakumin as hostile and aggressive in his relationships with individuals from the outside society. We discuss elsewhere the relationship of hostile behavior to ingroup solidarity. There is some evidence that in socialization practices the Burakumin actually do tend to be less restrained in the expression of aggression toward their children, and in many cases parents employ physical punishment. Whereas Buraku children do quarrel with one another, serious fighting tends to be discouraged. On the other hand, these children are not scolded with any severity when they fight with children outside the community, and are sometimes even encouraged to do so. The amount of hostility and aggression implanted in the outcaste children by the way they are controlled and the amount of direct aggression experienced may have something to do with how the majority Japanese evaluate the Buraku child, as well as the adult. Hostility, hate, and aggression developed within the family or peer group are readily displaced toward people of the outside community, who are judged to merit it because of their prejudice. The father's physical aggression toward his own children may be partially explained as a displacement in terms of hostility induced by certain relationships to the outside community. Our first-hand material, although extremely limited, would suggest that there may be greater experience of aggressiveness in interpersonal relationships by the Buraku child than is common

228

in the outside Japanese society. However, there is no valid quantification of these differences nor do we have any way of comparing the lower class in Japan generally in this regard.

The Buraku child is probably more overtly exposed to sexuality than is usual for the total Japanese society. There is less hiding of sexual relationships, and the children seem to develop less of a "latency period" in some respects than in the more restrained Japanese household. In general, although our sources of information are secondary, there would seem to be less stringent impulse control of either sexuality or aggression demanded of the Buraku child in his social role expectations. His perception of the nature of adult relationships shows him that adults do act impulsively and emotionally.

One reliable informant without Buraku background, who spent his childhood in the district near the outcaste community and had many friends of Buraku origin at school, stated that Buraku children are precocious and "know more about sexual matters than ordinary children." He thinks that there are two contributing factors: although the Buraku houses are no smaller than many non-Buraku houses, he had the impression that children have more opportunities to witness parental coitus. Also Buraku adults are more apt to talk openly about sex, so that children learn about sexual behavior both visually and verbally. The mechanism of repression is less operable in such an open atmosphere.

One informant from the Buraku told us that he does not remember being punished by his parents for his sexual curiosity and play when he was a child, though he engaged in sex play with both boys and girls. He recalled that in his early school days neighborhood children came to his house and all went together into a room upstairs and examined each other's genitals, shouting their comments freely. He remembers that in the living room downstairs there was always an adult who he believes must have had some notion of their activities, though no comments were made. He also noted that in the Buraku, the houses are rather small and there is little privacy, especially in summer when windows are left open all night. The informant recalls from childhood several experiences of witnessing adults in neighboring houses in the act of intercourse. In this way, Buraku children are exposed to sexual manners from a relatively early age.

DIFFERENTIAL ROLE EXPECTANCIES

In certain Buraku, at least among the lower strata of the community, there is considerable casualness about marriage ties and sexual fidelity. Temporary liaisons are reported to be common. For example, a husband who goes to a distant place to work for a year or two may find another partner there. His wife, instead of remaining alone with their family, will take another man if the opportunity occurs. In the majority society, a scandal would arise, whereas in the Buraku it is taken as a matter of course if the person who forms the temporary liaison is of their own community or a neighboring one. It is considered necessary for a woman to have someone to rely upon for income and training of children, as well as for her own pleasure which is an acknowledged part of the relationship of the sexes. Such "free" attitudes are not necessarily valued by the Burakumin themselves: we have seen, for example, that according to the opinion survey of the Japanese sociologist quoted in Cornell's chapter, Buraku people consider themselves to have lower sexual morals than the majority society. Rather, the attitude taken is a matter-of-fact one. One informant, now living in an outcaste community, told us that a husband's infidelity is taken for granted, especially if the man is a hard worker and supports his family. However, a noteworthy difference in social role expectation between the Buraku and the outside majority society would be the lenient attitude toward the sexual behavior of women in the former. In the majority society men traditionally could enjoy sexual freedom, but middle-class Japanese women were required to be loyal and chaste.

In the Buraku, according to one informant, premarital innocence is not generally expected of girls, and should a girl become pregnant, the general attitude, while disapproving, is protective. The baby is usually registered as its mother's brother or sister, or a marriage is quickly arranged between the mother and her lover or another man. In the case of marriage, the couple register the baby as their own.

The relative sexual freedom of Buraku women does not seem to carry over into formal equality of status between man and wife. The Buraku wife is expected to fulfill a role subordinate to a dominant household head. One of our Buraku informants illustrated the social attitudes in this regard by relating the following occurrence: In one of the outcaste communities of Kyoto, a husband liked a young woman who had been suspected of being a prostitute and made her his mistress. His wife got very angry, whereupon the couple quarreled and the husband ordered his wife to leave. She then decided to stand in front of her house on a wooden box and tell the gathering crowd the long story of a loyal and obedient wife's injuries. The crowd was amused but unsympathetic, the general understanding being that a good wife endures infidelity. She was supposed to accept whatever happened to her. This woman was acting in an unusual way, an unfamiliar way, and so was criticized. After this incident, the wife was driven from the house by her husband, who took his mistress in as wife. This incident reflects both the casual attitude about sexuality and the traditional or feudal concepts of the relative positions of women and men. Women among the Burakumin, as in the traditional society, are required or demanded to be subservient, docile, and non-aggressive toward their men; a husband beating an unruly wife is not uncommon.

Buraku men are allowed, if not expected, to be impulsive and physically aggressive, and the aggression is often directed toward their wives and children. Girls are spared no more than boys by their fathers, and both may be beaten by their fathers. Mothers are generally more physically aggressive than they are in the majority society, especially than in the middle class. Fights between women are within the experience of most of our informants.

Within the Buraku the upper class family patterns of aggression seem to be closer to those of the majority middle class society. General Buraku identification, however, makes for some feelings of vulnerability about inability to control one's passions, even among the middle class families of the Buraku.

SOCIAL SELF-IDENTITY AS A BURAKUMIN

Minority status requires an individual to cope continually with a negative self-image automatically internalized as he becomes socialized in a disparaging majority society. A self-image is not always conscious. Sometimes under stress a person comes face to face with attitudes toward himself that have been unconsciously repressed. The following material will illustrate, with case examples, the psychological experiences involved in self-discovery of Burakumin identity; the passive, intra-punitive, and conservative elements in conscious self-images; and certain unconscious and suppressed negative self-images.

Self-Discovery of Burakumin Identity

Perhaps our most poignant material concerning the social self-identity of the Burakumin deals with early experiences of children in discovering themselves and their families to be members of a disparaged group. An incident told to us by a university student with Buraku background well illustrates the experiences of self-discovery of a Buraku child's identity. It also illustrates the problem of having to internalize an image of oneself as a feared object, and of having to deal with fear both of others and of oneself. In this respect, there are some differences between the role of the Burakumin today and that of the American Negro. In relation to majority whites, the Negro has to handle within himself a complex pattern of hatred and fear. He well knows the stringent sanctions that have been used against

his race by the majority society in maintaining its dominance. At the
same time, he knows he is feared and that whites perceive him as
acting out impulses that they themselves feel but prefer to project
onto the Negro. In the self-identity of the Negro, therefore, is the fact
that he must be afraid of the white, while knowing that he is seen as
a potential sexual and aggressive threat to him. In the case of the
Burakumin there seems at present to be less acting out of aggressive
sanctions by majority Japanese against members of the outcaste group.
Whereas in the past Burakumin could with impunity be subjected
to violence by the samurai or even commoners, today aggressive
sanctions are not used to maintain dominance. The attitude both in
the distribution of relief funds and in other matters is nonviolent
and mollifying. The Burakumin, therefore, if he is at all permeable
to the role expectations of the majority group toward him, has to
cope with a self-concept that includes a potential display of aggression
toward the majority group individual. The incident which follows
illustrates how a small child tries to cope with the definition of himself as a fearful object.

One day our informant when four or five years old wandered out
of his community to a neighboring hill that separated the Buraku from
a residential district of ordinary folk. On his return he encountered
two children about his age who looked at him for a while, then suddenly screamed and started to run away. These two children must
have been told by their parents not to go beyond the hill where the
frightful, untouchable people lived. They must have been extremely
frightened when they realized this boy was from the prohibited area.
When they started to run, the children cried out the word, "yotsu,"
a harsh taboo word designating the outcaste group. The student remembers that he shuddered and felt a mixture of fear, sorrow, and
anger. He chased the children, caught them, beat them, and shouted
meaningless words at them, while they remained passive, pale with
fear. At a later date, our informant was again visiting the little hill,
and upon return he met a boy coming from the direction of his own
community. Without comprehending what he was doing, he cried out
"yotsu" and ran away from the boy. Somehow, he was attempting to
understand the overwhelming sense of fear that he had witnessed in
the other two children. In recounting the story, the emotional impact
of the word came back with extreme force.

Another informant, from a family that had successfully passed,
relates a number of episodes from his childhood that show feelings of
secrecy and shame relating to self-discovery. They also convey a sense
of discovery about the meaning of outcaste parental roles compared
with those of the larger society.

At about the time this informant was ready to go to grade school, his father decided to move out of the Buraku. The first step was to open up a small shoestore in a neutral neighborhood. In addition to selling new shoes, his father continued his previous occupation of repairing shoes and sandals. The boy went to a grade school with children of the outside society and was not known as an outcaste; in other words, he was passing at school, although in his immediate neighborhood his father's occupation made it evident that the family was of Buraku background. When in the second or third grade, he recalls that he drew a picture of his father at work for an art class. After showing the picture at school, he took it home and showed it to his parents, expecting praise. Instead, he noticed that they became very upset and forbade him ever to draw a picture of his family at work. From the serious reaction and tone of their voices, he sensed he had done something seriously wrong and that there was something about his father's job, some secret about his family that should be hidden from the eyes of some people. At this point he suddenly came to look upon himself not simply as another ordinary child in school, but as a Buraku person.

Another incident took place when he was in the fifth grade at school. When he delivered a pair of repaired shoes to a customer's house, the man brought out a bamboo stick and tied the money to one end of it which he then stretched out and proffered to the child, thus avoiding having the child come close to him or approaching the house. This was not an unusual way of giving money to the untouchable Burakumin. As he now recalls the incident, he was not angry, but felt very lonely and helpless, and wanted to be accepted more warmly as an ordinary child. It was not until after his family moved out of the Buraku that the small boy was exposed to the harsher attitudes toward Burakumin.

Internalized disparagement is often turned toward members of one's own group in times of stress or hostility. For example, not far from the family store of one of our informants was another small shoe-store. From the occupation, it was evident that the owner of this store and his family were Buraku people making an attempt to pass. Whenever the wife of the shoestore owner met our informant as a child, she would cry out, "eta, eta!" or "yotsu, yotsu!" repeatedly. The boy, sad and angry at the same time, told his mother who became incensed and asked him to tell her immediately the next time it occurred. When he did, his mother ran out and began to beat the woman wildly. The boy was frightened and ashamed; he had seen her before only as a calm, gentle woman, submissive to her husband. He recalls vaguely that back in the community from which he and his family had moved, he had seen other such wild fights between women.

This story reveals that this young man somehow had psychologically sought to separate himself from the community at a fairly early age. His reference group was no longer the Buraku but the outside society. Nevertheless, his mother's impulsive, passionate behavior destroyed a previous defensive idealization and caused him to feel consciously that he could not completely escape his past.

In a case of self-discovery Etsuko, an eighteen-year-old girl, committed suicide.[7] The newspapers reported different causes. *Mainichi* reported that the girl killed herself because she had been suspected of theft, while *Asahi* attributed her suicide to discrimination at school. The complete story was complex. One of Etsuko's friends at school, also a Buraku girl, was quoted as saying,

Etsuko was the only Buraku girl in her class; therefore it was she who was suspected of theft when stealing took place a number of times in her classroom. . . . She became very upset when she was suspected. Shortly before, a thoughtless inquiry had been made at the school to identify the Buraku students in every class. I am not saying that this inquiry made Etsuko kill herself, but it certainly was one of the causes. It was thoughtless of our school to make such an inquiry; instead of giving warmth or help to Etsuko who needed it, the school actually increased discrimination by carrying out such a strange inquiry.

Etsuko's father was of the Buraku but in an attempt to pass had moved away long before, and maintained very little contact with his former community. The children grew up without any knowledge of their outcaste background. Further, according to the friend, Etsuko herself had discriminatory feelings about the Buraku. However, shortly before her death, she had come to learn her own identity; in addition, there were some students who became suspicious of her background. The young girl must have developed a complicated, ambivalent feeling toward her own identity, and the inquiry at the school which made all the students aware of it must have been a strong shock. This state of affairs, followed by the suspicion of being a thief, is sufficient to explain the suicide.

Passive, Intra-punitive, and Conservative Elements in Conscious Self-Images

Some revealing materials have been gathered by Japanese social scientists concerning the Burakumin's conscious self-concepts. Koyama[8] cites four types of tension consciously experienced by Burakumin in their relationships with majority society. First, they are aware of their extreme poverty or economic handicap and often resolve their tension by supporting leftist policies. Second, many Burakumin have a strong

---

[7] From *Buraku*, November, 1957, pp. 2–9.
[8] Koyama, 1953.

sense of personal inferiority that leads to resignation or passive resentment. In critical situations, these resentments come to the surface and impulsive aggressive behavior emerges. The third tense attitude, found more in the educated, is a sense of injustice, which leads to a continual sense of indignation against the majority society. Few are able to overcome this personal indignation and sublimate their anger into more constructive channels. They function below their optimal capacities, debilitated by unresolved feelings. The fourth tension experienced by the more educated Burakumin is a continual anxiety over passing.

In research in Osaka City Koyama asked, "What do you think is the best way to abolish social discrimination against Burakumin?" He classified the answers into seven categories. Of 97 persons approached, 18.5 percent gave "don't know" answers; 11.3 percent gave "no solution" answers, such as "I know something must be done, but I don't know what to do"; 6.2 percent gave "avoidance" answers, such as "I do not want to think about it, I want to be left alone." These three groups, or over one-third the individuals approached, reveal a general attitude of passive resignation, helplessness, and avoidance of the problem of discrimination. The fourth group, or 29.9 percent, gave what Koyama terms "self-reflective" answers. These attitudes reflect some passive helplessness, a great deal of intra-punitive thinking, such as "We should behave better; we should give up our slovenly behavior and keep our houses and clothes clean; we should seek more education; we should cooperate with one another; we should move out of this dirty area; we should change our occupations to more decent and respectable ones." In contrast with these passive attitudes, the fifth group, 15.5 percent, gave "extra-punitive" responses, which put all the blame on the majority society: "We should destroy discrimination; we should make them learn that we are all equally Japanese; those who have prejudice should be legally punished." The sixth group, 10.3 percent, also militant, were too overwhelmed by their own anger and resentment toward the outside society even to verbalize their opinions. The last group, 8.2 percent, was considered by Koyama to be the most objective or realistic. Their answers pointed out the necessity of enlightenment on the part of the outside society and actual improvement in the Burakumin's life situation.

Men tended to be either intra-punitive or extra-punitive in their attitudes, while women tended toward "don't know" or avoidance answers. Self-reflective and objective-realistic answers were found most often among those between 30 and 55 years of age. People over 55 tended to be extra-punitive, and those under 30 tended to fall into the "passionate" group.

John Cornell, in his chapter, has cited some very interesting results of research carried out by Yamamoto on the Burakumin's self-image and image of the outside society that suggests that a conservative or traditionalist tendency is one way of insuring self and group acceptance.[9] The Buraku people consider themselves to be more filial, more respectful to ancestors, and more stringent in the observation of arranged marriages, more deferential toward persons of higher status when they compare themselves to the ippan (ordinary) outsiders. They also think they are harder working, more cooperative, and more egocentric than the outside people. They believe that outside people are better reared, more educated, more hygienic, better dressed, have higher and better sexual morals, and better speech habits. It is apparent that Burakumin use their traditionalist attitudes as a counterbalance to a self-disparaging image. According to our own informants, there seems to be a certain pride in being more traditional. Older and intellectual members of the community like to refer to a general deterioration of ethical standards among postwar youth and point out the importance of conservative Japanese conduct. In this respect the Burakumin in general inferentially put less emphasis on individualism or innovation and more emphasis on maintenance of traditionally sanctioned social-role behavior. These community attitudes serve to prevent anomic or deviant tendencies from becoming unduly disruptive in stabilized outcaste communities.

Unconscious and Suppressed Negative Self-Images

In the following chapter we shall discuss in detail the great difficulty experienced by a "passing" Burakumin in freeing himself from his own conceptions of himself as an outcaste person. To illustrate our argument here in reference to self-image we will anticipate this discussion by citing some examples of the unconscious presence of negative self-images in individuals who are attempting to change self-identity by passing.

In our first example, the informant is passing as a city official in the municipal government of Osaka, although he is still living with members of his own outcaste community in Kyoto. By taking a one-hour trip on a train, he changes his identity. At his bureau he is treated as an ordinary person, both by his supervisors and by those he supervises; at home, he remains an outcaste. He is looked up to in his community as a success and serves as a symbol of achievement for the outcaste people, particularly because he has not deserted them. When we asked this informant whether he thinks the Buraku people are visibly discernible, he answered that they were to other Buraku per-

---

[9] This tendency goes counter to the pressure toward deviancy and innovation suggested by Merton (1959) and others as operative on marginal or minority groups in society.

sons. He claims he can recognize a Burakumin who is successfully passing. When asked how he could tell, after some hesitation he told us
that living conditions within the outcaste community are terrible;
torn-down houses, unsanitary conditions, distasteful occupations, dirty
food, bad language, violence, fighting, laziness. These conditions produce "something vicious, something dirty, something unnameable, but
something which can be felt, like a strong odor. . . . This something
horrible permeates or gets into the people who are born and raised and
live in this area. It is something like a bad body odor. . . . Even when
an individual leaves the community, wherever he may go, this something horrible or discernible always accompanies him." He said that
this "something" may be recognized by speech, mannerisms, facial expression, gesture, and all those personal expressions usually not perceived consciously. Here, a man of considerable learning who is successfully passing, inadvertently told us that he himself has an image of
his people as somehow unclean. We could not assess how much of this
negative feeling is directed consciously toward himself.

The following incident was told by a young unmarried informant,
whom we will call Osamu, now successfully passing as a teacher. Although he did not know the traditional occupation of his own family,
he knew that they had long enjoyed upper class status within an outcaste community and had been very wealthy. In his grandfather's time
the financial state of his family suddenly declined and by the time
Osamu's mother came to his house as the young bride of his son, the
grandfather was reduced to repairing *geta,* the footgear of the outside
society. His father worked as an assistant to the grandfather, soon
taking his place. A virtuous, hard-working young man, he managed to
pay the grandfather's debts and eventually was able to rent a little
store of his own. This was a step in upward mobility, since there is
a big status difference between a person who walks around and repairs
shoes and a person who owns his own repair shop, however small.
When the building in which the store was located was put up for
sale he bought it and moved his family into it, but did not attempt to
hide his background. Passing had to wait until the next generation.
The business thrived, and almost twenty years after they moved out
of the community, the father owned one of the biggest shoestores in
the city.

The father was very much interested in his children's education. He
was stern to the point of harshness; his two sons were sent to good
private schools where they were always at the top of their classes, both
later graduating from the university.

As a child, Osamu went through some very painful experiences of
being discriminated against, laughed at, or being pointed out as a
four-footed animal (yotsu). When he complained, he was told by his

father that the only way to be freed was to achieve, to get ahead, to pass as a successful member of the majority society. To Osamu achievement and passing were identical words. "Unless you are successful in your achievement, you cannot be successful in your passing." However, Osamu told us that his father's attitude toward passing was rather contradictory because he was also told not to run away from insulting outsiders but to fight back. The father was telling his son two things— to hide his identity and be a successful passer, and also to strike back as an outcaste rather than hide his background. This "double bind" explains in part why Osamu remains basically ambivalent toward his own successful passing.

After going to the university near his own community, Osamu transferred to an institution in Tokyo where he faced keen classroom competition. He found life in the big city, away from friends and family, somewhat difficult, and began to feel inferior to others in his class. He became very depressed, and while on a train he suddenly noticed that a woman was looking at his face. Becoming panicky, he felt that everyone was staring at him, that he was becoming very ugly and that people were noticing the change and distortion taking place in his face. He mutely prayed for the people on the train not to look at him, saying to himself that he was a harmless person. He felt a strong surge of anger, but at the same time he felt very weak, and wished he could ask for the favor of not being stared at any more. In his panic, he was trembling and perspiring all over. He got off the train as quickly as possible and took a long rest in the station. Afterwards, this painful delusion of being stared at would come back occasionally. To avoid it, every time he boarded a train he would stand facing away from the other passengers close to the doorway, looking outside, or if this were not possible, he hid his face with a weekly magazine.

When he related his experiences, he obtained considerable cathartic relief. Some forgotten incidents came to mind. In the second grade he failed to become the top student, and when told by his teacher that he was second rather than at the top, he urinated in his pants. One free association to the face-changing was the memory of a long forgotten fearful experience. He once saw a movie in which the victim of a vampire becomes a vampire himself, and the face of the man gradually changes into the ugly, fearsome visage of a vampire. The change was shown in a closeup on the screen and the boy was so horrified he left the theater. That night he had a long nightmare, and for about a month he could not free himself from the horror produced by this particular film.

The interpretation of his fear of facial change is apparent in the light of the other material we have presented. The ugly face symbolized for him one aspect of his self-image of being an outcaste person. The man who passes may maintain the common prejudices of the majority society toward his own people. While he consciously thinks that since he is no longer functioning as an outcaste, he is free of the characteristics that supposedly stigmatize his people. Unconsciously, however, he has internalized these attributes as part of a disavowed self-image. In the example of Osamu, when under stress, when his sense of achievement was threatened, his security about successful passing also tended to become shaky. Anxiety over possibility of failure was experienced symbolically in a panic that the face would reveal his ugly identity. As a youth Osamu was so horrified by the vampire because it suggested that one's hidden or ugly impulses might disclose themselves; unconsciously he had identified with the fearsome creature who preyed on ordinary good folk.

A further possible reason for Osamu's experiencing a Jekyll and Hyde potentiality within himself, is that he had witnessed radical changes of behavior in other individuals. As a child he visited his grandfather and other relatives, all still living in the Buraku. He remembers very well that his mother showed a drastic change in speech, manner, and dress when she left their own house to visit the outcaste community. When she was outside the outcaste community, she identified with the ordinary middle class persons with whom she associated, and was proficient in adopting the behavioral patterns of middle class non-Buraku ladies. Yet when she returned to her own people, she spontaneously reverted to ruder forms of behavior. Osamu told us that the change was so drastic that sometimes as a young boy he wondered if his mother was a single integrated person. He felt as if he had had two different mothers, one within the outcaste community, the other outside.

There was once in certain locales the belief that the Burakumin bore upon their persons an inherited physical stigma—a bluish birthmark (aza), under each arm. The following poem written by a Buraku poet, Maruoka Tadao, depicts a tormenting part of his negative self-image, a sense of being branded with an inescapable stigma, carrying deep within himself a never-to-be-removed sense of his own despoiled nature.

Let Come the Day to Say "Once It Was So"

I heard whispering
Like the flow of wind from mouth to mouth
That under each armpit I am marked,
The size of an open hand.

Was it inherited from an ancient time?
My parents, so too I've heard
Were also bruised by nature's brand.

Yet of them no memory affords
Sight or feel of such a spot.

But in childhood I learned,
Through cruel heavy winks, how instinctively to hide.

What was it I so naively wrapped with rags,
And hidden, dragged, through dark months and years?

In these concealing rags, I had hid my heart,
When refound, it was sorely bruised
Shriveled red from stigma I sought to lose.

Without some fresh exposure, my songs would end in lies;
Tightly bound bruises but increase the inner plight.

Who marked my sides? For what unknown cause?
Why such a brand upon my very self and soul?
Even today, my ebbing thoughts,
So pale and cold, transparent as glass,
Hold me awake.

Chapter 12

GEORGE DE VOS AND
HIROSHI WAGATSUMA

Group Solidarity and Individual Mobility

Psychologically, group solidarity within the Buraku has three aspects: first, the security gained from belonging to and maintaining cohesiveness with group members; second, the sense of enmity toward the outside; third, the problems of individual and group identity related to changing reference groups and "passing" in the majority society. These attitudinal patterns have to be seen in the context of the general question of individuation in Japanese society. To become individuated, a person must have a great deal of inner security so that he need neither rely upon the group to maintain himself nor deny his origins, and so doing live a life of pretense.

A member of the outcaste Burakumin group must forge for himself a new social identity as well as become occupationally mobile in order to escape the stigma of the past. Essentially, the outcaste, consciously or not, makes one of three choices. The first and easiest path is to maintain an overt, direct identity with his minority status and its implications. He may be resigned to the way society defines him or he may seek increased advantages through concerted action with others sharing his status. Second, he can adopt a selective disguise in which he maintains affiliations within the Buraku but for occupational and other purposes disguises his origins from the majority population. A third possibility is to pass completely. If he seeks this, a complete loss of former identity, he must stop all overt contact with family and community by means of geographic as well as occupational mobility. He has to forge for himself an entirely new identity and in some cases fabricate a past so that he will not be disadvantaged by his lack of ancestry. Status in a majority population is difficult to achieve. The very act of passing cuts off meaningful primary and secondary family

241

relationships and the constant fear of exposure creates severe tension. To become individuated but at the same time to maintain a secure social self-identity is an extreme psychological challenge for the Burakumin.

INGROUP SOLIDARITY

In order to live vis-à-vis strong social discrimination, the ordinary Burakumin must rely heavily upon his own group. The individual cannot easily work in the majority society unless he has the capacity to pass successfully and most Buraku individuals instead remain and work within their own communities. A considerable number receive some form of public relief, having little opportunity for self-support.

Those who work within the outcaste community depend upon their employer. Usually the relationship with him is paternalistic, the traditional pattern of mutual obligation involving financial protection. The working conditions and income may be unacceptable to the employee, but he has no alternative. He may attempt to leave one job for another, that is, to change from slaughtering to shoemaking, or he may prefer to work as a daily laborer; however, the choice of occupation is limited. As long as he is loyal to his employer, he can enjoy some modicum of emotional and financial security, but repeated expressions of dissatisfaction may lead to dismissal and blacklisting. Thus, obedience and passivity on the part of employees is strongly sanctioned. As long as an employee remains passively loyal and hardworking, he will be protected. If he gets ill, or either his wife or child gets ill, his boss may help defray medical expenses. There is, within the group, strong discouragement of individuality for poor workers. Economic forces, therefore, induce the Burakumin to keep the outcaste community as his primary reference group.

Social solidarity is reinforced within the community in an area that, in itself, creates caste status—namely, by enforced endogamy. Ingroup marriage is still the rule: only occasionally will an individual take on the difficulties of marriage with a person of non-outcaste background.

As in all endogamous groups, the number of eligible individuals of proper age is limited by the size of the community as well as by relative status within it. This allows little room for individual choice—a situation particularly pronounced among the wealthier individuals within the group. And for individuals who are passing, a marriage arrangement becomes an especially crucial issue, for through necessary marriage arrangements otherwise well hidden backgrounds can be disclosed. Marriage is usually arranged between a boy of a passing family and an eligible girl of another passing family. Even in these situations, the prestige and status of both families is of considerable importance.

Thus, it is very difficult for a person from a wealthier Burakumin background to exercise any individual considerations in marriage.

Marriage negotiations between passing families are delicate and require tact. These families often try to avoid one another as a precautionary measure, for if a particular passing individual is unsuccessful, and people come to suspect his identity, undue contact with him may cause suspicion. In conversation there is anxiety about revelation, and each seeks to avoid reminders of his delicate social position. This type of delicacy in contact is not unknown in the world of homosexuals, where those individuals who are passing as normal and who maintain a façade of normal family ties, very often feel themselves on the edge of a precipice, where some unconscious revelation to another may be witnessed by a third person and understood. The role of the passing deviant in society is always fraught with danger.

Among the Burakumin, whether passing or not, certain individuals assume the role of matchmaker. Such a person must be one whom people can especially trust. Usually it is a middle-aged or older woman who fulfills this role and performs the necessary social function.

One of our passing informants told us of his younger sister's marriage. Before the girl was to finish high school, she was referred by a matchmaker to a boy of another passing family of equal status and wealth who was about to finish college. They were married immediately after their graduation, although until the day of their marriage they did not know each other. This is the traditional way marriages take place among the middle and upper status Buraku families. However, one informant, a college graduate, thought it was "too feudalistic to accept." So he went to the prospective bridegroom of his sister with an idea in his mind that if the boy turns out to be a wrong person, he would attempt the extremely difficult task of preventing the marriage. "Fortunately, he was a nice guy, I liked him right away, and I thought he would be all right for my sister. I think I was right; my sister is happy now." To our question why he did not have his sister herself meet the boy before marriage, he answered, "What is the point? My parents became very angry when they found out that I had met the boy. What would have happened if my sister had done such an indiscreet thing? Their marriage had been planned by both families for nearly ten years. It was almost a fixed fact. If my sister could have met the boy and if she had not liked the boy, what could she have done about it? She had no choice. The same with most of us."

A sense of group solidarity within the Buraku is certainly due in part to the fact that most of the individuals are related in one way or another because of the practice of endogamy. Expressions such as "We are like one family" are common. Everyone knows everyone else. Children are accepted in every house: when a child fears an angry father, he will flee into a neighbor's house and will at times sleep there or eat there on a very casual basis for days. Parents feel secure as long as they are sure the children are somewhere within the Buraku.

Social solidarity in the Buraku is also reinforced by participation in worship at a segregated Buddhist temple. In the middle of many Buraku, one will find a large, well-built Buddhist temple, probably belonging to the Shinshu sect, often in impressive contrast to the shabby houses in the vicinity. There is some indication that the Burakumin tend to adhere to their religion with a greater tenacity than is usual in Japan. Many are seemingly very pious and donate a considerable amount of money to their temple. Some Burakumin may adhere to the Shinshu sect because Shinran, its founder, taught that with Buddha's intercession they would receive full-fledged social status. However, as we have previously indicated, at one time during the Tokugawa period the government forced all the Eta to belong to the Shinshu sect. In the past, at least, some of the Burakumin believed that if they devoted themselves to the teaching of Buddha, they would be reborn as a non-Buraku person. Such belief in rebirth is rare in present-day Japan.

Parental ambivalence toward the meaning of achievement outside of the community, and the concern with the psychological and marital security, can lead to a child's enforced participation within the Buraku. The primary family can in this way maintain continuity and social solidarity, and can sanction the necessity for endogamy within the group. The following incident illustrates well a situation in which group identity triumphs over achievement in external society. The incident is described in a book written by a young woman doctor who worked for more than ten years among Burakumin.[1]

A son of Mr. Y finished a special high school for commercial and industrial training in Nara, then left the community for a job in a large company in Tokyo, full of buoyant expectation. During vacations he returned from Tokyo, apparently happy. However, about a year later the author found the young man back at home and in a depressed state. The father told her that he put pressure on his son to return home, and that after some uncertainty, he was successful; the mother added, "We feel relieved." The father said, "It is better that a boy of the Buraku comes back to his own community and learns how to make zōri; this is a Buraku industry." The boy's employer wanted to keep him and offered to have him transferred to Nara, thereby enabling him to commute from his own home to work. Nevertheless, the young man left. The father explained that even if his son should become a great man, successful in the majority society, his social intercourse would have to remain within the Burakumin. He cited the case of an outcaste who had become a professor and was forced to

---

[1] Kobayashi (1962).

remain unmarried since he could take neither an outcaste girl below his station nor a normal girl for a wife. The father stated that the more successful the Buraku individual becomes, the less happy he will be. Therefore he wanted his son to leave his job and return to his family.

Outgroup Enmity

It is too readily assumed that the problems caused by social discrimination can be resolved if only the outer society changes its attitudes. This assumption overlooks the nature of continuity in patterns of internalization and the development of self-identity. Strong forces in the socialization pattern of outcastes make the maintenance of their minority status important to their own psychological integration. Hostility toward the majority society becomes a part of the individual's total personality structure, and it is too simple to presume that it remains a simple reaction to discrimination. As stated in the previous chapters, fathers in the outcaste group frequently resort to physical punishment in disciplining their children. Counteraggression on the part of the children toward either parent is not permitted, and serious fighting among children within the community tends to be strongly discouraged. A Buraku child is often encouraged when fighting a member of the outside society, however. By such experiences, the direction and the nature of expressed hostility are behaviorally induced in modes that are perceived by the outside society as relatively aggressive. The hostility and aggression that are engendered by experiences within the community are readily displaced and turned toward the outer society. This is then justified in terms of the discrimination practiced against the outcastes. The reputation of the Burakumin for aggression thus seems to have some basis in fact. Outcaste children will even ambush children from outside the community and beat them. We may relate such activities to the nature of tensions arising in racial situations in the United States where Negro children are very often aggressive toward white children in newly mixed areas. Some Negro children are observed to continue expressing a great deal of sensitivity in newly integrated situations even though adults in both groups consciously attempt to get along. In the next chapter concerning attitudes of Burakumin toward outside authority, we will cite further evidence of outgroup enmity.

PASSING

Methods of Passing

Because the outcaste in Japan is not physically different, he can be identified with some degree of certainty only by knowing where he lives. Residence in an outcaste area of a city or town often identifies an individual as an outcaste, whether he is or not. Many try to hide their identities by, for instance, using public transportation only to some spot near the outcaste district, preferring to walk from there to the district itself. Such indirect means of avoiding identification are more common among the younger generation and the white-collar workers employed outside the community, both groups being the ones most interested in passing.

Some individuals who systematically seek to hide their outcaste background try to insure against revelation by changing their place of registry (*honseki*). The complicated legal procedures and their consequences are such, however, that relatively few Burakumin take advantage of this method. In a study by Suzuki of four different communities, 70 percent of the households investigated maintained their "honseki" in an obviously outcaste area.[2] Since the *koseki-tōhon* (record of registry) is much used and must be obtained from the office by use of one's *han* (seal) each time it is required, location in a ward office far from one's actual residence is extremely inconvenient. In addition, when a registry is changed, the previous address is recorded; therefore to erase any record of Buraku residence, at least two changes must be made in the honseki.

The lower class Burakumin, which constitutes the majority of the outcaste community, are not strongly enough motivated to initiate the complicated planning necessary to erase Buraku stigma from their records. They are too concerned with eking out their everyday existence to think seriously of passing. The effort to pass by changing registry takes planning that must start long before in order to be ready to present non-revealing credentials at the time of applying for a job. One must be coolly deliberate about one's plan of disassociation. Passing is of concern chiefly to the white-collar Burakumin. Individuals of lower class status within the community are caught in traditional bondage, both psychological and economic, to their *oyabun*. In everyday work situations they do not come into direct social contact with outsiders and are therefore not often exposed to overt rejection by members of the outside society.

The upper class family of a feudal boss, or other well-placed individuals within the community, have no compelling motivation for passing for other reasons. The upper class of the Buraku society is financially dependent in most instances upon the Buraku itself and those who work within it. Both their income and prestige depend upon the community. If they are particularly wealthy they can spent week ends or vacations at resorts where they are treated as ordinary guests. In effect, they can pass whenever they wish in their recreational activities.

---

[2] Suzuki (1952).

Passing takes a fair amount of financial as well as psychological independence. Affluence allows the education of children for white-collar or professional occupations. With such education, and with some financial backing, the children can move out of the community and attempt to overcome the external sanctions as well as the intra-psychic barriers to passing. For others, those who through personal enterprise have established a successful Buraku occupation, a change of occupation is still necessary before attempting to pass into the majority community. One informant outlined the steps taken by some members of his community in their attempt to pass. First, one works outside the community selling objects or repairing shoes, thus developing a clientele among the outside people. If successful in this enterprise, the individual then seeks to open a small store in the majority community, commuting daily from the outcaste community. Should he again be successful, he can expand his store, moving into a larger establishment and setting up living quarters in the rear. Since his expanded business is usually one stigmatized as a Buraku occupation, it is necessary at this point to buy out a business that is not related to his Buraku background. He may try to open a hardware or a grocery store or an inexpensive hotel or house of assignation. He may attempt to enter real estate or money lending. It is in the latter steps of passing that the individual and his family are most directly exposed to continuous discrimination since they are living alone in the outside community but are still clearly marked as Burakumin.

The tensions of passing are felt most strongly among those middle class families who have provided their children with sufficient education and support to enable them to have become established as white-collar workers. Working with people on the outside, these children are exposed daily to the disadvantages of being recognized as Burakumin. Visits to family and home community mean serious risks of discovery, yet Japanese culture emphasizes family relationships and interdependence within the family. As noted earlier, the culture does not socialize the individual toward an independent, individualistic life pattern. The dangers of anomic marginality are therefore always strong for the individual Japanese, and for a passing Burakumin this danger is particularly acute.

Should an individual (or a family) successfully maintain himself economically on the outside, and should he be able to break his emotional bonds to his old community, he still must re-face his problem in the marriage of his own children. In certain cases, neighborhoods may suspect the Buraku origin of a family, but because of their presentability and pleasing qualities, the suspicions may remain covert. Yet, should this family seek to establish a marital relationship in their new neighborhood, latent suspicions will become overt. It is particularly over the issue of intermarriage that the caste feeling toward the

Burakumin remains strong among middle class Japanese of the Kansai area.

Lateral Mobility Versus True Vertical Mobility[3]

A distinction needs to be made between the ambiguous movement of individuals (usually young men who do not expect to inherit property) to places of great occupational opportunity, and the definitive leap out of outcaste status. On the whole, and among the lower class Burakumin particularly, there is a great deal of movement laterally (on the same social level) to cities for temporary work: the so-called *dekasegi*, "going off to work." Such emigration does not in itself signal intention to cut home ties, but it puts the individual in an urban setting where he finds greater short-term freedom and considerably more anonymity—hence, more inducements to pass.

Since seasonal employment usually provides the impulse to emigration among Burakumin, the pattern of dekasegi does not normally imply permanent change of residence; it merely represents a tentative start in the process, and is associated almost entirely with young adulthood before career lines are firmly set. In his study of a Buraku in Fukuchiyama City (Kyoto Prefecture), Nishimoto[4] has found temporary outside employment experience to be common for both sexes between the ages of about fifteen and thirty; most of their venturing outside has been as manual laborers, shop clerks, or housemaids in Osaka. Over 40 percent of those between fifteen and twenty in 1956 were so engaged, and over one-third of the males were eldest sons, and therefore heirs, in farm households. Moreover, some 46 percent of the incumbent heads of households had spent an interim in dekasegi, and then returned permanently. Since going off to work in Fukuchiyama is common to all class levels, Nishimoto finds no reason to relate lateral mobility directly to serious intention to pass.

Cornell's findings in Matsuzaki, a large agricultural Buraku in the suburbs of Okayama, agree with those of Nishimoto. He finds it fair to say that every adult male has had at least some outside work experience, ranging from occasionally peddling goldfish or used clothing in Okayama or adjacent prefectures, to sojourns of a year or more in factory and construction labor in the cities of Kinki and Chubu. How many of these make a permanent change is difficult to say, but the consensus of his informants suggested that very few "pass" in this way; there are simply too few opportunities for people of their training and social background.

---

[3] The following materials on geographic mobility as it relates to the problems of passing were supplied by John Cornell on the basis of his field work in Matsuzaki.
[4] Nishimoto (1960), pp. 13–17.

Job discrimination, a major restraint on minority occupational mobility, is treated generally in Chapter 8. Locally, in Cornell's findings concerning Matsuzaki, the extent of unfair employment practices is suggested by failure of Matsuzaki young people to obtain jobs in situations where the personnel office requires the place of residence on the job application. In the prefectural government, too, as an Okayama Kaihō Dōmei official pointed out, hiring Burakumin is evidently done by quota, which, he complained, is set disproportionately low for their number in the prefecture. Even for those who do get respectable white-collar jobs by virtue of better education, advancement is difficult and they are first to be laid off when business is slow.

Some young men with special skills—for instance, concrete workers —work outside most of the time but always expect to return to the Buraku, where they leave their families, between jobs. Although such fixed-base, migratory work patterns are most typical of the poorest segment, even these have a guarantee of shelter and a tiny patch of garden. The more comfortable farmers, in fact, practice dekasegi as a sideline to agriculture when their labor can be spared at home.

As noted, a more serious measure of intent to pass than temporary change of residence is transfer of *koseki* (family registry). This may come before or after removal; however, a reasonably secure economic position for the family outside must be acquired before any move can be contemplated. In his study of Burakumin districts in Hiroshima City, Suzuki found that several transfers of koseki from one neutral ippan district to another might be tried to disguise the attempt to pass.[5] (About half the resident households in the Buraku were registered in majority areas in order to avoid embarrassment should their status be called into question.)[6] Of course, without influential connections, it is virtually impossible to succeed in so many moves, so that over 70 percent of these transfers were to majority areas in the same city, where presumably the outcastes could work through friends and relatives. Cornell's impression is that although the numbers transfering are smaller in Matsuzaki, the majority of those who do transfer are similarly limited to the metropolitan area.

One might suppose that the numbers passing would have increased with more positive individual freedoms and with some improvement in general mobility since the war. This does not seem to be the case. In Suzuki's Hiroshima Buraku, by 1951 the volume of registration transfers had noticeably declined from prewar and wartime rates. Earlier, a large share of the work of the *rinpo-kan* (block officer) had been the processing of Burakumin requests for transfer, and bribery was certainly involved in securing the cooperation of such

---

[5] Suzuki (1952), pp. 151–55.
[6] Suzuki (1952), p. 153.

officials. Moreover, one of the services of the Christian (Methodist) settlement house in the area had been to advise those who could not afford to pay a gratuity on how to arrange the koseki.

The recent history of the kaihō (liberation) movement offers a plausible explanation for this seeming puzzle of decline in rate of transfers. By the late 1930's the vigor of the Suiheisha effort had diminished because of the military emergency and the demand for national unity. Consciousness of kaihō as a political force ebbed at the Buraku level during that period, and there was more resort to purely private means of solution. Suzuki observes of postwar Hiroshima that ". . . in those districts where the kaihō organization is strong, interest in kaihō is universally high and there are not a great many transfers of registration. In districts where this is not true, transfers of registration are very frequent." Cornell was informed by a Kaihō Dōmei leader (of the local chapter) that in Matsuzaki such transfers are no longer common because the people are solidly behind the Dōmei's aim to work for universal liberation. While there is some question that the community is actually as strongly united as claimed, there is no doubt that as long as the Dōmei gives positive leadership and remains unsympathetic to private passing, the kaihō leadership can probably force outward compliance to its goal of collective rather than private emancipation.

In sum, passing—the private solution—would seem to have been impracticable for an individual; the effort of a whole family group is necessary. Japanese most familiar with the problem agree that individuals who are well educated and intellectually motivated have the best chance of success.

Psychological Barriers to Passing

After Feeling Freedom

When Spring comes
Young people go forth from their village—
Especially those from higher schools.

When alone away from home,
A young man feels suddenly in his breast (futokoro)
The increased weight of the home left behind.
Buraku is mentioned,
His breathing stops.
Pretending desperately not to be affected,
The young man secretly searches within his breast.

Keeping up with others in conversation,
Deep inside, more often than not, he finds
His bosom painfully smudged with blood.

Why Flee?

At one time
Alone, in a land of strangers,
I denied my childhood home.

Peter denied his Lord thrice.
How many more times did I deny
My humble place of birth?

Constantly threatened by an unknown lurking shadow,
Like an oppressive weight cutting off my breath,

I dwell alone, in a strange land,
Fearing to meet my kind, like a crab,
Ready to scurry away in dread of contact.[7]

Numerous individuals who are externally successful in passing cannot continue because of the intrapsychic tensions and difficulties over self-identity. When someone, even without an outcaste background, goes from a rural area to a big city like Tokyo, he has difficulty in adjusting himself to a strange environment. He may feel alone or awkward in his behavior—that people of the city are disinterested or even unkind. Ordinary new arrivals usually can endure such an adjustment period and gradually become able to function as city dwellers. Those young people who do fail and return to the rural areas attribute failure to inability to meet the requirements of city living. However, interpretations tend to be different with Buraku people. When a young man of Buraku background goes to the city to work, his difficulty in adjustment, seen objectively, does not usually result from differential treatment. Yet he remains prone to attribute his difficulty to his Buraku background. He tends to think that non-Buraku individuals from rural areas do not experience similar difficulties. In attempting to explain his difficulty in terms of prejudice and discrimination on the part of the majority society, he becomes disappointed and resentful and often returns home. He may then tell members of his community that he was mistreated and found it difficult to live in the city because he was known as an outcaste.

One informant, a university graduate who is successfully passing, not infrequently feels a strong impulse to declare himself an outcaste to those with whom he is talking or working. His attitude toward passing is extremely complicated and ambivalent. Although he is successful, he feels that passing is not quite morally right; to hide his Buraku background is to accept the prejudice of the majority society against his people, though he feels that discrimination is unjust. Of course

[7] The poems and the one quoted in Chapter 11 were translated into English by Hiroshi Wagatsuma and George DeVos with the assistance of Jill White. Maruoka Tadao, a poet from a Buraku in Yamaguchi Prefecture, published the first collection of his work in 1958. Unsatisfied with work that did not touch on his painful experiences of being a Burakumin, he decided to face his real problems squarely and began writing poem after poem describing the inner feelings of Burakumin. In the first poem, the word "futokoro," translated twice into "breast" and once into "bosom," originally means the place where the two lapels of the kimono meet on the chest. That is, the place where people keep their wallet and papers, as pockets in western dress. Futokoro also means, as in this poem, breast or bosom.

what he really wants of the majority society is to have them know his entire self, his origin, and still accept him. But he knows that if he disclosed his background, he would jeopardize his job and social relationships. He is very much aware of his guilt feelings. He feels he is not being fair to his relatives and friends in that he is being treated as an ordinary person while they are still suffering the disadvantages of outcaste status. He uses the Japanese word, "sumanai," a term expressing regret and a feeling of guilt. He also revealed that at heart he really hates everyone who doesn't have a Buraku background, and sudden attacks of silent hostility and anger toward outsiders often occur. It is particularly at these times that he is tempted to declare his background and frighten the others away, as he did when he was a child.

Another informant told about a friend who had tried to pass as a government officer but had somehow failed, left his job, and though a university graduate, is now running a store in a Buraku. He had changed his place of work several times because in each instance, after some time, people came to suspect his background. Wherever he went, the same thing happened. What actually occurred in the case is documented by the informant. The friend would somehow let those around him know about his background: when drunk, he would hint in various ways about his outcaste origin, or he would confide in someone whom he had no cause to trust.

MARRIAGE AND THE CASTE BARRIER

The following brief summaries are reported examples of the effect of social pressure on the lives of some who transgress caste and attempt intermarriage. They illustrate how intervention occurs. A number of reported suicides among known Burakumin are traceable to a rupture in love relationships brought on by discovery or disapproval of an inter-caste relationship. There is no way to substantiate speculation about the suicide rate among Japanese Burakumin as compared with the general population, since official statistics do not separate groups on this basis nor do they record suicide motivated by outcaste status.[8]

Often the rupture occurs with the discovery of background. In 1954, Matsumoto Kinue, a factory worker in Fukuchiyama City in Kyoto Prefecture, met Chihara Akira, a member of the Japanese self-defense corps, and mutual love soon developed. After having sexual relations,

---

[8] Burakumin probably share the motivational patterns of Japanese generally with respect to suicide. For further discussion of psychological motivational patterns to be found in Japanese suicides, see De Vos, "Role Narcissism and the Etiology of Japanese Suicide," unpublished MS.

they decided to marry. After inquiring about the family background of his fiancée, as is the custom in Japan, Akira discovered her Buraku past. He was shocked and ashamed, blamed her for secrecy, and his love quickly cooled. He showed no concern for the girl's feelings, nor would he take responsibility for their sexual intimacy. Kinue, overwhelmed by this harsh rejection, killed herself three days later.[9]

A Buraku youth fell in love with his employer's daughter. They lived together for 40 days, until the girl's parents found out and separated them. There was no possibility of marriage because of the boy's Buraku background. Shortly after, the boy killed himself.

The intervention of the majority group family is the usual cause of rupture. The act of suicide sometimes takes the form of a sacrificial removal of the self as a source of trouble for the beloved. For example, a Buraku girl 23 years of age died of poison. She left a message to her mother that the only possible way she saw to make her fiancé and others happy was to kill herself. The girl and her lover both had wished to marry, but without success. He worked for a company headed by his uncle who threatened to fire him if he persisted with his plan to marry a Buraku woman.[10] She killed herself despite the boy's reaffirmation of his love and renewed promises to marry her.[11]

The suicide often sees his or her act as a moral protest that may possibly help to alleviate future problems for others.

Knowing that he could not marry a non-Buraku girl, a Buraku youth tried to kill himself, leaving behind this note addressed to the *Mainichi News* in Osaka:

I sincerely hope that discrimination practised against three million Burakumin will be abolished by the power of the press. . . . I fell in love with a girl, and after six months of dating, I decided to marry her. But by that time, I had been found out to be a Burakumin, and our marriage was strongly opposed by the parents and relatives of the girl I love. Her mother said that she would not allow her daughter to marry a man with dirty blood. She even threw a handful of salt toward me.[12]

The boy had also left a will, addressed to his mother and brother: "I do not want to live further with the cursed brand of the Burakumin upon myself. I cannot love, because I am a Burakumin. The world is wrong. I kill myself in my protest against those who are wrong."

---

[9] From Mahara (1960), pp. 131–80.
[10] *Buraku*, July, 1951, p. 26.
[11] *Buraku*, June, 1961, p. 19.
[12] Throwing a handful of salt toward someone is a magical practice believed to purify the person who has done something polluting, like attending a funeral. When it is done to a Buraku person, it is probably simply to indicate that he is polluted. And it may also have the meaning of purifying the air which was "contaminated" by the presence of an outcaste. (From *Buraku*, April, 1962, p. 71.)

Suicides resulting from inter-caste love affairs may also occur as a protest by a thwarted parent.

In November, 1957, in Hiroshima, Mr. Tanaka, a fisherman, drowned himself in a well. He was opposed to his son's marriage to a nurse with a Buraku background, and there seemed to be no other solution.

In July, Mr. Tanaka's son had met a nurse in the hospital. They eventually fell in love with each other and decided to marry the following November. Soon before the date of their planned marriage, in the course of checking the girl's family background, the boy's family discovered that the nurse had come from a Buraku.

Mr. Tanaka and his wife spoke to the son about the marriage and also urged the girl to withdraw. Disappointed and depressed, the girl, who had seemingly not known about her own background, tried to kill herself but was unsuccessful. A little later the boy and the girl tried to commit a double suicide, but this was also unsuccessful. The Hiroshima branch of the Burako Kaihō Dōmei, learning about the problem, attempted to persuade Mr. and Mrs. Tanaka to allow their son to marry the girl. Mr. Tanaka, still stubborn but finding no way out, finally himself committed suicide, leaving a note saying, "Please solve the problem in such a way that everybody can become happy." The Social Welfare Department of Prefectural Government and City Office decided to conduct a full investigation of the case to prevent future occurrences.[13]

Outsiders noticing an inter-caste relationship are prone to interfere. Lacking the approval of family, it is hard for a love affair to survive the normal quarrels and discord when they occur.

A 24-year-old girl from a Buraku in Nagano Prefecture was working at a restaurant in Shinjuku, Tokyo, in 1954, where she met a student of Senshū University in Tokyo, who was also from Nagano Ken, though not from a Buraku. The girl and the student fell in love, and decided to live together in a nearby apartment, the boy knowing and professing not to care about the girl's background. The girl borrowed money from her own relatives to support the student, and also to pay for an abortion, which was requested by the boy though the girl was eight-months' pregnant. Doubtful of his sincerity, she decided not to return to Tokyo but was persuaded to do so by her lover and in 1956 gave birth to a boy. The youth then asked his mother to come up to Tokyo to see her grandchild. She discovered with shock that the woman was an outcaste and a few days later the boy received a letter from home threatening disownment if the association continued.

The boy and girl decided to appeal to the Buraku Kaihō Dōmei in Nagano Prefecture for help. The secretary of the Dōmei visited the

[13] Yamamoto (1963).

boy's parents in Nagano Prefecture and was given four reasons why the father was opposed to the marriage: his son had no job and no income; he was too young to marry; the couple could make no adequate preparation for their own marriage; and all the relatives were opposed to the marriage. The parents also made it clear that they would be unwilling to support the baby born to this woman. The boy's brother wrote him of the visit and attempted to dissuade him from the marriage.

The youth was then visited by the secretary of the Dōmei and the woman's brother, whom he told that although he loved his child and the woman, love itself was not enough for the marriage. He felt unable to marry against the will of his family. Soon after, the lovers quarreled; he struck her and she left, threatening suicide. The secretary of Kaihō Dōmei Nagano branch and the girl's father both went to talk with the lover and his brother. Though the conversation lasted for four hours, it brought about no change. The Nagano branch of the Dōmei decided to sue the boy and his brother for their failure to fulfill their responsibilities to the woman and her baby, and for the violence the boy inflicted on the woman. The Dōmei also demanded that the boy legally recognize the child as his own and become financially responsible for its upbringing.[14] (No subsequent report as to the final outcome of this case was published.)

Sometimes the rupture of a love relation occurs after a number of years of marriage. A recurring theme in many reports is that somehow the implications of Buraku membership were repressed or denied to consciousness.

A Buraku woman, named Niwa Mariko, sent her letter to the journal *Buraku*, describing her painful experience.

I was born in a Buraku, as a youngest daughter. Although my family was relatively well off in the Buraku, I had to work hard as soon as I finished junior high school. I found a job . . . in Kyoto, where I met my future husband. We fell in love with each other, and after talking it over with my brothers and sisters, I married him. . . . A few years after our marriage, my husband was promoted to a position of supervisor in his factory. I was happy.

Last year, I went to the factory to see my husband, and there I happened to meet a former acquaintance who knew I was a Buraku girl. She showed in an exaggerated manner her surprise at the fact that my husband was a factory supervisor. I felt disgusted at the expression on her face but I did not realize fully that the woman thought it was simply too much for a Buraku girl like me to be married to a factory supervisor. About ten days later, my husband came home sullen and morose. . . . From that night on my husband became a changed person. . . . He said, finally, that I was from a Buraku, and that it was all wrong. It may sound too naive, but until that time I had

14 *Buraku*, September, 1957, pp. 46–49.

not fully realized what it meant to be a Burakumin to those who are not. I had never been told very clearly that I was a Buraku woman, and was therefore the subject of discrimination. I later discovered that my old acquaintance had told everyone at the factory that I was from a Buraku. My husband finally forced me to leave his house. By that time, my previous intense love toward him changed into hatred.

I received a letter from my husband's brother telling me to sign a divorce paper so that my husband could marry someone else. I wrote back a letter that I would not consent to the divorce unless I was fully persuaded it was best for me. I went to my husband's house anyway to pick up my belongings. . . . There I found my bedding thrown into the garden like some objects of filth. While married, I had made for us bedding of the finest quality, but only the poorest set was given back to me. We also found two suitcases in the garden, which had been filled with the things I had used before my marriage. I could not meet with husband; he was out. I had been thrown out of the house, like filth. I trembled with anger and returned to my sister's home, angry, sad, and exhausted.

My husband and his brother still insisted that I sign the divorce document. I hated them, and had no intention of remaining his wife. And yet, I did not like to consent to a divorce, because the stated reasons for divorce . . . were all untrue. I did not believe that my husband had had any feelings of discontent before his discovery of my identity.

I had an opportunity to meet the man who was secretary of the Kaihō Dōmei. He told me that discrimination against Burakumin would never end unless Burakumin themselves fought back. He said I should overcome my own depression and fight for all the Burakumin, who were sufferers from discrimination. Also, one of my sisters, married to a non-Buraku man, wanted to keep our background hidden from her husband. If I stood up to fight, my sister's marriage would probably be threatened. I talked with the secretary of the Dōmei several times, and being ashamed of my indecisive attitude, I still cannot make up my mind. I know that eventually I will have to get over this conflict in myself and stand up and fight.[15]

Not all inter-caste love relationships, of course, end in rupture or divorce. Nevertheless, success in such a relationship demands much more of the partners than does success in a relationship sanctioned by family or social group; members of Japanese culture, with a strong sense of family belonging, are particularly vulnerable to family disapproval.[16]

FUTURE ASSIMILATION OF THE BURAKUMIN: AN UNRESOLVED PROBLEM

The Burakumin seeking to achieve his place in ordinary society must follow very strict rules when relinquishing the support of his

---

[15] *Buraku,* August, 1955, pp. 30–35.

[16] For further consideration of this subject see De Vos (1960).

group. It requires extreme self-reliance and extreme individual merit. Very few have the capability of overcoming, alone and unaided, the widespread though unstated selective discrimination.

Since only a few can hope to be recognized in ordinary society without consciously concealing their origins, most must either take a series of calculated steps to disguise their backgrounds, with the constant threat of exposure from within themselves as well as from the outside, or, with the great majority, content themselves with retaining an outcaste identity, however unpleasant the consequences.

Adherence to the group requires certain loyalty and support. With the appearance of Burakumin militancy in the 1920's came a renewal of what Wirth has called "secessionism." Organized Burakumin political action, first under the Suiheisha and later under the Kaihō Dōmei, has taken the position that liberation—kaihō—is the real goal, but that this must be accomplished by the group as a whole rather than privately. Joining such a mass movement does not signify pride of self; it does, however, indicate acceptance of a situation in which the Buraku and larger outcaste groups can negotiate for the minimal freedoms which are, for the mass of contemporary outcastes, the first essentials of self-interest and self-identity. Outcaste society today, therefore, seems to be drawing apart from ordinary society in order to press for the rights of citizenship, and the individual who participates must give up some personal goals.

In sacrificing some self-interest for the sake of group interest, the individual also assumes the psychological burden of status inferiority and tension in encounters with ordinary Japanese. The increasing rarity of overt displays of discrimination—sabetsu—does not mean any decrease of tension, for as a Matsuzaki informant observed to Cornell, "Ippan people show friendly faces on the surface but have strong discrimination underneath." [17]

The basic social mechanisms of group solidarity that strengthen the Buraku as the primary reference group, and the nature of internalized social self-identity and related psychological mechanisms are such that simply passing into the majority culture seems to offer no more solution for caste in Japanese society than in similar situations in the United States where racial visibility is a principal deterrent to assimilation. It is a poignant psychological and social fact that Japan's invisible race cannot simply pass and thereby end its own existence.

---

[17] Yamamoto (1959), p. 59.

Chapter 13

GEORGE DE VOS AND
HIROSHI WAGATSUMA

Minority Status and
Attitudes Toward Authority

From the standpoint of socialization theory[1] it is pertinent to understand the effects of social discrimination on minorities as manifested in social deviancy and lack of respect for constituted authority. Minority group members often lack the incentive to internalize conformist attitudes toward the law, but there are also active personal and community inducements to flout the rules of the majority society, either symbolically or by actual behavior. Finding methods to outwit authorities is a basic defensive maneuver of an individual who is in an exploited or discriminated role position that excludes equal participation. The minority group member salvages some aspects of self-esteem and "gets back" at an authority structure which he perceives as operating to maintain his degradation or to hinder his freedom. Therefore, the individual in a minority group role often tends to deviate from the standards set by the dominant groups in the society. He may not identify strongly with formal authority, as represented either in the school or in the legal system. He may not subscribe readily to the patterns of marriage stability set by the majority society. He may develop linguistic usages, language patterns that distinguish him from the majority society. He may be less apt to exercise, over either his aggressive feelings or his sexual urges, standards of impulse control that are maintained by individuals more motivated by needs to conform, who seek to keep their social status in the majority society.

Generally, the majority society is less apt to exercise police powers over the expression of impulses and sexual or aggressive activity among minority group members, since in its pejorative perception of a socially degraded group such behavior is expected and, as long as the injuries

---
[1] See especially Merton (1959), Chapter IV, "Social Structure and Anomie."

258

MINORITY ATTITUDES TOWARD AUTHORITY 259

suffered are by individuals within the group, covertly condoned. However, when there are assaults on the persons or property of the majority group, legal sanctions are apt to be interpreted more severely toward minorities and a sense of expected injustice on the part of these groups is thus deepened.

Discontent with discrimination has been expressed by Buraku individuals through concerted political action, as documented in previous chapters. Many Burakumin do find outlets for simmering discontent through leftist political organizations. Such movements seek to change social attitudes by creating a different pattern of political-legal sanctions within the society. As a result of involvement, the individual may participate in politically deviant behavior rather than resort to individual extra-legal deviancy. Far left political movements are socially integrative insofar as they seek means of effecting change without a denial of self-identity or a resort to expressions of hostility toward authority through extra-legal or unsanctioned behavior. The individual who takes political action is mobilizing his energy toward a cause rather than falling back from it in either resignation or apathy, as is the case with a great majority of the Burakumin.

EDUCATIONAL DEFICIENCIES
IN BURAKU CHILDREN

One striking parallel between the group situation of the American Negro and that of the Burakumin is that both American and Japanese cultures strongly stimulate and approve occupational and educational achievement. Yet, while a minority member is aware that he "should" apply himself to his own training and education, he also knows he will be faced with a highly problematical situation when he applies for work in his chosen profession or skill. He has to be willing to face self-deflation and rejection. Both cultures offer career blandishments, while at the same time offering a potential shock to a minority group member should a goal actually be sought. For instance, Mahara reports that in March, 1959, 166 non-Buraku children and 83 Buraku children were graduated from a junior high school in Kyoto.[2] Those who were hired by small-scale enterprises employing fewer than 10 workers numbered 29.8 percent of the Buraku and 13.1 percent of non-Buraku children. On the other hand, 15.1 percent of non-Buraku children could obtain employment in large-scale industries with more than 1,000 workers, while only 1.5 percent of Buraku children could do so. Working conditions in large-scale industries are generally much better than those in small-scale enterprises. The average first salary was 5,196 yen for non-Buraku children, and 4,808 for Buraku children.

[2] Mahara (1960), pp. 131–80; (1961), pp. 55–59.

At another junior high school near Kyoto, almost all the non-Buraku graduates found jobs in April following their March graduation, or in May at the latest, while only 39 percent of Buraku graduates could find jobs by April and May.[3] In many cases, Buraku children are actually unqualified for jobs. But it is also true that many employers are unwilling to hire them even when they are well qualified. Table 1,

TABLE 1

PERCENTAGE OF APPLICANTS AFTER GRADUATION FROM SCHOOL WHO ARE HIRED BY LARGE-SCALE INDUSTRIES COMPARED WITH LEVELS OBTAINED IN AN OBJECTIVE ACHIEVEMENT TEST

Objective Achievement	Non-Buraku	Buraku
Poor results (10–29 points)	25%	19%
Average results (30–49 points)	41	36
High results (50–69 points)	53	50

compiled from Mahara's results, illustrates this tendency. There is a consistent pattern for children of Buraku background to be less often hired. However, the higher the achievement results the less discrimination seems operative.

In the face of discrimination, the easiest solution is not to try, or to discredit the goal. A protective self-identity with a submerged group makes trying unnecessary. Although some minority individuals have the strength of purpose and the ego capacities to survive in spite of discrimination, a good number from a discriminated group react with general apathy and lack of involvement with the educational process.

There is scattered empirical support for the general impression that the Buraku children do relatively poorly in school, compared with majority group children. Their truancy rate is often high. We see an immediate parallel to the situation observed in California with respect to Negro and Mexican-American groups.

There are recent reports by Japanese psychologists that demonstrate a systematic difference in scores on IQ and achievement tests between majority and outcaste children attending the same public schools. The results of a Tanaka-Binet Group IQ Test, administered to 351 fifth and sixth grade children including 77 Buraku children at a school in Takatsuki City near Osaka, show that the scores of the Buraku children are much lower than those of the non-Buraku children (Table 2).[4] Recently reported test results from a small school in Fukuchiyama City show the same differences between Buraku and

---

[3] Ishida (1961), pp. 51–55.
[4] Tōjō (1960), pp. 11–12.

TABLE 2

COMPARISON OF BURAKU AND MAJORITY GROUP CHILDREN
ON THE TANAKA-BINET TEST IN A CITY NEAR OSAKA

IQ	Non-Buraku Children (N = 274)	Buraku Children (N = 77)
Above 125	23.3%	2.6%
124–109	31.8	19.5
108–93	23.3	22.1
92–77	11.7	18.2
Below 76	9.9	37.6

TABLE 3

COMPARISON OF TANAKA-BINET TESTS OF PRIMARY
SCHOOL CHILDREN IN FUKUCHIYAMA CITY

	N	Average IQ
Buraku boys	10	89
Buraku girls	9	87
Non-Buraku boys	10	105
Non-Buraku girls	12	103

TABLE 4

COMPARISON OF GRADE POINT AVERAGES OBTAINED IN FUKUCHIYAMA CITY

		N	Grade Point Average
Primary school	Buraku boys	12	2.29
	Buraku girls	10	2.59
	Non-Buraku boys	10	3.29
	Non-Buraku girls	15	3.16
Junior high	Buraku students	8	2.2
	Non-Buraku students	11	3.3

non-Buraku children (Table 3).[5] Also, the Buraku children in Fukuchiyama City are doing less well than their non-Buraku classmates at both primary and junior high schools (Table 4).[6]

Standard achievement tests devised by the Ministry of Education were given to a group of 247 students, 83 of them Buraku children, at a junior high school in Kyoto. Averages in four subjects consistently

[5] Nishimoto (1960), p. 71.
[6] Nishimoto (1960).

showed higher achievement by the non-Buraku than by Buraku students (Table 5).[7]

TABLE 5

COMPARISON OF STANDARD ACHIEVEMENT TEST SCORES
IN A KYOTO JUNIOR HIGH SCHOOL

	Non-Buraku Children N = 164	Buraku Children N = 83
Japanese	55.5	46.5
Humanities	61.8	46.6
Mathematics	49.9	36.4
Science	51.1	41.0

The more numerous studies in the United States similarly attest to the substandard functioning of children from culturally underprivileged ethnic backgrounds. Racists would argue that this reflects innate differences in ability. We would argue that in both cases, in Japan where there is no racial difference, and in the United States, the results, partly at least, reflect early damage to social self-identity and self-respect vis-à-vis cultural expectations held toward a traditionally disparaged group.

Perhaps the extreme example that makes our point clear is to be found in a most provocative report of systematic differences between children with regard to a superstition. In Izumo (Shimane Prefecture) on the Japan Sea in Southwestern Japan, there is a long tradition of belief in possession by foxes. The capability of being possessed by a fox descends along the family line, and families who are *kitsune-mochi* (those who have a fox) are labeled "black" in contrast with "white" families who do not have a fox. In many communities in this area, people are classified either as "black" or "white." Marriage across the black-white line is tabooed because it is believed that if a member of a white family marries a member of a black family, all the other members of the white family and their relatives become "black." Burakumin, of course, rank below the "black" families. Two tests were made of the intelligence of students in three junior high schools where members of all three groups matriculated.[8] On both tests and in all schools the results were uniform: "white" children averaged significantly higher than children from "black" families, and Buraku children, while not markedly lower than the "blacks," averaged lowest.

---

[7] Mahara (1961).
[8] Nomura, in Oguchi (1956), pp. 247–57

Truancy and Absenteeism in Buraku Children

Long-term absenteeism, truancy, and dropping out of school are all serious problems among Buraku children. Tōjō reports that in Kobayashi Buraku in Nara Prefecture, for instance, for the period between 1950 and 1953 after the establishment of a new junior high school under the revised educational system, a total of 740 students were matriculated to finish the obligatory three year period. Of these, 171 or 23 percent of the total number of students did not finish school and therefore were not recipients of the certificate of graduation. Of the 740 students, 237 were non-Buraku children but among those who did not receive a certificate of graduation only 9 were non-Buraku children; that is, a little more than 3 percent of the total non-Buraku students became dropouts. On the other hand, 162 of 503 Buraku children, or more than 30 percent of the total Buraku students, failed to graduate.

Sustained periods of absence from class is also a common occurrence. At the same school in Nara Prefecture, in 1953, 78 of the total 445 students were absent from school for extended periods. The research revealed that when they came of sufficient age to help their parents at work, students were increasingly absent from school.[9] As shown in Table 6, the research also revealed that the long periods of

TABLE 6

REASONS GIVEN FOR ABSENCE BY STUDENTS IN A
JUNIOR HIGH SCHOOL IN NARA PREFECTURE

Reasons	Non-Buraku Students N = 148	Buraku Students N = 297
Poverty	1	32
Work for family	0	11
Lack of parental understanding	0	9
Laziness	0	24
Physical disability	1	0
Total absent	2	76

absenteeism are explained in a majority of cases as the result of the poverty of Buraku families and the felt necessity for the children to work for their parents. Others explain absence in terms of "laziness."

According to the investigation carried out by the Welfare Department of the Kochi Prefectural Government in Shokoku Island, long-

[9] Tōjō (1960a), pp. 49–98.

term absenteeism is much more prevalent among Buraku children than non-Buraku children (Table 7).[10]

TABLE 7

COMPARISON OF ABSENCES IN BURAKU AND
NON-BURAKU CHILDREN

	Non-Buraku Children	Buraku Children
Primary school	0.49%	6.26%
Junior high school	1.38	32.9

Research in Nara Prefecture shows the same general prevalence of long-term absenteeism among Buraku children throughout the schools of the prefecture, as shown in Table 8.[11]

TABLE 8

COMPARISON OF ABSENTEE RATES OF SCHOOLS WITH AND WITHOUT
BURAKU CHILDREN

		Number of Schools	Number of Enrolled Children	Number of Absent Children
Primary schools	With Buraku children	63	34,254	419 (1.2%)
	Without Buraku children	254	59,516	480 (0.81%)
Junior high schools	With Buraku children	49	24,811	1,556 (6.2%)
	Without Buraku children	76	20,381	520 (2.06%)

RELATIVE INDICES OF DELINQUENCY AND CRIME

American evidence strongly associates delinquency problems with the social dislocations of mobility and migration, and ethnic minority status. In California, for example, the Mexican-American youth are committed to correctional institutions approximately five times more often, and the Negro approximately four and a half times more often, per population, than are whites of European background.[12]

---

[10] Tōjō (1960b), p. 15.

[11] Matsuda, Masutani, and Kudō Eiichi (1963), pp. 84–85.

[12] It must be noted that other minority groups have escaped a negative self-identity through the effectiveness of strong, cohesive, well-integrated communities that do not bring them into conflict with the majority society. In California the Japanese-American and the Chinese-American minority groups have the lowest delinquency

Table 9 shows that in Japan the delinquency rate (as well as the rate of households on relief) is higher in school districts with a heavy concentration of Buraku children than the average figure for Kyoto City as a whole. Although the districts shown do include varying

TABLE 9

COMPARISON OF DELINQUENCY RATES AMONG SCHOOL DISTRICTS
WITH BURAKU POPULATIONS

Name of District	Delinquency Rate[13]	Relief Rate[13]
Rakushi (Takagamine)	23.06	95.2
Tanaka	23.02	70.0
Sanjō	19.51	63.4
Sanjō	14.30	50.1
Sujin (Uchihama)	35.54	24.7
Kisshoin	16.70	40.5
Uzumasa (Saiin)	11.32	33.7
Mibu	22.45	24.7
Takeda	28.03	70.0
Average	*21.51*	*74.8*
Entire Kyoto average	*9.48*	*37.1*

numbers of non-Buraku children, some of whom certainly must be contributing to the rate of delinquency, we can still presume that Buraku children's delinquency rate is higher.

As part of our work on delinquency in Japanese youth we went through case files of a family court in a major city (Kobe) with a population of over one million, to learn more accurately the delinquency rate among Buraku children. When the case of a delinquent boy is first brought to the family court, his permanent address, home address, date of birth, the nature of his delinquent act(s), and the treatment received are all recorded on a file card. If the same boy is brought back to the court for further acts of delinquency, these incidents are added to his records. These cards, therefore, provide a general picture as to how delinquency is distributed in different residential sections of the population.

We examined a sample period with over thirteen thousand cards. All cases of traffic violation were excluded and every tenth card was

rate of any distinguishable group. (See California Department of Corrections Statistics.)

[13] Delinquency rate is calculated by dividing the number of different delinquent children of ages 12–20 by the total number of children registered in the district; dilinquents/total school children. The rate of relief: the number of households on relief/1,000 households. (Kyoto-fu Seishonen Mondai Kyogi Kai & Kyoto Daigaku Kyoiku Shakai-gaku-bu: Kyoto Prefecture Conference on Youth Problems & University of Kyoto, Dept. of Educational Sociology, 1960, p. 11.)

examined. The resulting 1,044 cards included boys whose residence
was unknown or outside the jurisdiction of the court from which we
derived our sample, and these cases were in turn excluded. We finally
obtained a sample of 633 boys, ages 14 through 19. Those who were
found to reside in districts known as "special," or Buraku, were identified as Buraku boys. Those living outside known Buraku districts
(passing or not passing) were *not* identified as Buraku boys. This
classification by residence in known Buraku would therefore include
a relatively small number of non-outcaste children. Conversely, a
probably larger number of children of outcaste families who were
attempting to pass were no doubt misclassified in the non-Buraku
sample. There was no way to avoid such probable misclassifications
since a boy's outcaste identity cannot legally be investigated nor documented in official records. The 633 boys included some Chinese,
Koreans, and a small number of other foreigners. We obtained estimates of the total population of Burakumin from this city's Welfare
Department. The population of Koreans and other foreigners was
obtained from the June, 1963, statistics of foreigners' registration.

The general population total in June 1963 was estimated from
the census of October, 1960. The number of boys in each category
was divided by the total estimated population for each group, thus
producing a rough rate of delinquents per 10,000 individuals. As
shown in Table 10, youth of Korean background have the highest

TABLE 10

ESTIMATED RATE OF DELINQUENCY IN MINORITY GROUP YOUTH IN KOBE

	Number of Cases	Total Population	Rate per 10,000
Those residing in majority areas	493	1,098,546	4.49
Those residing in ghettoed Buraku areas	71	47,023	15.10
Korean registrants	63	22,365	28.17
Other non-Japanese	6	10,468	5.73

delinquency rate—over six times that of the majority group. Those
identified as Buraku boys showed a rate of more than three times that
of the non-Buraku areas.

In Table 11, the boys of each group were classified as first offenders
and recidivists. This breakdown reveals that recidivism is highest
among those living in Buraku areas and is also higher among the
Koreans than among those living in majority areas.

The delinquent acts of the boys were put into different categories.
As illustrated in Table 12, those residing in Buraku areas show a very
high rate of threat, intimidation, and extortion. However, this prob-

TABLE 11

RELATIVE RECIDIVISM OF MINORITY AND MAJORITY
GROUP JAPANESE IN KOBE

	First Offenders		Recidivists		Total	
	Number	Percent	Number	Percent	Number	Percent
Those residing in majority areas	350	71.0	143	29.0	493	100
Those residing in ghettoed Buraku	42	59.1	29	40.9	71	100
Korean registrants	42	66.6	21	33.4	63	100
Other non-Japanese	4		2		6	

ably needs some qualification. In a number of the cases of threat and extortion the age of the delinquent boy is much lower than that of the individuals threatened. It is not unusual to find a boy 15 years old threatening a group of two or three older boys without the use of a weapon. In some cases the boy would simply tell the other children that he is from a feared Buraku. He thus evokes fear in the outside children and can obtain from them either money or goods on the basis of simple intimidation.

Community control seems to deflect delinquent activities to the outside so that they are rarely expressed within the Buraku itself. It is widely agreed by our informants that violence, theft, or other forms

TABLE 12

TYPE OF OFFENSE IN ARRESTS OF DELINQUENT BOYS OF MINORITY
AND MAJORITY GROUPS IN KOBE

	Buraku Residents	Majority Area Residents	Korean Registrants	Other Non-Japanese	Entire City
Theft	41.4%	55.5%	44.8%	41.7%	52.6%
Intimidation, extortion	42.9	22.8	26.1	16.7	25.3
Gambling, narcotics, prostitution, obscenity	0.7	2.2	1.9	16.7	2.2
Incendiarism, rape, robbery, murder	3.6	2.8	3.9	0.0	3.0
Fraud	0.7	1.4	1.3	8.2	1.4
Criminally inclined	9.3	8.8	8.4	0.0	8.7
Other*	1.4	6.5	13.6	16.7	6.8
Total	100.0	100.0	100.0	100.0	100.0

* Carrying guns and swords; light crime; breaking the Alien Registration Law.

of antisocial behavior rarely take place within the outcaste community itself, although the children will be verbally aggressive toward one another. Physical aggression is usually stopped by an interceding adult.

The Buraku people support the child, rather than outside authority, should a child be accused of delinquent behavior. It is more important, seemingly, that the children obey their parents than that they show allegiance to the majority society. In court, the obedience of children is cited by the parents as a mitigating factor.

It is customary that children on probation are put under the supervision of a so-called *hogo-shi* (supervisor) within their own communities.[14] The delinquent children under the hogo-shi within the Buraku do not manifest delinquent activities within their own communities; therefore, the hogo-shi actually supervises very little. He does not seem to be active in preventing the individual adolescent from again committing delinquent acts in the majority society: the recidivism rate is disproportionately high for Buraku children who are put on probation.

The community is not at all supportive of court decisions to place a child in a correctional institution. When such an incident occurs, sometimes a large number of adults will form an organized hostile protest at the court building. They may appeal to the court to put the boy instead on probation so that he is not compelled to leave the outcaste community.

A general attitude of hostility is directed toward the buildings that house the prefectural offices, police, and court. These institutions represent for the Buraku people the legal authority of the majority society. The prefectural office also represents the place where birth records or registry of Japanese families and individuals are kept— records of Buraku identity and background.

The police station and system face hostility related to alleged differential treatment. There is an implicit requirement among police that the social and family background of an officer's prospective bride

---

[14] In the Japanese court system, under Japanese juvenile law, there are two different forms of probation. One is probation in the custody of Family Court probation officers, the second is probation under the custody of probation officers belonging to the probation bureau of the Ministry of Justice. Probation by the Family Court officers is called *shiken-kansatsu;* the second type is called *hogo-kansatsu.* Usually when the prognosis of the delinquent case seems favorable the probation of the Family Court is used. When the children involved are probated to the Ministry of Justice, they are at the same time put under the supervision of some voluntary person in the community. The qualifications of these volunteers are carefully examined by the probation bureau, and those who pass scrutiny are appointed to work in the capacity of supervisor of children: these are the so-called hogo-shi. Many hogo-shi are school teachers, others are owners of small or middle-sized enterprises. Usually, the number of delinquent cases per probation officer is too large for him to handle personally and he is therefore heavily dependent on these lay volunteers. Very often the motivation for supervising a boy is that he will work at the factory or store of the supervisor.

be scrutinized very carefully and reported to a supervisor whose permission is necessary before any further step toward marriage is taken. One informant claimed that it was not unusual for a supervisor to deny a young policeman's application on the grounds that the girl had an unfavorable (Buraku) background. When the police are brought up in conversation, such incidents readily come to the mind of informants, suggesting the readiness to feel hostility toward police authority.

A criminal career may be one method of passing for members of the Buraku. If a youth is successful in becoming a member of a criminal gang or yakuza group, his outcaste background is discreetly forgotten, since professional criminals do not usually scrutinize the origins of associates. Therefore, the Buraku youth may feel more ready for this activity than for facing the discrimination that occurs in other occupations. In the same manner, Buraku women who become prostitutes find this an easy way to pass and to remove themselves from the Buraku.

BURAKUMIN ATTITUDES
TOWARD HEALTH AND WELFARE AUTHORITIES

Members of a minority group with a long tradition of discrimination develop certain characteristic ways of handling their relationships with dominant elements of the society. Not only do they develop a defensive hostility toward the dominant groups, but they are apt to develop ways of expressing ambivalent attitudes of dependency toward the economically dominant majority group members. The dependent feelings toward the majority group are expressed by deviousness in the ways of "taking." This allows the individual to maintain his self-respect, since he avoids feelings of helplessness that might otherwise accompany dependent needs. Individuals from the majority group sometimes are angered when they discover some form of "relief cheating." It confirms their prejudice concerning the worthless nature of the individuals who are being "helped" through the efforts of the beneficent elements within their community.

The Burakumin have developed certain expectations of economic assistance from the majority society. They tend to see it as a right that goes with their minority status. A woman doctor tells of an incident that well illustrates the "expediential-dependent" attitudes of the Burakumin toward welfare programs.[15]

A poor tailor, T, is married to an outcaste. T was not concerned when he learned of his wife's background, but she remained very much concerned and felt inferior to others. T tried to free her from her prejudice, and in

---

[15] Kobayashi (1962).

order to persuade her of his own feelings, he moved into her Buraku community.

Here, as an outsider, he met with discrimination and was not accepted. One day another man wandered into the community from the outside, poor and jobless, and T took him to be registered for relief. The public employees told T that the number of people who could receive unemployment relief money was limited and that he would have to wait. Then T found that people of the Buraku were being accepted and registered in the office, despite the fact that some had considerable income, and owned washing machines, telephones, and television sets. In anger he went to the public employment security office and criticized this discrimination against outsiders in the administration of relief among the Buraku. Through his efforts, his friend was accepted and registered for relief money, but nothing was done to rule out the wealthy Burakumin. T says that in this community receiving unemployment relief was considered a kind of job which the people "earned" by exerting political pressure on the ward office. If an individual has a large and influential family, strong support will enable him to secure relief funds. T himself completely rejected the clannishness of the Buraku people and their exclusive attitude toward members of the majority society.

Another example of the expediential "take what you can get" attitude of the Buraku toward the outside society is noted by the same doctor. Relatively poor Burakumin in her community use electricity generously, but pay only the basic fee, successfully adjusting the meters so they do not register the excess despite all efforts of the electric company. This cheating is practiced by almost every family, with no sense of wrongdoing.

As the only doctor living in this relatively poor community, the author of these reports was accepted and well liked by the people. However, she still could not make her patients pay medical bills though money was needed only for expenses—to maintain the clinic, drugs, and other supplies. Although they had sufficient financial resources, the social apathy of the community was such that they would not "give" even to a cause of direct benefit to them.

Burakumin seem to be prone to more illness and endemic disease than other communities, not because of a lack of effort on the part of public health officials, but rather because of resistance to governmental officials, whatever their purpose. According to the same doctor, trachoma was very common among the Burakumin: in 1953, at the junior high school attended by most Buraku children, 64 percent of the total 400 students were suffering from the disease. Despite the fact that after the district commission on education was alerted and the percentage dropped in one year to 30 percent, the health programs were still met with apathy and resistance.

Inoue, a well-known historian and active protagonist of Buraku liberation movements, also points out the frequency of "dependent-expediential" attitudes in older members of the Buraku:[16]

. . . in their campaigns aimed at the prefectural or central governments demanding further administrative measures for Buraku improvement, some of the older members of organized movements express the feeling that they have the right to demand things in compensation for a long period of discrimination, since they have not retaliated in any way against the majority society. . . . that they have a special right to ask for governmental help for improvement because they are Burakumin . . . but this is wrong. . . .

In this criticism of the Burakumin, Inoue virtually ignores the fact that this demanding attitude is a consequence of social discrimination extending through many generations. Such underlying antagonism to legitimate authority is particularly disturbing to majority Japanese, since within the culture it is traditional to conform to authority.

COMMENT

Evidence from Japan suggests direct functional parallels between deviant trends in traditionally disparaged minority groups in the United States and in Japan. An aggravated delinquency rate is but one symptom of a total situation influencing the internalization of social values. However, this internalization pattern in minority groups is influenced not only by the external pressures of discrimination but also by the nature of the response to minority status in terms of the sanctioning methods available to minority families and the community generally.

Not all minority communities react to discrimination by producing deviant members who flout socially expected behavior. The tradition of discrimination has to exist long enough to affect the socialization of the young. Only some minority groups that acculturate to a new society undergo disruptive changes. The Puerto Rican immigrants to New York, for example, cannot sustain their previous community or family relationships in their new setting. The Chinese in the United States, on the other hand, formed communities with strong sanctions that prevented any visible individual deviancy from the accepted standards of the majority. Some minority groups, on meeting a new situation of social discrimination, maintain active defenses against legal authority based on previous traditions. Mexican-American families and communities, in socializing the young, develop such defenses (legal authority being traditionally perceived as a hostile outside force). The Japanese, in contrast, on meeting discriminatory attitudes in the United States, socialize their young toward conformity to legal

---

[16] Inoue (1961), pp. 4–17.

authority. Through pursuit of the strong Japanese values of education and achievement, Japanese-Americans have been able to maintain a significantly low delinquency rate.

Some minority groups are based directly on a disparaged caste position in the society, to which the individual must respond by a form of self-evaluation that tends to incapacitate him for the ready assumption of socially expected roles. The parallel situation that we have documented in this chapter attests to how a tradition of such social disparagement continues even after discriminatory attitudes and practices are to some degree alleviated.

This is an example of what might be termed a psychological lag in a changing society, namely, that the effects of a particular social condition continue after the structural elements producing the condition have changed. This continuance occurs because there has been induced in individuals an internalization pattern that cannot as readily be changed, since internalized psychological mechanisms are involved. This internalization pattern occurs very often within the sanctioning practices of the primary family. In fact, the primary family itself may have been greatly influenced by certain types of minority status, as in the case of the American Negro, so that a serious disruption from the usual culturally prevalent family pattern has occurred. We have not discussed fully the types of evidence gathered concerning the free sexual practices and fragile family relationships that occur in the Japanese Burakumin. Nevertheless here also, on the basis of the impressions of some of our informants, we may note a direct parallel to the situation of the Negro.

There is some tendency for scholars seeking to define social problems within a sociological framework to neglect the psychological processes involved in socialization experiences within minority family groups. One cannot operate solely in terms of a theory based on social mechanisms if one is to understand such multi-determinant problems as delinquency in society. The primary family and its functions in socialization are a meeting ground for psychological and social theory.

Part Two:

Caste in Society:
A Comparative Structural
Analysis

Caste in Cross-Cultural Perspective: Organizational Components

INTRODUCTION

The word "caste" evokes an image of the system of social stratification characteristic of Hindu India. However, some social analysts have extended the word to apply to a variety of other societies exhibiting rigid social stratification. Controversy has arisen as to its applicability outside of South Asia, some claiming that it is uniquely South Asian, Indian, or even Hindu Indian, whereas others have held that systems of social stratification similar in some respects to that found in India, but dissimilar in other respects, can usefully be described as caste systems. Basically this is a problem characteristic of social science, namely, that of definition.

In the following two chapters I define caste broadly as a hierarchy of groups in a society, membership in which is determined by birth. So defined, in structural and functional terms, it refers to a type of social stratification that appears in a variety of cultures, scattered widely in space and time. But a distinction must be drawn between caste organization as a general principle and the widespread occurrence of pariah status, which is one manifestation of that principle—perhaps the most common and certainly the most spectacular manifestation.

Objections to application of the term outside of India have been many, largely directed to the notion that the cultural distinctiveness of Indian caste renders it incomparable to structurally similar social systems. I propose that this is a defensible position but one that is irrelevant to social scientific inquiry—that for such inquiry it is the

275

structural and functional similarities which are important and productive of useful generalizations. Some other notions used to substantiate the uniqueness of Indian caste, such as that it is non-conflictive and static in nature, are here held to be erroneous.

Caste as a principle of social organization can be contrasted to other principles—class, kinship, community (territorial groups) —with reference to the two key variables in the definition: mode of recruitment (birth ascription versus acquired membership) and hierarchy (ranked versus unranked groups). The contrast highlights the distinctive social organizational features of caste and leads to a consideration of the concomitants of caste systems. These concomitants include attitudes, values and personality characteristics, the social and individual mechanisms with which people respond to life in a caste society, and the broader behavioral implications of caste organization. The psychology of caste is treated in greater depth in Section VI of this book.

From the perspective of both social organizational principles and motivational determinants found in caste behavior, the basic point to be made is that in whatever cultural context caste occurs, it has common implications for those it involves. The attitudes and behaviors common to caste societies are too important to be overlooked, too similar to be dismissed as coincidental, and too widespread to be attributed to a common historical source. Their explanation is to be sought in the common nature of human social and psychological functioning under similar conditions.

The similarities of structure, function, and psychological effect among caste societies can be usefully analyzed cross-culturally without denying the real differences that occur in the cultures exhibiting them. Such comparative analyses are necessary to the advancement of knowledge and understanding of human society. As caste systems are increasingly confronted with egalitarian ideologies, even among those who comprise them, the understanding of this particular kind of social organization takes on a very practical significance.

G. D. B.

Chapter 14

GERALD D. BERREMAN

Structure and Function of Caste Systems

DEFINITION

Any definition of the term "caste" would be acceptable as long as it was clearly stated and consistently applied. Thus, caste can certainly be defined in terms that would restrict its occurrence to Hindu India. Similarly it can be defined so as to apply to societies that bear no historical connection to India. To define caste strictly with reference to its uniquely Indian attributes eliminates caste as a pattern of social structure that can be analyzed cross-culturally; and cross-cultural comparisons are essential to progress in social science. It is my belief that there are uniformities in structure, in functioning, in psychological and behavioral concomitants of certain social systems that can be usefully categorized together under the term "caste." It is these systems I wish to discuss in this chapter, explaining why they are categorized together and making explicit those things that are common, necessary, or perhaps inevitable in caste systems.

Even among authors who attempt to describe only the caste system of India, definition has been difficult. It has long been generally agreed that the concept is valid over most of India, but its precise referent has proved difficult to specify. Hutton states: "The truth is that while caste is a social unit and throughout India is consistent enough to be immediately identifiable, the nature of the unit is variable enough to make a concise definition difficult." [1] He does not venture to try. Ghurye says: "Owing to . . . [its] ubiquity and strangeness, the institution of caste has found many able scholars devoted to its study. With all [their] labors . . . , however, we do not possess a real, general definition of caste. . . . Any attempt at definition is bound to fail because

---

[1] Hutton (1946), pp. 44ff.

of the complexity of the phenomenon." [2] Another commentator, Blunt, attributes his own difficulty of definition to the fact that "castes are not all built on the same model. The system has grown up gradually and castes which are of different origin are also of different nature." [3]

However, many analysts of Indian society have attempted definitions, which have most often consisted of lists of characteristics of castes. Thus, N. K. Dutt (1931:3) says

it may be stated that the most apparent features of the present day caste system are that the members of the different castes can not have matrimonial connections with any but persons of their own caste; that there are restrictions, though not so rigid as in the matter of marriage, about a member of one caste eating and drinking with that of a different caste; that in many cases there are fixed occupations for different castes; that there is some hierarchical gradation among the castes, the most recognised position being that of the Brahmans at the top; that birth alone decides a man's connections with his caste for life, unless expelled for violation of his caste rules, and that transition from one caste to another, high or low, is not possible. The prestige of the Brahman caste is the corner-stone of the whole organisation.[4]

In addition to those listed above, the most frequently mentioned characteristics have been that castes are named groups, that they are historically, culturally, or racially distinct, that the system is based on religious concepts and sanctions, that there are specific rules restricting social interaction among castes, that castes have distinctive rituals, that there are self-regulatory bodies within castes that govern caste behavior, and that disabilities are imposed on the lowest castes. Such definitions represent varieties of a traditional view of Indian caste largely derived from orthodox Hindu views of the system as it is supposed to be. These definitions are associated with a view of the Hindu caste system as essentially static, admitting of no mobility, subject to no internal pressure, and afflicted with no conflicting aspirations among those within it.

Increased social scientific interest in India since the Independence has resulted in an increase in empirical and analytical studies of caste. A new view has emerged that emphasizes structures, functions, variations, and dynamic mechanisms within it. In addition to well-known formal attributes of the system, the newer view notes caste mobility, conflicting caste interests and aspirations, the nature of caste ideology, of caste ranking, and of inter-caste relations. Barber has commented on this new view of Indian caste in some detail,[5] and Bailey has sum-

[2] Ghurye (1952), p. 1.
[3] Blunt (1931), p. 1.
[4] Dutt (1931), p. 3.
[5] Barber (1961).

marized contemporary usages of the term as applied to India, and has suggested that it can be defined to apply outside of India.[6]

The literature on caste in India and descriptions of systems of social stratification in various parts of the world lead me to the conclusion that there is a range of types and specific instances of social organization that share common features and that can be usefully referred to as caste organization. That is, the concept has cross-cultural validity and analytical utility. This is not an original notion. Generalized and sometimes specifically cross-cultural definitions and discussions of caste have appeared frequently in the literature of social science. Among the best-known are those by Weber,[7] Kroeber,[8] Davis,[9] and Nadel.[10] An excellent recent discussion is by Bailey.[11] Gould presents an account emphasizing the social and cultural conditions under which caste organization has arisen.[12]

By any definition, there are sure to be borderline cases wherein the criteria of caste organization are met only to a questionable degree. Therefore, more useful than a rigid distinction between caste and non-caste societies is an "ideal type" model wherein castes and the caste system comprise an ideal type which any given society may approximate to a greater or lesser degree. In the following discussion this should be borne in mind because, for ease of presentation, I shall tend to speak as though caste were an absolute category—an "either-or" phenomenon—when in reality it is an ideal type.

I will here define a caste system as simply *a hierarchy of groups in a society, membership in which is determined by birth*. There are many concomitants and ramifications, but this is a useful minimal definition for my purposes. Its component elements require some explanation.

Recruitment by Birth

Endogamy (marriage within the group) has been almost universally considered a requisite for caste organization. I have defined it in this way myself.[13] Yet it is well known that inter-caste hypergamy (the practice of a man marrying a woman of lower rank than himself) occurs in some castes in various parts of India[14] and in other societies frequently described as having caste systems, such as the Natchez In-

---

[6] Bailey (1963), pp. 107–24.

[7] Weber (1946a), pp. 180–95 and (1946b), pp. 396–415.

[8] Kroeber (1930), pp. 254–57.

[9] Davis (1948).

[10] Nadel (1951), pp. 174ff.; (1954), pp. 9–22.

[11] Bailey 1963), 107–24.

[12] Gould (1960), pp. 220–38.

[13] Berreman (1960), pp. 120–27.

[14] Mandelbaum (1962), pp. 312f.

dians of the southeastern United States. In such instances the child derives its caste status from its father. Hypogamy, wherein a woman marries a man of lower rank than herself and the children derive their caste status from their mother, is a variation found more rarely in South Asia[15] and elsewhere.

In some areas, such as Swat in northwest Pakistan, a child shares the caste of its father,[16] while in others, such as the Malabar Coast, among the Nayars, the child shares the caste of its mother regardless of the rank of the other parent.[17]

It is often mentioned but rarely documented in India that membership in a particular caste may result from the union of parents of two different castes. Thus, a person of caste C may be the offspring of a father of caste A and a mother of caste B. Such inter-caste unions are frequently cited as the origin of particular castes (whose members thereafter usually marry endogamously). Von Fürer-Haimendorf has documented an instance of this sort in Nepal.[18] In the mountains of north India, it was reported that any child of mixed caste parentage was normally assigned the caste of his lower caste parent.[19]

Such instances as these constitute an embarrassment to any definition of caste that makes endogamy requisite. However, all of these instances share with endogamy the fact that they are unambiguous rules for assigning a child its lifelong affiliation with a ranked group on the basis of its birth. Endogamy is simply the most common mechanism toward this end. Thus, caste membership is determined by birth or descent, but castes are not necessarily endogamous.

Analogously, consanguineous or "blood" kin groups (for example, lineages, clans, phratries) also determine affiliation through birth. Some kin groups require endogamy and assign membership as a result of a bilateral rule of descent—through both parental lines. Many determine membership through only one parental line. In some societies (for example, Australian section systems) membership in a kin group is determined by parents' membership but is not the same as the membership of either parent. In these instances, as in caste systems, membership in a group is assigned unambiguously and permanently by birth. The mode of recruitment is therefore the same in the two instances

---

[15] von Fürer-Haimendorf (1957), p. 246.

[16] Barth (1960), pp. 132f.

[17] A Nayar woman may have a child legitimately by a Brahman "husband" and the child is a Nayar like its mother. The situation is actually more complicated than this since each woman has a Nayar "husband" of a different type (i.e., a ritual husband) as well, who is necessary in order for her to have any legitimate children at all, though he is unlikely to be the biological father of any of them or to play any role approximating that of social father as it is known in other societies. Gough (1959).

[18] von Fürer-Haimendorf (1957), pp. 247, 251.

[19] Berreman (1963), p. 157.

(castes and kin groups). Unlike castes, however, kin groups are usually unranked.

Hierarchy

A caste system is a system of social stratification; a system of rank. The bases for the ranking vary widely in detail from one society to another. The differences are frequently cited by those seeking to distinguish caste in India from other systems of rigid social stratification. It is well known that in Hindu India the basis for ranking is phrased in terms of a complex and detailed set of beliefs and rules regarding ritual purity and pollution. Srinivas comments, "The concept of pollution governs relations between different castes. This concept is absolutely fundamental to the caste system and along with the concepts of *karma* and *dharma* it contributes to make caste the unique institution it is." [20] Among the Swat Pathans of northwest Pakistan, Barth reports that the basis for rank is defined in terms of "privilege and shame." [21] It is widely known that in the United States the basis for ranking in Negro-white relations is the congeries of so-called racial attributes of which intelligence and morality are important components, closely associated with skin color and other physical attributes. In Japan the basis for the hierarchy is partly occupational and partly "racial" (that is, according to allegedly inherited physical characteristics).

The variety of bases for caste ranking can be reduced analytically to a common notion of a hierarchy of groups based upon differential degrees of shared, birth-ascribed *intrinsic worth,* which Weber has termed *honor,*[22] and De Vos has elsewhere in this volume called *purity* (in the context of purity and pollution wherein the impairment of purity constitutes pollution). Gould refers to "different amounts of moral goodness and badness possessed by the members of a society" as the basis of a "caste ethic." [23] These are equivalent concepts. Contact with less worthy (less honorable, less good, more polluted) groups can impair the worth (honor, goodness, purity) of one's own group. The social separation of castes is assured by fear of pollution by contagion. The particular criteria of intrinsic worth, honor, or purity, their manifestations, the ways in which they can be impaired or imperiled, and the mechanisms by which they are protected vary from culture to culture, but the fact that the paramount virtue is accorded differentially to birth-ascribed groups in a society is a common and distinctive characteristic of caste systems. That such virtue is so accorded, and

---

[20] Srinivas (1952), p. 28; and see Stevenson (1954), pp. 45–65.
[21] Barth (1960), p. 114.
[22] Weber (1946a), p. 189.
[23] Gould (1960), p. 224.

that it is always threatened by compromise, has implications, as we shall see, for individual psychology and group behavior in caste systems.

All members of each caste are assumed to share the attributes that determine the group's rank relative to other groups. All members of the group derive the benefits and disadvantages inherent in membership. The specific nature of these benefits and disadvantages varies from culture to culture just as definition of the group and definition of what confers status varies from culture to culture, but in each culture they are clear cut and well known to those who live the system. Caste-based differences in access to goods and services with resultant differential life-chances seem to be part of all caste systems, for intrinsically these are systems of institutionalized inequality.

Bases for Caste Distinctions

There are several factors that cause an individual to be placed in a caste hierarchy, and these must be sorted out if analysis is to be clear.

The necessity of distinguishing between the *criteria* by which a caste's rank is determined and the *idiom* in which a caste's rank is expressed has been noted by Barth.[24] Thus, in India, rank is said to be a function of the purity-pollution *criteria* and, in turn, it is expressed in an *idiom* that includes a particular configuration of deference behavior, ritual activity, interaction patterns, and life-styles. In the United States the criteria for Negro-white ranking are features that are allegedly genetic in origin, including morality and intelligence, while the idiom in which the ranking is expressed is our complex racial "etiquette."

The criteria for ranking are most relevant to discussions of the origin and the rationale of a caste's rank; the idiom in which ranking is expressed is most relevant to discussions of the actual functioning of a caste system. This is because, once a system is established, the idiom is perpetuated (and enforced) so as to obscure the criteria or create them artificially.

There is a difference between the criteria by which *groups* or castes are said to be ranked (as described above) and those by which *individuals* are ranked. In the first, individuals are assumed to share those attributes of their group that are important to caste ranking—the criteria—and even manifest deviation does not alter the caste rank of individuals. The shared intrinsic worth or purity implicit in membership in a given caste, rather than any individual attributes, determines a person's rank in the caste system. This, in turn, is determined once and for all at birth.

---

[24] Barth (1960), pp. 138f.

Often caste ranking is stated in terms of individual attributes as though these were the ultimate criteria. But they prove not to be. Thus, in the United States, it is frequently said that Negroes are discriminated against because of their color or because of their alleged stupidity and immorality. The fact is that if an individual is defined as a Negro, no matter how light, intelligent, and moral he may be, he is treated as a Negro by members of the society, and is generally so defined by himself as well. A Negro physician with skin lighter than that of his Caucasian neighbors is still a Negro in contexts where Negro-white distinctions are relevant, so long as he is known or believed to have Negro ancestry. In the same context, a Caucasian, no matter how dark, stupid or immoral he may be, if he is regarded as a Caucasian, is treated as a Caucasian. Within the Negro caste itself skin color is a criterion for status, but this is a matter of individual prestige quite different from the caste distinction between whites and Negroes. It might be noted that among whites skin color is also a criterion for status. In many areas a dark color indicative of exposure to the sun—presumably exposure to the sun under leisurely and often expensive circumstances—is a prestige symbol among Caucasians even where having the dark skin color attributed to Negro ancestry would relegate one to low caste status.

In India it is frequently said that castes are ranked according to their ritual and personal habits and associated attributes as these are defined in terms of purity and pollution. A person of shoemaker caste may be said to be of low status because he is ritually impure, and he is ritually impure because he handles dead animals, eats carrion, has impure personal habits and defiling religious and social customs. However, a person of shoemaker caste who becomes a school teacher or politician, who is a vegetarian, who is orthodox in his pursuit of Hindu ideals, who has never touched a dead animal or made a shoe, is still treated as a shoemaker in the caste hierarchy. He may be individually esteemed, but in the system he is an untouchable; he is ritually polluted like every other shoemaker and he is treated accordingly. Similarly, a man of high caste who is unorthodox, who eats meat, drinks liquor, and does other defiling things, so long as he is not expelled from the caste will be treated as a member despite his polluting activities.

Thus, an individual shares the putative attributes of his group in a caste society. He cannot, within the system, take advantage of personal attributes to change his position. Dissimulation or passing does not affect this generalization since it is an evasion of the system, not an exemplification of it. Similarly, outcasting, a possibility in India, removes an individual from a place in the caste system rather than altering his rank in it. The same is true of people who opt out of the system by becoming ascetics. It is possible for entire groups (castes) to change their position within the system in India by changing the behavior and other attributes of their members, and succeeding in having this change recognized, accepted, and validated by other groups in the system—by getting themselves redefined as being of higher rank than was previously the case. In the process, the shared attributes of the members of the group become redefined.

In addition to criteria of rank and idioms for its expression, and in addition to group and individual criteria of rank, there must also be *indicators* (signs or symbols) by which membership in a caste is recognized. People must know one another's caste in order to interact —in order to implement the caste idiom. In India, common indicators include occupation, speech, dress, social behavior, religious and ritual behavior, diet, style of life, and place of residence. Most of these are the same as the idioms that express rank. This is a virtual tautology since expressions of rank are conspicuous and hence are inevitably indicative of rank as well as expressive of it (that is, they are objective as well as subjective features of the system). The extent to which such indicators are effective for the functioning of a caste system is the extent to which they are indicative of ancestry—of actual caste affiliation. All of those listed above are useful and largely effective in India, but all are fallible since they are not inevitably tied to ancestry. The ultimate indicator of caste status is genealogy: actual credentials of heredity. The genealogy is publicly known and verifiable through personal acquaintance with an individual's background, through a priest's knowledge and affirmation, or through the activities of professional genealogists. In the United States, skin color is the paramount indicator of status in the Negro-white hierarchy (although other physical features and, in some regions, characteristic cultural forms, such as speech, are also symbols of racial affiliation). But even skin color is not infallible and the ultimate indicator in American race relations, as in Indian caste relations, is the genealogy.

It is important not to confuse group criteria, individual criteria, idioms, and indicators of caste ranking, even though they overlap significantly in some instances. They are conceptually and functionally distinct and are therefore analytically separable.

STRUCTURAL-FUNCTIONAL CHARACTERISTICS OF CASTE SYSTEMS

Having defined caste in the most elemental terms, I will turn to a discussion of features associated with caste organization—to the structural and functional characteristics of caste systems. Such a discussion amounts to an elaboration of the definition.

Groups and Group Membership

The ranked entities in a caste system as defined here are groups. In the context of the caste system individuals are ranked only as a result of their group membership. Caste groups are named, bounded, self-aware, publicly recognized entities composed of people who interact with one another actually, putatively, or ideally. They are not simply analytical categories of people or aggregates who share a common level of income or style of life as are some "classes" (to be discussed below).

If a caste system is to function, there must be no doubt as to the affiliation of every individual. For membership to be unambiguous, the groups must be *exclusive, exhaustive,* and *discrete.* Exclusiveness and exhaustiveness are among the criteria of stratification systems cited by Nadel [25] and whose relevance to caste systems has been stressed by Bailey.[26] This means that no individual can belong to more than one group (the groups are exclusive in their membership), and every individual must belong to some group (the groups are exhaustive in their membership). "Discreteness" refers to the fact that the ranked groups form a discontinuous hierarchy of bounded groups. There are no marginal individuals to introduce ambiguity into the system. The hierarchy can be made up of any number of groups. In India the number of interacting castes in the hierarchy of any region, or even of any particular village, ranges from five or ten to thirty or more. In other societies, such as that of the contemporary southeastern United States, the caste hierarchy may be a simple dichotomy. Whether there are many castes, a few, or only two, the "shape" of the hierarchy (that is, the relative distances between outcastes and the degree of grouping of castes into rank clusters) will have implications for the relationship among them and perhaps for the attitudes of one caste's members toward others.

Status Consistency

Caste systems have a uniquely high degree of status consistency among the individuals and groups comprising them. Barth has used the term "status summation" [27] derived from Nadel's phrase "summation of roles," [28] and has applied another term of Nadel's to describe caste systems as "involute" systems.[29] This simply means that there is

---

[25] Nadel (1951), pp. 174f.
[26] Bailey (1963), p. 109.
[27] Barth (1960), pp. 144f.
[28] Nadel (1957), pp. 63f.
[29] Nadel (1957), p. 68.

consistency among the statuses that members of a given caste occupy or among the roles they play and that there is consistency between such statuses or roles and the attributes exhibited by those who occupy them. A man who is well-to-do is also politically powerful, of high religious or ritual status, and socially respectable. A man who is poor is also politically weak and of low religious and social rank.

When incongruities occur, there is a tendency to adjust this embarrassing and threatening situation either by altering one or more of the statuses or by altering the discrepant attributes. Instances illustrating this can be cited from any culture where there is caste or caste-like social organization and probably from many clearly stratified non-caste societies. In the southern United States, for example, prior to World War II it was not uncommon for Negroes who possessed automobiles to wear chauffeur's caps when driving them in some southern cities to avoid being attacked by resentful whites to whom the Negro's low status was inconsistent with ownership of an automobile. Similarly, in India, low caste people have pointed out that they cannot show wealth even when they acquire it lest it be taken from them by resentful high caste people. In pre-Independence India there were many sumptuary laws prohibiting low caste people from display of certain kinds of behavior and goods thought to be inappropriate to them. For example, in many regions they were prohibited from wearing golden jewelry, from wearing certain kinds of clothing, from owning houses, from engaging in certain kinds of ritual, and from engaging in certain occupations.

The effects of the principle of status consistency can be seen in the mode of integration of some tribal groups into the larger Hindu society. Most tribal groups have been incorporated at the lowest caste levels. Some, however, characterized by conspicuous economic or political advantages, as for example the Raj Gonds of central India, have been incorporated at a high level in the caste hierarchy. Similarly, status mobility by caste groups within India has been sought through the acquisition of wealth or political power, as well as by adoption of high status religious and social usages.

The tendency to alter statuses or attributes in cases of discrepancies among them in a caste system accords with Festinger's concept of "cognitive dissonance" [30] and its implications for social change. According to this concept, when there is a disparity between the status accorded by others and that which one thinks is justified or correct, when there is perceived dissonance between the way one is treated and the way one hopes or expects to be treated, there is a tendency to strive to bring perception and reality together. This tendency may be even greater when the perceived disparity is visible to any observer than

---

[30] Festinger (1957).

when it is known only to the individual himself. Rowe has applied this concept to the analysis of an instance of caste mobility in India.[31]

Castes as Components of a Society

The ranked groups that comprise a caste system have been described in my definition as being "within a society." A caste system is exactly what the term denotes: a system. The groups comprising it are differentiated, functionally interdependent, and interacting—they are parts of a single society.[32] The nature of their interaction and interdependence varies widely, although it is always on a scale of superiority-inferiority, and it is always within the context of a single social system.

Indianists have often had difficulty in distinguishing castes from other ethnic groups in India, and especially in distinguishing castes from tribes.[33] Tribes have been identified variously by their economic organization, religion, social organization, racial composition, ethnic history, place of residence, and language. These identifications are inadequate in that they apply to only some of the social groups to which the term "tribe" is usually intended to apply.

A useful and broadly applicable variable in this context is one used here to characterize caste systems: castes are ranked components in a larger society comprised of analogous components. Tribes contrast to castes in that they are relatively independent and homogeneous systems of their own. They are not made up of interacting ranked groups nor do they participate in a larger system of such groups. In India there is a continuum from tribal to caste status so that, as Bailey has suggested, an ideal type model is most useful in defining tribes just as it is in defining castes.[34] Individual tribes have frequently become castes in a particular regional caste system. Some tribes are more independent than others, some are more homogeneous than others, some engage in interaction on a superior-subordinate basis with other groups in fewer contexts than do others. In each instance such groups would be more tribal than others, that is, nearer the ideal type labeled "tribal." Those with opposite characteristics would be more caste-like than others, that is, nearer the "caste" pole of the continuum.

Caste and Consensus

Castes are thus distinguishable from tribes and other contiguous but independent social groups partly because they are component parts

---

[31] Rowe (1960), pp. 73f.
[32] Cf. Nadel (1951), p. 176.
[33] Cf. Bailey (1961), pp. 7–19; and Sinha (1964).
[34] Bailey (1961).

of a single society. The distinction is partly a matter of self-definition and consensus. What of the instance in India, for example, where a group is often referred to in the literature as tribal and whose members themselves claim to comprise an independent social entity, but are defined by neighboring groups—those usually called castes—as simply one of many castes within the larger society? Whose word is to be taken as authoritative? Can (or must) the social analyst rely entirely upon observations of interaction, and if so, are such interacting groups to be described as castes in every instance?

On the problem of consensus and its relationship to societal integration it has been recently pointed out that value consensus is not crucial to successful social interaction but that behavioral articulation is essential.[35] The point is that behavioral articulation, behavioral complementarity, and behavioral conformity need not derive from common motives. A variety of motives can lead to common behavior.

The caste system in India has functioned for a very long time, race relations in the United States persisted (with changes) for a good many years, and there is ample evidence in both instances of lack of consensus from one component group to another (and particularly between groups low and high in the hierarchies) on the meaning, value, and bases of the hierarchy.[36] This does not mean that the groups did not articulate their behavior in such a way that a functional relationship was maintained, for the society was able to persist. And, of course, this proviso in turn does not mean that there were not seriously dysfunctional aspects of these systems, both in terms of social consequences and in terms of individual psychological consequences. The point is that people behaved in complementary ways, whatever they wished, whatever they felt, and whatever they believed. Ultimately and periodically changes occurred. There were slave revolts in the southern United States, there were religious movements and conversions away from the Hindu fold among low caste people in India—evidence that the systems did not work perfectly. However, the fact that the dominant system persisted as long as it did in each case indicates that the systems did work. Ultimately, I believe, the functioning of the systems depended upon considerations of relative power—upon enforcement, upon physical and economic sanctions at the disposal of the dominant groups. The effects of overt power were often supplemented by enforcement through other means, such as religious sanctions—the notion that supernatural punishment comes to those who fail to accept and conform to the social hierarchy, or that supernatural reward accrues to those who do conform to it. Such notions as these are not accepted by all members of low status groups, but frequently they are

---

[35] Wallace (1962), pp. 27f.; Mills (1960), p. 39.
[36] Berreman (1965).

accepted by some. Where they exist at all it is usually assumed and widely announced by high status groups that they are not only true and just but are acceptable to all.

In a caste hierarchy, ideological consensus is not crucial to the determination of status, nor even to the determination of whether or not a given group is a component in a caste hierarchy. What is crucial is behavioral conformity. If a group acts as though it were a caste in a hierarchy, if its members interact with the members of other groups (castes) in a manner conforming to publicly accepted expectations, then they are in effect within the system and their status is that which they act out. Thus caste status is largely a matter of social definition that in turn is dependent upon behavioral validation.[37]

An important distinction between subjective status, objective status, and accorded status was made by Hyman.[38] The first is an individual's personal and internal evaluation of his own (or his group's) place in a hierarchy—a place which often is not validated in practice. Objective status is his (or their) place in the hierarchy as determinable by observation and application of objective criteria of status. Accorded status is the status others give to the individual or group, validated by their behavior. In the functioning of a caste system these distinctions are extremely important. Whatever a person may think about his rightful place in the hierarchy, or even whether or not he is part of the hierarchy, the extent to which his claims are validated in the behavior of others is what counts in his daily interactions.

What a person thinks of his status is primarily important in so far as it leads to behavioral manifestations. If a person acts in a way that is incompatible with his status as defined by the dominant society, he may be subjected (and usually is) to severe sanctions from within his group (caste) or without. Such instances are often the result of a disparity between subjective status, on the one hand, and accorded status on the other, where the individual has attempted to objectify his subjective status and the attempt has not been validated by public approval—the new status has not been accorded him. He may then retreat to behavior appropriate to his publicly defined status or he may continue to defy public opinion, in which case he is likely to be brought sharply to account.

The self-definition of any individual—the self-images of the members of any group—is thus extremely important. There are those who insist that within a caste system, especially one as rigid as that in India or in the southern United States up until the last twenty years, there is little likelihood that individuals will attempt behavior inconsistent with the social definition of themselves, simply because they have

[37] Berreman (1965).
[38] Hyman (1942), pp. 5-7.

grown up with this definition, see no alternatives, accept it and perhaps even concur in it. There are others, and I am among them, who would suggest that this is a view more often advertised than realized. As a matter of fact, in both the southern United States and in India, the pariah groups can be shown to have a high incidence of active and intense resentment of their status, and a definition of themselves very different from that adopted by the dominant society.[39] Behavior that conforms to pariah status in these instances is attributable to enforcement rather than to acceptance of the negative self-definition. If enforcement ceases to be effective, changes in social relationships can be expected—changes toward greater objective (that is, attributional and behavioral) attainment of subjective status by the erstwhile low status groups.

Caste Mobility and Reference Groups

A caste hierarchy is one within which individual vertical social mobility—individual movement from rank to rank within the system —is impossible, at least in theory. That is, there is no legitimate mechanism by which an individual can move from one caste to another. There are instances in which individuals dissimulate and thereby pass as members of a caste other than the one into which they were born. There are instances of individuals who fail to conform to the behavior considered appropriate in their caste and are therefore outcasted. In some societies an individual may choose to leave the system (for example, in India by becoming an ascetic). But these are mechanisms that operate outside the caste system. In the first instance, the individual dissimulates. He is not accepted into another caste; he is simply assumed by those whom he is able to fool to be of another caste than that to which he legitimately (objectively) belongs. In the second instance he does not become a member of another caste; he is simply expelled from the system altogether. In the third, he enters a casteless state wherein he is treated as socially dead in the context of caste functioning.

This does not mean that vertical social mobility is impossible within a caste system. Mobility has attracted a great deal of interest among students of India in recent years;[40] they have amply demonstrated that social mobility in India is group mobility. A caste may raise its status in the hierarchy absolutely or relative to certain other castes, but no individual or family can do so alone. When a caste moves up within the hierarchy, every individual within it moves accordingly, since every

[39] Berreman (1960), pp. 120–27.
[40] Bailey (1957), pp. 220–26; Cohn (1954); Rowe (1960), pp. 56f., 299f.; Rowe (1963); Sinha (1959), pp. 9–32; (1962), pp. 35–80; Srinivas (1956), pp. 481–96.

member shares the status of the group. Mobility, therefore, requires concerted effort by all or most of the members of the caste. Usually this is accomplished by status emulation—emulation of high caste attributes and behaviors.[41] Members of the mobile caste simply adopt and exhibit characteristics inconsistent with their present status and consistent with a hoped-for higher status. These include occupations, material possessions, ritual performances, dietary restrictions, symbolic acts, attempts to interact with high caste people and to avoid those of low caste, and claims to heredity appropriate to the status to which they aspire. By adopting these symbols of high caste status they hope to gain public recognition and validation of their claims, for without such validation, their claims are empty. Validation is achieved when members of the upwardly mobile group are treated as though they were of the status they claim rather than of the status they were formerly accorded. In India this validation is observable and even measurable in terms of the kinds of interaction which occur among members of different castes.

Status emulation falls within the range of meaning of the phrase "reference group behavior" as it is used in social psychology. When a person's attitudes and behavior are influenced by a set of norms that he assumes are held by others, those others constitute for him a "reference group." [42] The norms may or may not be held by a group as such. Turner has distinguished two kinds of reference groups relevant to any discussion of status emulation and mobility: identification groups and valuation groups.[43] The identification group is "the source of the individual's major perspectives and values." "The individual takes the role of a member while adopting the member's standpoint as his own." [44] Valuation groups "acquire value to the individual because the standpoint of his identification groups designates them as points of reference" so that "the individual compares himself with [these] groups or notes the impression he is making on them or in some way takes account of them" without adopting their standpoints as his own.[45] For upwardly mobile groups in a caste society, a high caste or group of castes may serve as an identification group in that those who aspire to higher status adopt their values and behaviors— the process of emulation. At the same time, all or most other castes may be valuation groups in that it is their opinion and behavior that

[41] In the literature on India the term "Sanskritization" is frequently used in this context, since an important component of the process is usually adoption of orthodox, "Sanskritic" socioreligious attributes. Cf. Srinivas (1952), pp. 30f.; (1956), pp. 481–96.

[42] Newcomb (1950), p. 225; Berreman (1964), pp. 231–50.

[43] Turner (1956), p. 328.

[44] Turner (1956), p. 328.

[45] Turner (1956), p. 328.

can validate the mobile caste's claims to status. Reference group theory is a promising field for students of social mobility in any context, including caste mobility. It offers the prospect of a common theoretical basis for many discrete phenomena noted in mobility studies—such concepts as those which occur in studies of Indian society: Sanskritization, Rajputization, Hinduization, Islamicization, Christianization, westernization, urbanization, modernization, plainsward mobility (in the case of mountain people), etc. The crucial question is, upon what bases does a group choose reference group(s)?

Caste and Pariah Status

The difference between use of the term "caste" in India and its application outside India has often caused confusion. Within India caste refers to a great number of social groups, some of which are quite close to one another in public esteem—in social evaluation, ritual purity, or what I have called intrinsic worth—but which are socially distinct. These groups (castes or *jatis*) are regionally delimited and do not extend over very large areas.

Outside India the term "caste" has often been applied to a major dichotomous division in a society between pariahs and the rest of the members of the society. Obviously the Eta of Japan and the Negro in America are in positions of this sort with reference to the rest of the populations of those societies, and they have frequently been so described, as have blacksmiths in some parts of North and East Africa and the Middle East. Weber comments that the phenomenon of "pariah" peoples is found all over the world.[46] Pariahs are stigmatized people whose stigma is derived from their birth-ascribed group membership and is shared throughout their group.

This distinction is intrinsic in the classic Varna system of Hindu society, the modern form of which is composed of four major groupings of castes that are considered to be ritually clean and one major grouping, the so-called "untouchables" or "Harijans," considered to be ritually polluted and hence severely stigmatized, although few of them are literally untouchable. Bailey refers to the boundary between these untouchable or pariah groups and the rest of society as the line or barrier of pollution.[47]

One must distinguish between castes or a caste system in general and the special caste phenomenon that is pariah status. The general or universal characteristics of pariahs in their relations with non-pariahs may be quite different from the characteristics of castes where the pollution barrier is not a factor; where, for example, there are two

---

[46] Weber (1946a), p. 189.
[47] Bailey (1957), pp. 8, 13.

or more interacting castes of high status. Pariah castes and pariah-non-pariah relations are widespread and interesting phenomena within the category of caste organization, but care must be exercised not to attribute the characteristics of these phenomena to all caste societies or to assume that they are diagnostic of caste organization.

Since the term caste was first and most widely applied to Indian society, we cannot exclude from the meaning of the term, even by implication, the many groups comprising the caste system in India that are very close to one another in rank—and this would be the effect of adopting "caste" to mean "pariah" or "untouchable," or to refer exclusively to the pariah-nonpariah relationship. The more specific term "pariah" is preferable to designate the intrinsically polluted, stigmatized, denigrated, excluded caste status found in many societies.

Pariah groups the world over share many characteristics, one of which is that they do the necessary but dirty, demeaning, and unpleasant jobs for their social superiors. As a result they are contaminated, or perhaps because they are contaminated they are given these jobs. In any case because they are defiled, they are restricted in the contacts they may have with other members of society. Frequently they are defined as essentially "non-persons," a social definition that undoubtedly serves a number of social functions.

One function may be to assuage the guilt or alleviate the sympathy which high status individuals might feel if they were to believe that people like themselves were subject to the kind of defilement, and concomitant maltreatment, restriction, and deprivation they know pariahs experience. Guilt would be especially likely if it were believed that those in these positions were there unwillingly, as a result of force or necessity. By defining them as not fully human, behavior toward them can be excused that would be inexcusable if exercised toward real human beings. Thus, one need not worry about the hard work and poor living conditions of Negroes in the United States, or of untouchables in India, because that is what they are best suited for and that is all they really want anyway.

A manifestation of this kind of status is that described by Goffman in the relations between staff and inmates in total institutions.[48] He terms these relations "echelon" relations wherein "*any* member of the staff class has certain rights to discipline *any* member of the inmate class." He notes the similarity to adult-child relations in small American towns, where only children are subject to discipline and only adults can administer it (in some societies this relationship is restricted to that of people to animals). Similarly, any white can discipline any Negro in many localities in the southern United States, and any high caste Indian any untouchable in rural India. In each instance, the

---

[48] Goffman (1961), p. 42.

subordinate individuals are simply not defined as fully responsible persons. Conversely, they cannot be expected to behave appropriately or responsibly; they cannot be expected to get things done that they have been assigned to do. Pariahs sometimes use this concept to manipulate their situation to their advantage or to justify their own behavior: "I'm only a pariah"—not fully human, not fully adult, not fully responsible.

Pariah groups are widely spoken to in terms that explicitly or implicitly indicate that they are children. In India, linguistic forms for addressing low caste people are often the same as those for addressing children, and they are treated as children. In colonial states it is standard to speak of and treat the "natives" as children or childlike and to foster a kind of dependent role among them analogous to the child's role in the family.[49] In the southern United States, Negroes are called by their first names as are children or are addressed as "boy" regardless of age. In Mounds State Park in Alabama I have seen restrooms for whites labeled "Men" and "Women" while those for Negroes were labeled "Boys" and "Girls."

Another function served by defining pariahs as non-persons seems to be to enable them to observe the private lives of those of high status without constituting a viable threat. By the nature of their work (janitorial work, scavenging, menial service, personal service, and removal of refuse, body wastes, and dead bodies) members of some pariah groups are in a position to learn about the personal life of their social superiors. It is common in many societies to assign non-person roles to personal servants and others who must routinely be present in the intimate life of their superiors. It is also common to restrict their interaction with high status people to rigidly defined contexts (often virtually excluding relations with those for whom they do not work), thereby limiting their opportunities to communicate with those from whom their employers wish to keep secrets.

The non-person can move in and out of the lives of his superiors with impunity. He is among the stage hands necessary to put on the performance of the high status person, but he is personally irrelevant to that performance as it is seen by the audience. As a non-person, his observations of behavior that are inconsistent with the public image high status people attempt to project pose no threat. He is not in a position to communicate freely or effectively with those to whom the image is directed. He is not defined as eligible or competent to comment on high caste matters. If he ventures to do so, it is assumed or hoped that his comments will be ignored. The high status attitude is frequently expressed as follows: "Don't pay any attention, it's only a ———." Here one can fill in the name (usually derogatory) of the de-

[49] Mannoni (1964), pp. 39ff.

pressed group: "It's only an untouchable"; "it's only a pariah." Richard Wright has recorded a good example of such an instance when he described his job as a bellboy. "I grew used to seeing the white prostitutes naked. . . . It was presumed that we black boys took their nakedness for granted. . . . Our presence awoke in them no sense of shame whatever, for we blacks were not considered human anyway." [50]

Goffman cites children, drunkards, and the indiscreet as "performance risks" who are frequently treated as non-persons, both because they are a potential embarrassment, and to minimize the chance that any reports they may make will be taken seriously by members of the dominant society.[51]

There is always a danger that the communications of such people will be taken seriously. This makes necessary the maintenance of rigid controls over those who are in such positions, usually in the form of physical and economic sanctions that threaten the pariah group. The resentment, the reciprocal fear of exposure, and the threat of sanctions are important sources of the friction that universally exists between pariah and dominant groups; this friction is often concealed or minimized by the dominant group, who emphasize paternalism and reciprocal loyalty. They refer to a wide variety of philosophical, religious, moral, ethical, and biological dogmas to justify the relationship; dogmas rarely cited by members of the low status groups.

CASTE OUTSIDE OF INDIA?

We may briefly consider some of the characteristics of caste systems that, according to various students, make the term "caste" inapplicable to many of the societies outside of India to which it has commonly been applied.

Rationale for Caste

The most frequently cited unique characteristic of caste in India is its religious and philosophical rationale. If this becomes requisite for caste organization, then caste exists only in the Hindu religion. If comparative studies are to be made, however, the definition will have to be broader. In fact, it seems possible to analyze comparatively the structure, functioning, and social psychological implications of caste organization with little reference to the particular rationale underlying specific instances. This is not to underemphasize the similarities that exist cross-culturally even in this sphere. In the United States the southern racist quotes scriptures to justify his position just as in

---

[50] Wright (1945), p. 176.
[51] Goffman (1959), p. 91.

India the Brahman quotes scriptures to justify his position. It is the content of such explanations, rather than the fact of their existence, that differentiates the Indian system from all others. Barth in his study of a Muslim society in Northwest Pakistan has pointed out that while among Hindus the concepts of purity and pollution define the caste hierarchy to a large extent, among the Muslims other concepts, such as privilege and shame, serve as justifications.[52] Yet the social structure and associated behaviors he described are quite similar to those in Hindu India.

Static Nature

The next most widely cited distinguishing characteristic of caste in India is its alleged "nonconflictive," "nonpathological," "static" nature, with an absence of "aspiration and progressiveness." [53] Kroeber asserted that "the Hindu does not feel caste a burden as the individualistic occidental might. To him it seems both natural and desirable. . . . Whatever his caste, the Hindu is proud of it. . . . It gives him a sense of solidarity, and he does not seek to escape it." [54] This is a widespread opinion among those few American sociologists who object to the application of the term caste to the American situation. Thus, Simpson and Yinger stated that in the United States we lack a set of religious principles to justify a rigid system of social stratification and cause it to be willingly accepted by those at all levels.[55] Central to this opinion is the notion that caste in India is passively accepted and endorsed by all, whereas in America, Negro-white relations are characterized by dissent, resentment, guilt, and conflict.

Elsewhere I have attempted to demonstrate that this distinction is invalid, that caste relations in India are just as much characterized by dissent, resentment, guilt, and conflict as are race relations in the United States when the comparison is validly drawn.[56] I have also pointed out that there are in each instance strong vested interests on the part of the dominant groups in maintaining the status quo. I concluded that a comparison of the realities of caste attitudes and interaction in India and the United States suggests that no group of people is content to be low in a caste hierarchy, to live a life of inherited deprivation and subjection, regardless of the rationalizations offered them by their superiors or constructed by themselves.[57]

---

[52] Barth (1960), p. 114.
[53] Cox (1945), p. 360. Cf. Berreman (1960).
[54] Kroeber (1930), p. 256.
[55] Simpson and Yinger (1953), p. 328.
[56] Berreman (1960).
[57] Berreman (1960), p. 127.

An Indian Dilemma?

In contrasting Indian caste with American race relations it is sometimes claimed that the Indian system conforms to the basic values of the society whereas the American system contradicts the values of the society. Thus Cox says that "The difference between the racial attitudes of whites and the caste attitude so far as the social ideals of each system are concerned, is that whites *wrongfully* take the position of excluding groups from participating freely in the common culture, while castes *rightfully* exclude outsiders from participating in their *dharma*" (in this context dharma means moral duty).[58] Dumont has endorsed this view, summarizing and agreeing with Cox's contention that "the Indian system is a coherent social system based on the principle of inequality, while the American 'color bar' contradicts the equalitarian system within which it occurs and of which it is a kind of disease." [59] In response to this, I would quote Spiro's criticism of Myrdal's view of the "American dilemma":

The assumption of egalitarian culture norms is untenable unless one adopts an idealist conception of culture as ideal norms which are irrelevant to human behavior and aspirations. Actually discrimination against the Negro is not in violation of southern ideal norms; it is in conformity with them. The ideal norm of the southern American (and of many northerners, as well) is one of inequality, and his behavior is in accordance with his norm.[60]

India's constitution, like America's, espouses principles of equality, and among India's intellectual and political elite there is widespread advocacy of and even conformity to these principles—more widespread, one might note, than in the elite of the Southern United States today. If there is an American dilemma, as Myrdal has described it,[61] there is also an Indian dilemma. Because of the greater literacy, the greater education, and the greater communication of national ideology in the United States, the dilemma is doubtless more acute there than in India, but it is not qualitatively different.

Those who object to describing ranked hereditary groups outside of India as castes raise the point that the status conflict between Negroes and whites in the Southern United States, for example, reveals a lack of consensus on the nature, basis, and validity of the hierarchy, a lack that is not characteristic of a true caste system as exemplified in India. There is truth in this view. In rural India few question the caste system as such; what they dispute is their position (or their caste's

---

[58] Cox (1945), p. 367.
[59] Dumont (1961), p. 30.
[60] Spiro (1951), p. 34, see footnote 47.
[61] Myrdal (1944).

position) within it. They do not want to abolish the system; they want to move up in it. They seek superiority, not equality.

With the American Negro it is difficult to distinguish between objections to the system and objections to the Negro's position in it, since the system involves only the Negroes vis-à-vis whites. This makes comparison of attitudes in the two societies difficult, and it may constitute a real difference. However, it should be made clear that low castes in India do not happily accept their status. They dispute their low status, the bases by which it is assigned, and often also the supposed supernatural endorsement of it.[62] Contrariwise, perhaps even a southern Negro would not be averse to pariah status for dirty, ignorant, lazy, immoral, stupid people—he might simply deny that these were characteristics of himself and his race.

Very often behavioral conformity or complementarity is mistaken for consensus by those who believe that people in a caste system invariably exhibit consensus. Behavioral conformity or integration can result from widely differing beliefs and motives. The characterization of a caste system, even that in India, as necessarily based on widespread consensus is a distortion. To distinguish it from race relations, in the United States for example, on this basis is unjustifiable.

Cognitive Equivalence and Aspirations

Some analysts of Indian society have maintained that members of different castes see themselves as intrinsically so different as to preclude subjective comparisons among castes or aspiration for the status and advantages of higher castes. This is often held to account for the alleged nonconflictive nature of caste relationships. People who are unlike presumably do not compete with one another since they function in different worlds. This contrasts with situations where there is manifest competition for status, said to be a characteristic of non-caste societies. Of course, it is true that dominant groups often see themselves as intrinsically very different from groups lower than themselves, but to say that low castes see themselves as intrinsically so different from higher castes that they do not aspire to their status is to mistake the *behavior* of members of these groups for the *beliefs* of these members.

Low status groups (including castes) in every society seem to strive for upward mobility. Lipset and Bendix have noted, "The fact that there is constant striving for upward mobility in the most status-ridden society in the world (Indian society) adds considerable weight to the hypothesis derived from Veblen, according to which a

---

[62] Cf. Berreman (1960), p. 126; Kolenda (1964), pp. 75ff.; Mahar (1958), pp. 51–65; Sinha (1964).

system of stratification is a fundamental source of mobility motivation in and of itself. Apparently, there are imperatives which prompt men to resist and reject an inferior status and these imperatives persist regardless of the way in which any given society has legitimated inequality." [63]

It is a fundamental tenet of reference-group theory that in order for one group to aspire to the behaviors and other attributes of another group, they must see some equivalence between themselves and the members of the other group.[64] If these two things are true—that low castes strive or aspire upward and that striving implies perceived equivalence—then the notion that castes see themselves as being truly different is highly improbable. It sounds, in fact, like a high-caste rationalization. Low castes probably see themselves as fully human, high castes as fully human, and in fully human fashion they recognize and aspire to the advantages that those above them in the hierarchy enjoy.

Complementarity and Noncompetition

A number of more narrowly structural and functional features of Indian caste have been cited by various authors as distinguishing it inherently from other systems of social stratification which have sometimes been called caste. One of these focuses on the concept of occupational or other functional specializations within the society.

It has been pointed out that castes in India generally follow unique traditional occupations. By extension, Leach and others have pointed out that caste is therefore inherently noncompetitive; and therefore that caste organization results in groups of specialists that do not compete with one another; each has a monopoly on its traditional occupation.[65] According to Leach such noncompetitive groupings are a necessary and a distinguishing feature of caste societies.

Though this distinction has value, it is inadequate as a criterion of caste. By no means do all members within a caste engage in its traditional occupation.[66] There are numerous instances in India where two castes compete with one another in the same occupation. People of many castes compete with one another in caste-neutral occupations such as farming, farm labor, animal husbandry, trading, and public transportation. They also compete, of course, in noneconomic spheres —for status and power—not all of which are directly relevant to caste.[67]

---

[63] Lipset and R. Bendix (1959), p. 63.
[64] Cf. Merton and Kitt (1950), p. 61.
[65] Leach (1960), pp. 1–10.
[66] Cf. Sharma (1961), pp. 146–64.
[67] Cf. Silverberg (1959), pp. 148–62.

Leach has claimed that:

It is characteristic of class-organized societies that rights of ownership are the prerogative of minority groups which form privileged elites. The capacity of the upper class minority to exploit the services of the lower class majority is critically dependent upon the fact that the members of the underprivileged group must compete among themselves for the favors of the elite. It is the specific nature of a caste society that this position is reversed. Economic roles are allocated by right to closed minority groups of low social status. Members of the high status dominant caste, to whom the low status groups are bound, generally form a numerical majority and must compete among themselves for the services of individual members of the lower castes.[68]

This is an extreme instance of the emphasis on noncompetition as distinctive of caste societies, and one which no Indianist would take literally. Power in most villages lies in the hands of one or a few dominant castes. There is generally relatively little power in the hands of the occupational specialist castes, and the notion that they characteristically play off high caste people against one another is not borne out by the facts. The degree to which there is potential for exploitation by high caste people is of course dependent upon many circumstances, especially upon their economic power.

The potential for exploitation is increased when the worker is in a weak bargaining position in his relationship with his client as the result of such factors as lack of essential services to offer the client, lack of occupational monopoly, lack of an assured clientele, lack of independent or alternative sources of income, lack of occupational or residential mobility, lack of organization with fellows into a cohesive group that could withhold services as a means of obtaining its goals.[69]

Thus, it is possible for a given low caste, under favorable circumstances, to function like a trade union, but this does not seriously or consistently alter the distribution of power or the incidence of exploitation in village India.

It would seem that occupational specialization—functional complementarity—is characteristic of most caste systems. Whether or not this is a useful defining characteristic and whether or not it will exclude some societies heretofore described as caste societies remains to be seen. It depends partly on how rigidly the definition is applied. Is the Southern Negro, for example, an occupational specialist? Some occupations in the South have been virtual Negro monopolies and certainly the Negro competes with some segments of the society and not with others; certainly his economic role is in general complementary to that of whites and perhaps was more so in the past. But the lines are not as

---

[68] Leach (1960), p. 5.
[69] Berreman (1962a), p. 393.

clearly drawn, at least today, as they are for analogous groups in some other societies often described as exemplifying caste organization.

Corporateness

One characteristic of Indian castes that apparently does distinguish them from some other so-called caste groups in the world is the degree to which they are self-conscious, bounded, corporate groups. Most Indian castes are named. They see themselves as coherent groups. They are so organized as to constantly stress their group nature: members must marry within the group (or with reference to the group); members exclude outsiders on frequent formal and informal occasions; members can interact on a status-equal basis only among themselves; the behavior of each member reflects on every other and is therefore stringently prescribed. Some castes have formal administrative and judicial bodies that oversee the behavior of their members, resolve group conflicts and enforce group decisions and prescriptions regarding social and ritual conduct. They may supervise caste occupational matters, such as labor productivity, distribution of clientele, and allocation of raw materials. Upon occasion the caste at large may collect money to help a caste fellow fight a legal case or to stage a ritual performance. In contemporary India castes or associations of castes—usually made up of those close to one another in rank—are becoming increasingly important as self-interest groups: political entities, collective bargaining agencies, and lobbying groups.[70]

In their corporateness, castes in India differ from many of the social groups to which the term is applied in other parts of the world. The difference appears to be one of degree rather than of kind. The American Negro, or even the southern American Negro, in specific localities, probably does not comprise a corporate group to the extent described here. Negroes are aware of their identity and share some cultural features, but in other respects they are closer to a ranked category determined by birth than to a corporate group. In this respect the broad categories of castes in India, the traditional *varnas,* are more like the American Negroes than are the individual Indian jatis described above.[71] On the other hand, Negroes exhibit more group characteristics than do social classes as they are usually defined in American sociology. One could find, of course, more corporate characteristics among the Negroes of some regions than has been implied above, and one can also find jatis in India whose corporate nature is minimal. Yet few would wish to deny the applicability of the term caste to these

---

[70] Cf. Gould (1963), pp. 427–38; Harrison (1960); Rudolph and Rudolph (1960), pp. 5–22; Srinivas (1962), pp. 15–40.
[71] Cf. Mandelbaum (1960), pp. 437–48.

groups. Whether the American Negro and some of the other non-Indian caste-like groups must be ignored in a discussion of caste on grounds of insufficient corporateness, is a matter both of the definition and purposes of the researcher.

As suggested above, for a definition of caste we can best rely on the notion of ideal types, with "caste" at one extreme and class, and kinship or political groups at other extremes. We might say that corporateness is one criterion of caste organization but that it appears in varying forms and degrees. Caste organization may ideally be characterized by corporateness in the constituent groups, but it may sometimes appear in less extreme form. The same could be said for functional complementarity and noncompetition: they may characterize the ideal type but be found in varying degrees in specific instances of varying intensity of caste organization. The point here is simply that we have a continuum from caste to non-caste organization and it is characterized by a continuum in the manifestation of the various attributes of caste organization.

Indicators of Affiliation

Like the idiom in which caste differences are expressed, and like the rationale for caste differences, the specific indicators of caste affiliation have sometimes been cited as defining characteristics of caste organization. Thus, race and caste have been distinguished partly in terms of the allegation that races are genetically or physically distinct while castes are not.[72] I would maintain that this is irrelevant. Race is important in America not because of genetic or physical factors per se, but because these serve as indicators of social affiliation and hence, status. In India (where color is not altogether irrelevant) cultural differences serve the same function. A caste system can work equally well with any means for reliably determining the affiliation of all individuals within it.

Social interaction on a caste basis would be impossible if individuals could not identify one another's group affiliation and consequent rank. Bailey suggests that "Indian caste, in the absence of clear colour badges of rank, will be impaired by spatial mobility and diversification of social relations: more concretely, . . . there is necessarily a close-set limit upon the size and complexity of a society organized through a caste (jati) system." [73] That is, the caste system in India requires that the ancestry of all individuals be known in order that their caste status be known. Only where social interaction is largely on a face-to-face basis among a restricted number of persons who know one another will ancestry be unquestionable. Where the interaction is between people

---

[72] Cox (1945), p. 362; cf. Dumont (1961).
[73] Bailey (1963), p. 113.

whose ancestry one does not know and whose caste status is therefore unknown or suspect, passing is so easy as to make interaction on a caste basis impossible. This is presumably why Indian caste could not persist in a large-scale, impersonal milieu. If, however, there is an indicator of significant group affiliation that is conspicuous and not easily altered or dissimulated, the system can function perfectly well even though specific genealogies are unverifiable or unknown. Thus, if the symbol of caste affiliation is skin color, there is little opportunity for passing, and no need to know precise ancestry.

Cultural features are important symbols of caste affiliation. Most individuals have been enculturated by members of their caste; they interact frequently and intensely; they share a culture and, to a considerable extent, they share attitudes, values, and behavior. They share in the definition of themselves as members of their caste, and they share loyalty and commitment to it. Attributes appropriate to the caste are displayed naturally and voluntarily in most cases, but they are enforced when necessary by ingroup and outgroup sanctions.

In India there are many cultural symbols of caste status, such as dress, speech, posture, and style of life. These are learned and acquired attributes and they can be dissimulated. However, they are attributes which are learned or acquired early in life and which can be dissimulated only with skill and patience. For many people, dissimulation on these grounds is as impossible as would be dissimulation of skin color. Even within a relatively isolated Indian village there may be easily discernible differences between the styles of speech of the various castes.[74] These are unconsciously learned status symbols that are almost as reliable indicators as skin color. Appropriate learned or acquired indicators may be (and usually are) enforced upon those who should properly display them, if any tendency to significant deviation appears. Self-image, pride and loyalty to the group can similarly lead to behavior symbolic of social status, even when it might be advantageous to feign a different affiliation.

Thus, it is not essential that a caste society be small-scale and face-to-face in its relationships; it is only essential that its members be reliably and unambiguously identifiable as to caste status. One way to do this is to know all the individuals with whom you interact—to be positive of the caste to which they belong by knowledge of their genealogical credentials. Another way is to have an easily detectable and not easily dissimulable means of identifying caste affiliation.

Cultural Distinctiveness

The cultural differences among castes are often said to distinguish caste in India from so-called caste in other societies. Particular

---

[74] Gumperz (1958), pp. 668–82.

groups in India differ conspicuously in religion, for example, the kind of ceremonies performed, the content and complexity of the ceremonies, and the gods in whose honor they are performed. Associated with religious differences are differences in other customs. In many regions of North India bride price is found in the marriages of low castes, while dowry is found in the marriages of high caste people. Polygyny may be common among low castes and not among high. Ritual purity requires quite different behavior of high castes than does the lesser ritual purity of low castes. Women of high castes may be secluded, while those of low castes are not. The foods taboo to one caste are quite different from those taboo to another. Traditional and actual occupations differ. Speech differs from caste to caste. Style of architecture, dress, and ornament differ.

In other societies cultural differences between castes may be few. Whether they are ever altogether lacking is doubtful for, as has been mentioned, culture is made up of behavior that is learned, shared and transmitted. People who interact have the same culture, and people whose interaction is limited share commensurately less common culture. Within a caste people interact frequently and intensively on a status-equal basis and are restricted from doing so with others. Intensive, status-equal interaction leads to common culture to an extent that interaction which is limited to particular roles and contexts (such as is characteristic of interaction between groups of widely differing status) does not and cannot. Therefore, there is probably always greater cultural homogeneity within a caste than between castes; castes are culturally distinct.

On the continuum from the ideal type of caste organization to noncaste organization, cultural divergence between ranked groups in the society evidently lies toward the caste extreme. There is probably no absolute or even measurable amount of cultural divergence inherent in caste organization.

CASTE CONTRASTED TO OTHER PRINCIPLES
OF SOCIAL ORGANIZATION

The essential features of castes can be brought into focus by contrasting caste with class, kin, and community as organizing principles in human societies.

Caste and Class

The principle of social organization that is most frequently contrasted with caste by social scientists, and most commonly confused with caste by others, is class organization. Caste and class systems are both systems of social stratification; both refer to hierarchically ranked divisions of society. Classes are ranked categories of individuals who share certain attributes, especially income and style of life. They are distinguished from castes in that membership is not accorded by birth but is acquired as a result of attributes that are theoretically independent of birth. There is individual mobility from one class to another, although it may occur infrequently.

The fact that class systems are based on acquired characteristics is extremely important. Whatever the attributes considered to be indicative of status in a given society, it is the kind or amount of those attributes possessed by an individual that determines the class to which he belongs. A class is made up of people who share similar attributes and equivalent rank. Thus, where wealth is an important criterion of rank, an individual is accorded class status in accordance with his income. This may be mitigated by other factors—for example, by the source of his wealth, how long he has had it, how long his family has had it, the manner in which he uses it—but in general his rank is a function of his possession of this attribute. He may move to a higher class or drop to a lower one as a result of a perceived change in his possession of it. He may be of a different class than his father or son; more frequently he may be of a different class than his grandfather or grandson. The people with whom he will interact most frequently tend to be those with similar attributes—those who share his class status. He is most likely to marry within his class. Because of their upbringing and the rules of inheritance, his children may remain in his class. But these are statistical facts and not, in most instances, prescriptive rules. Class membership is acquired. In a caste system, as indicated, an individual's rank is determined by birth. If a man is high-born, he will be treated as though he were possessed of the valued attributes of his caste whether or not he has them. Thus, he will be treated as though he were wealthy if this is the stereotyped attribute of his caste (in the context of the caste system) even if he is not. Mechanisms may also be employed to bring his attributes into line with his inherited status.

Classes vary from culture to culture in the degree to which they are self-aware, sharply defined, and corporate groups, but generally this degree is much lower than in castes. There are individuals whose class membership is marginal or debatable whereas this is never the case for caste membership. Like castes, classes entail rank which is shared by categories or groups of people and is so defined. Caste hierarchies, however, are, by their nature, completely discontinuous; class hierarchies are not.

In some societies individuals are ranged in an apparently completely continuous hierarchy or spectrum of rank. Each individual is ranked according to his individual possession of valued attributes without reference to any group or category. In studying such situations, social analysts may find it useful to deal with segments of the hierarchy as categories. Usually these are simply termed "strata," and are defined in terms of criteria that seem to the analyst to be significantly similar among those who possess them. Strata differ from classes primarily in the fact that they are artifacts of the social analyst rather than generally recognized and often self-conscious divisions of society.

Caste and Kin

Another major principle by which people are organized is kinship. Here the discussion will be restricted to consanguineous kin, excluding affinal kin. Thus, we consider groups such as lineages, clans, and phratries—those whose members share common descent.[75]

Castes (like classes) are ranked divisions of society, whereas kinship groups are generally unranked divisions of society. Kin groups and castes share the fact that recruitment is by birth, and both thus contrast with class. I have discussed above the variety of rules for ascription by birth in castes and kin groups, noting that there is much similarity in the rules used for the two kinds of groups.

In many societies caste can be conceived of as ultimately a kinship group for the simple reason that the caste is endogamous. In such a society the caste is the maximum social unit within which ties of descent and marriage can extend. The caste is composed of kinship groups and it may be believed that everyone within the caste is descended from a common ancestor, so that caste fellows are kinsmen.

Caste and Community

A fourth principle of social organization, in addition to caste, class, and kin, is that of residence or territory—the community. The village is an example of a group so defined, as are a variety of political units, including most "tribes" in India (see above). People are members of a specific community because of their place of residence or property. It should be noted that castes are generally regionally delimited (certainly they are so within India). Also there are groups whose membership depends upon both kin ties *and* residence.[76] Some

---

[75] "Clan" is here used in its most common meaning: a group of putative consanguineal kinsmen whose relationship is traced unilineally. Lowie and Murdock have called such groups "sibs," and I have pointed out the utility of Murdock's distinction between sib (as unilineal descent group) and clan (as a group determined partly by descent and partly by locality) in the study of North Indian social organization. Lowie (1947); Murdock (1949); Berreman (1962b), pp. 524–28.

[76] Murdock calls these "compromise kin groups" because they use two criteria for membership. He designates such groups "clans." Murdock (1949), pp. 65–78; cf. Berreman (1962b).

communities are composed of, or in some cases are open only to, members of a given caste or kin group. The fact remains, however, that residence or territoriality is a principle that can and frequently does operate independently of the other principles described here and one that can be usefully contrasted with them.

Unlike castes and classes, but like kin groups, communities are generally unranked relative to one another. And, unlike castes and kin groups, but like classes, membership in communities is acquired—it can be changed with change of residence.

The Four Principles

Four principles of social organization have been described here: caste, class, kin, and community. They are not mutually exclusive in any societies in which they occur. All four, for example, occur in India even on the village level. Thus, a caste is generally also an extensive kin group; most castes are territorially delimited; kin and community principles of organization may be combined in compromise kin groups within castes; class distinctions commonly occur within castes, within kin groups, and within communities.

These are distinctive but not mutually incompatible principles of social organization. In this presentation they have been distinguished on the basis of two primary variables—ranking and mode of recruitment—although concomitant features have been described as well. The two variables serve to define caste organization in the broadest sense, and they also distinguish from one another the four principles of social organization.

Placed in the stereotypic fourfold table, the distinctive features of each of these four principles can be seen in terms of the two relevant variables. For comparative purposes, these distinctions are useful.

Ranked	*Unranked*	
Caste	Kin	*Ascribed membership (by birth)*
Class	Community	*Acquired membership*

Ranking and mode of recruitment appear to be especially important variables in the social psychology of groups and individuals, accounting, perhaps, for the widespread similarities in attitudes, values, beliefs, and behaviors found in societies sharing similar expressions of these variables (for example, caste societies). This point will be elaborated in the next chapter. To emphasize these distinctions is not to deny that great variation occurs in social structures that share the principles described here. It is simply an attempt to draw useful distinctions in terms of comparable variables in the hope of contributing to greater understanding through cross-cultural comparison.

Chapter 15

GERALD D. BERREMAN

Concomitants of Caste Organization

From a discussion of the structural and functional characteristics of caste, the inherent attributes by which caste organization is defined, I turn now to some of the concomitants of caste organization as they are manifested by individuals who live in caste societies; to beliefs, attitudes, values, and personality attributes, to mechanisms by which people respond to high and low caste status, and to the behavioral idioms in which cast status is expressed.

ATTITUDES, VALUES, AND PERSONALITY

A fundamental characteristic of a caste system is that it comprises a hierarchy of social groups ranked on the basis of intrinsic superiority and inferiority. There are numerous consequences for individuals in this kind of social hierarchy. One of these is the pattern of empathy and emulation. High caste members empathize with the low caste to the extent they may feel compassion or guilt. Those of low caste easily imagine the lives of the high caste people, wish for their advantages and often attempt to emulate them. Orans has pointed out that there is a potential conflict within emulating groups.[1] He calls this the emulation-solidarity conflict; that is, members of a low status group may on the one hand want to emulate members of a superior group and on the other may want or feel compelled to remain loyal to their own group—to its standards and to the maintenance of its integrity. Orans was speaking specifically of the absorption of tribal peoples into the caste hierarchy where the maintenance of group identity conflicted with the desire to emulate Hindu castes and to be absorbed into the Hindu religious and social system. In most instances of caste mobility

---

[1] Orans (1959), pp. 108–14.

in India, however, this does not seem to be a problem because the entire caste wants to move up within the system. Rather than wanting to be absorbed into a different religion, social system, or caste, thereby losing their identity, its members want both higher status and the maintenance of their group identity.

Other attitudinal concomitants of caste organization result from the nature of superior-subordinate group relations and the dependent role of the subordinates. Thus there is frequently an attitude of *noblesse oblige* among high caste groups. There is often a one-sided, paternalistic attitude wherein comfort, protection and material aid are granted to low status groups in exchange for loyalty, obedience, and service as well as the less explicit advantages to be derived from deference and sexual subordination. Herein we find the common tendency for high status-low status relations to approximate adult-child relations and the "echelon" relations of total institutions. Mannoni[2] has explored some of the implications of inferiority and dependence in the relationships between groups in colonial societies which in many instances approximate caste relations.

Perhaps the most crucial and widespread effect of caste status derives directly from the two defining attributes of caste cited here: *birth ascription* and *ranking* (of groups). Birth ascription of membership in groups with inherently different life chances and different public esteem—especially where these differences are great, as between pariahs and non-pariahs—seems to have some common psychological and behavioral results wherever it occurs. These results have been inadequately studied, but they surely include many of the responses, reactions, and mechanisms described for Negroes and whites in the United States[3] and for those who are subject to, or who exercise, colonial rule.[4] The biographical and novelistic literature on the American Negro, as exemplified in the works of such authors as James Baldwin, Ralph Ellison and Richard Wright (among many others), is replete with perceptive accounts of the human implications of pariah status in the caste system of America. The effects of such a system are evident in both high and low status groups, but have been most often described for the low groups. Cash and Smith have analyzed the effects of the American caste system on the dominant, high status (white) members of the society.[5]

The psychological effects of segregation and discrimination reported in the United States have analogues in India, and those reported in this volume for the Eta of Japan have analogues in both India and

---

[2] Mannoni (1964), pp. 39ff.
[3] See Allport (1958); Cash (1954); Hyman (1942); Kardiner and Ovesey (1951); Pettigrew (1964); Smith (1963).
[4] See Mannoni (1964).
[5] Cash (1954), and Smith (1963).

the United States. These are discussed in greater scope and depth in
other chapters of this book. Anyone familiar with untouchable status
in India will recognize in Kardiner and Ovesey's book on American
Negro personality, *The Mark of Oppression,* the low caste people he
has known in India. Those who know the American scene will see
similarities to the Indian situation in such accounts of untouchability
as the novel by Anand, the autobiography by Hazari, and the recent
journalistic account of mobile, educated untouchables by Isaacs.[6]

Thus, structural similarities among caste societies are evidently associated with psychological and behavioral similarities. Individuals in
high and low status groups into which they are born and out of which
they cannot move face common problems and react in common ways.
Therefore, ranking and birth recruitment of groups are crucial factors
in any cross-cultural definition of caste. They have attitudinal, valua-
tional, and behavioral as well as structural relevance.

MECHANISMS

Certain adjustive techniques are resorted to by people of denigrated and deprived groups whose position cannot reasonably be expected to be alleviated. One of these techniques is to deny the validity
of the status—a common phenomenon in India. In the region of my
research in northern India, low caste people explained their status
in ways quite different from those used by high caste advocates of the
system. Often the explanation was simply in terms of relative wealth
and numbers: "If we were wealthy and in the majority, we would
make the high castes untouchable." Three other kinds of explanations
were offered consistently by low caste people. These had the effect of
denying the legitimacy of their low caste position:

1. Members of the entire caste (or subcaste) group would deny that
they deserved the low status to which they had been assigned: "English-
men and Muslims are untouchables because they have an alien religion
and they eat beef. This is as it should be. We are Hindus and we do not
eat beef, yet we, too, are treated as untouchables. This is not proper.
We should be accorded higher status." No group would admit to being
lowest in the caste hierarchy.

2. People might grant that the caste of their clan, lineage, or family
was of low status but deny that their particular group really belonged
to it. I have not encountered a low caste group which did not claim
high caste ancestry or origin. Thus a typical comment is: "Yes, we are
drummers by occupation, but our ancestor was a Brahman who married a drummer woman. By rights, therefore, we should be Brahmans,
but in such cases the high castes here go against the usual custom and

---

[6] Kardiner and Ovesey (1951); Anand (1956); Hazari (1951); Isaacs (1964).

assign the child the caste of his low caste parent rather than of his father, from whom a person inherits everything else."

3. A person might admit that his own caste and even his lineage or family were of low status, but he would not take responsibility for his own assignment to that status. Explanations were supplied by Brahmans who, as the most privileged caste and the recipients of religiously motivated charity from all castes, have a vested interest in maintenance of the system and its acceptance by all levels. An individual's horoscope as read by a Brahman might describe him as having been of high caste and exemplary behavior in a previous life and therefore destined for even greater things in the present life. However, in performing some religiously meritorious act in his previous existence, he inadvertently sinned and was punished in this life with a low rebirth.

Thus, no one said, in effect, "I am of low status and so are my family members and my caste-fellows, and justly so, because of our misdeeds in previous lives." To do so would lead to a psychologically untenable position, though one advocated by high caste people and by orthodox Hinduism. Rationalizations or beliefs such as these form a consistent pattern—they are not isolated instances. Neither are they unique to the village or culture reported here: the literature reveals similar beliefs elsewhere in North India.[7] They evidently indicate something less than enthusiastic acceptance of caste position and, meanwhile, they perhaps alleviate or divert resentment.[8]

Origin myths of low castes consistently conform to the second or third type of explanation above.[9] Nearly always the low caste claims unrecognized high status. As Rowe indicated, "In parts of India castes of genealogists and mythographers exist whose function it is to maintain and even create genealogies for their patrons." [10]

Another reaction is to seek escape from low caste status or its more disturbing implications by simply avoiding high caste people as much as possible; by withdrawing into the group and limiting interaction to the highly stereotyped and impersonal interaction the system allows. Sometimes the escape takes the form of emigration to urban areas where it is supposed that caste is less important or where passing may be possible. Education and westernization may allow the low caste person to move into a milieu where caste is relatively unimportant or where his origins can be concealed.[11] Escape may also take the form of joining protest or reform movements: India has a long history of low

---

[7] Atkinson (1886), p. 446; Cohn (1954), pp. 112ff.; Majumdar (1944), p. 193. See also Berreman (1963), pp. 220ff.; Rowe (1960), pp. 61ff.; Karve (1953), p. 115.

[8] Berreman (1960), pp. 126ff.

[9] Karve (1953), p. 115; Rowe (1960), pp. 61ff.; Rowe (1964).

[10] Rowe (1960), p. 63; cf. Shah and Shroff (1959), pp. 246–76.

[11] Cf. Isaacs (1964).

caste conversion to casteless or anti-caste religious movements; to Jainism, Buddhism, Islam, Sikhism, Christianity and to Hindu reform movements, such as Arya Samaj. Recently Buddhism has reappeared as an escape from untouchability.

Other reactions to low caste status include grudging and minimal compliance with high caste expectations or demands; enacting the low caste role of irresponsibility, shiftlessness, and sometimes buffoonery and childishness. Commonly one finds resort to such passive accommodation, as Dollard has called it, coupled with ingroup aggression, especially where aggression toward the outgroup is dangerous or impossible: self-hatred is a concomitant of this pattern. Perhaps the most common reaction is to overtly accept one's position—to passively accommodate to it—while privately and among one's caste fellows, to express resentment, to fantasize, or even to plan to attain recognition of higher status through a variety of means, including aggression against higher castes. Low caste people frequently talk among themselves of resisting their accorded status or its manifestations at the hands of higher castes, but they rarely act upon it.

It has often been remarked that resistance to low status is much less common (some have said it is unknown) in India than in other caste-like societies, such as the southern United States. This, as previously indicated, has been cited as a fact that distinguishes caste from non-caste societies, and specifically Indian caste from American race relations. I believe this to be a false distinction based on inadequate knowledge of Indian caste.

Whether overt resistance occurs seems, in fact, more directly related to the power structure than to belief in the validity or justifiability of accorded status. In rural India power is heavily concentrated in the hands of people of high castes, and it is readily and ruthlessly used in the forms of economic, social and ritualistic sanctions, and in force and violence. For a weak low caste to defy its accorded status would be foolhardy. Precisely the same thing has been true, at least until recently, in the southern United States, particularly in such rural areas as the Mississippi delta. There, as in India, one finds a history of very little overt resistance, although in both instances resistance has occurred when the opportunity arose or when the oppression became intolerable. In India, with the advent of anti-discrimination legislation since Independence, overt resistance to the deprivations inherent in low caste status has increased, with resort to violent and non-violent resistance, litigation, and other mechanisms. Social legislation and its enforcement has altered the power structure so as to make effective resistance feasible. Again, precisely the same thing has occurred in the United States.

In most of India—excluding the most sophisticated and educated groups, especially in urban areas—resistance has traditionally taken the forms of attempts to change caste rank within the hierarchy rather than of attempts to eliminate the caste system altogether. People object to the status accorded them within the system rather than to the system itself. The Indian peasant's goal is superiority, not equality. In the United States, on the other hand, Negroes who are dissatisfied with the caste system, as most are, seek to eliminate it. This difference can be explained largely in terms of the social structure of the groups involved.

In most Indian villages and areas there are a great number of castes, most of which are relatively small in numbers and are competing for rank with other castes close to themselves in the hierarchy. There is often one dominant caste or a group of allied dominant castes of high rank. No single low caste has the numerical, political, or economic strength to exert its will over other castes in a power struggle. Since they compete with one another for status (and not infrequently for livelihood), low castes are unlikely to combine forces to attain common ends: they conflict because each wants to be above the other in rank; the closer in rank the castes, the greater chances for successful advance and the lower the risks. The lower in the hierarchy, the less powerful the castes, as a rule. In the rare case where a big jump in status is attempted, the mobile group usually has in some manner acquired great power (in numbers, education, wealth, land) to back up its claims.

If members of a caste were to advocate elimination of the caste system, they would possibly gain equality with higher castes, but at the cost of having to treat as equals other groups patently lower than themselves. Psychologically, their superiority to some castes is at least as important as their inferiority to others. No caste admits to being lowest in the hierarchy. Claims to prideful status are phrased in terms of superiority to certain other castes. Therefore, elimination of the system would be a mixed blessing at best. The advantage of equality with superiors would be mitigated or even eliminated by the disadvantage of equality with inferiors. Thus, in such a multiple caste system, attempts to move within the system seem more likely to be successful, and to be more advantageous if successful, than attempts to eliminate the system.

In the dual caste hierarchy of the United States power also lies clearly in the hands of the dominant and socially superior group. But abolition of the caste division is seen by Negroes as the only plausible remedy for their deprived position. To reverse the ranks—to make Negroes superior to whites—is an aim which would be highly unlikely to succeed even should it be desired, simply because of the power structure. (There are, of course, Negroes and organized groups of Negroes, including some of the black supremacist groups recently on the scene, who do apparently want to invert the caste hierarchy in the United States, but these are in the minority.) If the caste system in the United States were abolished, Negroes would have nothing to lose but their inferior status, and would gain equality with the high caste group. The difference between Indian and American aims and attitudes regarding changes in the hierarchy may therefore lie in the differences between a multiple and a dual caste hierarchy.

High castes as well as low reveal the effects of their status in their attitudes, values, beliefs, and behavior.[12] They exhibit feelings of social superiority—of greater intrinsic worth expressed in terms of such attributes as purity, honor, morality, and intelligence. They see lower castes as inferior and tainted. Prejudice, as described and analyzed in American race relations, is a manifestation of these values.[13] Perhaps prejudice and consequent discrimination toward pariah groups is found widely because of common structural facts in caste systems combined with common human psychological mechanisms. That is, denigration of a low caste may result from high caste people's displacement of their own internalized self-hatred that is the result of the guilt feelings they have acquired from their empathetic awareness (probably repressed) of low caste deprivations. Such denigration may also simply be rationalization for the deprivations imposed. Kardiner and Ovesey have remarked that "once you degrade someone in that way, the sense of guilt makes it imperative to degrade the object further to justify the whole procedure." [14]

Although low castes do not characteristically adopt a view of themselves entirely consistent with the negative view of their superiors, they cannot avoid being influenced by that view and its associated behavior. Gallagher notes for the southern United States that

By the attitudes of mingled fear, hostility, deprecation, discrimination, amused patronage, friendly domination, and rigid authoritarianism, the white caste generates opposite and complementary attitudes in the Negro caste. It is a touch of consummate irony that the dominant group should then argue that the characteristics which exhibit themselves in the submerged group are "natural" or "racial." [15]

The same can be said for high and low castes in India.

BEHAVIOR: THE IDIOM OF CASTE

Paternalism and reciprocal deference and service have been described as characteristic of caste systems. Associated with these are

---

[12] Cf. Cash (1954); Mannoni (1964); Smith (1963).
[13] Allport (1958).
[14] Kardiner and Ovesey (1951), p. 379.
[15] Gallagher (1938), p. 109.

prescriptions and proscriptions regarding certain kinds of interaction among castes. Most commonly these take the form of restrictions on marriage, sex relations, eating and sitting together, and on a variety of other forms of interaction symbolic of social equality. What makes up status-equal interaction varies from society to society, but all caste societies have regulations which define some kinds of interaction, some kinds of behavior, as appropriate only among those who are equal in status, while others are defined as appropriate for superiors vis-à-vis inferiors, and vice versa. Observance of the rules is essential because behavior, and especially behavior in inter-group contexts, is the idiom in which the caste system is expressed and validated.[16] Their importance is indicated by the stringency of the sanctions universally employed to enforce them. Even when the rules or etiquette bear no direct or obvious relationship to the rationale for differential status, their observance is crucial as an affirmation and therefore preservation of the system.

There is nothing in the religious-philosophical tenets of Hinduism, nor more narrowly in the purity-pollution concept, that requires the deferential terms of address and behavior that a person of low caste must use toward a person of any higher caste. Neither is there anything in the racial explanation of Negro status in the United States that justifies the similarly deferential behavior required of a Negro in his interaction with a white. Again, there is no explicit Hindu rationale for the former widespread prohibition against the wearing of gold jewelry and certain kinds of clothing among untouchables in India; yet it was enforced just as Negroes were for years prevented from owning automobiles in some parts of the United States. Behavior that contravenes these customs is as readily punished as behavior that in India is directly threatening to maintenance of ritual purity, or in the United States is explicitly identifiable as having to do with racial purity or other characteristics which are the rationale for the pattern of race relations. Observance is symbolic of the system and an endorsement of it; it is as such that it is important.

Eating seems consistently and cross-culturally to be crucial to the maintenance of caste purity, evidently because it requires relatively intimate interaction, normally within the family; perhaps also because it is closely identified with the ingestion of materials into the body, a procedure that can easily lead to pollution. The precise content of rules for eating vary from society to society, but their significance to notions of caste status are similar. In India and in Japan, as in the United States, eating together implies ritual and social equality. In India and Japan, a person who cooks for another and serves his food

---

[16] Gallagher (1938), p. 95, has noted that "A . . . pragmatic axiom of the caste system is the importance of etiquette in preserving the system. Observance of the etiquette [of inter-caste relations] implies acceptance of caste status."

must be equal or superior in rank to the recipient of the food; only thus can the person served avoid pollution. In the United States, however, a Negro may cook and serve, but not eat with the whites. As Gallagher says of the American case, "to break eating taboos is to defy caste. . . . The etiquette must be observed as evidence of the acceptance of caste." [17]

Other behaviors and types of interaction are regulated in caste societies to the degree that they are defined as relevant to caste status, to purity, or to maintenance of the system. In the United States, Negroes and whites can interact in many contexts so long as they are standing, but cannot interact when seated. Integration of facilities has sometimes been effected by the simple expedient of removing chairs. (This was reportedly the case when the libraries of Montgomery, Alabama, were integrated, and has been the case in the integration of lunch counters in some cities.) The term "vertical integration" is sometimes applied to this situation. In India there are also such rules. The height at which one sits, the place in which one sits, and whether one sits at all in the presence of others, are crucially related to status in the caste hierarchy.

Marriage and sex relations are among the most stringently regulated behaviors in a caste system. This is not surprising since caste membership is determined by birth, and birth is the likely result of marriage and sex relations. By inappropriate marriage or inappropriate sexual behavior, unacceptable ancestry may enter the group. This threatens the very foundation of the group's identity and claim to status. Prohibitions are much more stringent for high caste women than men, both in Negro-white relations in America and in high-low caste relations in India. This is not simply because paternity is unprovable while maternity is undeniable. More importantly, a high caste man who has sexual relations with a low caste woman does not threaten the integrity of his high caste group, for it is the woman who has the baby. A woman of high caste who has sexual relations with a man of low caste threatens her caste group vitally because she brings into it a new member of defiling ancestry.

In both India and the United States high caste women are jealously guarded by their men. Put on a pedestal, they are described as pure, honorable, and incorruptible; yet there is manifest anxiety on the part of their menfolk lest the women deviate from this image thereby jeopardizing the pride of the group and the purity of the progeny. It is also assumed (by the high castes) that low caste women are not virtuous and that they will be accessible to high caste men (this is evidently not the case in Japan). These assumptions are to some extent borne out because of the relative power in the high and low groups.

[17] Gallagher (1938), p. 96.

There is no doubt that low caste people in both societies resent the sexual exploitation of the woman.[18]

It is apparent that sexual exploitation is a common concomitant of caste organization. Other kinds of exploitation are probably equally common, particularly economic exploitation and the exploitation of social and psychological advantages that accrue to high status groups as a result of the fact that they claim the right to demand forms of behavior which serve to increase their own self-esteem. As Dollard has pointed out, "It must always be remembered that in the end this deference is demanded and not merely independently given." [19] Such exploitation is an overt feature of the caste system in India; one often mentioned by low caste people and readily recognized; in appropriate circumstances, it is described by high caste people as well. The same is true, of course, in the southern United States.

These aspects of the system are easily manipulated by those to whom they are advantageous, and there are even contexts in which groups to whom they are disadvantageous can manipulate the system for some minimal advantage; that is, for the latter there are compensatory gains. A low caste person, for example, may be able to avoid responsibility simply on the grounds that members of his caste are deemed irresponsible. He may be able to gain leisure from time to time simply because low caste people are assumed to be lazy. It should be noted, however, that such compensatory gains are cited much more often by high caste advocates of caste systems than by those who are alleged to enjoy them. They are gains common in authoritarian systems everywhere and are usually subject to the will of the dominant groups. Very rarely can these gains be realistically described as equivalent to those of the high status and dominant groups.

One rather convincing indication of the lack of equivalence is that status emulation or mobility striving occurs in all societies and that it occurs in only one direction: upward. If it were true that low status groups derived advantage from their low status—that they derived great comfort, security and satisfaction from their position, as some insist is the case—one would expect to find them generally content with their lot, and to find high status groups striving downward on occasion. Only when the situation is drastically altered, as when in contemporary India special privileges have been invented for low status groups (in the form of legislation giving them certain conspicuous advantages such as scholarships, reserved seats in the legislature, and special economic advantages), has low caste designation not been resisted. In this circumstance, interestingly enough, some groups in certain regions of India are striving to be defined as low status in order

[18] Cf. Berreman (1960).
[19] Dollard (1957), p. 174.

to acquire the conspicuous material advantages that will help them toward upward mobility in a modern, Western (sometimes urban, sometimes industrial) context at the cost of downward mobility in the traditional ritual hierarchy. This is possible, of course, because the traditional ritual hierarchy is losing its relevance for many whereas the modern social hierarchy, based on criteria of wealth, education, and Western life-styles, is becoming the important one.[20] The aim, as always, is higher status, but its definition and the appropriate path to it is new.

CASTE AND THE EQUALITARIAN CREED

Caste systems, despite their putative rigidity are, like all social systems, dynamic. One way in which they change is in the functions of their constituent parts. In India, for example, with urbanization, modernization, and Westernization, castes have increasingly become self-interest groups in the context of party politics, the welfare state, urban employment, and Western education, and their role as arbiters in traditional social and ritual matters has diminished proportionately.[21] Additionally, castes change in structure. Thus, local castes (jatis) have been for many purposes submerged in larger caste clusters or "associations" that did not exist in traditional rural India.[22] Castes have also occasionally split into traditional groups and mobile groups that come to comprise separate castes.

The most vital dynamic force in caste societies lies in the mobility striving inherent among their members. Low castes resist the status accorded them, with its concomitant disabilities and discrimination, and strive for higher accorded status and its attendant advantages. High castes attempt to prevent such striving and the implicit threat to their position. In this conflict of interests lies the explosive potential in all caste societies. The passivity of depressed groups, like the peacefulness of the system, is deceptive, for it is dependent upon the unremitting (but often subtle and covert) threat of sanctions; the unstinting exercise of power by those who possess it. As long as the balance of power is clearly and stably in the hands of the advantaged groups, the potential for conflict is unlikely to be realized. But if the balance shifts, the potential becomes suddenly actual and when this happens— when people see the possibility of throwing off their degradation and achieving their aspirations for dignity, opportunity, security and life itself—the myth of the contentment of low castes is rudely exposed.

Low caste rejection of their status is expressed in movements to alter

[20] Srinivas (1956), pp. 481–96.
[21] Cf. Gould (1963), pp. 427–38; Harrison (1960), pp. 96–136; Rudolph and Rudolph (1960), pp. 5–22; Srinivas (1962), pp. 15–40.
[22] Rudolph and Rudolph (1960), pp. 5–22.

their position within the system (as is characteristic of rural India) and in movements to alter the system itself (as in the United States). The determination and militance with which such movements seek their goals have usually come as a shock to the theretofore complacent, but suddenly threatened, elites, who respond with resistance, anger, and repression. This pattern has occurred repeatedly in recent years in caste societies as disparate as those in Alabama and Andhra. The Negro's classic struggle for social equality is only the best known of many such movements.

The greatest threat to caste systems in the modern world is the increasing prevalence of an egalitarian ideology. Such an ideology strikes a responsive chord among those who suffer from the existence of caste, either as victims of low status or as victims of the empathy-guilt syndrome exhibited by some high caste individuals and groups. When such an ideology becomes widespread, it has usually been promulgated by sophisticated social revolutionaries (as in the southeastern United States and in South Africa), or by official governmental sources (as nationally in the United States, Japan, and India). Often (but not always) effective governmental advocacy has only been a belated response to the demands of social revolutionaries and their aroused followers.

Broad public support for equality is generally not immediately forthcoming. Those who stand to benefit most may fail to understand the ideology or may fear to endorse it lest they suffer the powerful wrath of their social superiors. Though these fears have generally proved to be well grounded, in the modern context they have failed as deterrents to egalitarianism simply because of the increasing access to power among denigrated groups, their increasing awareness of alternative systems, and the consequent urgency of their demands for opportunity. When egalitarianism captures the enthusiasm and evokes the support of low status people (and those who empathize with them) who see it as a means to alleviate their condition, it is usually resented and harshly resisted by those of high status who see it as a threat to their vested interests.

In caste societies, the most militant advocates of equality tend to be those who are most educated and who have the most sophisticated awareness of the world beyond their own communities. They include people of all strata, but since educated, sophisticated people come largely from the advantaged castes, many active advocates of equality are of high status. Thus, in India, the leaders of anti-casteism in the Congress Party and in various recent reform movements have been members of the Western-educated elite. Those most active in the movement for Negro rights in the United States have included educated people of both races.

The equalitarian creed is an ideal which, in the form referred to here, has largely grown out of the Western tradition, a tradition that has been communicated through Western languages and specifically through Western education. Its spread has accompanied the spread of Westernization, improved education, improved mass communications, and the increased influence of Western-educated people in non-Western nations. It is a result also of the fact that nations are becoming increasingly "other-directed." They are subject to scrutiny and even sanctions from formerly little known, powerless, and therefore irrelevant peoples and nations. Many of these peoples and nations until recently suffered acutely from political, social, and economic domination and the manifold discriminatory practices accompanying such domination. To them the egalitarian creed takes on special importance. Thus, the creed becomes a matter of national policy.[23] It is incumbent upon any nation, religion, or ethnic group whose members wish to secure the respect, cooperation, or support of the world community to follow this creed. Even those who privately feel threatened may find it prudent to pay lip service to it, or at least to remain silent.

With increasing frequency and urgency caste societies are confronted with the challenge of an egalitarian ideology. Such a confrontation is extremely traumatic; it consistently results in drastic social changes. Basically, it means that powerful elite groups whose advantages are dependent upon the status quo are challenged by aroused low status groups whose goals are dependent upon the destruction of the status quo. This is the dilemma of the caste society in an era of equality. The results are manifold but remarkably consistent. Overt conflict is well known in India and in the United States despite attempts to wish the problem out of existence or sweep it from view. Such conflict has taken the form of violence, nonviolent resistance, and the application of other sactions of varying degrees of subtlety. The effectiveness of nonviolent resistance has been vividly manifest in the United States recently, where the Indian precedent has been followed and elaborated upon. How the problem might be resolved without resort to such costly and debilitating measures has been a matter of considerable interest and most are by now aware that fundamental social change is needed. The problem then becomes one of how to effect such change and with a minimum of trauma. Many observers have suggested that it is impossible to legislate attitudes and that before low caste grievances can be resolved, those who oppose their resolution must themselves undergo a change. Education is usually advocated as the means to accomplish this, combined with a recommendation that a concerted effort be made by those who are denigrated to become worthy of respect by changing their ways of life. It might be noted that such observers are

[23] See Fallers (1963), pp. 158–219.

singularly loath to advocate the means by which this might be accomplished—namely, provision of equal and undifferentiated opportunity for all.

Most social scientists would agree that changed attitudes are an ultimate goal of equalitarian ideologies, but they would insist that the immediate complaints of denigrated people hinge not on attitudes but on behavior. American Negroes, for example, often insist that they want jobs, houses, education, the vote, and medical care more than the love of whites. Behavior—in this case discrimination—can be influenced by legislation, and attitudinal change follows behavioral change if the situation is properly handled—if the behavior involves status-equal contact in meaningful contexts.[24] Low caste people can achieve equal treatment, or very nearly so, even when they are not loved or liked equally. They are evidently willing to wait for the latter if they can achieve the former.

Wallace and Mills have pointed out that any given behavioral pattern can stem from a variety of motives.[25] An untouchable, for example, might be given a white collar job because he is personally qualified, because he is entitled to it by law and the law is respected, because the employer thinks it the moral thing to do, because the untouchable is liked, or because the employer is afraid to deny him the job. Thus, for an untouchable to get a job or an education, or the vote, it is not necessary that prior moral consensus be achieved in the society. It is only necessary to induce someone to hire him, to allow him into the school, or the polls. Later, as a result of the fact that he has been in this context, the attitudes of those around him are likely to change to accord with their behavior.

But if an equalitarian creed is to be realized, the fundamental features of caste must be eliminated: its hereditary, hierarchical nature. This can be most effectively accomplished by the elimination of discriminatory behavior through appropriate legislation, vigorously enforced; and by the provision of means by which low caste people can escape the vicious cycle of denigration, self-doubt, and lack of opportunity. By providing them education, jobs, houses, and political participation, low caste people are enabled to escape many of the immediate consequences of their status and also to achieve a way of life inconsistent with the stereotypes of low caste behavior; they thus may gain opportunities for new self-definition, for higher accorded status, and for material advantages.

India has made the most determined legislative effort of any nation to implement an equalitarian creed in a caste society, and against the greatest odds.[26] Unambiguous legislation against discrimination has

---

[24] Cf. Rose (1949), pp. 61–67; Simpson and Yinger (1953), p. 675; Williams (1947).
[25] Wallace (1962), pp. 27ff.; Mills (1960), p. 39.
[26] Galanter (1963), pp. 544–59.

been combined with preferential opportunities for people of disadvantaged groups through a system of quotas for scholarships, jobs, and seats in legislative bodies. It is assumed that they will thereby be able to gain power and destroy stereotypes. This "reverse discrimination" causes some hardship to individual high caste candidates for such opportunities, but India has chosen to pay this calculated cost to close the gap between the castes and bring more rapid realization of the egalitarian ideal.

This step has not been taken in the United States. Evidently the hope is that in time Negroes will accomplish the same end despite the immense social, economic, and political disadvantages with which they enter competition. Only the civil rights movement in this country has undertaken a task similar to that undertaken by the government in India: to see that Negroes are provided with special opportunities to rise out of their disadvantaged position through programs of special education, and campaigns to get jobs for Negroes in formerly closed or restricted places, and so on. But in both countries the effectiveness of legislation for equality has been greatly mitigated by the weakness of enforcement. It has been left to equalitarian movements to seek the enforcement of the laws and the use of legal channels as well as to lobby for more and better laws and to advocate voluntary equalitarian behavior where no laws exist. When these means have proved ineffective or unsatisfactory, direct action of various sorts has resulted.

Thus, as caste systems confront equalitarian creeds, attitudinal changes need not precede the social changes that the confrontation demands. It is evident that complementary behavior—"public conformity"—is primary; that equalitarian behavior can be successfully achieved by statutory means vigorously enforced, and that changes in attitudes—"private acceptance"—can come later. Behavioral changes need not wait on attitudinal changes, and the latter can and probably will follow if equalitarian behavior occurs or is enforced in meaningful, functional contexts, especially among people of similar life-styles where equal and undifferentiated opportunities exist. This, in turn, can be realized most quickly and effectively in caste societies when special opportunities are provided for those to whom they have been traditionally denied until such time as those granted them stand on an equal footing with others.

If caste organization is an anachronism in the modern world, it is an extremely important one, with human implications only now becoming fully realized as a result of the fact that such organization is being vigorously challenged (and vigorously defended) in many parts of the world. Unless it is understood, the problems it evokes are unlikely to be resolved.

CONCLUSION

Among societies composed of ranked groups, membership in which is determined by birth, there are similarities covering a broad range of individual and group characteristics. They are sufficiently consistent to suggest that they are not due to chance. Thus comparisons among such societies can be expected to lead to useful generalizations about the nature and consequences of their common features, termed collectively, caste organization. This should lead to a better understanding of the societies and ultimately of human behavior in general.

To compare caste societies is not to ignore, deny, or belittle the fact that there are important differences among them. These differences, like the similarities, can be revealed only by investigation. Their structural, functional, and psychological implications can also be revealed only by research. Earlier chapters in this book have described and analyzed a caste system that has received relatively little attention. Despite enormous differences in cultural context in Japan, the United States, and India, structural similarities appear; these are defined as caste and provide a basis for productive comparisons.

Because there are differences in the caste organization manifested in different societies and because the cultural context in which it occurs differs in each society, some observers have held that comparisons are impossible. Most often they have urged that the term caste be reserved for the system of social stratification found in Hindu India, in all of its complexity and richness of cultural detail. But social science, like any science, requires that part of reality be ignored while other parts are emphasized. Otherwise, comparisons and generalizations are impossible.

Social reality is everchanging and, for practical purposes, infinite. Part of it is brushed aside in the very act of observing, describing or analyzing. Every social reality is unique. This is true not only as between India and the United States and Japan, but as between North India and South India, as between village A and village B within India, and as between family X and family Y in a single village. But if one cannot ignore certain differences in favor of similarities, which are thought to be important for a given purpose, then one cannot talk about social subgroups, institutions, kinship systems, or ceremonies, for example, but only about unique events. This is an acceptable position, but it cannot result in anything likely to be describable as social science.

Only by reference to common features of society and culture can significant generalizations be made concerning social processes and principles in societies as unlike as those of Japan, India and the United States. The hereditary system of ranked social groups—the caste system—is one important common feature, with common implications for the people who live these three cultures. Without analysis of the common aspects of caste organization, the striking similarities that, upon close investigation, prove to exist among these societies—and in other caste societies as well—would be likely to be overlooked or dismissed as coincidence. The similarities of form, function and structure and of individual behavior and attitudes among caste societies as they have been defined here are too great and too consistent to allow them to be dismissed so lightly.

The comparison of similar social facts—such as caste organization in its manifestation in many cultural contexts—leads to genuine understanding, which the study of unique facts cannot. As caste systems are increasingly confronted with equalitarian ideologies, even among those who comprise them, understanding of this type of social organization takes on acutely practical significance.

Motivational Components of Caste

INTRODUCTION

The final two chapters develop two theoretical propositions: first, that in personality structures as well as in the social structure itself, there are determinants of behavior in particular cultures that permit a definition of caste as a type of expressive social behavior; and second, that racism can be defined as a particular form of caste ideology.

The foregoing material on the Japanese Burakumin must be considered as one historical instance of the development of caste phenomena in a hierarchical society. At first glance, a direct comparison of social discrimination in Japan, India, the United States, Germany, and South Africa, with their very different historical and social origins, would seem to be unwarranted. Yet there are underlying structural similarities that maintain caste or racist attitudes in the social-cultural matrix operative in all these modern national states. A comparative approach demonstrates that caste is a reappearing form of social phenomenon that periodically reveals itself institutionally in highly disparate times and places.

There are some who would limit the appearance of caste to Hindu India and exclude other examples of independent development of endogamous occupational social hierarchies. One could possibly make a case for the existence of Japanese caste from what is termed in anthropology a "diffusionist" standpoint. As indicated in the chapter on the origins of the pariah caste in Japan, one can trace some of the religious proscriptions defining caste in Japan to indirect contact with Indian culture through the medium of Buddhist religious doctrines. Although itself an attack on caste, Buddhism as a protest against social inequity never completely eliminated concepts of ritual pollution from religious doctrine. On the contrary, it transmitted concerns with pollution by its sanctions against the taking of life, especially the killing of animals for food and the use of hides for leather products.

Such an historical-cultural diffusionist plea for considering what appeared in Japan as a legitimate instance of caste, however, would not be satisfactory. It would not explain why China, the direct source of Japanese Buddhism, did not more fully develop comparable institutions, nor would it give sufficient weight to the indigenous Japanese concerns with purity and pollution found in the Shinto cult.

One might even make a more speculative diffusionist foray into the unknowns of Japanese prehistory and suggest that the Shinto concern with purity and its vague notions of the supernatural indicate similar cultural origins as those of the concepts of taboo and mana found scattered throughout the islands of Oceania. These vague religious conceptions could have been brought into Japan with some influx of population from a coastal locality in the Southeast Asian continent.

The inclusion of Japan among those societies exhibiting caste is not based on any such concepts, however, but is more securely based on the structure of traditional Japanese society itself. The "functional" role that came to be played by the outcaste within the Japanese social hierarchy is of far more importance than any possible historical adaptation of caste concepts from an external cultural source. While espousing a functional theory of the role of the outcaste I must hasten to indicate that my form of functionalist theory is based on considerations not only of social structure but of psychological structure and history as well. It is, therefore, a theoretical position that encompasses a knowledge of both cultural and psychological dynamics, considered diachronically through time.

The proposition espoused by Berreman and myself, that caste is structural and not the unique feature of Indian culture, makes us partisans in a conflict nowhere near resolution. The purpose of this volume therefore is not limited to the presentation of the descriptive material from Japan. We strongly contend that the existence of the Burakumin can only be interpreted as a historical instance of caste. The first step, taken in the previous section by Berreman, was to further the understanding of the structural nature of caste from the standpoint of social organizational principles. From this, I shall take the argument further,[1] to explain why, in caste as contrasted to class phenomena, one must also consider psychological structural determinants.

Caste behavior is peculiarly irrational when compared with class behavior. One can demonstrate the continued presence of caste in

[1] Berreman in his exposition of the social-organizational components of caste did not concern himself with the psychological nature of the pollution barrier suggested by Bailey and others as an essential feature of inter-caste behavior, a consideration to which I shall devote more attention below.

societies where it no longer receives vital support from social structural elements; caste can be manifestly dysfunctional. This latter phase of our argument may be opposed by some who are sympathetic to a social organizational approach but see no value in calling on psychological determinants to solve what they believe to be a strictly social problem.

The following chapter begins with an examination of the various organizational requisites of caste in order to demonstrate the need to consider psychological determinants as criticial in differentiating it from other systems of social stratification. Caste can be considered synchronically—in its present functioning, without reference to questions of origin, development, or change. Freed from cultural-historical contexts, valid cross-cultural generalizations can be made. In the second section of this chapter, however, we move on to criticize the idea that structural theory as it now stands, without reference to psychological determinants, can adequately discuss.caste diachronically especially when it is affected by radical social change.

In the final chapter we briefly sketch the theory that caste is expressive rather than instrumental behavior and therefore of necessity is properly studied only by a dual sociological-psychological examination.

The proposition of Berreman and myself that, entirely aside from questions of origin or development, the caste concept is structural and not unique to one culture, brings us into direct conflict with the theoretical positions taken by a number of others. The refusal by some authorities[2] to extend the concept of caste to other analogous structural situations is based on the holistic view that one cannot arbitrarily select as caste only certain of the total network of traits organically interrelated into a total culture. They are impressed more with unique centrality of caste ideology, values, and social perceptions to the Indian social system than with the structural analogies elsewhere to Indian caste.

Such a concept of cultural uniqueness could also be applied to particular forms taken by social class in one culture as contrasted with another. Yet the concept "class" is found useful in comparing disparate

---

[2] We cite for a specific instance the position taken by the eminent British anthropologist, E. R. Leach, who has given considerable thought to the subject of caste. Leach says:

. . . I do not accept the view that, because caste is a structural phenomenon, it is therefore a concept which has world-wide application. Caste, in my view, denotes a particular species of structural organization indissolubly linked with what Dumont (Dumont and Pocock, 1957) rightly insists is a Pan-Indian civilization. Consequently I believe that those who apply the term to contexts wholly remote from the Indian world invariably go astray. The specific character of caste systems lies in the peculiar nature of the systemic organization itself.

Leach (1960), p. 5. Leach's position following that of Dumont seems to be somewhat inconsistent with the Durkheimian sociology to which both owe some debt in other facets of theory.

societies with one another. The Portuguese word caste, used to describe Hindu social organization, has become not only convenient but necessary to describe situations other than that in India, in which societies are hierarchically segmented by sanctioned endogamy justified by an ideology stressing intellectual and moral as well as physical differences in biological inheritance, whether these justifications be in religious or secular terms.[3] This syndrome designates caste whether it occurs in the political states of present-day India, South Africa, or the United States, or in smaller folk societies that evidenced similar phenomena in the past. These structural similarities become more apparent when the comparative analysis is extended to an examination of the congruence in psychological structures underlying various appearances of race and caste phenomena.

From the standpoint of a dual framework of culture and personality, what is often termed a synchronic social structural approach in modern social anthropology appears to be insufficient for explaining the recurrence of caste phenomena. It cannot account for the appearance or modification of caste segregation in any particular society, nor can it explain why a society or culture remains peculiarly resistant to its disappearance after the loss of many of its economic, political or social functions.

Along with a general loss of interest in an outmoded evolutionist approach, anthropology has in recent decades tended to neglect theories concerned with the origin of institutions within culture. Most of today's leading social anthropologists tend to remain ahistorical in their approach to social structure. They are essentially uninterested in problems not only of origins but also of social change as it influences structural theory. This neglect of the development and change within culture that affects specific institutions is somewhat arbitrary; to understand present functions fully one must at some point consider how institutions develop or decay through time.

Sometimes within a critical period of social or cultural change, one finds clearly outlined tensions and disequilibria within a given social institution. Such dislocations tend to highlight the structural mechanisms at work, just as critical states of intrapsychic tension and disequilibrium in the individual help to define in their extremity the structural mechanisms operative in personality organization. In many instances the conditions of social disequilibrium themselves must be partially defined in psychological terms. A culturally oriented concept of personality structure is essential to social theory since there are critical forms of social behavior within given cultures determined by

---

[3] I agree with Berreman's proposal to use the word "pariah caste" to designate disparaged outgroups. I would claim the necessity of using the word "caste" as the general term designating relations across the social pollution barrier. Without this pollution barrier, there would be no caste society in India.

socialization processes that gain through time some functional autonomy from other institutional influences. In every culture, therefore, one finds continuities in behavior from one generation to the next that resist changes brought about by fluctuations in economic or political organization, or even sweeping changes in the status hierarchy of the society caused by such external disruptions as war and conquest.

This duality in behavioral determinants related to social structure on the one hand and personality on the other can give rise to situations of chronic as well as acute dysfunction within the social structure itself. As in the instance of caste as we have documented it in Japan, situations of psychological lag occur that cannot easily be eradicated by legal efforts or concerted social planning.

Our evidence from Japan amply documents the inadequacy of a rigid, single-minded social structural approach in situations of social change. The simple fact is, seen *instrumentally,* caste is no longer functional in Japan; yet it continues to exist. So, too, racial prejudice in the United States has become dysfunctional and disruptive. It has become a "disease" of the society, fostering various forms of conflict rather than social accommodation. Not only is it unnecessary for the continuity of American society, it has become explosively dangerous and corrosive to other widely accepted social values. Such social incongruity among economic, political, and social forms of interaction when found in a culture must be understood in terms of individual and social psychological mechanisms as well as in sociological terms.

One may suppose that ultimately social attitudes will again become more congruent with social structure. But in stages of transition a sociologist relying only on an analysis of structural dynamics cannot cope with the persistence of attitudinal patterns nor explain them sufficiently without some recourse to a psychological analysis.[4] The level of abstraction available to sociologists is more appropriate theoretically when applied to explanations of the society with a high degree of integration and stability, but it obviously fails to provide adequate, thorough understanding for societies in transition or in a state of internal disorder caused by value conflicts. Moreover, even in a stable society, a strict sociological approach fails to explain fully the ordering function of traditional expressive relationships. The expressive life of a culture, which includes its art and religion, is often carefully excluded from too careful an analysis within a social structural approach, not only synchronically but as an aspect of social change.

In the final chapter I have tried to pull together from a psychological perspective several theoretical concerns which at first may seem to be totally unrelated.

First, there is an instrumental-expressive dichotomy in human be-

---

[4] From this standpoint one can criticize the recent statements of Dumont (1964).

havior which may be juxtaposed to the essential distinction between magic and religion. This instrumental-expressive dichotomy helps to differentiate between the exploitation in class societies and that in caste segregation. When extended in the context of developmental psychology to a consideration of magic and religion, it helps us to view magic as a form of mechanical technological *instrumental* pre-causality. Religion, on the other hand, is more characteristically a form of *expressive* pre-causal thinking related to a developmental stage in social morality. Magic is an attempt at manipulation or control of things, whereas supernatural religions are forms of relating to beings and as such are attempts at establishing moral laws. Religion involves both the projection of anthropomorphic extensions of inner experiences of human motivation and emotion onto natural events, and the creation of a mythology to explain the origin, vicissitudes, and destiny of mankind in sacred rather than secular terms. It is not surprising therefore to find a link between expressive religious beliefs and caste as an expressive institutionalization of human feelings about elevation and degradation.

Second, from the expressive functions of religion we can turn to examine psychologically how cognitive and affective residues become institutionalized into expressive "meaning" in the more specific religious or secularized collective representations of the socially disavowed. The content of these representations includes unresolved, often unconscious, emotionalized states. These states result from activations of the autonomic nervous system, which influences the nature of the symbolic associations that occur during early periods of cognitive development. From this psychological perspective the conceptualizations of W. Robertson Smith and Emile Durkheim concerning the role of the "sacred" in society are valid. They conceive of the sacred as part of an essential ambiguity found in what Freud called primary process thinking. This ambiguity remains visibly operative in primitive religious representations of ritual purity and pollution.

Third, what can be recognized individually as psychoneurotic syndromes become institutionalized in the collective representations justifying caste segregation. Compulsive insistence on purity and insulation from some fearful form of contamination are parts of what become a collective psychological defense system underlying the pollution barrier in a caste society. The rigidity of this barrier is a function of the degree to which what I term status anxiety is present in the dominant caste. This term, "status anxiety," is a conceptual bridge stressing the interpenetration of social structural determinants and psychological structural determinants in caste behavior. It must be stressed again, however, that it is the expressive aspects, not the instrumental aspects, of social status that are most involved in the caste barrier.

Status anxiety in one sense also operates in the social segregation of women at historical periods in particular cultures. Concepts of purity and pollution tend to become part of occupational or other limitations placed on women as participants in a social structure.

Whereas the institution of caste may develop gradually or abruptly in situations where there is considerable congruence of instrumental and expressive determinants, such as the conquest of one culture or group by another, caste segregation seems to be symptomatic of some form of collective self-justification by a dominant group related to status anxiety. This justification may be a defensive reaction to some internal or external threat to the secure self-identity of members of a particular culture. Such recent situations of threatened social identity can be documented historically in Germany, South Africa, and the American South; they have led in each instance to the espousal of a racist ideology as a basis for caste.

Fourth and finally, as has been well described in the literature of social prejudice, a caste system permits some institutionalization of scapegoating as a form of expressive exploitation of a despised outcaste group. On this basis, caste relationships develop a functional autonomy independent of economic or occupational changes in social structure. The expressive psychological features involved in status anxiety and in projective scapegoating can continue after changes in the instrumental structure of the social system have made caste dysfunctional or disruptive. One can, therefore, in periods of transition observe the phenomena of psychological lag manifest in the persistence of caste relations occurring in modern industrializing societies.

In summary, the following two chapters will sketch very briefly in a number of sections the pertinent dimensions of an integrative theory of caste. Some of these sections are little more than speculative incursions into particular subjects demanding far more exposition than is possible in the present volume. My aim is to provoke further explorations of the subject of caste by others from a more broadly based unified perspective.

G. D. V.

Chapter 16

GEORGE DE VOS

Essential Elements of Caste: Psychological Determinants in Structural Theory

THE REQUISITES OF CASTE

There have been numerous attempts to examine caste for its essential elements, the peculiar combination of which results in a working caste system. From the standpoint of a culture and personality framework we believe that there are six basic requisites for the presence of caste. Four of these are related to the peculiarities of the social structure in which caste phenomena occur; while these requisites have psychological as well as social dimensions, the social structural determinant factors are crucial. The other two requisites in a particular culture are related to the emphasis given by that culture to the peculiar psychological mechanisms underlying caste. These mechanisms provide the motivating force that gives continuity, from one generation to the next, to caste attitudes within a society.

From ethnographic reports of various social situations suggesting the presence of caste, we find that it occurs only when (1) there is a unified social-political structure, (2) it is organized on a fixed hierarchical basis, in which (3) certain occupational specializations exist. These three factors can be called "prerequisites of caste," but they can also be found in many societies without any caste structure. In order to have a true caste system, hierarchically ordered occupational specializations within a given society must be carried on (4) by groups defined by birth ascription (usually by endogamy) and kept distinct by strong social sanctions. These sanctions must be sustained and justified (5) by unquestioned assumptions of intellectual, moral, and aesthetic inferiority as an inherited, unchangeable aspect of particular human groups. This latter assumption is emotionally supported by (6) deeply felt fear of pollution or contamination as a result of unguarded contact of the more "pure" with the less "pure" individuals. These three latter factors—enforced or sanctioned birth ascription, fixed ideas of group inferiority in human heredity, and supposed hereditary state of relative purity—can be considered the basic elements found in any institutionalized caste system. Social justifications for the system may differ widely. They can be premised on varying religious or secular, quasi-scientific social beliefs.

In the simplest forms of caste one finds either of two types of social division. The first is a ritually pure superior caste, isolated from the main group of the society so that it may perform special magical-religious tasks necessary to the continuity of the entire group. Examples of this type were found in the South Pacific in societies with a kingly caste that has a concentration of religious or magical power.[1] The second simplest form of caste is a separated group of individuals who perform some social functions that are considered innately contaminating, again in accordance with ritual or religious definitions of purity and impurity. This type of outcaste or pariah status, found throughout Asia in various societies, is the form of caste with which we are principally concerned as it occurred in Japan. We shall forego further consideration of the caste-like segregation of "saints" or ritually "pure" groups within specific cultures. However, from the standpoint of attitudes toward inherent purity or pollution there are possible caste barriers related to elevation as well as to degradation.

Institutionalized Inequality Within a Unified Culture or Political Structure

Endogamy by itself does not lead to caste without some form of political or cultural cohesion in the endogamous groups. It is the usual condition for maintaining separation between geographically adjacent distinct cultures or social-political entities. Endogamy sometimes even helps maintain distinct cultural groups within the same geographic area without resulting in the formation of a caste structure. For example, although endogamous, the Gypsies in Europe have resisted becoming a true caste, since their separate society has with rare exceptions remained outside the political social structure of the countries in which they resided: generally they performed only peripheral nonessential functions as itinerants within European societies.

The maintenance of an ethnically distinct or submerged and conquered social group within a culture as a slave population also does not constitute caste. One can cite as an example the Jews in Egypt who,

---

[1] See the description of Fiji in Hocart (1950).

though slaves, did not evolve into a caste minority within Egyptian society.[2] In India, the Parsis or Sikhs are not castes but are perceived as ethnic, religious minorities keeping themselves separate on the basis of their religious beliefs.[3] The tribal groups within Indian society are also, properly speaking, not castes, although there is some tendency to integrate them as castes whenever possible.

Therefore, a requisite of a working caste system is that the caste division must occur between groups of a recognizable single culture, not between distinct cultural groups simply coexisting in some form of enforced or crescive symbiosis. From the standpoint of psychology it must be pointed out that caste is most visibly operative in those situations wherein a sense of cultural self-identity is shared in spite of the segregating effect of caste in human relationships. The Japanese Burakumin, the American Negro, the South African colored, and the Indian Harijan, all identify themselves as members of their society despite their outcaste status.

Fixed Hierarchy

Some form of hierarchy or differential social status exists in all societies. The basis of the hierarchy varies somewhere between the polarities of assigned and achieved status. The more hierarchy is based of fixed hereditary considerations, the more one approaches the type of society that might produce caste attitudes. However, even when hierarchy or status positions within a society are based mainly on heredity, there is provision for some form of social mobility in exceptional cases. When such exceptions are barred by some form of absolute prohibition we find a caste rather than a class society.

In medieval Europe, although social status was generally determined by inheritance and one could talk about the caste-like exclusiveness of the aristocracy, there were numerous unusual individuals who were able to change their status given proper circumstances. Commonly held beliefs ascribed inherited noble traits to the high-born, and ignoble ones to the lowly, but should an individual prove himself exceptional, a breach in the natural order did not evoke the type of acute discomfort noticed when there is a breach in a true caste structure. In *The Inequality of Human Races*,[4] Gobineau was attempting to develop a racist theory to espouse a caste status for the French aristocracy, true "Germanic" people, innately superior to the "Celts" and

---

[2] The Jews in medieval Europe almost became a true caste insofar as they came to perform essential functions related to money that were forbidden to the majority Christian society.

[3] The Parsis today are called neither *mlechha,* meaning outsider, nor *jati,* meaning caste, but are distinguished as a separate people, *parsi-loga* (or *parsi*-people).

[4] Gobineau (1915).

"Mediterraneans" that made up the ordinary folk of France. The society as a whole did not support these views but they were later readapted by Hitler's Germany in its attitude toward the neighboring Slavic peoples. These same ideas of racial purity were more immediately used as justification for the systematic genocide of the unclean, contaminating Jews and Gypsies. Hitler's "Aryans" were to become the dominant caste in a restructured but integrated European society and the Hindu-Buddhist swastika, adopted as the Nazi emblem, was symbolic of the new Aryan state that openly espoused caste barriers of enforced endogamy as a basis for social segmentation. Theirs was a self-conscious identification with the Indo-European-speaking Aryan invaders who conquered Dravidian India and supposedly initiated the caste system to keep their blood pure.

The basic difference between a class and a caste society lies in the fact that the presence or relative intensity of socially induced psychological attitudes in the members of a caste society in itself comes to constitute a qualitative difference in immutability and rigidity. These attitudes resist modification even in the face of contrary social experiences. Class societies permit change of class position with changes in economic and political power. An illustrative case is that of Dr. B. R. Ambedkhar, who after receiving education in the United States, England, and Germany—including a Ph.D. from Columbia University— attempted to overcome the stigma of his status, that of *harijan* (untouchable) upon his return to India. Although never socially accepted, he eventually became a successful lawyer in Bombay, entered politics, and became the spokesman for the untouchables in their efforts to secure better treatment from their fellow Hindus. He further became minister of law in Nehru's first cabinet and headed the committee that drafted the Indian Constitution. In despair, shortly before his death he and many of his followers became Buddhists, feeling that the stigma of being from the untouchable caste could not be resolved within Hindu society.

Finally, caste is not slavery. Slavery has appeared numerous times in history without the appearance of the particular emotional attitudes, transmuted into fixed social institutions, essential to the development and maintenance of a caste society. The institution of slavery in Greek or Roman societies, to illustrate, never included the idea of ritual pollution. Slaves are not repulsive or untouchable by nature, nor does a slave group generally become an outcaste group with a change in the social structure of a society. Something more is necessary to explain the appearance and continuity of caste phenomena. Caste takes root and grows only in a specific type of psychological as well as social soil. Unlike the Graeco-Roman situation or that of aristocratic France, the abortive attempt to reorder European society on a caste basis by Nazi

Germany cannot be explained by a naive theory about the nature of social structure. It must rather be attributed to deeply felt emotions shared by a sufficient number of the population to have made this attempt more than the simple, shared madness of a small group. Fixed hierarchy is essential but not sufficient to an institution of caste. It must be supported by a particular type of psychological attitude.

Occupational Specialization Combined with Endogamy

There is evidence that caste in its development is of necessity linked at some time to some form of occupational separation within the society. Nevertheless, later developments within a caste system may not hold strictly to this pattern as an invariant characteristic of caste. Many outcastes in modern caste societies can achieve nonhereditary occupational roles. It is, in effect, this inconsistency that helps to define the continual operation of caste within some modern societies, for in spite of the possibility of change in occupation, an outcaste member of a society is bound by social sanctions to consummate marriage only within his hereditary social group, not his acquired occupational group. This differentiates a modern caste society from a class society which, although it may severely discourage social mobility, allows for intermarriage in a manner not possible in a true caste society.

Occupational specialization in endogamous caste divisions can be negative in the form of *exclusion*. To illustrate: there has been exclusion of American Negroes from particular occupations rather than a positive inducement for them to maintain some form of traditional specialization to be passed on within families. What appears in American caste is, more properly speaking, occupational exclusion rather than specialization.

In a positive sense, occupational specialization is often related to religious ritual in the highly evolved, interdependent, caste-occupational, closed organic system, such as exists in India. Caste membership is defined positively by religion rather than by economics; for example, a Brahman who is ritually of the priestly caste may be a farmer, or even a merchant. There is much evidence to indicate that in some caste societies the passing-on of a particular occupational role meant the passing-on of magical religious knowledge that at one time was inseparable from the secular aspects of the special occupation. This seems to have been true to some extent in Japan.[5]

---

[5] We can best illustrate this interblending of the religious and the secular by citing at length from a very perceptive essay by Warner (1958, pp. 18–23) on the relation of the indigenous Japanese nature religion, Shinto, to the specialized arts and crafts of the people. Warner brings out in a very cogent fashion the inseparable intertwining of the religious and the secular in the occupational specialization of Japanese artisans.

A fact lost sight of by most historians of art is that Shinto has always been the

In respect to the essential nature of caste, however, such specialization does not of itself necessarily imply hereditary occupations, or endogamy within groups that follow such occupations. To become related to caste the religious specialization inherent in a particular occupation must somehow be tied to degrees of purity or impurity for those carrying out the task. Individuals must in a positive sense be delegated certain tasks or in a negative sense disqualified from performing them on the basis of caste-linked inherent characteristics.

In its most primitive form, occupational role definitions probably first appeared in very simple, small societies on the basis of sexual

---

artist's way of life. Natural forces are the very subject matter for those who produce artifacts from raw material or who hunt and fish and farm. Thus Shinto taught succeeding generations of Japanese how such forces are controlled and these formulas have become embedded in Shinto liturgies. Dealing, as this body of beliefs does, with the essence of life and with the spirits inhabiting all natural and many artificial objects, it came about that no tree could be marked for felling, no bush tapped for lacquer juice, no oven built for smelting or for pottery, and no forge fire lit without appeal to the *Kami,* resident in each (pp. 18–19).

Even in the dim days before the trades were separated, there must have existed a basis on which specialization would become inevitable. Growing knowledge of the controls and formulas needed in dealing with a variety of natural forces implied the formation of guilds with their separate mysteries and trade secrets at an early period.

The correct (religious) way to build a house, forge a sword, or brew liquor had been, from earliest times, in Japan as elsewhere, imbued with a peculiar guarantee of success through its dependence on a divine patron who established rules and divided labor and in whose honor the chanties were sung. To be right has always, until lately, been to be religious (p. 19).

It was by rules of Shinto that the jobs of fellers and haulers of timber were distinguished from those of carpenters competent to build with it. Shinto chanties hoisted the roof beam into place, timed the movements of gang labor and preserved the necessary orderly progress that marks the stages of any construction job. Failure to observe the logical stages halts the work and therefore becomes impious, an evidence of divine disapproval (p. 20).

The more hidden and complicated the natural processes involved, the more necessary are the mnemonic and religious devices to preserve correct procedure. In early times the craftsman of the greatest skill (the master) was naturally the one on whom the duty fell to make sacrifice and perform the purifications to insure the success of the job in hand, whether it was a building, or a boat, or a sword, or the cure of the sick, or the difficult pouring of bronze for an image, or the communal rice planting in the spring (p. 21).

To invoke the nature gods correctly meant that the farmer must be weather wise, and the smith experienced in the precise shade of cherry-red when the blade must be drawn from the forge and quenched in its bath. Further, the correct prayers and songs and ceremonial gestures must be employed. This, of course, was a kind of priestcraft, an ability to control the nature gods (p. 22).

A man skilled in such formulas was not only the head of his shop or guild. He was a priest in the very act. The Shinto priesthood, recognized as such today, no longer includes these master craftsmen. But even the recognized ones are still called on to invoke the spirits of weather and crops as well as the gods who hold the welfare of the nation and of the imperial family in their power. Until a few decades ago, however, the head of the guild performed priestly offices in special robes and was, on such occasions, sacred. Even today some villages can be found where a preeminence in boat building or fishing implies a temporary priesthood with its accompanying and religious distinction (p. 23).

differentiation. To insure success and to allay anxieties, man is most apt to attach some ritual to his adult functions that provide livelihood. In many simple cultures, women are not permitted to perform certain activities lest they incur the wrath of some god. The more this activity has a ritual as well as a secular aspect, the more rigorously it may be forbidden to women. Most often, the prohibition was related to the periodic "pollution" inherent in menstruation and childbirth. Although divisions based on the relative purity of the sexes cannot be related directly to caste thinking, the separation of a society into rigidly defined sex-occupational roles often derives its emotional validity from feelings about purity and impurity related to sex that in other, more complex, segmented societies are re-directed toward the maintenance of a caste structure.

While these social elements—endogamy, occupational specialization, and rigid social hierarchy—help define caste from a social-structural standpoint, they do not by themselves evoke the particular emotional atmosphere nor the essential ideology of caste.

Justification by Unquestionable Sacred Tenets

Endogamy (or other methods of birth-ascribed group membership), important as it is from the standpoint of social structure, by itself cannot produce a viable caste system, even when linked directly to occupational specialization within a society. In traditional societies, only when occupational specializations are limited by the necessity to perform sacrificial practices or rituals, or to deal with ritually polluting objects, does caste begin to appear operative.

It is in the appearance of types of endogamy related to sacred or ritual functions that one finds numerous instances in which social interaction tends toward the creation of both ritually elevated as well as ritually polluted groups. In societies in which social hierarchy is defined in sacred rather than secular terms there is a need to separate certain groups of individuals who periodically deal with supernatural, sacred elements, both in an elevating and polluting way.

The system of maintaining an elevated caste seems to have functioned best over a long period of time in some Polynesian societies that were able to maintain a form of caste endogamy for the kingly group.[6] Efforts in European societies to establish and maintain the "divine" right of kings by maintaining endogamy among the hereditary nobility were continually vitiated by the nobility itself, whose sexual interests strayed beyond the acceptable women of higher status. The sacred Pharaohs of Egypt were pressed to an endogamy so nar-

---

[6] Cf. Hocart (1950).

rowly defined that brother-sister marriages became the favored marriage liaison.

Caste-type thinking, therefore, related to religious concepts of purity or impurity, tends to appear most often in reference to either extreme of a hierarchy. The word *hier-archy* itself implies a religious rather than a secular stratification of society. Frazer, in *The Golden Bough*, cites numerous societies in which the role of the king was a sacred one.[7] The sacred functions of kingship required the continuity of blood within the kingly line to insure the well-being of his entire group.[8]

People tend to place their beliefs in beneficence beyond the priestly or kingly group to the supernatural. Nevertheless those individuals who become holy, by example or ascetic withdrawal, partake of a special quality that sets them aside from ordinary individuals. This type of priestly specialization, however, is more often related to celibacy than to endogamy, since such asceticism is more an act of adult will than of simple birth. Therefore, there is perhaps less historical occasion for the formation of a successfully endogamous elevated group than for the periodic occurrence of the opposite, a polluted and debased outcaste minority within the society.

Occupational and ritual specializations, when combined in specific groups, imply that relative prestige is based both on the distribution of power within the community or political stratification, and on the religious hierarchy. It is difficult to conceive of societies that involve systems of ritual purity that do not involve a concomitant system

---

[7] Frazer (1959).

[8] In a most perceptive book, De Grazia (1948) illustrates how the role of the ruler in many respects resembles that of a deity in providing for the security and well-being of his subjects:

Political authority accumulates in the hands of those who are believed to have outstanding skill in the most hazardous and fortuitous elements of provisioning the community. Success in extracting nutriment from the peculiar conditions of land, sea and air is the supernatural quality of kings, be it called *mana* as in Polynesia, *iddhi* as in India, or *wakan, manitow*, or *orenda* as in Indian North America. The ancient Babylonians looked to their kings for abundance. In Fiji kings carried the title of *Sri*, which means both prosperity and food. In Polynesia the word *sau* signifies king, peace, and prosperity. Homeric mythology held kings responsible for the food supply. The Burgundians held their king responsible for the fortunes of war. Under the Roman Empire, power over crops and prosperity became specially connected with the emperor. From the time of Augustus Roman coins bore such inscriptions as: "The prosperity of Augustus." . . . The Malays have faith that their king possesses a personal influence over the works of nature, such as the growth of crops and the bearing of fruit trees. Drought, dearth, or defeat in war notified the Khazars of southern Russia that the natural powers of their king were on the wane (p. 19).

A peculiar historical occurrence in India very early split the sacred from the secular functions of kingship noted elsewhere and the sacred functions became the specialization of the Brahman caste. Cf. Dumont (1962), pp. 48-77.

of political hierarchy. Theories concerning the origin of caste differ as to the roles played by political hierarchy and ritual purity in the development of the caste structure. Most theories emphasize either the force of secular power, usually resulting from the conquest of one group by another, or the religious power of a priestly monopoly.

A DIACHRONIC APPROACH TO CASTE

Theories of the Origins of Caste in Society

One may oversimplify somewhat by dividing the theories concerning the origin of caste into two orientations. There are those that emphasize caste structures as resulting from a conquest of one group by another. Such theories are usually related to more general theories on the origin of the state; in our terminology such theories emphasize instrumental exploitation. Conversely there are theories that emphasize the religious origin of caste in relation to social segments performing ritually pure or ritually polluted occupational specializations. Roughly, these latter theories implicitly stress the presence of "expressive exploitation." [9] Origin theories therefore emphasize either the force of the secular power wielded by a political, economic, or social group resulting in the appearance of caste; or the force of supernatural religious power, sometimes increased by a politically dominant group, which reinforces social values related to ritual purity. These theories differ somewhat in their consideration of the time sequence of caste formation. The former stresses the abrupt occurrence of conquest and a subsequent sustained aftermath that firmly establishes caste as a long-lasting accommodation. The latter theory sees a more organic and crescive gradual institutionalization of religious concerns without necessarily envisioning the intervention of group conflicts.

One theory of caste in India that has a number of adherents holds that caste institutions have arisen because conquerors have sought to preserve their position as an elite group by invoking rules of endogamy. According to this theory, warriors set themselves up as a dominant group (aided and assisted, or even sometimes dominated, by the magico-religious, intellectual elite of the priesthood) and impose themselves upon a less militarily effective group. In such a situation the value of the agricultural and mercantile functions might be sufficiently recognized to permit agricultural communities and groups of merchants to

---

[9] This distinction between instrumental and expressive exploitation follows a useful distinction concerning role behavior found in Parsons and Bales's volume *Family, Socialization and Interaction Process* (1955). Instrumental activities are those that are goal oriented—behavior is directed toward the realization of some goal. Instrumental behavior, therefore, is primarily a means to an end. As an ideal polar opposite, expressive behavior is something that exists for itself. The primary satisfaction in expressive behavior is the emotional release secured.

become classified among the "good people," whereas especially demeaning occupations might come to be carried out by a slave group drawn from among the conquered.

The more crescive, organic theory stresses the slow development of ritual specialization within endogamous occupations in which religious and secular behavior cannot be artificially separated. Since there was no separation in the minds of those performing the acts, work and religion were an inseparable organic whole. Caste evolved out of the deeply felt religious proscriptions and taboos concerning pollution and purity. These proscriptions became increasingly rigidified.

Our illustrations for caste phenomena so far have been India and other parts of Asia. Nadel provides an incisive theoretical overview based on a brief description of the caste-type social relations that appear in many African societies, suggesting both types of origin are possible.[10]

In certain circumstances, situations of conquest in Africa seem to have evolved into rigidified caste structures.

Nadel advances several instances which he believes to fit this pattern. He cites the case of the Nupe in North Nigeria, who by the seventeenth century were a kingdom of about half a million inhabit-

---

[10] Nadel (1954), pp. 9-22:
I am only concerned with extracting the basic principles underlying caste stratification and to discover the conditions and processes (social as well as psychological) which appear necessary for its emergence. Differently expressed, I am comparing *types* of society and wish to show that the same "type" (namely, caste-stratified society) can occur in widely different cultures and areas of the world, given certain common conditions or processes.
Exemplifying the conquest theory of the state, he quotes from Gumplowitcz's *Outlines of Sociology* (1899):
There is still another natural characteristic of the state, although it has hitherto been wholly overlooked; there are always ethnical differences between the ruling class and the ruled. . . . States have never arisen except through the subjection of one stock by another. . . . This is not accidental; it is essential—no state has arisen without original ethnic heterogeneity. . . . Universally there is a ruling minority and a subject majority; this is the essence of the state as it is the essence of sovereignty. But what is the ruling minority disposed to do? There is but one thing it can wish, viz., to live in better circumstances with the services of the subject majority than it could do without them. The result is a common industrial enterprise conducted under compulsion in which the greater burden, all the unfree service, falls upon the subject class. Always, the life of the state is summed up in this common though unequal labour.
[Always also there are these] two fundamental social processes—satisfaction of human needs and exploitation of services of foreigners. . . . [This] evolution cannot cease, for nature has provided that man's needs shall not stand still, while at the point where natural ethnic distinctions arise to perpetuate the antagonism of human groups. Human desires never fail and there are groups differing in stature, colour, and odour, in diet, morals and religions, or in possessions, conditions, calling, occupation and interests. . . . The life and death struggle between ethnically heterogeneous hordes becomes a contest between social groups, classes, estates and political parties. . . .

ants. In this society there is a rigid social stratification separating a conquering elite from a submerged group.

The social stratification is partly one of *caste*—if by caste we mean the rigid and unalterable apportionment of social privileges on the grounds of descent. Partly the stratification is only one of class, based on a differentiation in political and economic power which is not rigid, but permits of movement between the strata, in accordance with capability, with services rendered— especially in war—with success and luck; that is, it permits "social mobility." [11]

One might question whether this example is not one of class rather than caste. Neither strict endogamy nor consistent social attitudes of genetic purity characterize this society.

His next example, the Beni Amer, however, seems to meet the criteria of caste much better.[12] They are an Arabic people living with a conquered lower social stratum who perform demeaning occupational tasks. No intermarriage is permitted between the two strata of this society: the Beni Amer can take serf women as concubines, but should a Beni Amer woman become intimate with a serf she would at once be relegated to the status of a common prostitute as punishment. In either case the offspring is assigned to the serf caste. As in other caste situations, such as the southern United States, the Beni Amer take the concept of racial purity literally. Like the Nupe, but with more reason in history, they make a fetish of pure blood lineage. As in the case of the American Negro, there is considerable influx of blood from the upper caste and there are many individuals among the serfs who are identical with the Beni Amer in appearance.

Nadel sees the Beni Amer society as clearly representing more than a simple class structure, since it admits no mobility and makes no concessions to talent or outside marriage. He emphasizes that historically it is obvious that this stratification occurred as a result of the conquest of one ethnic group by another, and therefore asks whether this does not answer the question he raised at the beginning of his article, namely, "Is this the only way in which caste arises—as a side issue of a government by conquest?"

To demonstrate the converse situation Nadel turns to another example taken from African society, that of the Tira, a tribe living in the Nuba Mountains of the Central Sudan. This is a community of about 10,000 subdivided into a number of descent lines or clans, each tracing descent back to a common ancestor. Occupationally there is no differentiation, all being farmers and owners of livestock. However, the clans are distinguished from one another by certain food taboos and ritual observances. Each clan is believed to possess certain super-

[11] Nadel (1954), p. 13.
[12] Nadel (1954), pp. 13ff.

natural powers peculiar to it and to no other clan and each clan, there-fore, assumes control of some part of the life space or universe of the Tira. Each clan exercises this control not only for its own benefit but for the benefit of the tribe as a whole, so that together they insure in a supernatural sense the ultimate survival of the social structure and its welfare. All the clans are thus mutually interdependent in con-trolling the weather, the fertility of the soil, the animal world, and health and disease within the group. This apportionment of super-natural powers of which all are aware involves not only privileges but duties: each clan is expected to perform its particular ritual faithfully on appropriate occasions as its contribution to the common welfare.

In two of the Tira clans another feature enters the picture which suggests the type of pollution barrier found in caste. One of the clans affected is believed to possess the power to control storms and to cure or ward off psychotic behavior. These powers are considered vital to the maintenance of the tribe at large and this clan is expected to per-form the regular rituals peculiar to it so as to protect the community from the possibility of these dangers. Yet the people who perform these essential rituals are, for the very reason of their power, feared and avoided. There is a belief that the food that they grow is somehow tainted, and that an outsider eating it would be struck by insanity. In consequence, no one will eat or drink with them or visit their houses. Other people are even afraid to farm too close to them lest they become exposed to some form of contamination. In practice, then, the members of this clan have become "untouchables" and are isolated from the general life of the community.

Nadel notes that these clans are clearly not castes in the Indian sense. First, they are still exogamous and marry into other clans, al-though there is a marked reluctance on the part of members of other clans to marry into these groups, with the result that they tend to take husbands or wives not wanted by others. Second, he points out that there is a differentiation of mystic duties, not of occupations in the strict sense of the word. On this point, however, as we have indicated earlier, it is the ritual aspect of a so-called occupation rather than its secular aspect that is essential for caste.

Third, Nadel points out that the clans are not strictly despised; rather they are feared and therefore avoided. The contamination comes from some awesome power harmful to all not born to its use. This point of the fearfulness of the uncanny will be developed in our final chapter on the psychology of caste segregation. Nadel has here clearly found a type of social structure that, given possible future changes, could develop through time into a recognizable caste struc-ture. The marriage pattern, for example, could develop further into one of some more limited form of endogamy. Nadel summarizes:

To return once more to our first question—whether all forms of caste strati-fication are a consequence of government by conquest. Some are clearly of this kind—Beni Amer society for one, and certain castes in India probably also. But others, as we have seen, can arise from the internal differentiation of societies, in the absence of any ethnic heterogeneity or any "struggle of races." It would suggest that such conditions as I have described for certain African societies are also responsible for the emergence of a full-fledged caste system like that of India.

Let me, in conclusion, summarize these conditions. First, there must be a differentiation of social tasks which is permanent and rigid and which makes the different segments of the society interdependent. In other words, there must be a rigid division of labour. Secondly, this division of labour must be sanctioned by religion, conceived of as pre-ordained, and invested with mystic meaning; and this arises most easily where the allocated tasks themselves are of a mystic kind—be it command over rain or disease or over some rare skill like that of working iron. But thirdly, these tasks, though vital for the welfare of the society, involve also some attitude of fear and awe, or some belief that the powers and skills in question go together with unclean, spiritually de-grading qualities.

In this last respect African and Indian societies have gone somewhat dif-ferent ways. In Bharat India the conception of spiritual purity and perfec-tion dominates the picture, so that caste differentiation in turn expresses the ideas of pollution, contagion, and segregation between people of different degrees of perfection. In Africa the dominant conception is more pragmatic and in a sense materialistic; it revolves upon fear and the need of keeping away from magic powers and dangerous gifts. But in either case the social consequences are alike; they lie in the shunning of sections of the population in spite of the fact—indeed, because of the fact—that their contributions are vital for the rest of the society.[13]

We have quoted extensively from Nadel since he affords us the pos-sibility of capsulizing many of the essential issues concerning the pos-sible origins of caste in society. He cites examples of concern with group purity resulting from a secular mythology as well as from abhorrence toward a given group because of necessary but possibly contaminating ritual functions.

Using the leverage afforded by the above examples, it is possible to criticize the conquest theory of caste origins as of itself insufficient to explain the formation of an untouchable caste. Our principal criticism is not of any assumption held of the invariant necessity for a conquest to occur to produce caste; rather it arises from the same criticism we have been directing toward what we perceive as a weakness of strict sociological theories generally. They overly emphasize the "instrumen-tal" functions of caste—such as using a submerged group to perform tasks considered repugnant to a dominant group—without examining sufficiently the continuing expressive functions of caste or their de-

---

[13] Nadel (1954), p. 18.

velopment. Such a conquest theory by itself, as it is usually elaborated, lacks any emotional or psychological depth. It does not help us understand how the expressive emotional psychological features that accompany caste develop diachronically, or how the emotionally toned religious or secular racist reinforcements or justifications of caste come to wield such emotional force.

The evidence from Japan leads us to conclude that the use of slaves in ancient Japan of itself did not lead to caste. Occupational specialization in ritually impure activities is a more likely origin. There are numerous cases other than Japan where conquest and slavery of itself did not result in the appearance of endogamous castes, or where distinctions between plebeian and patrician social segments, as in Rome, disappeared. A history of enslavement of outgroups does not of itself seem to predispose a society to develop a caste structure. Egyptian, Greek, or Roman societies were founded on slave or quasi-slave populations that never became true castes in any sense.

In more recent history, slavery, related specifically to different social structures with different value systems in the Spanish and Portuguese American colonies, did not become transformed into a social caste system in Latin America as it did in the American South.[14]

Throughout Latin America, former slaves did not become the scapegoats of the society. They were not considered to be contaminated by unclean proclivities or made impure by a tainted heredity, nor did the end of slavery involve the type of defensive self-identity on the part of a dominant group troubled by status anxiety. Slaves were not made, because of convolutions of social justification and guilt, scapegoated embodiments of what was disavowed within the self.

Mediterranean cultures have not sought to assuage a sense of guilt by transmuting it into a necessity for personal accomplishment as a means of self-justification. The instrumental exploitation of slaves did not lead to their concomitant expressive exploitation. To the Romans, for example, enslaved barbarians were considered uncouth but not contaminating or unclean. Racial considerations in the Mediterranean world and later those of colonial Spain were not based on any cultural concepts related to personal cleanliness or concepts of feminine purity defined racially.

Stanley Elkins[15] very cogently develops the thesis first brought forth by Frank Tannenbaum[16] that the nature of instrumental exploitation in the American, British, and Dutch institutions of slavery was unchecked by the presence of religious or other values institutionalized sufficiently to act as a base for at least a partial control over slavery.

---

[14] Tannenbaum (1963).
[15] Elkins (1959).
[16] Tannenbaum (1963).

Elkins' analysis of the effects of the unrestricted exploitation of the American Negro, although phrased in different terminology, is congruent with our espousal of the necessity of theoretically differentiating between instrumental and expressive functions and their institutionalization in the social structure. Elkins, in line with Tannenbaum's thesis, shows that American slavery was based on a rationalist, free enterprise, capitalist, social philosophy that could consider labor simply as a commodity. The philosophy of the Southern planter therefore did not differ from the rationalist conception of human institutions found in Marxian theory. The economic and political institutions of the society are conceived of as the ultimate determinants of behavior. Expressive institutions are considered as illusory and derivative, rather than capable of an autonomous continuity of their own or of providing values counter to those of the marketplace. In contrast, the Spanish and Portuguese cultures, despite their desire to maximize the instrumental exploitation of human labor, could not free themselves completely from the force of their religious institutions, which insisted that whatever the bondage of the body, the human soul was free to achieve other expressive goals. In the Spanish and Portuguese colonies, therefore, the Catholic church developed a compromise with slavery that forced the slave to be treated as a man, guaranteeing his right of marriage, limiting the taking of his life, and placing some limitation on the use of his time.

In the Spanish dominions unlike in the United States, the brutalizing effect of slavery did not strip the former African of every vestige of his culture. Whatever the conditions of economic servitude, he was considered more than a thing, an instrument to be manipulated in the ultimate rationalization of the economic laws. He was a being and as such was subject to a moral law independent from laws promulgated by the dominant groups in the state. Furthermore, the Spanish and Portuguese cultures had as their ultimate value some concept of "glory" rather than simple economic "success." The American culture, on the other hand, showed some remnants of Protestant Calvinistic thinking in its readiness to embrace social Darwinism, with the unsuccessful and the unfit easily associated with the morally unclean. The self-righteous Protestant refused to identify himself with those who were inferior in his eyes. He needed to deny the humanity of those he exploited—they were not his brothers but a subhuman species. He could patronize them but not relate to them as moral equals.

The present form taken by the American caste system did not immediately follow upon the emancipation of the Negro from slavery. During slavery in the American South there had been a sustained intimacy between the master and at least some of his slaves. The development of legal proscriptions against casual, impersonal contact with Negroes in public places occurred considerably after the Reconstruction Period. Woodward documents at length the concept of segregation as, contrary to popular impression, a relatively recent development that occurred concomitantly with the American political expansion into territories occupied by non-white inhabitants, such as the Philippines and Cuba at the end of the nineteenth century.[17] The Americans were at this time assuming the white man's burden overseas.

What was initiated as a hysterical insistence on keeping the Negro "in his place" began to change to more total systems of avoidance with the social segregation of children. From a psychological standpoint, such early segregation fostered an increase in projective concerns with cleanliness and fear of contamination. No longer permitted to patronize the Negro, the Southerner managed his strong unresolved feelings by insisting more and more on the maintenance of social distance. The succeeding generations of Southern white children were being socialized in such a way as to emphasize the polluting nature of contact with the Negro caste. Easy intimacy with slaves in the course of fifty years was being gradually transmuted into strong feelings about caste segregation, rationalized and buttressed by fears of racial pollution that were idealized positively as a concern for the purity of white womanhood. Racism based on simpler rationalizations concerning innate inferiority have imperceptibly changed psychologically to a system of caste relations based on unresolved anxieties concerning contact. Many white Americans, both northern and southern, make expressive emotional use of the Negro as a visual representation of unconscious equations such as "black equals dirt." Further, the Negro has come to represent in the collective unconscious of the American what is primitively aggressive and sexual, if not what is racially and ritually unclean and debasing.

This process of making a separate caste out of the American Negro has by the secularized nature of modern society been stopped short of what in a previous age would have become an even more religiously based rationale for segregation. We can speculate that modern-rational-international-cultural interpenetration has stopped short a process toward what could have become institutionalized definitions of racial ritual purity resembling those evolved as part of the Aryan heritage in India.

In the following chapter we examine those ontogenetic aspects of psychological development that make man, no matter what this culture, prone to have recourse to the expression of religious dread of the demonic and the unclean.

---

[17] Woodward (1957).

EXPRESSIVE MOTIVE FORCES ESSENTIAL TO AN UNDERSTANDING OF THE SOCIAL STRUCTURE OF CASTE

A number of present explanations of caste from a strict social-structural standpoint are weakened by their failure to consider the emotional attitudes supporting caste endogamy. Most social anthropological theories of human behavior do not sufficiently consider psychological motivational forces as autonomous determinants that, in concert with social economic factors, develop, elaborate, or maintain certain value aspects of a social system. For example, a strict social-structural theory of endogamy relates ingroup marriage to kinship functioning, and perhaps to the continuity of necessary, interdependent occupational groups. It does not explain how or why endogamy satisfies certain expressive psychological characteristics.

If we apply a dichotomous distinction between the primacy of instrumental or expressive role behavior to social-structural theories of endogamy related to caste, we see that such theories rely solely on instrumental explanations of behavior for either the individual or the social group. In such theories endogamy is seen operative only from the standpoint of how occupational roles are interdependent, how accommodation and job security, rather than competition, are fostered, and so forth. Such a structural theory lacks a source of energy which would give the structure life.

I propose that the expressive motivation involved in caste determine the basic social segregation in caste cultures, at least in some stages of their development or decline, is a separation of the unclean from the ordinary, or the ordinary from the super-pure. Further elaborations or distinctions tend to blur these essential separations.[18]

---

[18] To clarify further the proposition that caste is a form of social segregation based on expressive psychological functions, it would be necessary to enter into a more extended critique of the related but contradictory positions taken by a number of present-day theorists. Such a discussion would not be germane to the more general purposes of the present volume. I could cite very briefly points of disagreement with E. Leach (1960), R. F. Bailey (1963), L. Dumont and D. Pocock (1958), rather than the large areas of agreement with what they have to say about the structure and function of caste in India.

For example, Leach (1960), while following Dumont and Pocock (1958) in insisting on a "cultural" definition of caste (that is to say, "caste" is a unique feature of Hindu culture), nevertheless appears closer to Frederik Barth, a social structuralist critic, in that he sees caste more as an interdependent economic structure than as an *hier-archy*—a society stratified in religious terms. Leach (1960) states:

The caste society as a whole is, in Durkheim's sense, an organic system with each particular caste and subcaste filling a distinctive functional role. It is a system of labour division from which the element of competition among the workers has been largely excluded. The more conventional sociological analysis which finds an analogy between castes, status groups, and economic classes puts all the stress upon hierarchy and upon the exclusiveness of caste separation. Far more

Properly speaking there tends to be, in psychological terms, only a dual or at most a tripartite caste system: that is, socially, stratification among the ordinary members of society, as an extension and elaboration of caste, can be ranked according to relative states of purity, though political or economic power will influence the ranking order. The two extremes of purity in a religious system comprise first those who represent saints or holy people whose behavior or birth assures them to be the most ritually pure and therefore eligible to practice the most elevated or prestigious of the rituals in relation to the supernatural, and second, the most debased outcaste groups who, by virtue of birth or behavior are consigned to perform or engage in activities that are defined as ritually polluted. Sanctions preventing

---

fundamental is the economic inter-dependence which stems from the patterning of the division of labour which is of a quite special type.

Compare this with a quote from Dumont and Pocock (1958, pp. 32ff.):

In the caste system we have to do preeminently with religious ideas connected with purity. . . . The caste system can only be understood when we realize that it is permeated by essentially religious conceptions and further that these religious conceptions are based upon a social apprehension of the pure and the impure. . . . In order to understand the distribution of occupations in India we have to go to beliefs of a religious nature. . . . It is above all religious ideas rather than economic values which establish the rank of each group.

Bailey (1963) points out that if this latter statement is to be empirically testable it should hold true even if there is a change in the economic positions among castes. He suggests then that this statement is only partly true and goes on to demonstrate that although prestige and social position are maintained by an impoverished Brahman or a wealthy untouchable, in the middle ranges of the caste system a change in the wealth of the caste members is followed by a change in the rank accorded the caste. On the other hand, to see status as deriving from economic power will not explain why particular Brahmans, although impoverished, do not lose ritual rank. Bailey says:

I am saying only that such an approach (namely a system of defining caste as a system of religious beliefs) leaves a large area of social relations unanalyzed and that it is this area which most requires analysis in a comparative study of social stratification, and finally that such a structural analysis can be undertaken with or without subscribing to the definition of caste as a system of religious beliefs. (P. 116)

I would disagree with Leach's and Bailey's emphasis. From the psychological standpoint there is some support for Dumont's and Pocock's emphasis on ritual purity and pollution as the basis of caste.

Nevertheless none of these authors, whatever their differences, sufficiently meets the psychological factors that could possibly explain the phenomenon noted by Bailey—that the two extremes of the caste hierarchy do not respond to economic changes, whereas the middle ranges of Indian caste do.

Indian endogamy is sometimes reported to be less stringently enforced among the various intermediate caste segments of the society who have moved from the village to urban settings. Intermarriage, while discouraged, may be condoned among contiguous castes above the level of the untouchable. Although the present system may be consistently described as a thorough caste society, it is in effect perhaps slowly becoming a combination of a class and a caste society, with intermarriage increasingly possible. One could perhaps find historically just as rigid a separation among social segments within European class hierarchies as that which now exists de facto above the untouchable level in urban India.

intermarriage are most strongly invoked against these two extremes and are not subject to the numerous exceptions nor modified by other considerations that operate in the intermediate levels of the caste structure.

The foregoing explains the fact that the loosening of sanctions with social change is most apparent first in the intermediate segments of the population. F. G. Bailey's description (1963) of change of caste in India, as caste is modified from what he terms a closed organic system toward a closed segmental system, suggests that the first castes that become mobile, as competing, self-seeking, segmented social organizations, are those found in the intermediate ranges of the caste structure.

It is at the extremes that the "expressive" functions of caste remain most operative, and a psychological approach allows us to perceive why. The two possible extremes of any caste society play a more forceful, continuing, interdependent role in the emotional life of the total group, apart from the utilitarian questions usually considered in a standard sociological analysis.

The appearance of castes at the extremes of a sacred hierarchy is noted by Fredrik Barth in his report on caste in the Muslim state of Swat in North Pakistan.[19]

In contrast to Hinduism, Islam is an egalitarian religion; and an elaborate hierarchy of ritual rank has no meaning in an Islamic framework. This is not to say that there is no development of a concept of pollution; but, according to Islam, ritual pollution, which derives from body processes such as elimination, sexual intercourse and death, applies equally to all. All men are equally cursed with such sources of pollution, and purity can only be maintained by repeated purificatory acts on the part of the individual. As a ritual system Islam is thus unsuited to produce hierarchical distinctions between social strata. However, this ideal ritual equality does not imply that Moslem societies are without ritually based systems of social stratification.

In Swat, as in Hindu societies, the notion that pollution derives from body processes marks off certain castes as occupationally polluted. In the cases of Sweepers this pollution is so strong that the profession as such has been rejected by Pathan society. The only Sweepers to be found in Swat are members of a Pamjabi caste who have been brought in and protected by prominent chiefs. The indigenous polluted castes include Washermen, Barbers (who are concerned with shaving, nailparing and childbirth), and Thong- and Sievemakers (who work with the guts of animals); these three groups are everywhere despised and form the lowest stratum of society. The caste of Dancers also falls in this category, since they are associated with prostitution and other morally bad practices.

The criterion of purity/pollution thus gives a tripartite ranking of castes in the categories (1) *polluted*, embracing the four lowest castes, (2) *ordinary*, representing the bulk of the castes, and (3) *sacred*, represented by the highest caste, the Saints.

[19] Barth (1960), pp. 113–46.

Barth reports how in Swat, in spite of the Muslim egalitarian ideology and opposition to caste, one finds "holy men" forming an elevated caste, and sweepers and other untouchables forming a pariah group in which hypergamy does not occur. In the middle ranges of the stratification system of Swat there is a positive correlation between ritual status, and political and economic status.

Neither Barth nor Bailey convincingly explains why the extremes of the religious status system do not respond to social processes that would tend to create consistency in economic, political, and religious status positions. The explanation of why this does not occur for specific groups is related to Durkheim's understanding of the duality found in the sacred. From our standpoint, caste, in psychological terms, tends to apply only to either or both extremes of a hierarchy of religious or biological purity. Further complications or elaborations are cultural historical developments.

This hiatus in theoretical perception is somewhat general to sociostructural approaches in sociology. The laws of social interaction tend to be reduced to a type of mechanical causality in which—in spite of Dumont's and Pocock's insistence, after Weber[20] and Durkheim,[21] on the fundamental role of ideology or "values"—the society is reduced to a set of somewhat mechanical relationships. Culturally determined motivational patterns per se, that is, "subjective" motivations, are not perceived as having any continuing autonomy from one generation to the next and are excluded from an explanation of the continuity of social processes. I would stress, as necessary to understanding, in Durkheimian terms, knowledge of underlying collective unconscious motivations as well as resultant collective representations. I would submit that to exclude motivation is artificial, since behavior patterns not directly related to social structure must also be subject to examination. This holds true for such traits as language systems, and for those more subtle culture traits related to the socialization of personality systems of control over affects or drives underlying patterned likes and dislikes, desires and abhorrences. Such culture patterns develop self-perpetuating structures that tend to insure cultural continuity from one generation to the next. Prevailing patterns tend to be interrelated with culturally available cognitive patterns and thereby continuously influence the mutual perception of social roles.

Some of these patterns of behavior are codified into what might be termed "moral laws" or "shared values" observable in the social traditions of specific societies. This is not to transmute social science theory into moral philosophy, but merely to indicate that there is continuity in what may be termed the moral "forces" in society and

[20] Weber (1920–1923), 3 vols.; see also the discussion of Weber in Parsons (1949), especially pp. 506ff.
[21] Durkheim (1947 and 1949).

that this continuity must be accounted for in satisfactory causal explanations of cultural behavior be it caste or other social institutions.

The usual explanation of the symbolic content of art or religion, following the Durkheimian theory, is that it represents those values united in conflict, accommodation, or compromise that maintain social solidarity. Such application of theory misses the point that the collective representations found in religion or myth are also symbolic of underlying intra-psychic conflicts and accommodations or compromises. Not only are these of universal psychological import, but some of these intra-psychic concerns are found with relative intensity within specific cultures.

In sum, although Durkheimian sociologists, such as Dumont, Pocock, and Leach, rightly distinguish between structural and cultural definitions of caste, in apparent inconsistency with their own interests in comparative structural theory they mistakenly insist on the uniqueness of caste in India. Moreover, they do not look sufficiently beyond the instrumental approach to social structure to understand the force of expressive feelings related to underlying personal motivations institutionalized in concepts of ritual pollution that, when related to endogamy, constitute a syndrome we believe to be the essential nature of caste. Dumont does not slight the role of ritual pollution, but there are other limitations to his theoretical approach seen from the standpoint of dynamic psychology. These limitations become even more apparent when caste is examined diachronically in respect to historical vicissitudes. We contend that any thorough explanation of social institutions must provide for the possibility that at certain times in history social institutions were maintained by expressive psychological motivations even though they cease to be directly relevant to the social structure itself. My own approach to caste, further developed in the following chapter, is that of a broadened definition of structuralism that emphasizes psychological determinants related to expressive behavior. Caste must be related to a theory of social change that includes sufficient attention to the tensions appearing between what is instrumentally relative to social functioning and what is expressively satisfying in given social institutions.

Chapter 17

GEORGE DE VOS

Toward a Cross-Cultural Psychology of Caste Behavior

This final chapter attempts a rather difficult synthesis: relying on a dual cultural psychological framework, a number of topics are juxtaposed that at first glance may seem to be quite unrelated. A theory of caste attitudes may seem to have little to do with such diverse topics as the distinction between magic and religion; the prelogical thought processes of children; rules of pollution and taboo in primitive societies; the relation of occupational restrictions and women's lower status to menstrual taboos; ritual acts of communion and commensality; the psychological mechanisms involved in scapegoating; racial prejudice; and individual psychoneurosis. However, it is necessary to understand the dynamic elements in all these topics in order to understand the appearances of caste from the dimension of human motivation given the proper social structural conditions and historical circumstances already discussed.

From the viewpoint developed out of our two ordering ideas—first, that expressive as well as instrumental behavior is institutionalized in systems of social stratification, and second, that psychological needs for self-justification or self-protection in given social circumstances can lead to forms of "status anxiety" rigidified in fixed systems of social segregation—caste can be expected to appear periodically in a variety of human cultures with its justification embedded in religious belief and ritual, or more recently in pseudoscientific mythologies.

To develop these general propositions, the preceding discussion of the instrumental-expressive dichotomy in social relations which distinguishes caste from class is related to a psychological distinction between religion and magic. This distinction has long been a problem that has concerned anthropologists attempting to apply structural theory to the nature of religion. From this step I relate the expressive symbols of religion to the cognitive and affective developmental sequences occurring during childhood socialization. I then examine more specifically how symbols of the impure and the disavowed contribute to the underlying emotional attitudes perpetuated in caste segregation.

THE INSTRUMENTAL-EXPRESSIVE DICHOTOMY IN COLLECTIVE REPRESENTATIONS

The Developmental Sequence in Symbolic Thought

To understand how symbolic representations of ritual pollution or racial contamination can become an essential part of social segregation, one must resort to some form of psychodynamic theory of a developmental sequence in symbolic thought. One part of the socialization process observable in every culture is the learning of what Durkheim called the collective representations that come to constitute the social reality of the individual. Some of these representations remain characteristic of one or another structural level of cognitive immaturity. Even though it may never be possible to arrange the evolution of social thought in any neat chronological sequence, one can, nevertheless, trace ontogenetically from childhood to adulthood some sequences that lawfully occur in individual maturation, regardless of the influence of culture on the total inhibition or facilitation of causal or logical thinking in its collective representations.

According to Piaget's conclusions[1] derived from an intensive investigation of the developing thought of children, one finds in children sequences from pre-causal magical concepts to an adult capacity for scientific logic. This sequence from magic to science is in an evolutionary sense, a sequence in instrumental means-ends thought processes toward a greater and more orderly control and prediction of events in the natural environment. Modern technology has removed many of the terrors of the unknown that primitive man sought to control by magical formulae.

Coexistent but distinct, one finds also in the developmental life of children a sequence of development starting from inchoate representations of motivational forces which go through early pre-causal forms similar to what one observes in various religious beliefs concerning supernatural forces. These forces are more or less anthropomorphized or "personalized" by being endowed with human emotions and motivations. These early representations are derived from attitudes and prac-

---

[1] See Piaget (1928, 1930, 1948, 1954). See also Rapaport (1951). The natural laws of mechanical causality gradually become objectified and freed of egocentric personalizations or investments of mystically conceived sources of power.

tices learned in the course of relating to other motivated beings while in a helpless and dependent childish state. There is an observable sequence in the maturation in children from more primitive forms of social morality toward more objective, reciprocal forms of social relationships. However, the feelings engendered and the methods employed by children in dependent primary relationships may be retained without further development in respect to how the supernatural is represented in particular cultures. In man's continued experience of helplessness toward the mysteries of birth and death and the uncontrolled vagaries of the natural environment, feelings of dependent awe and methods of supplication or achieving merit or approbation by unquestioned obedience are transmuted to modes of relating to the inferred wishes of transcendental powers. In some respects at least the childish modes of "heteronomous" relating (in Piaget's term) can with cultural facilitation be modified into gradual realization of adult forms of reciprocity in social relationships and an increasing secularized "autonomous" conception of social morality freed from internalized absolutes. Social relationships for the most part, in psychologically mature adults, come to be based on a growing capacity for mutual sympathy rather than on an egocentric search for security obtained in a relationship to an omnipotent force. The social basis of adult morality is a reciprocal understanding that finds satisfaction in the mutual facilitation of *expressive* needs in some socially acceptable form.

The recognition of the continuing role of the expressive features of social life and their maturation through the cultivation of the "humanities" receives less emphasis in our technologically preoccupied civilization than does the attainment of a greater instrumental control over the political or economic institutions of the social structure. To some extent the social theory of modern materialistically preoccupied social sciences tends to reflect such preoccupation with the functioning of instrumental role behavior in social institutions and thereby leads to an overevaluation of the political and economic aspects of human culture, deemphasizing the force of artistic and religious-moral traditions which also impart a persistent quality to particular societies.

Marxian theory, for example, would deny any functional autonomy to such determinants of behavior related to the expressive needs in human interaction as are passed on through generations in a cultural heritage.[2] In Marx's theory religious expression is reduced to an "opiate" that distracts man from his necessary preoccupation with his material well-being, which depends ultimately on the instrumental control of human relationships. Awareness of expressive needs and their representations in social thought finds more explicit acknowledg-

---

[2] Parsons (1949).

ment in the sociological systems of Max Weber,[3] Emile Durkheim, and Talcott Parsons.[4]

Although Weber explicitly recognizes the influence of values or what he calls "meaning" in the differentiation of one culture from another, he gives rather scanty development to this concept. Durkheim extends this line of inquiry further. Ultimate cultural values (Durkheim's "sacred") embody the expressive aspects of social behavior. The "spirit" of a particular culture tends to be embodied in such collective representations rather than simply in the particular instrumentalities of power, prestige, or wealth as ends in themselves. Parsons moves even further to incorporate the psychodynamic considerations of a personality system in his theoretical analysis.

The instrumental-expressive dichotomy is essential to investigate particular problems of social change. There are societies that protectively maintain their integrity by clinging to highly emotionalized, rigid beliefs not readily amenable to change or modification. These beliefs are not instrumentally oriented but are expressive of the collective defensive psychology of the group. In studying situations of culture contact we find several historical examples where such rigid belief systems caused the eventual dissolution of a society rather than its instrumental adaptation and modification. The study of social change, therefore, must take into account how values and beliefs may or may not allow for change in any specific direction.

Belief systems supply directives for what is experienced as moral social behavior. What is sacred to a society resembles what is sacred or taboo to the individual conscience. And what are perceived to be eternal truths are protected and made untouchable or unapproachable to critical evaluation by internal barriers of emotion as well as by explicit external sanctions that warn the individual daring to approach that any direct challenge would result in his own destruction. For many an individual member of a culture, belief in the collective representations of his group may be based on maintaining an intrapsychic balance or integration, and therefore a belief system can be conceptualized as a necessary integral part of a rigidified personality structure. This is not to say that for others such belief may not simply reflect conformity to the acceptable belief system of the social group as a mark of conformity as well as social self-identity. (In the later discussion of status anxiety we will return to this subject.)

Malinowski, on the basis of his sustained first-hand contact with the Trobriand Island culture, adequately disposed of the view that there is something structurally different about mental processes, in what are termed primitive cultures compared with those found in modern civil-

---

[3] Parsons (1949).
[4] Parsons (1949).

ization. He suggests that any pre-literate group is as eager to apply causal thinking to the sequence of events as are individuals living in a modern society. The difference lies in what is traditionally available in the way of knowledge within a culture. Nevertheless, life in a primitive culture is much more subject to uncontrollable natural forces than is life in the protected artificial environment of a modern urbanized culture.

Conversely, psychoanalytic psychology amply demonstrates the persistence, conscious as well as unconscious, of pre-causal magical thinking both in modern man and in so-called primitive man. Modern man resorts to certain representations despite readily available knowledge to the contrary. In spite of cultural changes in available knowledge he, just as his primitive counterpart, is still subject to thinking distortions in situations of duress. Caste segregation in this sense can be perceived as part of a belief system protecting against a sense of threat to religious or social status.

Socialized representations have their inchoate origin in the immature psychological structures of the ontogenetic if not the phylogenetic infancy of Homo sapiens. To date, Jean Piaget[5] in the most systematic formulation of the maturation of cognitive systems of thought and rationality in developing children in present day psychology illustrates in both cognitive and moral development the series of developmental stages through which children go in their attempts to comprehend the world about them. Incomplete development of mental processes at some stage of maturation causes children to perceive their environment and related events in ways that are directly congruent to the type of representations found in pre-literate cultures, in their limited comprehension of the natural world, and in their beliefs concerning the structure and function of the supernatural. Without a thorough understanding of this sequence in the maturation of thought processes, one cannot arrive at any understanding of the psychological basis for the symbolic behavior observed by the anthropologists embodied in various forms of religious myth and ritual including those related to the disavowed or demonic.

A careful study of Piaget's reports on cognitive maturation allows one to distinguish instrumental-phenomenological magical forms of pre-causality from expressive forms of pre-logical thinking found in religious belief systems.[6] Piaget, however, does not examine how affec-

---

[5] Piaget (1928).

[6] See, for example, Piaget (1930), pp. 285ff. To illustrate, Piaget stresses the presence of "adherences," such as attributions of inner muscular states into natural forces as they appear in animistic beliefs or forms of "participation," in which one's thoughts or gestures seem to influence causal sequences in the environment. Such thinking is structurally identical to that occurring in institutionalized practices of sympathetic magic found almost universally in primitive folk cultures. There are several forms of pre-causal thought structurally similar to thought

tive valences govern pre-logical associations. For this one must turn to Freud's formulations concerning unconscious symbolic associations.

Unconscious processes of thought as discussed by Freud are residues of the first conceptual means available to a developing ego structure in the early stages of separating out the self from the surrounding environment. The mental processes accompanying the earliest functioning mental mechanisms, termed by Freud introjection and projection, are governed by the laws of association (similarity and congruity) as they are described in behaviorist theories of learning. Similarity and congruity govern the earliest flow of symbolic thought. They remain manifest in magical beliefs and practices.

Psychological Distinctions between Magic and Religion

Malinowski in refuting possible structural differences in the mentality of non-literate groups illustrates how so-called primitive man is not limited to pre-causal forms of thought, but can draw adequate causal conclusions from the sequence of events. He knows that if he plants and tends he can grow his taro and yams, but he also knows that his success is subject to interference by forces or occurrences over which he has no control. In the face of an anxiety-producing drought, therefore, he resorts to magic.

Modern man, too, will resort to magic given a similar lack of control in a situation of stress. For example, until very recently a rain-maker might be called in if a drought became severe enough, thus flying full in the face of what has become available in scientific knowledge about the magical nature of such practices. A modern Catholic facing the known hazards of highway driving is wont to place a St. Christopher's medal in his automobile to help along his own statistical chances of escaping harm.

Moral-religious beliefs in a personalized supernatural force may also be aroused by crisis experiences. The idea of a drought as one god's punishment for unsavory moral conditions within the suffering community might become increasingly persuasive as the drought continued. One finds, therefore, in modern as in primitive man, forms of pre-causal thought of both a magical and personalized religious nature in the recesses of the mind, available in those situations where the usual capacity for logical processes begins to fail.

In spite of the structural similarities in the adult mental capacity for logical thought regardless of culture, there are normative differences

in institutionalized religious beliefs. The principal one is "motivational" pre-causality, the attribution of personalized motivational forces which respond to the child's behavior by punishment or reward. There is also "artificialism," the attribution of the origin of natural objects to the handiwork of a creator god.

among cultures in magical or scientific teaching. Instrumental, goal-oriented human activity is dependent not only on the state of scientific knowledge available to a particular culture but also on the values of the culture itself. A future time orientation and concern with economic maximization can stimulate the conceptual use of logical means-end relationship.[7]

Magical practices are replaced gradually as increased knowledge affords better methods of instrumental control, but greater knowledge of mechanical types of causality can never substitute completely for the types of satisfactions sought for in man's expressive life. Whereas science can replace magic, it cannot replace the expressive features of man's cultural life. These expressive aspects of human relationships become institutionalized in various forms of family and social interaction, and become crystallized in the art and religious practices as well as the ideology of any culture. These expressive aspects of social relationships are often excluded from too careful a content analysis within a sociologically oriented social structural approach since such theory cannot adequately cope with the peculiar content of expressive behavior.

The usual explanation given for particular art forms, religious ritual, or even prevailing types of psychoneurotic behavior found in a culture, according to some followers of Durkheimian theory, is that they must somehow be related ultimately to representations either of social solidarity, or the interaction of the society with the natural or supernatural environment that governs the course of events. This form of explanation although generative of understanding does not supply a well differentiated theory of psychological motivation.

The essential point made concerning the social nature of religion is valid. Religious rites are social concerns, for they are generally symbolic affirmations of the important life crises, the major periods or stages of social life. They are, therefore, often rites of passage concerned with conception, pregnancy, fertility, birth, puberty, adulthood, marriage, death, and the types of change in status that move the living member of the society into some form of afterlife.[8] Religion also concerns itself with the origins of society in human existence and the values and meanings mythologically symbolized in relation to the origin of a particular group. Malinowski,[9] without developing it explicitly, comes very close to defining as one of the basic differences between magic and religion a distinction between instrumental and expressive behavior. He sees magic essentially as instrumental activity, while religion, in addition to being a form of assurance of the deity's

---

[7] Mannheim (1959).
[8] van Gennep (1960).
[9] Malinowski (1948), p. 20.

help in reaching desired goals, is even more concerned with the expressive emotions essentially and eternally present in human nature. While he does not use our terminology, the meaning of the following passage is abundantly clear.

A closer scrutiny of the facts allows us to make from the outset a preliminary classification into two main groups. Compare a rite carried out to prevent death in childbed with another typical custom, a ceremony in celebration of a birth. The first rite is carried out as a means to an end, it has a definite practical purpose which is known to all who practice it and can be easily elicited from any native informant. The post-natal ceremony, say a presentation of a new-born or a feast of rejoicing in the event, has no purpose; it is not a means to an end but an end in itself. It expresses the feelings of the mother, the father, the relatives, the whole community, but there is no future event which this ceremony foreshadows, which it is meant to bring about or to prevent. This difference will serve as *prima facie* distinction between magic and religion.

It is this expressive aspect of religion that Durkheim interpreted functionally as a collective social moral affirmation of the society. But though it may have this function, the behavior must also be related to psychological structures. The specific behavioral content of many ceremonies does not make sense if analyzed only in terms of societal symbols. The behavior is also a derivative of unconscious symbolism, and of psychosexual developmental experiences.

Malinowski's view of religion is essentially directed toward a consideration of its positive representations of the social and personal needs of propagation, sexuality, and nutrition. He does not pursue the essential role taken by religion in disavowing the "evil" potentials in human nature, be they sexual or aggressive, and in denying the destined death and putrefaction of the human body, whatever its idealization. These concerns permeate the vital anxieties of all men, and as such are related to what is religiously disavowed in every society—the unholy and the uncanny. These religious disavowals are a starting point for thinking about how psychological needs become institutionalized as expressive caste behavior sanctioned in religious terms.

INSTITUTIONALIZATION OF SYMBOLS OF THE IMPURE AND THE DISAVOWED

Pre-Causal Symbolism

What becomes part of the sacred of a society, its purposes, goals for life, definitions of values—the very structure of society, be it in the form of kin groups or occupational segments—is somehow represented in religious beliefs. However, inextricably interwoven into the same beliefs and rituals are also the representations of the socially disruptive or disavowed. Improper or incestuous relationships, reprehensible behavioral trends, forms of destruction (interpersonal or directed against nature) that are found intolerable to the society, disavowed usages of the body and its urges, what is proper or improper in nutritive incorporation or in excretion—all are diffused through forms of symbolic representations of what is desirable and what is to be shunned. Germane to our subject are those representations related to what is polluting, befouling, and contaminating. The socialization processes that come to direct the individuals' concern for the moral and immoral, clean and dirty, are reinforced on a symbolic religious level by the practices and demands embodied in the religious code learned in the later stages of socialization.

What becomes sacred in societies that emphasize feelings of purity or untouchability in segregating one human from another must be related somehow to deflections of early representations of oral, sexual, and anal functions into the affective tone accompanying specified forms of later social contact. In given societies where associations of purity and impurity in respect to particular foods or even particular classes of individuals are particularly emphasized in infancy and childhood one will also find related symbolic representations in the religious beliefs and practices of adults.

Psychoanalytic theory was the first to draw attention to the links in the psychosexual life of children between oral, anal, and genital functions. Later, physiological psychology discovered that such links indeed occur within the diffuse organization of the autonomic nervous system and the very structure of the brain itself. Unfortunately, there has been little systematic psychophysiological study to date on the developmental sequences of autonomic functioning and its relationships to cognitive development at various stages in early childhood. If more knowledge were available, we would no doubt be able to trace explicitly how representations of ritual pollution originate in early personality mechanisms. It would then be possible to trace their evolvement from their early physiological bases.

The autonomic nervous system, which in its functioning interrelates oral, anal, and genital functions, also intimately relates bodily experiences and early symbolic associations resulting from tactile and oral contacts with things external to the organism. Autonomically involved bodily reactions are inescapably related to both positively and negatively toned, affectively associated, symbolic representations that can be transferred to later social situations.

The negatively toned experiences start with primitive reflexes serving to protect the organism from noxious stimuli, be they approaching the body or actually part of what would be ingested as food. The etymology of the word "revulsion" suggests a pulling away from, a drawing back related to sensations of tactile aversion. The word "repulsion" has in it the idea of creating distance between the experiencing individual and an object. The word "disgust" is more specifically related to sensations of repelling something noxious from the mouth. These primitive reflexes themselves can become stimulated by highly emotionalized situations not involving food in any way.[10]

Symbolized ideas such as "coldness" toward a person, for example, are related to autonomically induced physiological phenomena such as the withdrawal of circulation from the surface level of the skin. Such withdrawal can occur in fear situations or in other affectively stressful states in which the blood supply on the dermal level of the body diminishes. Thus, basic early developmental levels of autonomic functions are related to later socially inculcated representations and can be formulated as fears of social contamination.

In considering how these fears of social contamination or pollution are structured in the adult, one must further explore how the earliest tactile and oral reflexes and their symbolic representations become interwoven with anal and sexual representations. The word "pollution" connotes either a surface coverage with material considered to be filthy or some actual penetration of the body by noxious or disagreeable material. When the polluting object remains on the surface, some act of cleansing is possible. Pollutions that enter in and become part of the individual are more frightening, since they cannot be as readily removed.

The feeling of revulsion toward "dirty" is related very obviously, in Western culture at least, to the types of attitudes inculcated in the socialization of anal controls. The child learns to be repelled by his own feces. It must not be overlooked that culturally learned revulsion, however, is not only directed toward what comes from within the body but also toward objects that can be placed in the mouth by babies or toward other objects, animals, and people. The difficulty of making adequate distinctions between inside and outside is one of the early problems of developing a self-structure or ego, which assists the individual in precisely locating the source of sensations and perceptions.

For example, in the fear of a neurotic who must wear gloves in order not to be contaminated, one finds an extreme of symbolized anxiety concerning contamination by touch. In psychoanalytic therapy, the complexity of the emotionalized experiences that underlie such neurotic symbolism has been well illustrated in individual case histories.[11] Neurotic rigidities resulting in compulsive behavior are ex-

---

[10] For example, some of the judicial party that visited the Auschwitz death camp as part of a trial of war criminals could not help vomiting at what they saw.

[11] See Fenichel (1945).

treme examples of individual feelings of vulnerability to permeation by objects from the outside environment. In our discussion of status anxiety, we shall suggest that such neurotic mechanisms become socially justifiable when an institution of caste exists. They appear consciously as a neurosis only when the individual gives up an adherence to the belief system sanctioning caste. The point at which the child directs his feelings into conceptual channels provided by the society is, of course, something that has not been well studied in detail but remains one of the future tasks of a comparative cultural psychology.

Culturally prevalent confusions related to the diffusion or interpenetration of concepts of pollution, dirt, disgust and contamination, sexual arousal, or destructive mutilations, originate in body functioning itself. In addition to the learned avoidance of noxious outside objects of putrefaction, or other forms of unpleasantness, the developing individual learns to dissociate himself from his own excretions as well as to disavow essentially revolting improper ideas originating in his own mind related to aggressive drives or body needs that are not admissible within the types of self-concept condoned within his culture. If these impulses and urges are so overpowering as to force themselves into an acknowledged part of the ego, the individual must choose some deviant role among those available within his culture.

Given this framework, we can also understand why there is an inducement in a minority group such as a disparaged caste to give vent to what is unacceptable in the majority culture. Since they are already seen as acting out disavowed elements, if such socially unacceptable urges have any force within a particular individual, it becomes more difficult to resist some partial identification with a socially disparaged image. There are secondary gratifications making the acceptance of disparaged patterns rewarding to some degree as well as contributing to a conscious or unconscious negative self-image.

It is to be noted also that the concept of ritual pollution goes beyond the concept of ordinary dirt or contamination and is interpenetrated by feelings of awe and fear. The confusion of awe in pollution has to do again with the nature of the early primitive confusion in symbolic representations characteristic of infantile associative mental processes. Feelings of awe and fear are especially pertinent to the mysteries of sex, birth, and death. One of the pioneering, major insights of Robertson Smith was that the holy and the unclean, in their most primitive forms, are not readily distinguishable.[12] Freud suggests an

---

[12] Smith (1894), pp. 447–48:

    Holy and unclean things have this in common, that in both cases certain restrictions lie on men's use of and contact with them, and that the breach of these restrictions involves supernatural dangers. The difference between the two appears, not in relation to man's ordinary life, but in the irrelation to the gods. Holy things are not free to man, because they pertain to the gods;

analogous confusion occurs in early stages of maturation of the mental processes of children. Robertson Smith attempts by his evolutionist approach to Semitic religions to trace how these earlier ambiguities concerning the sacred are separated with the development of moral rules in later religious formulations. These rules became embodied in codes of behavior derived from a belief in a personal relationship to a deity.

The fact that all the Semites have rules of uncleanliness as well as rules of holiness, that the boundary between the two is often vague, and that the former as well as the latter present the most startling agreement in point of detail with savage *taboos*, leaves no reasonable doubt as to the origin and ultimate relations of the idea of holiness. On the other hand, the fact that the Semites—or at least the Northern Semites—distinguished between the holy and the unclean marks a real advance above savagery. All taboos are inspired by awe of the supernatural, but there is a great moral difference between precautions against the invasion of mysterious, hostile powers and precautions founded on respect for the prerogative of a friendly god. The former belong to magical superstition—the barest of all aberrations of the savage imagination—which, being founded only on fear, acts merely as a bar to progress and an impediment to the free use of nature by human nature and industry. But the restrictions on individual licence which are due to respect for a known and friendly power allied to man, however trivial and absurd to us in their details, contain with them the germinate principles of social progress and moral order. To know that one has the mysterious powers of nature on one's side, so long as one acts in conformity with certain rules, gives a man strength and courage to pursue the task of the subjugation of nature to his service. To restrain one's individual licence, not out of slavish fear, but from respect for a higher and beneficent power,

---

uncleanliness is shunned, according to the view taken in the higher Semitic religions, because it is hateful to the god, and therefore not to be tolerated in his sanctuary, his worshippers, or his land. But that this explanation is not primitive can hardly be doubted, when we consider that the acts that cause the uncleanness are exactly the same which among savage nations places a man under taboo, and that these acts are often involuntary, and often innocent, or even necessary to society. The savage, accordingly, imposes a taboo on a woman in childbed or during her courses, on the man who touches a corpse, not out of any regard for the gods but simply because birth, and everything connected with the propagation of the species on the one hand, and disease and death on the other, seem to him to involve the action of superhuman agencies of a dangerous kind. . . . The affinity of such taboos with laws of uncleanness comes out most clearly when we observe that uncleanness is treated like a contagion, which has to be washed away or otherwise eliminated by physical means. Take the rules about the uncleanness produced by the carcases of vermin in Leviticus XI, 32ff.; what they touch must be washed; the water itself is then unclean, and can propagate the contagion; nay, if the defilement affects an unglazed earthen pot, it is supposed to sink into the pores, and cannot be washed out, so that the pot must be broken. Rules like this have nothing in common with the spirit of Hebrew religion; they can be only remains of a primitive superstition, like that of the savage who shuns the blood of uncleanness and such things as a supernatural and deadly virus.

is a moral discipline of which the value does not altogether depend on the reasonableness of the sacred restrictions.

This description by Robertson Smith is almost a direct representation of Freud's concept of identification, in which the child learns to suppress and repress the disavowed as a means of enjoying the love and approval of parents. Through a denial of the disavowed, the child brings within him a feeling of identification with the powers that regulate the moral order, be it the parents, or later when he assumes the religious beliefs of his group, either a beneficent guiding deity or a jealous and terrible god ready to visit pestilence, starvation or natural catastrophe upon his wayward subjects.

Nowhere is the unconscious psychological symbolic nature of ritual behavior more clearly apparent than in the ritual acts of purification that follow contamination. Most religions have incorporated some such ritual. As pointed out earlier, Shinto used forms of ablution in cleansing related to the purity of white as a color and to the use of water for ablution. In Christianity, baptism symbolically cleanses the individual from sin. To understand, therefore, the thinking related to ritual pollution, one must see that certain representations tend to have universal symbolic value and that such actual forms of cleansing as occur with water can be transmitted to ritualistic representations as well.

There are series of representations that are forms of equivalents common to many societies. Moral virtues, or goodness, are almost universally identified with physical cleanliness. There are chains of associations such as superior-good-virtuous-clean-white-pure-harmless, and the converse—inferior-bad-corrupt-dirt-black-defiled-dangerous. Individual associations in any one part of this chain can lead to the symbolic diffusion into other parts.

The psychological factors underlying ritual pollution are well represented in the almost universal concern with menstrual blood and childbirth. We note the especial abhorrence concerning menstruation as it is related to the demeaned social status of women as a result of what can be considered the status anxiety of men. According to the theoretical perspective we are propounding, the institutionalized social segregation of women is an example of expressive exploitation understandable in terms of such status anxiety.

Purity and Awe: The Social Segregation of Women

In the historical material on Japanese caste it was related how in Japan, as almost universally elsewhere, there were institutionalized strong feelings concerning the pollution of menstruation and childbirth including, at one time, use of special menstrual huts. Some form of temporary ritualistic segregation of women is reported throughout most sections of the world. In Chapter 16 we suggested that the feelings underlying this type of segregation must be intimately related to those appearing in the social segregation of polluted, endogamous groups. Feelings of contamination related to women's sexual functioning must be, in effect, psychologically similar to those feelings that reinforce caste attitudes. There is no way of separating women permanently in all areas of life; nevertheless, in many societies in which a priesthood is established, women are not allowed to partake of the most elevated sacred functions. The belief that women are impure is sufficient to justify the prevention of their participation in many forms of ritual life.

The ritual impurity of women is best documented in the Semitic religions, both those that preceded Judaism and in early forms of Christianity. Robertson Smith[13] documents the antiquity of the Hebrew taboos concerning menstruation. He also shows that there was not only a concern with impurity per se among the Arabs, but there were a variety of supernatural powers supposedly attaching themselves to menstruating women. The menstrual blood was one of the strongest of charms; along with such other unclean things as dead men's bones, menstruous rags used to be tied on children to help them avoid the *jinn* or the evil eye. Such practices again appeared among the tantric groups in India where the use of abhorrent materials bestowed supernatural powers. In later Judaism the Pentateuchal code ordained that a menstruous woman should be considered unclean for seven days from the beginning of her period.[14] During the course of these seven days she is contaminatory to every object with which she comes in contact. There is a treatise in "Niddah" that elaborates the regulations and rules concerning a woman in childbirth (see also Leviticus 12). Moreover, degrees of impurity vary according to whether the woman bears a male or a female child (Leviticus 12), for the codification includes those unusual circumstances where the birth is hermaphroditic or the delivery is premature or results in a miscarriage. In early Christian culture, sexual functions were described by the early Church fathers as dirty in the same language as used to describe acts of defecation. The medieval treatise on witches, *Malleus Maleficarum,* shows why women are particularly prone to witchcraft and why among witches it is particularly the midwives who are to be feared.[15] The argument put forward is that women, like ecclesiastics, are given to extremes, especially in the realms of the sacred.[16]

---

[13] Smith (1894), pp. 447–48.

[14] *The Jewish Encyclopaedia* (1905), p. 301.

[15] Henricus Institoris (1928).

[16] Henricus Institoris (1928), p. 42:

For some learned men propound this reason: that there are three things in nature, the tongue, the ecclesiastic, and a woman, who know no moderation in

One can perceive an irony of history by juxtaposing the present concern with the purity of white women, which prevails so in the pre-occupations of American racists, and the early Christian-Judaic attitudes concerning women's essential impurity. The gradual development of the cult of the Virgin Mary has indeed been a revolutionary force in religious mythology, leading to a profound idealization of virginity and motherhood in the West. It is a complete denial, not only of the sexual functions of womanhood, but of death itself. One can find no psychological remnant of those aspects of awe and terror that made the more animalistic representations of primitive goddesses so terrifying. If one juxtaposes the Virgin Mary to Kali or Durga in Hindu religion, one sees the extreme polarities of religious representations of female nature. The appearance of witches in the West up until two centuries ago provided some outlet for the representation of the demonic in female nature. But the unconscious projections in Northern Europe in more recent times seem to have been diverted more to racial representations than to representations of women as a source of projection of the animality present in the depths of human nature.

How are we to understand this preoccupation with menstrual flow and the blood and fluids accompanying human childbirth? It is perhaps difficult in this modern age with the modern possibilities of inconspicuous sanitary napkins and the scientific and sterilized methods of hospital childbirth to recapture what must have been the experiences of small children witnessing menstrual bleeding and childbirth.

---

goodness or vice; and when they exceed the bounds of their condition, they reach the greatest heights and the lowest depths of goodness and vice. . . .

The argument about women's polluted nature also sounds very similar in some respects to arguments related to differences in inferior castes heard today. For example (p. 44):

For as regards intellect, or the understanding of spiritual things, they seem to be of a different nature from men. . . . Women are intellectually like children. . . . But the natural reason is that she is more carnal than a man, as is clear from her many carnal abominations.

Women are cursed by heredity with being defective in nature.

And it should be noted that there was a defect in the formation of the first woman, since she was formed from a bent rib, that is, a rib from the breast, which is bent, as it were, in a contrary direction to a man, and through this defect she is an imperfect animal, she always deceives. . . . (P. 24)

On page 46, the author quotes Valerius:

You do not know that woman is chimaera, but it is good that you should know it; for that monster was of three forms; its face was that of a radiant and noble lion, it had the filthy belly of a goat, and it was armed with the virulent tail of a viper. And he means that a woman is beautiful to look upon, contaminating to the touch, and deadly to keep.

He concludes, summarizing the sources of witchcraft and its motivation in women:

All witchcraft comes from carnal lust, which is in women insatiable. See Proverbs XXX. There are three things that are never satisfied, yea, a fourth thing which says not it is enough; that is, the mouth of the womb, wherefore for the sake of fulfilling their lust, they consort even with devils.

These realities must be considered in understanding the strong feelings and the symbolized derivatives concerning sexual functions related to destruction, as well as creativity.

The most basic feelings of awe are related to concepts of power and creativity. In the history of religions there are numerous occasions when these were combined symbolically in a female deity. Sometimes power, however, was split from creativity with the bright-forceful-thrusting-maleness, all combined symbolically with power, and the generativity of women combined with the dark-mysterious-awesome that governs passage into the world by birth, and out of it by death. There has been no successful alternative to the schemes offered by psychoanalysis to explain how these concepts come to influence the individual. One finds in the prehistory of mankind that the earliest artistic representations of which we have record have to do with the killing of animals and the fecundity of women.[17] It is no accident that the most defiling aspect of the washerman caste in India is the fact that they are responsible for the washing of menstrual clothes, that this is the function that pollutes them beyond the barbers and others of the lowest of the untouchables.[18]

The explicit manner in which menstruation and childbirth came to have symbolic implications of awe and destruction has never been worked out in detail. Some of the material presented by Bruno Bettelheim from his experience with psychotic children at the orthogenic school at the University of Chicago, however, is relevant.[19] Bettelheim was able to observe in the overt thinking processes of psychotic children what must occur unconsciously or at earlier maturation of cognitive levels in a normal child. He was able to show the feeling in specific children of awe and danger related to menstruation.[20] Some psychotic girls flaunt their menstruation, making sure that others are aware of their menstrual flow. Some know that this display of female animal nature makes boys shudder and recoil. Some feel that it gives them some mysterious power over men.

But whatever gives power is also potentially dangerous, what can make others anxious is a potentially destructive power; and if it can harm others it might also destroy its owner. A girl who experiences her menses in this way has not really accepted or emotionally mastered the function and remains partly at its mercy. She is not in control of her "sorcery," but at best a "sorcerer's apprentice" who at any moment may find herself subject to her own witchcraft.[21]

---

[17] Death and birth and the sexual act, as Robert Graves points out, comprise the affective forces underlying the essential symbolism of poetry. (Graves, 1948.)

[18] See for example, Banks (1960), pp. 61–77.

[19] Bettelheim (1962).

[20] Bettelheim (1962), pp. 27ff.

[21] Bettelheim (1962), p. 27.

Some girls act as if their blood is a potentially potent poison. They become obsessed with the disposal of the soiled napkin, and sometimes Bettelheim observed the development of elaborate compulsive rituals around this disposal. Bettelheim states that "many normal women, even those who do not consider menstruation a 'curse,' regard it as something weird and their attitude toward their own menstrual discharge is ambivalent; sometimes a mixture of fascinated interest and deep revulsion." [22] It must be noted that the word curse itself has connotations suggesting the supernatural and hence a mysterious power. It also suggests a curse of demeaned social position and an innate physiological handicap. Bettelheim makes the interesting connection between these attitudes and the fact that feminine envy sometimes ends in a wish that boys should also bleed from their sexual organs.[23]

A recent cross-cultural study of the severity of menstrual taboos indirectly concerned itself with the possible confluence of the social as well as the psychological determinants of status anxiety. In the research of Stephens' indices of sexual anxiety are implicitly related to both the maintenance of male dominance over women and unresolved Oedipal feelings related to sexual fear.[24] By a compelling use of statistical techniques he was able to point out a direct relationship between the degree of sexual anxiety found in men of particular cultures and the institutionalization of menstrual taboos. For Stephens, menstrual taboos are a central index of Oedipal anxiety in adults. He found a significant correlation between a scale measuring the degree of severity of menstrual taboos and a scale measuring other forms of sexual anxiety. In turn, both these scales related positively to the institution of polygyny; hence, menstrual taboos are somehow related both to social structure and to other symbolized forms of sexual anxiety. In polygynous societies the position of women vis-à-vis men is lower generally than in monogamous societies. There would, therefore, be a possible fear of retribution from women as a submerged and disparaged social group.

Both in societies that have severe caste proscriptions and in those with severe menstrual proscriptions it is the higher caste or the dominant males that enforce the social sanctions. We may assume, therefore, that not only are social sanctions related to questions of ritual

---

[22] Bettelheim (1962), p. 28.

[23] Bettelheim (1962) relates these concerns in symmetrical fashion to his theory of the unconscious meaning of circumcision rituals also found strangely universal in man.

[24] Stephens (1962). Stephens did not explicitly attend to the influence of man's dominant social role over women as related to symbolic anxiety concerning sexual functions, since his major concern was the demonstration that menstrual taboos were an institutionalized expression of sexual anxiety.

impurity, but also in both cases these sanctions are related to underlying tensions resulting from a fear of retribution. In other words, social dominance begets fear and the fear itself begets greater sanctions, and in turn the sanctions themselves repeat the vicious cycle of unresolvable psychological concern with a nonsymmetrical social relationship.

COMMUNION AND COMMENSALITY: SYMBOLIC EXCLUSION OF THE OUTCASTE

The outcaste in India and Japan is differentiated from others by what he eats as well as by what he does. It is necessary to make some further speculations as to how caste segregation is related to the eating of food together in a society. In addition to avoidance of the eating practices of the outcastes, there are some other cultural psychological symbolic features to the abhorrence of commensality across a caste barrier.

The Symbolic Nature of Communion.—Malinowski points out how magic and religion are both related to the procuring and distribution of food; not only are there magical rites to facilitate the procurement of food instrumentally, but in most single cultures there is some type of expressive ceremonial act involved in the distribution of food and the holding of feasts. These ceremonies are of a religious as well as an economic nature. In some types of sacrifice, discussed in detail by Robertson Smith and Durkheim,[25] these religious acts of sacrifice and thanksgiving also symbolize the continuity of social integration within the society.

Primitive man, never free from the threat of starvation even under the best conditions, attempts to alleviate anxiety not only by the practice of magic but also by seeking the intercession of and offering thanksgiving to a god or a supernatural force symbolically included in the act of eating. Sacrifice and communion, the two main forms in which food is ritually administered, are found in some form throughout the world's cultures. These rites must therefore be of universal significance to society.

The symbolic nature of communal eating has profound meaning in terms of an interpenetration and sharing necessary within the intimate social group. Eating with a member of another caste is therefore symbolically giving up caste separation. The abhorrence of commensalism with members of an outcaste group is, in many of the instances reported, much greater than that involved in acts of sexual congress. Eating together is a deeply social act symbolizing a form of communion, whether it exists as part of a ritual or as part of the daily habits

---

[25] See Smith (1894) and Durkheim (1947).

of life. It is from this standpoint that in caste situations commensality remains particularly abhorrent.[26] It symbolizes ritual fraternity, identification, and mutual permeability.[27] Even though the individual is not conscious of this, it represents vulnerability to other forms of interpenetration that cannot be tolerated where there is a deep fear of contamination, be it rationalized in religious terms or in terms of disease and dirt.

We may also speculate how unconscious mental processes are inextricably involved in the obtaining of food. Man as a hunter or eater of meat must of necessity kill and mutilate animals for food. As long as there is no sense of identity with other forms of life these acts can be performed without a sense of destructiveness which may be turned toward one's fellow man. The psychological implications of totemism are not germane to our present analysis; suffice it to say that psychologically special forms of identification occur with specific animals. This type of relationship to animals, be it in the creation of animal deities or in proscriptions against eating, is evident in numerous cultures and are embedded almost universally in sacrificial ritual. Acts of sacrifice induce the participation of a beneficent deity to share, in this sense, and bless not only the eating of the food but also the necessary act of mutilation and destruction that precedes it. One may suppose that the communal feast occurring with God's blessing relieves man's horror of his own impulses as a killer. This feeling of kinship toward all living creatures has been worked out in the most excruciating detail in Indian culture: it is not simply coincidental that we find the appearance of extreme preoccupations with purity and pollution as well. The deep repression of destructive behavior in the individual very often results in the appearance of obsessive-compulsive symptomatology.

If one reads in detail the material in Robertson Smith and others, one can see what pains man has taken, in some cultures at least, to divest himself of the responsibility of taking an animal's life. In Hindu culture the development of a stringent vegetarianism is not unrelated to the general search after purity as a means of salvation. The Jain religion illustrates the extremes to which compulsive avoidance practices can be institutionalized, not only with respect to alimentary cleanliness but also to killing, even of the casual insect.

For the present adherents of the orthodox Jewish faith, meat to be eaten must first be purified or *kosher*. To take away the curse of impurity, animals must be ritually blessed by a rabbi at the slaughter.

---

[26] Weber (1953).

[27] The converse is also true—the outcaste protects his identity by resisting penetration by the majority society. See Chapter 11, where we discussed the resistance to penetration on the part of the Japanese outcaste by educative and welfare interference from the dominant group.

The act of killing is thereupon deemed a good rather than an impure act. The ordinary man is not sufficiently sanctified to remove the taint of general unconscious destructive feeling which may motivate his taking of life.

Communal Eating: An Act of Belonging.—Not only does eating signify the taking in or introjection of aliments; the manner of eating can also reinforce and reassure one's sense of status in society. Every society develops rules for eating that when breached can become a symbolic threat to an individual's status or sense of cultural identity.[28]

In many societies men eat apart from women, not only from the standpoint of possible differences in purity but as marks of status. The woman serves the food to the man. Even in the rural frontier in the early nineteenth century in America, the man would finish eating before his wife was permitted to do so. One can state, therefore, that social self-identity as well as sexual identification may be guarded by how, where, and with whom eating occurs.

In situations of culture contact social identity may be symbolically maintained by continuing food habits. There is a tendency for many individuals to be revolted by foods other than those familiar since childhood. In many instances these revulsions are not under the control of the individual experiencing them. Even today there are many who fear traveling because of the lack of "proper" food in other lands. In the American armed forces in Japan, provision was made for importing American beef in spite of the frank acknowledgment by the buyers of meat that the Japanese beef was superior and less expensive. The families of many servicemen refused to use the local beef.

SCAPEGOATING:
PERSONAL AND SOCIAL ADAPTATIONS

One predominant defense mechanism that pervades the symbolism of caste as well as other forms of nonsymmetrical social relations is projection. An institutionalized representation of this mechanism is scapegoating, which occurred literally in Semitic religions. There are numerous examples of ceremonials in which a goat or other animal was symbolically infused in the course of a religious ritual with particular sins, diseases, or forms of ritual contamination and then either killed or driven out into the desert. What we see represented in lateral terms in ancient ceremony is what occurs in modern times in more subtle displacements of human problems or unresolved issues onto the backs of a vulnerable individual or group that cannot defend itself.

Such projection involves treating as external what was originally

---

[28] The Englishman, dressing for dinner in a tropical colony, nightly reaffirmed his sense of identity as an Englishman.

part of the body or the self. Disavowed, repressed aspects of the self are projected out and experienced as something external, to be found in depraved or debased creatures who are therefore unlike oneself. But unlike objects that are truly external, what is projected cannot be avoided by simply creating some form of physical or social distance to relieve tension. The contaminated dead can be buried, but the unresolved, internal affective states they caused in others while still alive, cannot. Particular dead may come back to haunt the living. So too repressed feelings continually threaten to return, whether as tendencies arising from within, or as projections perceived as part of another individual. The energy necessary to maintain a projection is continual, and in those individuals bedeviled by processes with which they cannot cope, the need for some form of external scapegoat remains unceasing. This hated scapegoat can be an external enemy, disloyal subversives within one's own community, the devil and his emissaries, or witches who dwell among us. In modern form in a national state it is more likely to be disloyal neighbors, suspicious minority groups, or a debased social caste.

Bettelheim and Janowitz, in a systematic study of both anti-Semitism and anti-Negro attitudes in the United States,[29] find that the presence of prejudice is inversely related to the strength of ego integration.[30] People with weak egos usually cannot manage inner conflicts without resorting to some form of projection or displacement. This is the source of intrapsychic tension from which institutionalized scapegoating draws its continuity. They found that projection and displacement are general social phenomena in intergroup relationships.[31]

Collectively held and socially reinforced representations do help sustain individual psychic structures. By resorting to historically available sustaining group beliefs, the individual can gain some relief from his own tensions, since the energy demanded to believe in a collectively held social myth is much less than necessary to create and main-

---

[29] Bettelheim and Janowitz (1965).
[30] Cf. the similar conclusion of Jahoda (1960).
[31] Bettelheim and Janowitz (1965), p. 261:
This projection of guilt, which makes individual members of the group projecting the guilt feel persecuted, is by no means restricted to phenomena of ethnic intolerance. In most wars known to history, each warring group has accused the other of having "started" the war, i.e., of having persecuted the other group. This was usually explained as "hypocrisy" on the part of one or both warring parties. The view that this phenomenon is a rationalization by means of which each group tries to justify its case offers only a partial explanation. The justification of aggression by rationalization is only in addition to the primary phenomenon of guilt projection. Most members of the warring groups simply feel guilty about their own aggressions set loose. They project this persecution by their own superegos onto members of the other group, who thus become, psychologically speaking, the true persecutors. The fight against them then becomes true self-defense, i.e., defense of the self against tendencies which threaten its integration.

tain a projective system individually. The true believer in some form of socially accepted prejudice is less threatened and can maintain a level of acceptable social adjustment and solidarity with others who may be faced with similar internal stresses. Whereas the weight of maintaining individual projections might be unbearable and might lead to psychopathological behavior, projections shared collectively can permit a more easily maintained psychic balance. The continual expressive social function of some form of an institutionalized scapegoat, therefore, is apparent. Just as the conscience or the superego, during childhood socialization, comes to direct behavior toward what is elevating or ideal and prevents the occurrence of what is disavowed or repressed, what is sacred to the society defines the ideals and directives of the social group and what is despised and reprehensible.

In some respects the West, in contrast with the East, has been preoccupied with individual motivation and the universal presence of original sin. Concepts of individual responsibility for behavior and individual salvation derive from this tradition.[32] Nevertheless, the idea that evil arose out of the impulses of the individual could not always be sustained. The devil was a necessary representation of the disavowed, and his hordes represented personalized forces which, residing outside, might periodically "possess" the ordinary man just as God might "inspire" him. But in Western tradition, the saint or the witch was for the most part individually considered, and a state of pollution or holiness resulted from acts of will more than from acts of birth. In Japan the holy man through the enlightenment of Buddha could attain to a state of detachment from his society; he did not, however, form a self-perpetuating caste as did the Brahman in India. But Indian and Japanese society both ascribed to its outcastes the continual transgressive behavior (performance of polluting tasks) not allowed to individuals who wished to maintain acceptable status within the society. They were on the one hand necessary to the society, and on the other, in violation of its moral standards. The outcastes or untouchables personified all that was disavowed or unclean. The outcaste as scapegoat is consigned to his level as an accident of his birth rather than as an attributed embrace of the unclean or demonic as an act of will as is often the case in witches. The pariah has no choice in the matter. He has been degraded by an unhappy destiny; he grows up unclean with tainted blood that cannot be cleansed by any symbolic act.

It is interesting to note how the outcastes in Japan were differenti-

---

[32] This tradition was more evident in Protestant than in Catholic Europe. Calvinism, however, with its doctrine of predetermination, tended to retreat from this aspect of individualism and interpreted prosperity and positive social position as indicative of God's approval and auspicious for future salvation, in some respects approaching the religious justification found in Indian caste.

ated into two groups. The Hinin of Japan were essentially individuals whose pollution was a result of individual will, so that under extraordinary conditions, they could have recourse to an act of symbolic foot-cleansing that would reinstate them in the regular society. They were not outcastes but literally "outcasts"; social renegades who, given extraordinary acts of contrition, could find some form of reinstatement. But the Eta were defiled by destiny. A true caste is hereditary, whatever its role as scapegoat.

The scapegoat functioning of an outcaste group is dependent upon historical events. As demonstrated in preceding chapters, in the earliest period majority group farmers frequently turned on the Burakumin neighbors, venting their frustrations over the ill-understood social processes of change into which they had been swept. It is difficult for the outcaste to escape his role as scapegoat, since being of the lowest[33] status he finds it difficult to strike back politically, economically, or by use of force.

From a psychological standpoint it is not entirely fortuitous that in modern times those societies that manifest most concern with performance, cleanliness and self-righteousness also are more prone to a fear of dirt and contamination in developing or maintaining caste attitudes.[34] Concern with proper cleanliness is induced early in the socialization process—the middle class Japanese, like the German and the American, develops feelings of self-righteousness around meeting expectations of hard work and the pursuance of long range goals. Those who show less diligence, dedication, self-control or concern with daily hygiene are readily considered as inferior and it is difficult for those so trained not to despise such individuals. The strictness of taboos about dirt, if inculcated in childhood during the period in which other forms of obedience are learned, can become part of a syndrome of compulsive traits. More relaxed attitudes on the part of others may stir up unconscionable feelings of submerged rage and rebellion against the severe requirements placed on the self in meeting demanding standards of performance. One cannot identify with such people without danger to one's own equilibrium but must consider them beneath oneself.

It must be noted in contrasting the history of the Negro in North and South America that there has been in Latin-American cultures

---

[33] Projections are symbolically related to what is *beneath*. Man's "higher" senses are in his head. An erect posture is directed up. What is dirty is to the rear and beneath.

[34] The American soldier, accustomed to similar standards of cleanliness, felt more "at home" in Germany than in France or other parts of southern Europe. The degree of preoccupation with bathing and personal cleanliness on the part of the Japanese finds no direct reflection in Koreans or Chinese who are not considered "clean" people by Japanese standards.

less concern with cleanliness, hard work, and self-righteousness, and caste feelings around dirt did not develop in respect to Negro slaves subsequent to their emancipation.

Although all outcastes used as scapegoats are considered in one way or another to be unclean, there are differences in emphases on what is disavowed or projected within various cultures. What is negatively projected is a reflection of what is positively valued in the society. In the case of the Burakumin, although there is ample evidence of looser sexual behavior than in the majority society proper, it is not this aspect of their behavior that causes the most revulsion; it is their "unclean" habits in reference to food, language, and manners, as well as their supposed tendency to be inordinately violent and aggressive. They are also seen as disease-ridden, a reflection of a hypochondriacal concern that permeates Japanese culture.[35] Within Japanese society sexuality is tolerated under the right conditions, but there is a great need to disavow the appearance of direct aggression, and an even greater need to stress specified rules of propriety than is true for Western culture.

If we turn to the Negro in the South we find that while there is ample emphasis on "dirtiness" and "aggressiveness" in stereotyping and in justifying outcaste status for the Negro, even more pressing is the supposed primitive sexuality of the Negro. Dollard, in his now classic work, points out how the Negro in the South is subject to the projected sexual fantasies of the majority white population.[36] In this sense, expressive exploitation of the Negro in the South has been sexual as well as economic. The Southern white developed and attempted to maintain an ideal of womanhood wherein the white woman was put upon a special pedestal representing biological and social purity. The Negro woman conversely became an outlet which permitted the Southern white to divide his sexual image between primitive and refined women. In Japanese culture, in contrast, the Burakumin was not used as extensively in sexual fantasy by the dominant society. Rather, a well-elaborated system of semi-public prostitution not related to caste served to split the sexual familial functions of wife from that of sex as entertainment. There is some indication that with the change in attitude toward public prostitution there may be greater future use of the outcaste as a source of sexual fantasy.

SPECULATIONS ON THE ROLE OF STATUS ANXIETY IN CASTE SEGREGATION

It would be well to consider the possible historical role played by status anxiety in the institutionalization of more rigid control of so-

---

[35] De Vos and Wagatsuma (1959).
[36] Dollard (1957).

cial contact across a pollution barrier of caste. There are few individuals who do not need some form of symbolic reassurance periodically from the society concerning the nature of their status. The social roles provided by society not only provide patterns of behavior, but in a sense they also provide ready-made patterns of thought and feeling that help the individual maintain some form of self-identity. A man becomes selectively permeable in what he "takes in" from those about him. The primitive psychological symbolism of incorporation changes characteristically the type of psychological internalizations related to early forms of identification, but this process never ceases. The individual at adult levels still needs a constant form of communication with significant others who help maintain his sense of self.[37]

There are times in the history of groups when there is a collective development of status anxiety related to a threat from within the society or from some external political entity. The sense of cultural belonging is reinforced on such occasions where there is more stringent insistence upon the proper symbolic behavior defining group membership. This is true not only for minority groups, as discussed in the previous chapter, but also for dominant social segments of a culture.[38] An adult's social self-identity defines not only his occupational role but also a sense of personal commitment to his social group. Some form of psychological identification theory would be helpful to an understanding of the development of nationalism and theories of state. Society is not simply a power structure maintained by external sanctions as Hobbes would have it in his analysis of man's political structure in *The Leviathan,* societies, rather, are kept together by internalizations of social roles as well as the expectations reinforcing these roles in others.[39]

Any dynamic view of cultural historical trends must relate to how and under what circumstances a self-conscious sense of social belonging arises and is maintained. One aspect of this very complex subject touches on the use of caste position or an insistence on racial superiority as a form of social self-justification and belonging to a group. In this context it might be of interest to a historical specialist to document recent developments of racism in Germany. I would suppose that the development of racism in Germany can, in some part at least, be traced back to a situation of cultural self-justification, not too dis-

---

[37] Elkins (1959) develops a striking analogy between the breakdown of social behavior and sense of self systematically experienced by the inmates of concentration camps in Nazi Germany, and the type of development of a sub-adult social role by the Negro during slavery.

[38] The extended function of these mechanisms of introjection and identification into later forms of social self-identity have been developed theoretically and from both a sociological and a psychoanalytic standpoint in the theoretical writings of Erikson (1950).

[39] Hobbes (1960).

similar from that following the defeat of the American South in the Civil War.

Prussia was founded as a German state on the sandy wastes south of the Baltic, beginning in the eleventh century with a slow conquest by Teutonic knights of the agricultural Slavs living in this area. Those Slavs who were not exterminated were reduced to the position of serfs living under the domination of a foreign feudal nobility. (The etymology of the word for Slave comes from the German Sklave or Slave, obviously related in origin to the view held of Slavic people by their German overlords.) These conquerors had no economic resources other than those obtained by the exploitation of land and people. Through a culturally developed talent for military organization, the Prussians were able not only to maintain themselves, but also to aggrandize their territory and establish a strong spartan military state. This state had as its sustaining and integrating ideology belief in its own inherent ability and the superiority of the German "race" over the inferior Slavic-speaking peoples, both those within its own territory, and those living on the vast steppes to the east. These German overlords were not subjected to any of the softer blandishments of Western culture; rather they gloried in their own toughness and in a sense of superiority that stemmed from the continuous inculcation of strict discipline that permeated their socialization from childhood. This harsh but compelling ideology provided a rigid armature on which could be united the patchwork of independent duchies and small states in which the German-speaking peoples to the west and south of Prussia were divided. It was the elitist Prussians who offered the first serious resistance to the thrust of the French under Napoleon, and their view of life and the virtue of military discipline received a severe challenge when they were defeated in 1807. Some defensive recoil seems to have occurred throughout the disunited German states: a growing sense of national identity became intertwined with an assertion of the racial superiority of those united by the German language. The intellectual justification of racial superiority as a part of national identity can be traced in the writings of the social philosophers who held chairs at the University of Berlin subsequent to this period of defeat. Fichte, and later Hegel, espoused at length the virtues of a superior elite that was to head Germany and cleanse it of the influences of the decadent races in their midst that had prevented the national self-assertion of the Germans. Later social philosophers, such as Nietzsche and Schopenhauer, in their deprecation of the ordinary man, were simply following attitudes already expressed by Hegel and others whose voices could be heard by the elitist youth attending the German universities.

It is interesting to compare this series of historical events from a social psychological standpoint with what was occurring in the American South after its defeat. For the Southerner, his cause was lost, but not his need for a sense of social self-justification. What had been, under slavery, an easy assertion of superiority, in the post-slavery period became a more fanatical insistence on racial and individual superiority.

Attitudes of cultural superiority were less defensively organized, but nevertheless present, in the colonial expansion of the national states of France and England. Yet for them, in one sense at least, an expansive cultural superiority became more important than a unified cultural heritage that had to be defended from genetic incursions from the outside. No one became German, but strangers could become British or French should they demonstrate sufficient identification with the language and culture to attempt complete assimilation. In contrast, the German social belief became more exclusivist in its insistence on blood and heredity as necessary to maintain purity from foreign contamination.

In more recent German history, Bettelheim and Janowitz point out how the support of Nazism came in great part from German militant groups experiencing status anxiety.

The socially and economically downward-moving lower middle class groups (frequently referred to as "squeezed out groups") were the followers of Hitler, while the "respectable" relatively secure, and static middle classes (those who had not yet experienced downward mobility) held apart from this extreme form of nationalism (and anti-semitism). Before Hitler, there were the followers of *Stahlhelm,* of the conservative parties who embraced stereotyped and social anti-semitism without being outspokenly intolerant. All this changed with the advent of Hitler. Then anti-semitism became not only respectable, but the social norm. Moreover, these middle classes which had formerly enjoyed relative security now themselves became part of the squeezed out group, first by the new ruling group of National Socialists, then by the war mobilization economy. At this point, most of them became intensely hostile to the Jews, both because they were again following the accepted and successful pattern and also because they needed more violent oulets for the hostility aroused by sudden and severe frustration.

These authors also observed that this response, although general, was not universal. While the vast majority reacted to the rapid loss of secure status with an increase in prejudice, a small minority became even more tolerant but at the price of a great increase in personal anxiety. This anxiety was avoided by those who readily accepted Hitler and could discharge their pent-up feeling toward a minority group scapegoat.[40]

In the United States, the early history of slavery did not emphasize Negro untouchability. The Negro slave in the old South could be a

[40] Bettelheim and Janowitz (1965), p. 164.

body servant, a wet nurse to children, and a sexual consort to the white master with the firm definition of unequal status in slavery as a protection. Caste attitudes of the more untouchable sort developed subsequently with the Southern attempts to keep down the emancipated Negro. Because of Northern interference, the Negro became for the Southerner a more threatening source of fear and guilty projection. One white bigot, presently an eloquent editor of an influential Southern newspaper, expressed the Southern feelings about caste segregation without consciousness of the implications of his remarks: "Three elements when combined are unconscionable or distasteful to the white Southerner in the mingling of races—when contact is intimate, sustained, and on the basis of equality, it becomes insufferable." He pointed out that interracial contact where one of these three elements was missing was quite possible, but intimacy and sustained contact when combined with status equality was something that was emotionally intolerable. His statement reveals that for many Southern whites the segregation of the races became necessary with the increase in possibilities for individuals to come into sustained contact on an equal basis. As long as the relationship in the old South was very clearly defined as one of superior and inferior, the white Southerner did not feel contaminated by contact. But the growth of Jim Crow legislation at the end of the nineteenth century was symptomatic of a need for symbolic assurance of status, especially for those whites who were economically close to the impoverished blacks.

One can therefore suggest that despite historical trends that are now contravening with greater force, the South had been steadily developing toward a true caste society as a protective device to prevent, as Berreman points out cogently, the necessity for the white to consider the black American as a fellow citizen rather than as a non-person socially available as a scapegoat.

Concern with the "purity" of white womanhood and the innate brutishness of Negroes took on a more fearful quality as the opportunity for social contact was protected by legal institutions. Under slavery, sexual congress between white men and Negro women could occur without social consequences. After emancipation, such relationships were frowned upon since the consequences became more observable and more serious. Without the intervention of the stronger social forces that obtain in a modernizing world, one can conjecture that Southern society left to itself could have drifted further into a more fixed caste structure of fixed occupations, with intermediate castes perhaps developing among the Negroes themselves on the basis of color differentiation and specialized occupations.

The continual secularization of modern society prevents the further development of religious justification of such caste status. There were indications of this type of development in the more fundamental Southern Christian churches, which use Biblical interpretations to dignify and justify the maintenance of caste segregation. In certain instances within the Negro group itself incipient caste segments had made some appearance in such areas as New Orleans, which recognized gradations in color and status.

It is noteworthy that the idea of eating at the same table with a Negro in public or eating at a Negro restaurant or home is one of the most abhorrent features of the new Civil Rights legislation to Southern whites. Many Southerners experience a feeling of vague discomfort that is translated into autonomic reactions of physical disgust. In addition, the idea of group interracial bathing causes particular distress to many whites, both in the North and South. Stringently defined superiority of social position, when it was very firm, acted as a form of physical protection against possible feelings of contamination. Once this is removed, the anxious individual is apt to react with uncontrolled feelings, translated into neurotic symptoms.

This juxtaposition of neurotic compulsion and what we have described as status anxiety is well represented in a recent article by an editor of *Look* magazine, who is by birth and upbringing a Southern white.[41]

The madness associated with segregation takes several forms; all involve the failure of perception, the inability to make sense from the information presented to the senses. We had no trouble "understanding" our servants or our friends' servants. As long as a Negro is a servant or slave—that is to say, not a human being—we can face him. If we should confront him as a human life ourselves, however, we might feel what he feels, and that would be unbearable.

Strange things pop up at us like gargoyles when we are liberated from our delusions. Madness never seems so real as when we first escape it. My own liberation came through fortunate circumstances while I was still in my teens, even before I joined the air corps in 1942. When I first began meeting Negroes as equals, I thought I was entirely prepared, emotionally and intellectually. But at the beginning, something happened, so embarrassing to me I have never before been able to tell anyone. Each time I shook hands with a Negro, I felt an urge to wash my hands. Every rational impulse, all that I considered best in myself, struggled against this urge. But the hand that had touched the dark skin had a will of its own and would not be dissuaded from signalling it was unclean.

That is what I mean by madness. Because, from the day I was born, black hands had held me, bathed me, fed me, mixed dough for my biscuits. No thought *then* of uncleanliness or disease.

---

[41] Leonard (1964), pp. 16, 18.

These symptoms are not unique to the person who is reporting this with honesty. In neurotic attitudes held toward Negroes, the idea is often expressed that somehow the black skin color rubs off on the other person. Somehow it will contaminate the person touching it. Ninomiya, as we pointed out when discussing the mythology concerning the Japanese outcastes, states that one popular myth was that the outcaste could somehow walk barefoot because dirt did not stick to his feet. In other words, whereas an ordinary person is somehow contaminated by possible permeation by dirt, the outcaste, being of the nature of dirt himself, is free from penetration by the dirt on which he walks.

Revulsions felt toward an outcaste person or group are not simply related to some rational appraisal of the presence of what is contaminating, but to feelings symbolic of some other form of anxiety or guilt. Status anxiety operative in inter-caste relations can become symbolized as dread of contact. In spite of the individual's conscious attempts to overcome the barrier of caste within himself, he is still victimized by his own unconscious psychological processes that reach the conscious level as a concern over dirt or disease, which he himself recognizes as irrational.

In modern society, with the knowledge we have gained of individual psychological processes, we have come to view irrational dread as a form of individual neurosis prompted sometimes by unconscious guilt. Nevertheless, there are still social groups who maintain themselves by prejudice and seek social justification for doing so. There is a need to maintain self and status by symbolically maintaining distance from those who are perceived as inferior. A tendency to resort to inflexible automatic psychological defenses to maintain the security of a selective identity through symbols of distance is common.

Sociologically, societies are to be viewed in terms of processes of group inclusion and exclusion. Psychologically, the processes examined are those of identification and distantiation. An individual has to learn psychologically not only to identify with his own group, but in a segmented society to avoid very strong identification with segments to which he owes lesser allegiance. There is a constant tension in social identity between belonging and alienation. The processes of socialization taking place during childhood are selective and help to determine the relative impermeability of the individual not only to aliens but also to meaningful experiences with members of one's own society belonging to other social segments.

The needs and fears of the dominant group itself are structured by cultural traditions. Sanctioning systems—specified behavior as to acceptability or dissonance within particular roles and statuses—are controlled and manipulated by the dominant power segments of the society toward realization of their own purposes. However, it must be recognized that they themselves become subject to such sanctioning systems and that they cannot escape internalized patterns that limit their freedom of action.

The capacity to internalize feelings and identify with the needs of others leads to a source of tension and dissension among the dominant members of the society. On the one hand, there are those who become directed by moral imperatives and thereby seek to protect the weak with whom they identify and thus to artificially prolong their survival. On the other hand, many members of a dominant group will seek to increase the gains to be derived from the prerogatives of dominant status and continue to exploit the weaker segments of the society.

Sensitive to some inner awareness of the motivations attributable to socially submerged groups, men in dominant positions find it difficult to avoid feelings of possible retribution from exploited segments of their own society. The greater the political dominance the greater the fear, and consequently the greater the need to maintain barriers securing social status. Generally, the greater the exploitation of subordinate groups psychologically in caste, or instrumentally in class structures, the greater the social need to maintain external symbols of status differentiation.

The more inflexible the prejudice one finds in a society, the more it can be presumed to be a defensive attempt to maintain the advantages of exploitation while warding off a common sense of shared social guilt. Such defensive use of legal sanctions by dominant yet insecure socially self-segregating racial caste enclaves, be they on the level of small communities or larger nations, can only be resolved by bringing about in their members a broader, more secure basis for social self-identity which sustains the individual's dignity as it frees him from the burden of his unacknowledged past guilt.

The mark of Cain to which the Southern white bigot is apt to refer in calling on Biblical justification for his degradation of the Negro is actually on his own head. Whereas it is yet invisible to him, others have become able to read the sign for what it is. He, too, must be liberated from his past sins.

The authors, not as social scientists but as an American and as a Japanese completing this book together in 1966, would like to end on a moral and philosophical rather than a scientific note. The answer to the outcaste problems in society, although possibly clarified by scientific objectivity, depends ultimately on moral maturation.

We know that man individually, if not collectively, is capable of reaching levels of maturation that make it possible to obliterate historical barriers between communities and nations. Buttressed further with both psychological and sociological knowledge, we can come to understand why and how problems occur in society and we can seek ways of overcoming them. Whereas advanced social legislation can put us on the right path to stop commonly acknowledged instances of prejudice, we must find further means of assuring that other groups or individuals do not become social scapegoats.

The profundity of Buddhist philosophy, which in some curious ways anticipated what modern science has taught us about natural laws, would temper any optimism about an ultimate resolution of the human condition. There can be no force without counterforce, no matter without antimatter, no positive numbers in mathematics without negative ones, and no blind espousal of an elevated good without a blind rejection of a submerged evil. The higher man builds his castles of sand, the deeper he digs his pits.

Good creates evil—and yet, do we not live under the necessary illusion that there has been and can be moral progress toward a broadening of human understanding? Or is it simply that out of familiarity we prefer, to the simpler forms that preceded them, the more complex convolutions and entanglements composed from the skeins of modern social life?

Human culture has produced a capacity to symbolically internalize the outer world; and hence, the need to separate self from non-self, a consciousness of self counterposed by an unconscious non-self, a capacity for closeness balanced by a sense of distance, a consciousness of group countering a sense of alienation.

Whatever we can say about the necessary ultimate balance of natural forces, the appearance of man's moral conscience as an interference with nature has created a new dimension of social purpose. This sense of purpose can be unraveled or reduced to its mechanical physiological elements; but man has developed sensibilities only to a total configuration of purpose to which he is constrained to respond.

Our volume treats of a special type of institutionalized societal and psychological immaturity. When greater social maturity is a goal, personal immaturity becomes more visible. When a sense of justice develops, injustice becomes intolerable. By creating ideals, man has become subject to self-contempt; fearing his own self-contempt, he seeks justification. His ideals, at times unattainable and punishing, make him want to see himself better than his animal progenitors and he flees his past evil by present disavowal—he comes to clothe his naked self by clutching to him some fragile robe of dignity, be it even the flayed skin of a fellow sufferer.

Bibliography

Bibliography

INTRODUCTION TO SECTION I (pp. 3-5)

Eberhard, Wolfram
- 1942 *Kultur und Siedlung der Randvölker Chinas,* Leiden: E. J. Brill.

Ninomiya Shigeaki
- 1933 "An Inquiry Concerning the Origin, Development, and Present Situation of the *Eta* in Relation to the History of Social Classes in Japan," *Transactions of the Asiatic Society of Japan,* Vol. 10, pp. 47-154.

Passin, Herbert
- 1955 "Untouchability in the Far East," *Monumenta Nipponica,* Vol. 2, No. 3, pp. 27-47.

Ch'ü T'ung-tsu
- 1947 *Chung-kuo fa-lü yü Chung-kuo she hui,* Shanghai: Commercial Press.

CHAPTER 1 (pp. 6-30)

Cornell, John B.
- 1961 "Outcaste Relations in a Japanese Village," *American Anthropologist,* Vol. 63, No. 2, pp. 282-96.

Donoghue, John D.
- 1956 "An Eta Community in Northern Japan: A Study of Intra-Group Relations," unpublished Ph.D. dissertation, University of Chicago.

Eberhard, Wolfram
- 1942 *Kultur und Siedlung der Randvölker Chinas,* Leiden: E. J. Brill.
- 1965 Personal communication.

Hall, Robert B., Sr.
- 1962 "A Map of Buraku Settlements in Japan," *Papers of the Michigan Academy of Science, Arts and Letters,* Vol. 47.

Hayashiya Tatsusaburō *et al.* (eds.)
- 1962 *Buraku-shi ni kansuru Sōgōteki Kenkyū* (An Integrative Study of Buraku History), Vol. 3, Kyoto: Buraku Mondai Kenkyūjo.

Ishii Ryōsuke
    1960   *Edo Jidai Manpitsu* (Notes of the Edo Period: Edo Playgirls and Others), Vol. 2, Tokyo: Inoue Tosho.
Kanzaki Kiyoshi
    1964   "Tokyo no Buraku Mondai: Sono Atarashi Men to Furui Men" (Tokyo's Buraku Problem: The New and Old Aspects), *Asahi Journal*, Vol. 6, No. 46, pp. 191–97.
Kikuchi San-ya
    1923   *"Eta-zoku ni kansuru Kenkyū"* (A Study Concerning the Eta Race), Tokyo: Sansei-sha.
Ninomiya Shigeaki
    1933   "An Inquiry Concerning the Origin, Development, and Present Situation of the *Eta* in Relation to the History of Social Classes in Japan," *Transactions of the Asiatic Society of Japan*, Vol. 10, pp. 47–154.
Ōe Taku
    1919   "Eta Hinin Shogō Haishi no Temmatsu o nobete Eta no Kigen ni oyobu" (Description of the Process of Abolishing Eta and Hinin Status with Reference to the Origin of Eta), *Minzoku to Rekishi* (Race and History), Vol. 2, No. 1.
Passin, Herbert
    1955   "Untouchability in the Far East," *Monumenta Nipponica*, Vol. 2, No. 3, pp. 27–47.
Reischauer, Edwin O., and Fairbank, John K.
    1960   *East Asia: The Great Tradition*, Boston: Houghton Mifflin.
Ueda Masaaki and Harada Tomohiko
    1960   *Buraku no Rekishi* (Buraku History), Vol. 1, Kyoto: Buraku Mondai Kenkyūjo.

CHAPTER 2 (pp. 33–67)

Buraku Mondai Kenkyūjo (Research Institute for Buraku Problems) (ed.)
    1955   *Buraku no Rekishi to Kaihō Undō* (Buraku History and Emancipation Movements), Kyoto: Buraku Mondai Kenkyūjo.
Fujitani Toshio
    1960   "Kindai Nihon to Buraku Mondai" (Modern Japan and Buraku Problems), in Buraku Mondai Kenkyūjo (ed.), *Buraku no Rekishi* (A History of the Buraku), Kyoto and Tokyo: San-itsu Shobō, pp. 21–52.
Harada Tomohiko
    1963   "Dōwa Gyōsei no Kaiko to Tenbō" (Integrationist Measures in Retrospect and Prospect), *Buraku*, August, pp. 7–11.
Inoue Kiyoshi
    1959   *Buraku Mondai no Kenkyū: Sono Rekishi to Kaihō Riron* (A Study of Buraku Problems: History and Emancipation Theories), Kyoto: Buraku Mondai Kenkyūjo.
Inoue Kiyoshi and Kitahara Taisaku
    1964   *Buraku no Rekishi* (A History of the Buraku), Tokyo: Rironsha.

Kimura Kyōtarō
  1951 "Omoide no Tatakai" (Memorable Battles), *Buraku,* July, pp. 17–23.
Kitahara Taisaku and Kimura Kyōtarō
  1956 "Guntainai no Sabetsu to Jikiso Jiken" (Discrimination in the Army
      and the Direct Appeal Incident), *Buraku,* January, pp. 47–53.
Koyama Keikan
  1934 *Seigantai wa Ikani tatakatta ka?* (How Did the Petition Troop
      Fight?), Hamamatsu: Zenkoku Suiheisha Shizuoka Rengōkai.
Kyōchōkai (Harmonization Society) (ed.)
  1929 *Saikin no Shakai Undō* (Recent Social Movements), Tokyo: Kyō-
      chōkai.
Matsuda Keiichi, Masutani Hisashi, and Kudō Eiichi
  1963 *Buraku Mondai to Kirisutokyō* (The Buraku Problem and Christi-
      anity), Tokyo: Nihon Kirisuto Kyōdan Senkyō Kenkyūjo (United
      Church of Christ of Japan Research Institute for Missionary Work).
Matsumoto Jiichirō
  1948 *Buraku Kaihō e no Sanjū Nen* (Thirty Years Towards Buraku
      Emancipation), Tokyo: Kindai Shisō Sha.
Naimushō Keihōkyoku (Police Bureau, Ministry of Internal Affairs)
  1931 *Shakai Undō no Jōkyō* (Social Movement Conditions), Tokyo:
      Naimushō Keihōkyoku.
Nishimitsu Mankichi *et al.*
  1961 "Suiheisha no umareru made, II" (Until the Birth of the Suiheisha,
      Part II), *Buraku,* May, pp. 34–44.
Sakamoto Seiichirō *et al.*
  1961 "Suiheisha no umareru made, I" (Until the Birth of the Suiheisha,
      Part I), *Buraku,* April, pp. 34–43.
Totten, George O.
  1960 "Buddhism and Socialism in Japan and Burma," *Comparative
      Studies in Society and History,* Vol. 2, April, p. 302.
Yamamoto Katsunosuke and Arita Mitsuho
  1950 *Nihon Kyōsanshugi Undō Shi* (A History of the Japanese Commu-
      nist Movement), Tokyo: Seiki Shobō.

CHAPTER 3 (pp. 68–87)

Buraku Henshūbu (Editorial Staff of *Buraku*)
  1957   "Hiraoka Chūgaku ni okeru Sabetsu" (Discrimination at Hiraoka
      Junior High School), *Buraku,* No. 7, pp. 4–15.
  1961a "Kenpō Dōri no Seikatsu to Kenri o" (Demanding the Life and
      Rights Guaranteed by the Constitution), *Buraku,* No. 10, pp. 16–23.
  1961b "Kanzen Kaihō ni mukatte" (Toward Complete Liberation),
      Buraku, No. 11, pp. 22–25.
  1961c "Buraku Mondai o konponteki ni Kaiketsu suru tame no Chūō
      Seifu ni taisuru Seigan-sho" (Requests to the Central Government
      for the Purpose of a Complete Solution of Buraku Problems),
      Buraku, No. 11, pp. 75–87.

Cole, Allan B., George O. Totten, and Cecil H. Uehara
  1966 *Socialist Parties in Postwar Japan,* New Haven: Yale University
        Press.
Inoue Toshio
  1962 "Ōru-Romansu Tōsō to sono go no Kaihō Undō" (All Romance
        Struggle and Later Liberation Movement), *Buraku,* No. 7, pp. 27–
        35.
Inoue Kiyoshi and Kitahara Taisaku
  1964 *Buraku no Rekishi* (A History of the Buraku), Tokyo: Rironsha.
Kitahara Taisaku
  1960 "Buraku Mondai to Kaihō Undō" (Buraku Problems and Liberation
        Movements), *Buraku,* No. 8, pp. 4–15.
Miyazawa Toshiyoshi *et al.*
  1957 "Nenkan Kaiko: 1957" (Review of 1957), *Jurisuto* (Jurist), No. 144,
        pp. 2–29.
Nakanishi Yoshio
  1960 "Sengo no Buraku to Kaihō Undō" (Postwar Buraku and Liberation
        Movements), in Buraku Mondai Kenkyūjo (ed.), *Buraku no Rekishi,
        II* (History of Buraku, Part II), Kyoto and Tokyo: San-itsu Shobō,
        pp. 183–277.
Naramoto Tatsuya
  1961 "Buraku Kaihō no Tenbō" (Review of Buraku Liberation), *Buraku,*
        No. 1, pp. 4–7.
Nishimoto Sōsuke
  1960 *Buraku Mondai to Dōwa Kyōiku* (Buraku Problems and Assimila-
        tion Education), Tokyo: Sōbunsha.
Osborne, John
  1950 "My Dear General," *Life Magazine,* Vol. 29, No. 22, pp. 127–39.
Taniguchi Shūtarō
  1961 "Umoreta Yōkyū o dō Soshiki suruka" (How to Organize Hidden
        Needs), *Buraku,* No. 10, pp. 4–7.
Tōjō Takashi
  1959 *Sabetsu: Buraku Mondai Nyūmon* (Discrimination: Introduction to
        Buraku Problems), Tokyo and Kyoto: San-itsu Shobō.
Yamamoto Masao
  1962 *Buraku Kaihō Undō Hihan* (Criticism of Buraku Liberation Move-
        ments), Tokyo: Dōwa Taisaku Kenkyū Kaigi.
  1963 *Dōwa Kyōiku no Kihon Mondai* (Basic Problems of Assimilation
        Education), Tokyo: Dōwa Mondai Kenkyūjo.

CHAPTER 4 (pp. 88–109)

Abe Isoo
  1959 "Shakai Shugi-sha ni naru made" (How I Became a Socialist),
        quoted in Kudō (1959).
Diffley, Francis
  1964 Personal communication.

Fujitani Toshio
1961 "Bukkyō to Buraku Kaihō" (Buddhism and Buraku Liberation), in
      Kōza Kindai Bukkyō (Series on Modern Buddhism), Vol. 5, Tokyo:
      Hōzō-kan, pp. 133–50.
Jōdo Shinshū Honganji-ha, Dōhō Kai
1957 *Nihon no Minshu-ka to Bukkyo no Gō Shisō* (Democratization of
      Japan and Buddhistic Theory of Karma), Kyoto: Jōdo Shinshū
      Honganji-ha, Dōhō Kai.
1959 *Dōhō Undō no Susumekata* (How to Promote Brotherhood Cam-
      paign), Kyoto: Nishi Honganji.
Kagawa Toyohiko
1916 *Hinmin Shinri no Kenkyū* (Study of the Psychology of the Poor),
      Tokyo: Keisei-sha Shoten.
1920 *Seishin Undō to Shakai Undō* (Spiritual and Social Movement),
      Tokyo: Keisei-sha Shoten.
Kudō Eiichi
1959 *Nihon Shakai to Purotesutanto Dendō* (Japanese Society and Protes-
      tant Missionaries), Tokyo: Nihon Kirisuto Kyōdan Shuppan-bu
      (United Church of Christ of Japan Press).
Kyoto-shi Dōwa Kyōiku Renraku Kyōgi Kai (Kyoto City Coordinating Council for Assimilation Education)
1959 *Dōwa Kyōiku ni Kansuru Shōgakkō Kyōshi no Ishiki Chōsa* (Re-
      search Report on the School Teachers' Attitudes in Regard to
      Assimilation Education), May.
Matsuda Keiichi, Masutani Hisashi, and Kudō Eiichi
1963 *Buraku Mondai to Kirisutokyō* (The Buraku Problems and Chris-
      tianity), Tokyo: Nihon Kirisuto Kyōdan Senkyō Kenkyūjo (United
      Church of Christ of Japan Research Institute for Missionary Work).
Miura Kin-ichi
1961 "Hyogo-ken Dōwa Kyōiku no Ayumi: Jūyonen no Kaiko to Tenbō"
      (The Review of Assimilation Education in Hyogo Prefecture for
      the Past Ten and Some Years), *Hyogo Kyōiku*, Vol. 13, No. 8, pp.
      18–22.
Mombu Shō Dōwa Kyōiku Kenkyū Kai (Ministry of Education Research Association for Assimilation Education)
1942 *Kokumin Dōwa no Michi* (The Path Toward National Assimilation),
      Ministry of Education.
Mori Ryūkichi
1959 *Honganji,* Tokyo and Kyoto: San-itsu Shobō.
Morita Yoshinori
1960 "Dōwa Kyōiku no Hansei" (Vicissitudes of Assimilation Education),
      in Buraku Mondai Kenkyūjo (ed.), *Dōwa Kyōiku* (Assimilation
      Education), Tokyo and Kyoto: San-itsu Shobō, pp. 5–48.
Nishimoto Sōsuke
1961 "Dōwa Kyōiku no Konnichi-teki Kadai: Toku-ni Jissen no Tachiba
      kara" (The Present-Day Task of Assimilation Education, Especially
      from the Practical Standpoint), *Hyogo Kyōiku*, Vol. 13, No. 8, pp.
      10–16.

Nishimura Kan-ichi
  1952 "Buraku Mondai to Watakushi" (The Buraku Problem and I),
         Kirisuto Shinbun (Christian Newspaper), March 17.
Satouchi Tetsushi
  1957 "Shinshū-shi to Buraku" (Shin Sect History and Buraku), in Jōdo
         Shinshū Honganji-ha, Dōhō Kai (ed.), *Nihon no Minshu-ka to
         Bukkyō no Gō Shisō* (Democratization of Japan and Buddhistic
         Theory of Karma), Kyoto: Jōdo Shinshū Honganji-ha, Dōhō Kai,
         pp. 215–97.
Sugimoto Shin-yū and Onga Kazuo
  1961 "Dōwa Kyōiku o kataru" (Dialogue About Assimilation Education),
         Hyogo Kyōiku, Vol. 13, No. 8, pp. 28–34.
Sumiya Mikio
  1954 Nihon Shakai to Kirisutokyō (Japanese Society and Christianity),
         Tokyo: Tokyo Daigaku Shuppan Kai (University of Tokyo Press).
Thompson, Lawrence
  1964 Personal communication.
Tōjō Takashi
  1960 "Sengo no Dōwa Kyōiku" (Postwar Education for Assimilation), in
         Buraku Modai Kenkyūjo (ed.), *Dōwa Kyōiku* (Assimilation Educa-
         tion), Tokyo and Kyoto: San-itsu Shobō, pp. 49–98.
Tomeoka Kōsuke
  1963 "Suiheisha Undō" (Levelers' Movement), quoted in Matsuda, Masu-
         tani, and Kudō (1963).
Yamamoto Masao
  1963 *Dōwa Kyōiku no Kihon Mondai* (Basic Problems of Assimilation
         Education), Tokyo: Dōwa Mondai Kenkyūjo (Research Institute for
         Assimilation Problems).

        CHAPTER 5 (pp. 112–129)

Chūō Seishōnen Mondai Kyōgikai (Central Committee on Youth Problems)
  1962 *Seinen Hakusho* (Youth White Paper), Tokyo.
Hall, Robert B., Sr.
  1962 "A Map of Buraku Settlements in Japan," *Papers of the Michigan
         Academy of Science, Arts and Letters,* Vol. 47, pp. 521–27.
Inoue Kiyoshi
  1954 *Buraku no Rekishi to Kaihō Undō* (History of Buraku and Libera-
         tion Movements), Kyoto: Buraku Mondai Kenkyūjo.
  1960 *Buraku Mondai no Kenkyū* (Study of Buraku Problems), Kyoto:
         Buraku Mondai Kenkyūjo.
Mahara Tetsuo
  1960a "Buraku no Sangyō to Shigoto" (Industry and Work in
         Buraku), in Buraku Mondai Kenkyūjo (ed.), *Buraku no Genjō*
         (Present Situations in Buraku), Tokyo and Kyoto: San-itsu Shobō,
         pp. 93–130.
  1960b "Buraku no Shakai" (Buraku Society), pp. 131–80 in above.
  1960c "Buraku no Kurashi" (Buraku Living), pp. 181–212 in above.

Ninomiya Shigeaki
1933 "An Inquiry Concerning the Origin, Development, and Present Situation of the *Eta* in Relation to the History of Social Classes in Japan," *Transactions of the Asiatic Society of Japan*, Vol. 10, pp. 47–154.
Ōhashi Kaoru
1962 *Toshi no Kasō Shakai* (Urban Lower Society), Tokyo: Seishin Shobō.
Smythe, Hugh H. and Tsuzuki Chūshichi
1952 "The Eta: Japan's Indigenous Minority," *Sociology and Social Research*, Vol. 37, No. 2, pp. 112–14.
Suzuki Jirō
1953 "Burakumin no Chiikisei, Shokugyō, Kekkon" (Regional Characteristics, Occupation, and Marriage of Buraku People) in Nihon Jinbun Kagakukai (ed.), *Shakaiteki Kinchō no Kenkyū* (Studies on social Tensions), Tokyo: Yūhikaku, pp. 369–94.
Tōjō Takashi
1960 "Mura ni aru Buraku" (Buraku in Rural Areas), in Buraku Mondai Kenkyūjo (ed.), *Buraku no Genjō* (Present Situations in Buraku), Tokyo and Kyoto: San-itsu Shobō, pp. 13–58.
Watanabe Hiroshi
1963 *Mikaihō Buraku no Shiteki Kenkyū* (A Historical Study of the Unemancipated Buraku), Tokyo: Yoshikawa Kobunkan.
Yamamoto Masao
1963 *Dōwa Kyōiku no Kihon Mondai* (Basic Problems of Assimilation Education), Tokyo; Dōwa Mondai Kenkyūjo.

CHAPTER 6 (pp. 130–137)

Warner, W. L., and Lunt, Paul S.
1941 *The Social Life of a Modern Community*, Yankee City Series, Vol. I, New Haven: Yale University Press.

CHAPTER 7 (pp. 138–153)

Ishino Iwao
1953 "The Oyabun-Kobun: A Japanese Ritual Kinship Institution," *American Anthropologist*, Vol. 55, pp. 695–707.
Ishino Iwao, and Bennett, John W.
1953 *Types of the Japanese Rural Community*, Interim Technical Report No. 6, Research in Japanese Social Relations, Ohio State University.
MacIver, R. M.
1948 *The More Perfect Union*, New York: Macmillan Co.
Merton, Robert K.
1949 *Social Theory and Social Structure*, Glencoe, Illinois; The Free Press.
Myrdal, Gunnar
1944 *An American Dilemma*, New York: Harper and Bros.

Stoetzel, Jean
    1955 *Without the Chrysanthemum and the Sword,* New York: Columbia
    University Press.

    CHAPTER 8 (pp. 154–183)

Beardsley, Richard K., John W. Hall, and Robert E. Ward
    1959 *Village Japan,* Chicago: University of Chicago Press.
Cornell, John
    1960 "Status and the Community among Outcastes in Modern Japan:
    Report on Grant No. 2291," *American Philosophical Society Year-
    book,* 1959, pp. 310–16.
    1961 "Outcaste Relations in a Japanese Village," *American Anthropolo-
    gist,* Vol. 63, No. 2, pp. 282–96.
    1963 "Individual Mobility and Group Membership: The Case of the
    Burakumin," prepared for the Second Conference on Modern
    Japan: Changes in Japanese Social Structure, held at Bermuda, Janu-
    ary 19–25, 1963.
Donoghue, John
    1957 "An Eta Community in Japan: The Social Persistence of Outcaste
    Groups," *American Anthropologist,* Vol. 59, No. 6, pp. 1000–1017.
Nara-ken Minsei Rōdōbu (Nara Prefectural Government, Bureau of Public
    Welfare and Labor)
    1953 *Mikaihō Buraku no Jisshōteki Kenkyū* (An Empirical Study of Un-
    liberated Communities), Nara: Dōwa Mondai Kenkyūjo.
Nihon Jinbun Kagakukai (Japan Humanities Association) (ed.)
    1953 *Shakaiteki Kinchō no Kenkyū* (Studies on Social Tensions). Tokyo:
    Yūhikaku.
Passin, Herbert
    1955 "Untouchability in the Far East," *Monumenta Nipponica,* Vol. 2
    No. 3, pp. 27–47.
Smythe, Hugh H.
    1952 "The Eta: A Marginal Japanese Caste," *American Journal of
    Sociology,* Vol. 58, pp. 194–96.
Suzuki, Jirō
    1952 "Hiroshima-ken, 'O'-gumi no Chiikisei, Shokugyō, Kekkon ni tsuite:
    Buraku Mondai Shiryō Sono-ichi" (Characteristics, Occupation, and
    Marriage in 'O' District, Hiroshima Prefecture: Contributions to the
    Buraku Problem, I), *Philosophia,* Vol. 33, pp. 142–70.
    1953 "Burakumin no Chiikisei, Shokugyō, Kekkon (Regional Character-
    istics, Occupation, and Marriage of Buraku People) in Nihon Jinbun
    Kagakukai (ed.), *Shakaiteki Kinchō no Kenkyū* (Studies on Social
    Tensions), Tokyo: Yuhikaku, pp. 369–94.
Yamamoto Noboru
    1959a "Sabetsu Ishiki to Shinriteki Kinchō: Mikaihō Burakumin no
    Ishiki ni kansuru Kenkyū" (Discrimination Consciousness and Psy-
    chological Tension: A Study of Attitudes Among Unliberated
    Burakumin), *Jinbun Kenkyū* (Studies in Humanities), Vol. 10, No. 12,
    pp. 35–59.

1959b "Koyō Kankei kara mita Shakaiteki Kinchō: Okayama Kenka no Mikaihō Buraku no Baai" (Social Tensions Among Elementary Schoolmates: Studies of Outcaste Buraku in Okayama Prefecture), unpublished manuscript.
1958 Personal communication.

CHAPTER 9 (pp. 184–199)

Ishizuka Takatoshi
1959 Personal communication.
Makino Shinnosuke
1938 *Tochi oyobi Shūraku Shijō no Shomondai* (Problems in History of Land and Community), Tokyo: Kawade Shobō.
Matsuo Sōtarō
1931 "Chūgoku Chihō no Tetsuzan Gyōsei to Chihō Keizai" (The Iron Mine Administration and the Local Economy in the Chūgoku District), *Rekishi Chiri* (History and Geography), Vol. 58, No. 4, pp. 46–58; No. 5, pp. 65–85; No. 6, pp. 59–68.
Mutō Tetsuzō
1933 "Akita Katagi ni tsuite" (About the Akita Spirit), *Minzokugaku* (Ethnology), Vol. 5, No. 12, pp. 81–92.
Ninomiya Shigeaki
1933 "An Inquiry Concerning the Origin, Development, and Present Situation of the *Eta* in Relation to the History of Social Classes in Japan," *Transactions of the Asiatic Society of Japan*, Vol. 10, pp. 47–154.
Noguchi Takenori
1958 "Ebune no Shakaiteki Seiyaku" (Social Restrictions of Ebune), *Nihon Minzokugaku Kaihō* (Newsletter, Japanese Society of Ethnology), No. 4, pp. 27–32.
1959 Personal communication.
Yamaguchi Yaichirō
1939 "Aizu Chihō ni okeru Kiji Goya" (Woodworkers' Huts in Aichi District), *Minzokugaku Kenkyū* (Study of Ethnology), Vol. 5, No. 2, pp. 10–27.
Yanagida Kunio
1911 "Itaka oyobi Sanka," *Jinruigaku Zasshi* (Journal of the Japanese Association of Anthropology), Vol. 27, No. 6, No. 8.
1912 "Itaka oyobi Sanka," *Jinruigaku Zasshi* (Journal of the Japanese Association of Anthropology), Vol. 28, No. 2.
Yoshida Keiichi
1941 "Nihon ni okeru Ebune-teki Shūraku no Chōsa (Research Report of Ebune-type communities in Japan), *Tōa Jinbun Gakuhō* (Reports of East Asiatic Studies), Vol. 1, No. 1, pp. 181–207.

CHAPTER 10 (pp. 200–227)

Merton, Robert K.
1949 *Social Theory and Social Structure*, Glencoe, Illinois: The Free Press, Chapter IV, "Social Structure and Anomie."

CHAPTER 11 (pp. 228–240)

Buraku
1957   November, pp. 2–9.
Erikson, Erik
1950   *Childhood and Society,* New York: W. W. Norton.
1959   "Identity and the Life Cycle: Selected Papers," *Psychological Issues,*
        Vol. 1, No. 1, pp. 1-171.
Kardiner, Abram
1939   *The Individual and His Society: The Psychodynamics of Primitive
        Social Organization,* New York: Columbia University Press.
Koyama, Takashi
1953   "Buraku ni okeru Shakai Kinchō no Seikaku" (The Nature of Social
        Tension in Outcaste Communities) in Nihon Jinbun Kagakukai (ed.)
        Shakaiteki Kinchō no Kenkyū (Studies on Social Tensions), Tokyo,
        Yūhikaku, pp. 395–410.
Merton, Robert K.
1959   *Social Theory and Social Structure,* Glencoe, Illinois: The Free
        Press.
Sherif, Muzafer
1948   *An Outline of Social Psychology,* New York: Harper and Bros.
Shibutani Tamotsu
1961   *Society and Personality,* Englewood Cliffs, N. J.: Prentice Hall.
Whiting, J. W. M., and Child, I. L.
1954   *Child Training and Personality: A Cross-Cultural Study,* New
        Haven: Yale University Press.

CHAPTER 12 (pp. 241–257)

Buraku
1951   July, p. 26.
1955   August, pp. 30–35.
1957   September, pp. 46–49.
1961   June, p. 19
1962   April, p. 71.
De Vos, George
1960   "The Relation of Guilt Toward Parents to Achievement and Ar-
        ranged Marriage Among the Japanese," *Psychiatry: Journal for the
        Study of Interpersonal Processes,* Vol. 23, No. 3, pp. 287–301.
n.d.   "Role Narcissism and the Etiology of Japanese Suicide, unpublished
        manuscript.
Kobayashi Ayako
1962   *Buraku no Joi* (A Woman Doctor in a Buraku), Tokyo: Iwanami.
Mahara Tetsuo
1960   "Buraku no Shakai" (Buraku Society), in Buraku Mondai Kenkyūjo
        (ed.), *Buraku no Genjō* (Present Situations in Buraku), Tokyo and
        Kyoto: San-itsu Shobō, pp. 131–180.

Nishimoto Sōsuke
 1960 *Buraku Mondai to Dōwa Kyōiku* (Buraku Problems and Assimilation Education), Tokyo: Sōbunsha.
Suzuki Jirō
 1952 "Hiroshima-ken, 'O'-gumi no Chiikisei, Shokugyō, Kekkon ni tsuite: Buraku Mondai Shiryō Sono-ichi" (Characteristics, Occupation, and Marriage in 'O' District, Hiroshima Prefecture: Contributions To the Buraku Problem, I), *Philosophia*, Vol. 33, pp. 142–70.
Yamamoto Masao
 1963 *Dōwa Kyōiku no Kihon Mondai* (Basic Problems of Assimilation Educaion), Tokyo: Dōwa Mondai Kenkyūjo.
Yamamoto Noboru
 1959 "Sabetsu Ishiki to Shinriteki Kinchō: Mikaiho Burakumin no Ishiki ni kansuru Kenkyū" (Discrimination Consciousness and Psychological Tensions: A Study of Attitudes Among Unliberated Burakumin), *Jinbun Kenkyū* (Humanistic Research), Vol. 10, No. 12, pp. 35–59.

CHAPTER 13 (pp. 258–272)

Inoue Kiyoshi
 1961 "Kaihō Undō no Rekishi ni manabu" (Lessons We Receive from the History of Liberation Movements), *Buraku*, No. 9, pp. 4–17.
Ishida Shinichi
 1961 "Shinro Shidō to Kōkō Zennyūgaku Mondai" (Guidance and the Problem of an Entire Class Entering High School), *Buraku*, No. 9, pp. 51–55.
Kobayashi Ayako
 1962 *Buraku no Joi* (A Woman Doctor in a Buraku), Tokyo: Iwanami.
Kyoto-fu Seishōnen Mondai Kyōgi Kai and Kyoto Daigaku Kyōiku Shakai-gaku-bu (Kyoto Prefecture Conference on Youth Problems and University of Kyoto, Department of Educational Sociology)
 1960 *Shōnen Hikō no Shakaigaku-teki Chōsa Hōkoku:* Kyoto-shi ni okeru Hikō no Shakai Bunka-teki Haikei no Bunseki (Report of the Sociological Study of Juvenile Delinquency: Analysis of Socio-Cultural Background of Delinquency in Kyoto).
Mahara Tetsuo
 1960 "Buraku no Shakai" (Buraku Society), in Buraku Mondai Kenkyūjo (ed.), *Buraku no Genjō* (Present Situations in Buraku), Tokyo and Kyoto: San-itsu Shobō, pp. 131–80.
 1961 "Buraku no Kodomo to Shinro Shidō" (Buraku Children and their Guidance), *Buraku*, No. 9, pp. 55–59.
Matsuda Keiichi, Masutani Hisashi, and Kudō Eiichi
 1963 *Buraku Mondai to Kirisutokyō* (Buraku Problems and Christianity), Tokyo: Nihon Kirisuto Kyōdan Senkyō Kenkyūjo (United Church of Christ of Japan, Research Institute for Missionary Work).
Merton, Robert K.
 1959 *Social Theory and Social Structure*, Glencoe, Illinois: The Free Press, Chapter IV, "Social Structure and Anomie."

Nishimoto Sōsuke
   1960   *Buraku Mondai to Dōwa Kyōiku* (Buraku Problems and Assimilation
          Education), Tokyo: Sōbunsha.
Nomura Nobukiyo
   1956   "Tsukimono no Shinri" (Psychology of Fox Possession), in Oguchi
          (1956) pp. 247–57.
Oguchi Iichi (ed.)
   1956   *Shūkyō to Shinkō no Shinrigaku* (Psychological Studies of Religion
          and Beliefs), Tokyo: Kawade Shobō.
Tōjō Takashi
   1960a "Sengo no Dōwa Kyōiku" (Postwar Education for Assimilation), in
          Buraku Mondai Kenkyūjo (ed.), *Dōwa Kyōiku* (Assimilation Educa-
          tion), Tokyo and Kyoto: San-itsu Shobō, pp. 49–98.
   1960b *Dōwa Kyōiku Ron* (Debate on Assimilation Education), Tokyo: Shin
          Hyōron Sha.

CHAPTER 14   (pp. 277–307)

Bailey, F. G.
   1957   *Caste and the Economic Frontier, Manchester:* Manchester Uni-
          versity Press.
   1961   " 'Tribe' and 'Caste' in India," *Contributions to Indian Sociology,*
          No. 5, pp. 7–19.
   1963   "Closed Social Stratification in India," *Archives of European Soci-
          ology,* Vol. 4, pp. 107–24.
Barber, Bernard
   1961   "Social Mobility in Hindu India," paper presented at the 13th An-
          nual Meeting of the Association for Asian Studies, Chicago, March
          1961; amplified version, Barnard College, Columbia University, New
          York (mimeographed).
Barth, Fredrik
   1960   "The System of Social Stratification in Swat, North Pakistan," in
          E. R. Leach (ed.), *Aspects of Caste in South India, Ceylon and
          Northwest Pakistan,* Cambridge Papers in Social Anthropology, No.
          2, pp. 113–46.
Berreman, G. D.
   1960   "Caste in India and the United States," *American Journal of Soci-
          ology,* Vol. 66, pp. 120–27.
   1962a "Caste and Economy in the Himalayas," *Economic Development and
          Cultural Change,* Vol. 10, pp. 386–94.
   1962b "Sib and Clan Among the Pahari of North India," *Ethnology,* Vol.
          1. pp. 524–28.
   1963   *Hindus of the Himalayas,* Berkeley: University of California Press.
   1964   "Aleut Reference Group Alienation, Mobility, and Acculturation,"
          American Anthropologist, Vol. 66, pp. 231–50.
   1965   "The Study of Caste Ranking in India," *Southwestern Journal of
          Anthropology,* Vol. 21, pp. 115–29.
Blunt, E. A. H.

1931   *The Caste System of Northern India,* London: H. Milford, Oxford University Press.

Cohn, B. S.
1954   "The Camars of Senapur: A Study of the Changing Status of a Depressed Caste," Ph.D. dissertation, Department of Sociology and and Anthropology, Cornell University, *and* Ann Arbor: University Microfilms.

Cox, Oliver C.
1945   "Race and Caste: A Distinction," *American Journal of Sociology,* Vol. 50, pp. 360–68.

Davis, Kingsley
1948   *Human Society,* New York: Macmillan Co.

Dumont, Louis
1961   "Caste, Racism and 'Stratification,' Reflections of a Social Anthropologist," *Contributions to Indian Sociology,* No. 5, pp. 20–43.

Dutt, N. K.
1931   *Origin and Growth of Caste in India.* London: Kegan Paul.

Festinger, Leon
1957   *A Theory of Cognitive Dissonance,* Evanston: Row, Peterson.

Ghurye, G. S.
1952   *Caste and Class in India,* New York: Philosophical Library.

Goffman, Erving
1959   *The Presentation of Self in Everyday Life,* New York: Doubleday.
1961   *Asylums: Essays on the Sociology of Mental Patients and Other Inmates,* Garden City, New York: Doubleday.

Gough, Kathleen
1959   "The Nayars and the Definition of Marriage," *Journal of the Royal Anthropological Institute of Great Britain and Ireland,* Vol. 89, Part I, pp. 23–34.

Gould, Harold
1960   "Castes, Outcastes and the Sociology of Stratification," *International Journal of Comparative Sociology,* Vol. 1, pp. 220–38.
1963   "The Adaptive Functions of Caste in Contemporary Indian Society," *Asian Survey,* Vol. 3, pp. 427–38.

Gumperz, John J.
1958   "Dialect Differences and Social Stratification in a North Indian Village," *American Anthropologist,* Vol. 60, pp. 668–82.

Harrison, Selig S.
1960   *India: The Most Dangerous Decades,* Princeton: Princeton University Press.

Hutton, J. H.
1946   *Caste in India,* Cambridge, England: Cambridge University Press.

Hyman, Herbert
1942   *The Psychology of Status,* Archives of Psychology, No. 269, New York.

Kolenda, Pauline Mahar
1964   "Religious Anxiety and Hindu Fate," *The Journal of Asian Studies,* Vol. 23, pp. 71–81.

Kroeber, A. L.

1930   "Caste," in E. R. A. Seligman and A. Johnson (eds.), *Encyclopaedia of Social Sciences*, New York: Macmillan Co., Vol. 3, pp. 254–57.

Leach, E. R.

1960   "Introduction: What Should We Mean by Caste?" in E. R. Leach (ed.), *Aspects of Caste in South India, Ceylon and Northwest Pakistan*, Cambridge Papers in Social Anthropology, No. 2, pp. 1–10.

Lipset, S. M., and Bendix, R.

1959   *Social Mobility in Industrial Society*, Berkeley: University of California Press.

Lowie, R. H.

1947   *Primitive Society*, New York: Liveright.

Mahar, Pauline M.

1958   "Changing Caste Ideology in a North Indian Village," *The Journal of Social Issues*, Vol. 14, No. 4, pp. 51–65.

Mandelbaum, D. G.

1960   "Social Perception and Scriptural Theory in Indian Caste," in D. Stanley (ed.), *Culture in History: Essays in Honor of Paul Radin*, New York: Columbia University Press, pp. 437–48.

1962   "Role Variation in Caste Relations," in T. N. Madan and G. Sarana (eds.), *Indian Anthropology: Essays in Honor of D. N. Majumdar*, Bombay: Asia Publishing House, pp. 310–24.

Mannoni, O.

1964   *Prospero and Caliban: The Psychology of Colonization*, New York: Frederick A. Praeger.

Merton, Robert K., and Kitt, A. S.

1950   "Contributions to the Theory of Reference Group Behavior," in R. K. Merton and D. F. Lazarfeld (eds.), *Continuities in Social Research*, Glencoe, Illinois: The Free Press, pp. 40–105.

Mills, C. Wright

1960   *The Sociological Imagination*, New York: Grove Press.

Murdock, G. P.

1949   *Social Structure*, New York: Macmillan Co.

Myrdal, Gunnar

1944   *An American Dilemma*, New York: Harper and Bros.

Nadel, S. F.

1951   *The Foundations of Social Anthropology*, Glencoe, Illinois: The Free Press.

1954   "Caste and Government in Primitive Society," *Journal of the Anthropological Society of Bombay*, Vol. 8, pp. 9–22.

1957   *The Theory of Social Structure*, Glencoe, Illinois: The Free Press.

Newcomb, T. M.

1950   *Social Psychology*, New York: Dryden Press.

Rowe, William L.

1960   "Social and Economic Mobility in a Low-Caste North Indian Community," Ph.D. dissertation, Department of Sociology and Anthropology, Cornell University *and* Ann Arbor: University Microfilms.

1963   "The New Chauhans: A Caste Mobility Movement in North India,"

Center for South Asia Studies, University of California, Berkeley (mimeographed).

Rudolph, Lloyd I., and Rudolph, Susan H.
1960 "The Political Role of India's Caste Associations," *Pacific Affairs,* Vol. 33, pp. 5–22.

Sharma, K. N.
1961 "Occupational Mobility in a North Indian Village," *Southwestern Journal of Anthropology,* Vol. 17, pp. 146–64.

Silverberg, James
1959 "Caste-Ascribed Status Versus Caste-Irrelevant Roles," *Man in India,* Vol. 39, pp. 148–62.

Simpson, G. E., and Yinger, J. M.
1953 *Racial and Cultural Minorities,* New York: Harper and Bros.

Sinha, Surajit
1959 "Bhumij-Kshatriya Social Movement in South Manbhum," *Bulletin of the Department of Anthropology* (Calcutta), Vol. 8, No. 2, pp. 9–39.
1962 "State Formation and Rajput Myth in Tribal Central India," *Man in India,* Vol. 42, pp. 35–80.
1964 "Tribal Transformation in Central India," paper presented before the Inter-University Summer Program in South Asia, at the University of California, Berkeley, June 25.

Spiro, Melford
1951 "Culture and Personality: The Natural History of a False Dichotomy," *Psychiatry,* Vol. 14, pp. 19–46.

Srinivas, M. N.
1952 *Religion and Society Among the Coorgs of South India,* Oxford: Clarendon Press.
1956 "A Note on Sanskritization and Westernization," *Far Eastern Quarterly,* Vol. 15, pp. 481–96.
1962 *Caste in Modern India and Other Essays,* Bombay: Asia Publishing House.

Stevenson, H. N. C.
1954 "Status Evaluation in the Hindu Caste System," *Journal of the Royal Anthropological Institute of Great Britain and Ireland,* Vol. 84, pp. 45–65.

Turner, Ralph
1956 "Role-taking, Role Standpoint and Reference-group Behavior," *American Journal of Sociology,* Vol. 61, pp. 316–28.

von Fürer-Haimendorf, C.
1957 "The Inter-relations of Castes and Ethnic Groups in Nepal," *Bulletin of the School of Oriental and African Studies,* University of London.

Wallace, A. F. C.
1962 *Culture and Personality,* New York: Random House.

Weber, Max
1946a "Class, Status, Party," in *From Max Weber: Essays in Sociology*

(H. H. Gerth and C. W. Mills, trans. and eds.), New York: Oxford University Press, pp. 180–95.

1946b "India: The Brahman and the Castes," in *From Max Weber: Essays in Sociology* (H. H. Gerth and C. W. Mills, trans. and eds.), New York: Oxford University Press, pp. 396–415.

Wright, Richard
1945 *Black Boy*, New York: Harper and Bros.

CHAPTER 15 (pp. 308–331)

Allport, Gordon H.
1958 *The Nature of Prejudice*, Garden City, New York: Doubleday.
Anand, Mulk Raj
1956 *Untouchable*, Bombay: Jaico Publishing House.
Atkinson, E. T.
1886 *The Himalayan Districts of the North-Western Provinces of India*, Allahabad: The North-Western Provinces and Oudh Press.
Berreman, G. D.
1960 "Caste in India and the United States," *American Journal of Sociology*, Vol. 66, pp. 120–27.
1963 *Hindus of the Himalayas*, Berkeley: University of California Press.
Cash, W. J.
1954 *The Mind of the South*, Garden City, New York: Doubleday.
Cohn, B. S.
1954 "The Camars of Senapur: A Study of the Changing Status of a Depressed Caste," Ph.D. dissertation, Department of Sociology and Anthropology, Cornell University, *and* Ann Arbor: University Microfilms.
Dollard, John
1957 *Caste and Class in a Southern Town*, New York: Doubleday.
Fallers, Lloyd
1963 "Equality, Modernity and Democracy in the New States," in Clifford Geertz, (ed.), *Old Societies and New States*, New York: The Free Press of Glencoe, pp. 158–219.
Galanter, Marc
1963 "Law and Caste in Modern India," *Asian Survey*, Vol. 3, pp. 544–59.
Gallagher, Buell
1938 *American Caste and the Negro College*, New York: Columbia University Press.
Gould, Harold
1963 "The Adaptive Functions of Caste in Contemporary Indian Society," *Asian Survey*, Vol. 3, pp. 427–38.
Harrison, Selig S.
1960 *India, the Most Dangerous Decades*, Princeton: Princeton University Press.
Hazari
1951 *An Indian Outcaste: The Autobiography of an Untouchable*, London: Bannisdale Press.

Hyman, Herbert
    1942   *The Psychology of Status,* Archives of Psychology, No. 269, New York.
Isaacs, Harold R.
    1964   *India's Ex-Untouchables,* New York: John Day Co.
Kardiner, Abram, and Ovesey, L.
    1951   *The Mark of Oppression,* New York: W. W. Norton.
Karve, Irawati
    1953   *Kinship Organization in India,* Deccan College Monograph Series 11, Poona: Deccan College Postgraduate and Research Institute.
Majumdar, D. N.
    1944   *The Fortunes of Primitive Tribes,* Lucknow: University Publishers.
Mannoni, O.
    1964   *Prospero and Caliban: The Psychology of Colonization,* New York: Frederick A. Praeger.
Mills, C. Wright
    1960   *The Sociological Imagination,* New York: Grove Press.
Orans, Martin
    1959   "A Tribe in Search of a Great Tradition: The Emulation-Solidarity Conflict," *Man in India,* Vol. 39, pp. 108–14.
Pettigrew, Thomas F.
    1964   *A Profile of the Negro American,* Princeton: D. Van Nostrand Co.
Rose, Arnold M.
    1949   "You Can't Legislate Against Prejudice—Or Can You?" *Common Ground,* Vol. 9, pp. 61–67.
Rowe, William L.
    1960   "Social and Economic Mobility in a Low-Caste North Indian Community," Ph.D. dissertation, Department of Sociology and Anthropology, Cornell University, *and* Ann Arbor: University Microfilms.
    1964   "Myth as Social Charter: The Assignment of Status in Hindu Caste Origin Stories," Paper presented before the 63rd Annual Meeting of the American Anthropological Association, Detroit, November 20.
Rudolph, Lloyd I., and Rudolph, Susan H.
    1960   "The Political Role of India's Caste Associations," *Pacific Affairs,* Vol. 33, pp. 5–22.
Shah, A. M., and Shroff, R. G.
    1959   "The Vahivanca Barots of Gujerat: A Caste of Genealogists and Mythographers," *Traditional India and Cultural Change,* Philadelphia: American Folklore Society, pp. 246–76.
Simpson, G. E., and Yinger, J. M.
    1953   *Racial and Cultural Minorities,* New York: Harper and Bros.
Smith, Lillian
    1963   *Killers of the Dream,* New York: Doubleday.
Srinivas, M. N.
    1956   "A Note on Sanskritization and Westernization," *Far Eastern Quarterly,* Vol. 15, pp. 481–96.
    1962   *Caste in Modern India and Other Essays,* Bombay: Asia Publishing House.

Wallace, A. F. C.
 1962 *Culture and Personality,* New York: Random House.
Williams, Robin M.
 1947 *The Reduction of Intergroup Tensions,* New York: Social Science
        Research Council.

INTRODUCTION TO SECTION VI (pp. 325–331)

Dumont, Louis
 1964 "Change, Interaction, and Comparison," *Contributions to Indian
        Sociology,* No. 7, pp. 7–17.
Dumont, Louis, and Pocock, D.
 1957 "For a Sociology of India," *Contributions to Indian Sociology,*
        No. 1, pp. 7–22.
Leach, E. R.
 1960 "Introduction: What Should We Mean by Caste," in E. R. Leach
        (ed.) *Aspects of Caste in South India, Ceylon, and Northwest Paki-
        stan,* Cambridge Papers in Social Anthropology, pp. 1–10.

CHAPTER 16 (pp. 332–352)

Bailey, F. G.
 1963 "Closed Social Stratification in India," *The Archives of European
        Sociology,* Vol. 4, pp. 107–24.
Barth, Fredrik
 1960 "The System of Social Stratification in Swat, North Pakistan," in
        E. R. Leach (ed.), *Aspects of Caste in South India, Ceylon, and
        Northwest Pakistan,* Cambridge Papers in Social Anthropology, No.
        2, pp. 113–46.
De Grazia, Sebastian
 1948 *The Political Community,* Chicago: University of Chicago Press.
Dumont, Louis
 1962 "The Conception of Kingship in Ancient India," *Contributions to
        Indian Sociology,* No. 6, pp. 48–77.
Durkheim, Emile
 1947 *The Elementary Forms of the Religious Life* (J. W. Swain, trans.),
        Glencoe, Illinois: The Free Press.
 1949 *The Division of Labor in Society* (George Simpson, trans.), Glencoe,
        Illinois: The Free Press.
Elkins, S. M.
 1959 *Slavery,* Chicago: University of Chicago Press.
Frazer, Sir James George
 1959 *The Golden Bough,* New York: Criterion Books.
Gobineau, Arthur de
 1915 *The Inequality of Human Races* (Adrian Collins, trans.), London:
        William Heinemann.
Hocart, A. M.
 1950 *Caste—a Comparative Study,* London: Methuen Co.

Leach, E. R.
1960 "Introduction: What Should We Mean by Caste?" in E. R. Leach (ed.), *Aspects of Caste in South India, Ceylon, and Northwest Pakistan*, Cambridge Papers in Social Anthropology, No. 2, pp. 1–10.
Nadel, S. F.
1954 "Caste and Government in Primitive Society," *Journal of the Anthropological Society of Bombay*, Vol. 8, pp. 9–22.
Parsons, Talcott
1949 *The Structure of Social Action*, Glencoe, Illinois: The Free Press.
Parsons, Talcott, and Bales, Robert
1955 *Family, Socialization and Interaction Process*, Glencoe, Illinois: The Free Press.
Tannenbaum, Frank
1963 *Slave and Citizen: The Negro in the Americas*, New York: Vintage Books.
Warner, Langdon
1958 *The Enduring Art of Japan*, New York: Evergreen Books.
Weber, Max
1920–1923 *Gesammelte Aufsaetze zur Religionssoziologie*, 3 vols., Tübingen: J. Mohr.
Woodward, C. Vann
1957 *The Strange Career of Jim Crow*, New York: Oxford University Press.

CHAPTER 17 (pp. 353–384)

Banks, Michael
1960 "Caste in Jaffna," in E. R. Leach (ed.), *Aspects of Caste in South India, Ceylon, and Northwest Pakistan*, Cambridge Papers in Social Anthropology, No. 2, pp. 61–77.
Bettelheim, Bruno
1962 *Symbolic Wounds*, New York: Collier Books.
Bettelheim, Bruno, and Janowitz, Morris
1965 *Social Change and Prejudice*, New York: The Free Press of Glencoe.
De Vos, George, and Wagatsuma, Hiroshi
1959 "Psycho-Cultural Significance of Concern over Death and Illness Among Rural Japanese," *The International Journal of Social Psychiatry*, Vol. 5, No. 1, pp. 6–19.
Dollard, John
1957 *Caste and Class in a Southern Town*, New York: Doubleday.
Durkheim, Emile
1947 *The Elementary Forms of the Religious Life* (J. W. Swain, trans.), Glencoe, Illinois: The Free Press.
Elkins, S. M.
1959 *Slavery*, Chicago: University of Chicago Press.
Erikson, Erik
1950 *Childhood and Society*, New York: W. W. Norton.

Fenichel, Otto
  1945   *Psychoanalytic Theory of Neurosis,* New York: W. W. Norton.
Graves, Robert
  1948   *The White Goddess,* New York: Farrar, Straus, and Cudahy.
Henricus Institoris
  1928   *Malleus Maleficarum* (trans. with Introduction by Montague Sum-
          mers), Suffolk, England: John Rodker.
Hobbes, Thomas
  1960   *The Leviathan,* Oxford: B. Blackwell
Jahoda, Marie
  1960   "Race Relations: A Psychoanalytical Interpretation," Chapter 6 in
          Philip Mason (ed.), *Man, Race, and Darwin,* New York: Oxford
          University Press.
The Jewish Encyclopaedia
  1905   "Niddah" (Menstruous Woman) in *The Jewish Encyclopaedia,* Vol.
          9, New York: Funk and Wagnalls, p. 301. (From Pentateuchal Code,
          Leviticus 15.)
Leonard, George B.
  1964   "A Southerner Appeals to the North: Don't Make Our Mistake,"
          Look, Vol. 28, No. 16, pp. 16, 18.
Malinowski, Bronislaw
  1948   *Magic, Science and Religion and Other Essays* (selected and with
          an introduction by Robert Redfield), Glencoe, Illinois: The Free
          Press.
Mannheim, Karl
  1959   *Ideology and Utopia,* New York: Harcourt, Brace, and World.
Parsons, Talcott
  1949   *The Structure of Social Action,* Glencoe, Illinois: The Free Press.
Piaget, Jean
  1928   *Judgment and Reasoning in the Child,* New York: Harcourt, Brace.
  1930   *The Child's Conception of Physical Causality,* London: Kegan Paul.
  1948   *The Moral Judgment of the Child,* Glencoe, Illinois: The Free Press.
  1954   *The Construction of Reality in the Child,* New York: Basic Books.
Rapaport, David
  1951   *The Organization and Pathology of Thought,* New York: Columbia
          University Press.
Smith, W. Robertson
  1894   *Lectures on the Religion of the Semites,* London: Adam and Charles
          Black.
Stephens, W. N.
  1962   *The Oedipus Complex: Cross-Cultural Evidence,* New York: The
          Free Press of Glencoe.
van Gennep, Arnold
  1960   *Rites of Passage,* Chicago: University of Chicago Press.
Weber, Max
  1953   *From Max Weber: Essays in Sociology* (H. H. Gerth and C. W. Mills,
          trans. and eds.), New York: Oxford University Press.

Index

Abe Isoo, 93
Ainu, 12, 16, 183
All Romance incident (*Oru Romansu*), 76, 77
Allport, Gordon H., 309, 314
amabe (menial workers), 20. *See also* Outcaste (in Japan): outcaste Japanese groups
Anand, Mulk Raj, 310
Anarchists (Japanese), 49, 50, 52
Antidiscrimination activity. *See* Outcaste (in Japan); Shin sect antidiscrimination efforts; Christian antidiscrimination activity
ashi arai (foot-washing), 21
Atkinson, E. T., 311
Australia, 280
Authority: attitudes against, 258–272

Bailey, F. G., 279, 285–302 *passim*, 349, 350
Baldwin, Roger, 71
Banks, Michael, 368
Barber, Bernard, 278
Barth, Frederik, 280–282 *passim*, 285, 296, 350
be-min (*be*-people), 20. *See also* Outcaste (in Japan): groups in Japan
Beardsley, Richard K. *et al.*, 155
Beni Amer, 342
Berreman, G. D., 279, 280, 288–291, 296, 298, 300, 306, 311, 317

407

Bettelheim, Bruno, 368, 369; and Morris Janowitz, 373, 379
Bisaku Heimin Kai (Bisaku Common Peoples Association), 38
Black Robe League, 91
Blunt, A. E. H., 278
Buddhism: as Japanese state religion, 88; and outcastes, 88; similarities to Shinto, 16, 17
Buraku, Burakumin (Japanese outcastes): non-Eta, 183–200, and *passim*
Buraku (periodical), 234, 253, 255, 256
Buraku Henshūbu, 82–84 *passim*
Buraku Kaihō Dōmei. *See* Kaihō Dōmei
Buraku Kaihō Zenkoku Iinkai (National Committee for Buraku Liberation), 67, 71
Buraku Liberation League (Buraku Kaihō Dōmei), 73, 74
Buraku Mondai Kenkyūjo (Research Institute for Buraku Problems), 10, 11, 34
Buraku Problems Research Institute (Buraku Mondai Kenkyūjo), 10, 11, 34

Cash, W. J., 309, 314
Caste:
  characteristic aspects of: complementary behavior and noncom-